Unequal Chances

Unequal Chances

FAMILY BACKGROUND
AND ECONOMIC SUCCESS

Edited by Samuel Bowles, Herbert Gintis,
and Melissa Osborne Groves

RUSSELL SAGE FOUNDATION
New York
PRINCETON UNIVERSITY PRESS
Princeton and Oxford

Published by Princeton University Press, 41 William Street, Princeton,
New Jersey 08540

In the United Kingdom: Princeton University Press, 3 Market Place,
Woodstock, Oxfordshire OX20 1SY

And the Russell Sage Foundation, 112 East 64th Street, New York, New York 10021

LIBRARY OF CONGRESS CATALOGING-IN-PUBLICATION DATA

Unequal chances : family background and economic success / edited by Samuel Bowles,
Herbert Gintis, and Melissa Osborne Groves.
p. cm.
Research from a workshop, "Persistent Inequality in a Competitive World," and from
other projects funded by a grant from the Russell Sage Foundation to the
Santa Fe Institute.
Includes bibliographical references and index.
ISBN 0-691-11930-9 (cl : alk. paper)
1. Income distribution—Social aspects.   2. Family—Economic aspects.   3. Inheritance
and succession—Social aspects.   4. Equality—Psychological aspects.   5. Social
status—Psychological aspects.   6. Social mobility—Psychological aspects.
I. Title: Family background and economic success.   II. Bowles, Samuel.
III. Gintis, Herbert.   IV. Osborne Groves, Melissa.
HC79.I5.U515 2005
339.2′2—dc22   2004050521

British Library Cataloging-in-Publication Data is available

This book has been composed in Sabon

Printed on acid-free paper.∞

www.pupress.princeton.edu

Printed in the United States of America

1 3 5 7 9 10 8 6 4 2

CONTENTS

PREFACE

THE research reported here is part of the resurgence of scholarly interest in inequality and the role of parental status in the processes by which individuals come to occupy particular rungs in the ladder of economic success. Interest in the subject extends far beyond academic circles, as is indicated by the lively controversy in the United States about the appropriate level of taxation of inheritances and the centrality of intergenerational equity in the rhetoric of the British Labour Party.

A grant from the Russell Sage Foundation to the Santa Fe Institute to study "Persistent Inequality in a Competitive World" allowed us to convene a workshop of the authors to discuss initial drafts of the papers. We are grateful to the Foundation, and especially to Eric Wanner and Suzanne Nichols. Other projects funded by that grant include studies of the role of inequality as a possible impediment to cooperation in the protection of local environmental commons, the poverty traps that contribute to persistent inequality among families, nations, and ethnic groups, and the impact of globalization on egalitarian redistribution by nation-states. We are also grateful to Andi Sutherland, Margaret Alexander, Bae Smith, Tim Taylor, and others on the staff of the Santa Fe Institute for their contributions to this project and for the support given to the preparation of this volume by the John D. and Catherine T. MacArthur Foundation, through the Research Network on the Nature and Origins of Preferences. Finally, we extend our thanks to Peter Dougherty and Tim Sullivan of Princeton University Press, who turned a complicated manuscript into a beautiful book.

SAMUEL BOWLES, HERBERT GINTIS,
AND MELISSA OSBORNE GROVES, Santa Fe Institute
Santa Fe, New Mexico
March 2004

Unequal Chances

INTRODUCTION

SAMUEL BOWLES, HERBERT GINTIS, AND
MELISSA OSBORNE GROVES

INTERGENERATIONAL INEQUALITY MATTERS

Citizens of modern democratic societies hold strongly meritocratic values. Equal opportunity for educational and occupational advancement can and should ensure that each child have a fair chance of economic success. At the same time, parents have the right and the duty to prepare their children as best they can for a secure economic future. These two values may conflict, but a moderate positive correlation between the economic success of parents and children is arguably compatible with both, since this may be interpreted as a sign that most parents are preparing their children well, and that only a small minority are exceptionally advantaged or disadvantaged.

As amply documented in this volume, however, there are quite strong tendencies for children of those at the bottom of the income distribution to find their children at the bottom, with a parallel tendency for those at the top of the income distribution to find their children also at the top. (see figure I.1).

Many will read the data provided in this and succeeding chapters and conclude, with us, that children from the least well-off families do not have a fair chance at attaining the level of economic security most other families manage to attain. This book not only analyzes the extent of economic mobility. It equally seeks to uncover the factors accounting for the success of some families (and the failure of others') attempts to ensure their children an auspicious economic future. Much of what we have learned through this research makes us optimistic concerning the power of social policy to enhance equality of opportunity. For instance, we find that little intergenerational inequality is due to parents passing superior IQ on to their children, and much is due to parents passing their material wealth to their children, at least for those at the top of the income distribution. On the other hand, we find that children may well inherit genetically based behavioral characteristics that strongly affect their labor market success, though the extent of this aspect of the intergenerational transmission process cannot be estimated with much precision, and we are just beginning to find out what those characteristics are. While the evidence for a genetic aspect of the intergenerational

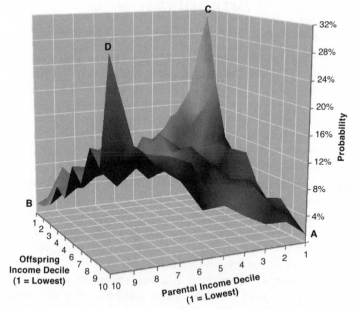

Figure I.1 Probability of offspring attaining given income decile, by parents' income deciles, United States. Based on total family income for black and white participants in the Panel Study of Income Dynamics who were born between 1942 and 1972, and their parents. The income of the children was measured when they were aged 26 or older, and was averaged over all such years for which it was observed. The number of years of income data ranged from 1 to 29 with an average of 11.5; the median year of observation was 1991. Parents' income was averaged over all observed years in which the child lived with the parents. The number of years of income data ranged from 1 to 27 with an average of 11.9; the median year of observation was 1974. The simple age-adjusted correlation of parents' and children's incomes in the data set represented in the figure is 0.42.

Source: Hertz, this volume.

transmission process is suggestive, a major role for the environmental influences of family, neighborhood, and schooling is beyond a doubt. However, conventional measures of schooling attainment do not capture key aspects of this process.

BETTER DATA, NEW CONCLUSIONS

For many years, the consensus among economists was that in the United States, one's income is only very weakly dependent upon the economic success of one's parents.[1]

Early research on the statistical relationship between parents' and their children's economic status after becoming adults, starting with Blau and Duncan (1967), found only a weak connection. For example, the simple correlations between parents' and sons' income or earnings (or their logarithms) in the United States reported by Becker and Tomes (1986) averaged 0.15. Becker (1988) expressed a widely held consensus when, in his presidential address to the American Economics Association, he concluded, "[L]ow earnings as well as high earnings are not strongly transmitted from fathers to sons." (10)

More recent research, some of which is presented in this volume, demonstrates that the estimates of high levels of intergenerational mobility were artifacts of two types of measurement error: mistakes in reporting income, particularly when individuals were asked to recall the income of their parents, and transitory components in current income uncorrelated with underlying permanent income (Bowles 1972; Bowles and Nelson 1974; Atkinson et al. 1983; Solon 1992; Zimmerman 1992). The high noise-to-signal ratio in both generations' incomes depressed the intergenerational correlation. As Bhashkar Mazumder shows in chapter 2, when corrected for these two types of measurement error, the intergenerational correlations for economic status appear to be substantial, many of them three times the average of the U. S. studies surveyed by Becker and Tomes (1986).

The higher consensus estimates of the intergenerational transmission of economic success has stimulated empirical research. The relevant facts on which most researchers now agree include the following: brothers' incomes are much more similar than those of randomly chosen males of the same race and similar age differences; the incomes of identical twins are much more similar than fraternal twins or non-twin brothers; the children of well-off parents obtain more and higher-quality schooling; and wealth inheritance makes an important contribution to the wealth owned by the offspring of the very rich. On the basis of these and other empirical regularities, it seems safe to conclude that the intergenerational transmission of economic status is accounted for by a heterogeneous collection of mechanisms, including the genetic and cultural transmission of cognitive skills and noncognitive personality traits in demand by employers (see Melissa Osborne Groves's contribution, chapter 7), the inheritance of wealth and income-enhancing group memberships such as race (see Thomas Hertz's contribution, chapter 5), and the superior education and health status enjoyed by the children of higher-status families.

The transmission of economic success across generations, however, remains something of a black box. Basing our arguments on the consolidation of several data sets, we report in this introduction that the combined inheritance processes operating through superior cognitive performance and educational attainments of those with well-off parents, while important, explain at most half of the intergenerational transmission of income. Moreover, while genetic transmission of earnings-enhancing traits appears to play a role, the genetic transmission of IQ appears to be surprisingly unimportant.

It might be thought that the relative unimportance of IQ in intergenerational inequality is an artifact of poor measurement of the intervening variables relative to the measurement of the income or earnings of parents and offspring. But this does not seem to be the case. Years of schooling and other measures of school attainment, like cognitive performance, are measured with relatively little error. Better measurements will of course help; but we are not likely to improve much on our measures of IQ, and recent improvements in the measurement of school quality have not offered much additional illumination. Our weakness in accounting for intergenerational economic status transmission is not due to measuring the right variables poorly, but to missing some of the important variables entirely. What might these be?

Most economic models treat one's income as the sum of the returns to the factors of production one brings to the market, like cognitive functioning and education. But *any* individual trait that affects income and for which parent-offspring similarity is strong will contribute to the intergenerational transmission of economic success. Included are race, geographical location, height, beauty or other aspects of physical appearance, health status, and some aspects of personality. Thus, by contrast to the standard approach, we give considerable attention to income-generating characteristics that are not generally considered to be factors of production.

In studies of the intergenerational transmission of economic status, our estimates suggest that cognitive skills and education have been overstudied, while wealth, race, and noncognitive behavioral traits have been understudied. As a partial corrective, in chapter 7, Melissa Osborne Groves includes explicit personality variables in modeling intergenerational status transmission. Using the National Longitudinal Surveys, she finds that the inclusion of personality accounts for a larger component of the intergenerational transmission process than measured IQ. Adding a single personality variable—fatalism—reduces the unexplained persistence of earnings by more than four percentage points—more than twice that of cognitive performance. In addition, the transmission of personality contributes to the transmission of earnings between father and son, comparable to estimates of the portion attributed to the inheritance of IQ.

In chapter 1, Greg Duncan, Ariel Kalil, Susan Mayer, Robin Tepper, and Monique Payne describe the extent of resemblance between parents and children and attempt to account for resemblances with traditional measures of family background such as socioeconomic status, educational level, and even general parenting skills. On the basis of two data sets containing seventeen detailed measures of parental behavioral characteristics measured in adolescence and the same characteristics of their children, they find that parents pass on *specific* rather than *general* competencies to their children. Family background and parenting explain only a small part of intergenerational correlations. It follows that disaggregation of individual behavioral characteristics may significantly improve our understanding of intergenerational status transmission.

MEASURING THE INTERGENERATIONAL TRANSMISSION OF ECONOMIC STATUS

Economic status can be measured in discrete categories—by membership in hierarchically ordered classes, for example—or continuously, by earnings, income, or wealth. The discrete approach can allow a rich but difficult-to-summarize representation of the process of intergenerational persistence of status using transition probabilities among the relevant social ranks (Erikson and Goldthorpe 1992). By contrast, continuous measures allow a simple metric of persistence, based on the correlation between the economic status of the two generations. Moreover, these correlations may be decomposed into additive components reflecting the various causal mechanisms accounting for parent-child economic similarity. Both approaches are insightful, but for simplicity of presentation we rely primarily on the continuous measurement of status. For reasons of data availability, we use income or earnings as the measure of economic status, though income (the more inclusive measure) is preferable for most applications. We use subscript p to refer to parental measures, while y is an individual's economic status, adjusted so that its mean, $\bar{y}$, is constant across generations, β_y is a constant, and ε_y is a disturbance uncorrelated with y_p. Thus

$$y - \bar{y} = \beta_y(y_p - \bar{y}) + \varepsilon_y; \qquad (1)$$

that is, the deviation of the offspring's economic status from the mean is β_y times the deviation of the parent from mean economic status, plus an error term. The coefficient β_y is a measure of intergenerational income persistence. In the empirical work reviewed below, earnings, income, wealth, and other measures of economic success are measured by their natural logarithm unless otherwise noted. Thus, β_y is the percentage change in offspring's economic success associated with a 1 percent change in parents' economic success. The influence of mean economic status on the economic status of the offspring, $1-\beta_y$, is called *regression to the mean*, since it shows that one may expect to be closer to the mean than one's parents by the fraction $1-\beta_y$ (Goldberger 1989).

The relationship between the intergenerational income elasticity, β_y, and the intergenerational correlation P_y is given by

$$\rho_y = \beta_y \frac{\sigma_{y_p}}{\sigma_y},$$

where σ_y is the standard deviation of y. If y is the natural logarithm of wealth, income, or earnings, its standard deviation is a common unit-free measure of inequality. Thus, if inequality is unchanging across generations, so $\sigma_{y_p} = \sigma_y$, then $\rho_y = \beta_y$. However, the intergenerational income elasticity exceeds ρ_y when income inequality is rising, but is less than ρ_y when income inequality is declining. In effect, the intergenerational correlation coefficient ρ is affected by changes in the distribution of income while the intergenerational income elasticity is not. Also, ρ^2 measures the fraction of the variance in this generation's measure of economic success that is linearly associated with the same measure in the previous generation.

Estimates of the intergenerational income elasticity are presented in Mulligan (1997), Solon (1999), and Harding et al. (this volume). The mean estimates reported in Mulligan are as follows: for consumption 0.68, for wealth 0.50, for income 0.43, for earnings (or wages) 0.34, and for years of schooling 0.29. Evidence concerning trends in the degree of income persistence across generations is mixed. Most studies indicate that persistence rises with age, is greater for sons than daughters, and is greater when multiple years of income or earnings are averaged. The importance of averaging multiple years to capture permanent aspects of economic status is dramatized in Mazumder's contribution to this volume (chapter 2). Mazumder used a rich U.S. Social Security Administration data set to estimate an intergenerational income elasticity of 0.27 averaging a son's earnings over four years and a father's earnings averaged over two years. But the estimate increases to 0.47 when seven years of the fathers earnings are averaged, and to 0.65 when sixteen years are averaged.

Do intergenerational elasticities of this magnitude mean that rags to riches is no more than a fantasy for most poor children? The intergenerational correlation is an average measure, and may be unilluminating about the probabilities of economic success conditional on being the child of poor, rich, or middling parents. Calculating these conditional probabilities and inspecting the entire transition matrix gives a more complete picture. The results of a study by Tom Hertz, reported in chapter 5, appear in figure I.1, with the adult children arranged by income decile (from poor to rich, moving from left to right) and with parents arranged by income decile along the other axis. The height of the surface indicates the likelihood of making the transition from the indicated parents' decile to the children's decile.

Though the underlying intergenerational correlation of incomes in the data set that Hertz used is a modest 0.42, the differences in the likely life trajectories of the children of the poor and the rich are substantial. The "twin peaks" represent those stuck in poverty and affluence (though we do not expect the term "affluence trap" to catch on). A child born to the top decile has a 29.6 percent chance of attaining the top decile (point D) and a 43.3 percent chance of attaining the top quintile. A indicates that the child of the poorest decile has a 1.3 percent chance of attaining the top decile, and a 4.3 percent chance of attaining the top quintile. C indicates that children of the poorest decile have a 31.5 percent chance of occupying the lowest decile, and a 51.3 percent chance of occupying the lowest quintile, while B shows that the child of the richest decile has a 1.5 percent chance of ending in the poorest decile, and a 3.5 percent chance of occupying the lowest quintile.

Mobility patterns differ dramatically by race, as reported by Hertz in chapter 5. In particular, the rate of persistence in the bottom decile, a measure of the severity of the intergenerational poverty trap, is much higher for blacks than for whites. Other studies (Corak and Heisz 1999; Cooper et al. 1994) also suggest that distinct transmission mechanisms may be at work at various points of the income distribution. For example, wealth bequests may play a major role at the top of the income distribution, while at the bottom, vulnerability to violence or other adverse health episodes may be more important.

Sources of Persistence: Cultural, Genetic, and Bequest

Economic status does persist substantially across generations. We seek to uncover the channels through which parental incomes influence offspring incomes. We do this by decomposing the intergenerational correlation (or the intergenerational income elasticity) into additive components reflecting the contribution of various causal mechanisms. This will allow us to conclude, for example, that a certain fraction of the intergenerational correlation is accounted for by the genetic inheritance of IQ, or by the fact that the children of wealthy parents are also wealthy.

It is a remarkable fact about correlation coefficients that this can be done. Moreover, the technique we use does not require that we introduce variables in any particular order. Suppose that parents' income (measured by its logarithm, y_p) and offspring education (s) affect offspring income (also measured by its logarithm, y). Like any correlation coefficient, this intergenerational correlation $r_{y_p y}$ can be expressed as the sum of the normalized regression coefficients of measures of parental income $\beta_{y_p y}$ and offspring education β_{ys} in a multiple regression predicting y, each multiplied by the correlation between y_p and the regressor (which, of course, for parental income itself is 1). The normalized regression coefficient is the change in the dependent variable, in standard deviation units, associated with a one standard deviation change in the independent variable. The *direct effect* is the normalized regression coefficient of parental income from this regression. The education component of this decomposition of the intergenerational correlation is called an *indirect effect*. Figure I.2 illustrates this breakdown,[2] which gives

$$r_{yy_p} = \beta_{y_p y} + r_{y_p s}\beta_{ys}.$$

As long as the multiple regression coefficients are unbiased, the decomposition is valid whatever the relationship among the variables. Specifically, it does not require that the regressors be uncorrelated. This decomposition allows us to be more precise about our "black box" claim. When we reported that the standard schooling, cognitive level, and other variables account for less than half of the observed parent offspring similarity of income, for instance, we mean that the direct parental effect is least half of the intergenerational correlation in a number of studies allowing this comparison (Bowles 1972; Bowles and Nelson 1974; Atkinson et al. 1983; Mulligan 1997).

Our strategy is to estimate the size of these direct and indirect effects. Note that the decomposition uses correlations between parental incomes

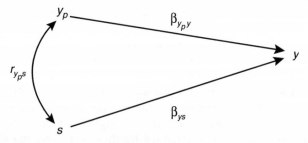

Figure I.2 Representing a correlation as the sum of direct and indirect effects.

and other variables—schooling, in the example—thought to be causally related to the income-generating process. These correlations with parental income need not, of course, reflect causal relationships. But the above decomposition can be repeated for the correlations between parental income and the causes of offspring income, in some cases permitting causal interpretations. For example, a study of the role of wealth in the transmission process could ask why parental income and offspring wealth are correlated. Is it bequests and inter vivos transfers or the cultural transmission of savings behaviors that account for this correlation? Or do we simply not know why parent and offspring wealth is correlated, and as a result should avoid giving the data a causal interpretation? Likewise, parent-offspring similarity in human capital may be due to genetic or cultural inheritance of whatever it takes to persist in schooling and to acquire skills and behaviors that are rewarded in the labor market. Unlike models of parental and child behavior that account for persistence, pioneered by Becker and elaborated by Graw and Mulligan (2002), our approach is more diagnostic, not giving an adequate causal account of the transmission process, but indicating where to look to find the causes. The next sections will explore such decompositions.

The Role of Genetic Inheritance of Cognitive Skill

One of the transmission channels deserves special attention not only because of its prima facie plausibility, but also because of the extraordinary attention given to it in popular discussions of the subject. This is the genetic inheritance of cognitive skill. The similarity of parents' and offspring's scores on cognitive tests is well documented. Correlations of IQ between parents and offspring range from 0.42 to 0.72, where the higher figure refers to measures of average parental vs. average offspring IQ (Bouchard and McGue 1981; Plomin et al. 2000). The contribution of cognitive functioning to earnings both directly and *via* schooling attainment has also been established in a variety of studies that estimate determinants of earnings using IQ (and related) test scores. The direct effect of IQ on earnings is estimated from multiple regression studies that typically use the logarithm of earnings as a dependent variable, and that estimate the regression coefficients of a variety of explanatory variables, including performance on a cognitive test, years (and perhaps other measures) of schooling, a measure of parental economic and / or social status, work experience, race, and sex. The indirect effect of IQ operating through its contribution to higher levels of educational attainment is estimated using measures of childhood IQ (along with other variables) to predict the level of schooling obtained.

We have located sixty-five estimates of the normalized regression coefficient of a test score in an earnings equation in twenty-four different studies of U.S. data over a period of three decades. Our meta-analysis of these studies is presented in Bowles, Gintis, and Osborne (2001b). The mean of these estimates is 0.15, indicating that a standard deviation change in the cognitive score, holding constant the remaining variables (including schooling), changes the natural logarithm of earnings by about one-seventh of a standard deviation. By contrast, the mean value of the normalized regression coefficient of years of schooling in the same equation predicting the natural log of earnings in these studies is 0.22, suggesting a somewhat larger independent effect of schooling. We checked to see if these results were dependent on the weight of overrepresented authors, the type of cognitive test used, at what age the test was taken, and other differences among the studies, and we found no significant effects. An estimate of the causal impact of childhood IQ on years of schooling (also normalized) is 0.53 (Winship and Korenman 1999). A rough estimate of the direct and indirect effect of IQ on earnings, call it b, is then $b = 0.15 + (0.53)(0.22) = 0.266$.

Do these two facts—parent-child similarity in IQ and an important direct and indirect causal role for IQ in generating earnings—imply a major role for genetic inheritance of cognitive ability in the transmission of intergenerational economic status? One way to formulate this question is to ask how similar would parental and offspring IQ be if the sole source of the similarity were genetic transmission. Also, how similar would the incomes of parents and offspring be if there were no other transmission channel?

For this we need some insights into genetics (the details are in the appendix and in Bowles and Gintis [2002]), and a few terms— *phenotype, genotype, heritability*, and the *genetic correlation*. A person's IQ—meaning, a test score—is a *phenotypic* trait, while the genes influencing IQ are the person's *genotypic* IQ. *Heritability* is the relationship between the two. Suppose that, for a given environment, a standard deviation difference in genotype is associated with a fraction h of a standard deviation difference in IQ. Then h^2 is the *heritability of IQ*. Estimates of h^2 are based on the degree of similarity of IQ among twins, siblings, cousins, and others with differing degrees of genetic relatedness. The value cannot be higher than 1, and most recent estimates are substantially lower, possibly more like a half or less (Devlin et al. 1997; Feldman et al. 2000; Plomin 1999). The *genetic correlation* is the degree of statistical association between genotypes of parents and children, which is 0.5 if the parents' genotypes are uncorrelated (random mating). But couples tend to be more similar in IQ than would occur by random mate choice (assortative mating), and this similarity is associated with an unknown correlation m of their genotypes. The effect is to raise the genetic correlation of parent and offspring to $(1 + m)/2$.

Using the above method of decomposition, the correlation γ between parental and offspring IQ that is attributable to genetic inheritance of IQ alone is the heritability of IQ times the genetic correlation. Thus we have $\gamma = h^2(1 + m)/2$. The correlation between parent and offspring income attributable to genetic inheritance of IQ is simply this correlation, times the normalized effect of IQ on the income of parents, times the analogous effect for the offspring, or γb^2. Another way to see this is to note that the correlation between parental income and offspring IQ, which we would observe were the genetic inheritance of IQ the only channel at work, is γb, and this times the effect of offspring IQ on earnings, which is b, gives the same result.

Using the values previously estimated, we see that the contribution of genetic inheritance of IQ to the intergenerational transmission of income is $(h^2(1 + m)/2)(0.266)^2 = .035(1 + m)h^2$. If the heritability of IQ were 0.5 and the degree of assortation, m, were 0.2 (both reasonable, if only ball park estimates), and if the genetic inheritance of IQ were the only mechanism accounting for intergenerational income transmission, then the intergenerational correlation would be 0.01, or roughly 2 percent the observed intergenerational correlation. Note the conclusion that the contribution of genetic inheritance of IQ is negligible is not the result of any assumptions concerning assortative mating or the heritability of IQ: the IQ genotype of parents could be perfectly correlated and the heritability of IQ 100 percent without appreciably changing the qualitative conclusions. The estimate results from the fact that IQ is just not an important enough determinant of economic success.

Might the small contribution of genetic inheritance of IQ to parent-offspring similarity of incomes be the result of measurement error in the cognitive measures? There are two issues here. First, what is the *reliability* of the test: whatever the test measures, does it measure well? Second, what is the *validity* of the test: does the test measure the right thing? The concern that the tests are a very noisy measure is misplaced. In fact, the tests are among the more reliable variables used in standard earnings equations (reliability is measured by the correlation between tests and retests, between odd and even numbered items on the tests, and by more sophisticated methods). For the commonly used Armed Forces Qualification Test (AFQT), for example—a test used to predict vocational success that is often used as a measure of cognitive skills—the correlation between two test scores taken on successive days by the same person is likely to be higher than the correlation between the same person's reported years of schooling or income on two successive days.

The second concern, that the tests measure the wrong thing, is weightier and less easy to address with any certainty. Could it be that cognitive skills not measured on existing test instruments are both highly heritable and have a major impact on earnings, thereby possibly explaining a more substantial fraction of the transmission process? The search for general cognitive measures that are substantially uncorrelated with IQ and predictive of success in adult roles began with Edward Thorndike's (1919) paper on "social intelligence." Some alternative test instruments, such as Robert Sternberg and collaborators' "practical intelligence" (Sternberg et al. 1995; Williams and Sternberg 1995) predict economic success in particular occupations. But despite the substantial fame and fortune that would have accrued to success in this area, the quest that Thorndike launched three generations ago has yielded no robust alternative to IQ, let alone one that is highly heritable. Thus, the possible existence of economically important but as yet unmeasured heritable general cognitive skills cannot be excluded, but should at this stage be treated as somewhat wishful speculation.

Indeed, we are inclined to think that available estimates *overstate* the importance of general cognitive skill as a determinant of earnings, since in many respects taking a test is like doing a job. Successful performance in either case results from a combination of ability and motivation, including the disposition to follow instructions, persistence, work ethic, and other traits likely to contribute independently to one's earnings. This is the reason we eschew the common label of a test score as "cognitive skill" but rather use the more descriptive term "cognitive performance." Eysenck (1994, 9), a leading student of cognitive testing, writes, "Low problem solving in an IQ test is a measure of performance; personality may influence performance rather than abstract intellect, with measurable effects on the IQ. An IQ test lasts for up to 1 hour or more, and considerations of fatigue, vigilance, arousal, etc. may very well play a part." Thus some of the explanatory power of the cognitive measure in predicting earnings does not reflect cognitive skill but rather other individual attributes contributing to the successful performance of tasks.

Genetic and Environmental Inheritance

Although the genetic inheritance of IQ explains little of the intergenerational transmission process, this does not rule out the possible importance of other genetically transmitted traits. Indeed, the remarkable income similarity of identical twins compared to fraternal twins suggests that genetic effects may be important. We will use the similarity of twins to estimate the genetic heritability of income as well as the environmental component of intergenerational transmission.

But two words of caution are in order. First, as we will demonstrate, our estimates are quite sensitive to variations in unobserved parameters. Second, it is sometimes mistakenly supposed that if the heritability of a trait is substantial, then the trait cannot be affected much by changing the environment. The fallacy of this view is dramatized by the case of stature. The heritability of height estimated from U.S.-twin samples is substantial (about 0.90, according to Plomin et al. 2000). Moreover there are significant height differences among the peoples of the world: Dinka men in the Sudan average 5 feet and 11 inches—a bit taller than Norwegian and U.S. military servicemen and a whopping 8 inches taller than the Hadza hunter-gatherers in Southern Africa (Floud et al. 1990). But the fact that Norwegian recruits in 1761 were *shorter* than today's Hadza shows that even quite heritable traits are sensitive to environments. What *can* be concluded from a finding that a small fraction of the variance of a trait is due to environmental variance is that policies to alter the trait through changed environments will require nonstandard environments that differ from the environmental variance on which the estimates are based.

Consider the case of South Africa, where in 1993 (the year before Nelson Mandela became president) roughly two-thirds of the intergenerational transmission of earnings was attributable to the fact that fathers and sons are of the same race, and race is a strong predictor of earnings (Hertz, 2001). That is, adding race to an equation predicting sons' earnings reduces the estimated effect of fathers' earnings by over two thirds. Because the physical traits designated by "race" are highly heritable and interracial parenting uncommon, we find a substantial role of genetic inheritance in the intergenerational transmission of economic status. Yet, it is especially clear in the case of South Africa under apartheid that the economic importance of the genetic inheritance of physical traits was derived from environmental influences. What made the genetic inheritance of skin color and other racial markers central to the transmission process were matters of public policy, not human nature, including the very definition of races, racial patterns in marriage, and the discrimination suffered by nonwhites. Thus, the determination of the genetic component in a transmission process says little by itself about the extent to which public policy can level a playing field.

Our estimates of heritability use data on pairs of individuals with varying degrees of shared genes and environments. For example, identical and fraternal twins are exposed to similar environments during their upbringing but fraternal twins are less closely related genetically than identical twins. Under quite strong simplifying assumptions (explained in the appendix to Bowles and Gintis 2002), one can exploit the variation in genetic and environmental similarities among pairs of relatives to estimate heritability of a trait such as income, years of schooling, or other standard economic variables. Taubman (1976) was the first economist to use this method. The model underlying the following calculations assumes that genes and environment affect human capital, which produces earnings, as the equation below indicates, but the effects of wealth and other contributions to income are unaffected by genes and environment, and will be introduced subsequently.

Here are the assumptions. First, genes and environments have additive effects—genes and environment may be correlated, but the direct effect of "good genes" on earnings (its regression coefficient) is independent of the quality of the environment, and conversely. Thus an individual's earnings can be written

$$\text{earnings} = h(\text{genes}) + \beta(\text{environment}) + \text{idiosyncratic effects.}$$

Second, within-pair genetic differences (for the fraternals) are uncorrelated with within-pair environmental differences (for example, the good-looking twin does not get more loving attention). Third, the environments affecting individual development are as similar for members of fraternal sets of twins as for the identical sets. Fourth, the earnings genotypes of the two parents are uncorrelated (random mating). Given these assumptions, the heritability (h^2) of earnings is twice the difference between the earnings correlations of identical and fraternal twins. As the difference between these two correlations is 0.2 in the best data sets available (the Swedish Twin Registry studied by Anders Björklund, Markus Jäntti, and Gary Solon in chapter 4, and a smaller U.S. Twinsburg data set studied by Ashenfelter and Krueger [1994]), these assumptions give an estimate of h^2 equal to 0.4.

Because the correlation of genes for the fraternal twins is 0.5 (due to random mating), the implied correlation of fraternal twins' earnings due to genetic factors is $h^2/2$. The fact that the observed correlation of twins' earnings exceeds this estimate is explained by the fact that twins share similar environments. Thus, once we know h^2, we can use information about the degree of similarity of these environments to estimate how large the environmental effects would have to be to generate the observed earnings correlations.

The assumptions concerning random mating and common environments are unrealistic, and can be relaxed. First, we need an estimate of m_y, the correlation of parents' earnings genotypes. The relevant measure is the earnings *potential* (the correlation of actual earnings would understate the degree of assortation, because many women do not work full time). The degree of assortation on phenotype is likely to be considerably larger than on genotype for the simple reason that the basis of the assortation is the phenotype not the genotype (which is unobservable), and the two are (for the case of earnings, as we will see) not very closely related. Assuming that the genotype for potential earnings of parents is half as similar as are the actual incomes of brothers, the correlation would be about 0.2.

Second, note that because it was assumed that the environments experienced by the two identical twins are not, on the average, more similar to the environments of the two fraternal twins, the fact that within twin-pair earnings differences are less for the identical twins must be explained entirely by their genetic similarity. But if the identical twins experience more similar environments (because they look alike, for example) than the fraternals, the estimate will overstate the degree of heritability.

It is likely that identical twins share more similar environments than fraternal twins and other siblings (Loehlin and Nichols 1976; Feldman et al. 2000; Cloninger et al. 1979; Rao et al. 1982). Estimates of the extent to which identical twins environments are more similar than those of fraternal twins are quite imprecise, and we can do no better than to indicate the effects of using plausible alternative assumptions. Just how sensitive the estimates are to reasonable variations in the assumptions concerning differences in the correlations of twins' environments can be estimated by assuming some degree of statistical association of genes and environment, with the correlated but not identical genes of the fraternal twins giving them less correlated environments than the identical twins.

Table I.1 presents estimates based on various magnitudes of this genes-environment effect. As the assumed correlation between genes and environment increases, the correlation of the environments of the identical twins rises, and because this then explains some of the earnings similarity of the identical twins, the resulting estimate of heritability falls.

The Swedish Twin Registry data set assembled by Björklund, Jäntti, and Solon, analyzed in chapter 4, has data not just on twins, but on many pairs with varying degrees of relatedness (half-siblings, for example) and may allow for more robust estimates using the methods developed by Cloninger et al. (1979), Rao et al. (1982), and Feldman et al. (2000).

We take the third numerical column of table I.1 as the most reasonable set of estimates. Using these, two striking conclusions follow. First, the heritability of earnings appears substantial. Second, the environmental effects are also large. The normalized regression coefficient of environment on earnings is $\beta_e = 0.38$, which may be compared with the normalized regression coefficient for a measure of years of schooling in an earnings equation, from our earlier meta-analysis, which is 0.22. Thus, these estimates suggest that while educational attainment captures important aspects of the relevant environments, it is far from exhaustive.

TABLE I.1
The Effect of the Assumed Correlation of Genes and Environment on
Estimates of the Heritability of Earnings

	Assumed Correlation of Genes and Environment			
	0.00	0.50	0.70	0.80
Heritability of Earnings	0.50	0.29	0.19	0.13
Normalized Regression Coefficient:				
Genes on earnings	0.71	0.54	0.44	0.36
Environment on earnings	0.29	0.33	0.38	0.44
Correlation of Environments:				
Fraternal twins	0.70	0.70	0.70	0.70
Identical twins	0.70	0.80	0.90	0.97

Notes: The association of genes with environment is represented by the normalized regression coefficient of genes on environment. This table assumes that parental earnings-determining genes are correlated 0.2, and the correlation of fraternal twins' environment is 0.7. We use the correlations of income for identical twins of 0.56 and of fraternal twins of 0.36, taken from the U.S. Twinsburg Study, and assume that these are also the correlations of earnings.

What is the intergenerational correlation of earnings implied by our estimate of β_e and h? To answer this question, in addition to h and β_e, we require the correlation of parents' earnings with genes (which is already implied by our estimates) and the correlation of parents' earnings with environment. The first column in table I.2 gives our estimates. The genetic contribution is simply h times the correlation between parental earnings and offspring genotype, or $h^2(1 + m)/2$. The environmental contribution, similarly, is β_e times a correlation of parents' earnings and

TABLE I.2
Contribution of Environmental, Genetic, and Wealth to
Intergenerational Transmission

	Earnings	Income
Environmental	0.28	0.20
Genetic	0.12	0.09
Wealth		0.12
Intergenerational correlation	0.40	0.41

Notes: The income column and the estimated contribution of wealth are discussed below. The environmental vs. genetic breakdown assumes the figures in the third numerical column in table I.1.

environment (namely 0.74) selected to yield a total intergenerational earnings correlation of 0.4.

The estimate that genetic inheritance may account for almost one-third of the intergenerational correlation is somewhat unexpected, in light of our negative findings concerning the inheritance of IQ. The surprising importance of both environment and genes points to a puzzle. If the genetic contribution is not strongly related to IQ and if the environmental contribution is much larger than the contribution of years of schooling, what are the mechanisms accounting for persistence of income over the generations? We shall return to this puzzle, but will turn to data other than twin studies first, to show that the same puzzle arises elsewhere.

HUMAN CAPITAL

Because schooling attainment is persistent across generations and has clear links to skills and perhaps other traits that are rewarded in labor markets, an account of the transmission of intergenerational status based on human capital has strong prima facie plausibility. The data already introduced allow a calculation of the portion of the intergenerational income correlation accounted for by the more extensive schooling received offspring of high-income parents (measured in years). This is just the correlation of parent income and offspring schooling (about 0.45) multiplied by the normalized regression coefficient of schooling in an earnings equation (0.22 from our meta-analysis) or 0.10. This is a substantial contribution, particularly in light of the fact that it is restricted to the effects of years of schooling operating independently of IQ (because our estimate of 0.22 is from earnings functions in which the regressors include the AFQT test or a similar instrument). The full contribution—including the effect of schooling on IQ and its effect on earnings, as well as the direct effect of schooling on earnings holding constant IQ—is 0.12.

It used to be commonly assumed that once adequate measures of schooling quality were developed, the only effects of parental economic status on offspring earnings would operate through effects on cognitive functioning and schooling, and that the direct effect of parental status on offspring earnings would vanish. But even as the measurement of schooling quality has improved over the years, the estimated direct effect of parental incomes (or earnings) on offspring earnings has turned out to be remarkably robust. For example, Mulligan (1999), using early 1990s data from the (U.S.) National Longitudinal Study of Youth, first estimated the effect of a change in the logarithm of parental earnings on offspring's logarithm of earnings without controlling for any other factors, and then controlled for a large number of measures of school quality, as well as the AFQT and standard educational and demographic variables. He found that between two-fifths and one-half of the gross (unconditional) statistical relationship of parental and offspring earnings remains even after controlling for the other factors.

These results just reaffirm the black box puzzle using entirely different data and methods: more than half of the intergenerational transmission coefficient is unaccounted for.[3]

Taking account of the better health enjoyed by the children of the well-to-do than that of poor children (Case et al. 2001), along with the fact that poor health has substantial effects on incomes later in life (Smith 1999), would probably account for a substantial part of the intergenerational transmission process. The role of health in the process is particularly striking because parental incomes appear to have strong impacts on child health that are not accounted for by either the health status of the parents nor by the genetic similarity between parents and children. Moreover, as John Loehlin shows in chapter 6, while there are modest but highly significant intergenerational correlations of personality and attitude variables, these correlations are unlikely to account for more than a small part of the intergenerational correlation of incomes, given our current ability to measure accurately these individual characteristics.

WEALTH EFFECTS

Economic success can be passed on in a family through the inheritance of wealth as well as inter vivos wealth transfers to children. Remarkably little scholarly attention has been given to this mechanism, in part because no representative panel data-set with adequate measures of other earnings determinants exists, in which the second generation has reached the age whereby the inheritance of wealth typically has been completed. We are aware of only one study that addresses this problem by following the second generation to their deaths, and it estimates a much higher intergenerational wealth correlation (Menchik 1979). But while inheritances of wealth clearly matter for the top of the income distribution, we doubt whether such transfers play an important role for most families. Very few individuals receive inheritances of significant magnitude. Mulligan (1997) estimates that estates passing on sufficient wealth to be subject to inheritance tax in the United States constituted between 2 and 4 percent of deaths over the years 1960–95. Even though this figure leaves out quite substantial inheritances as well as transfers that occur during life, it seems unlikely that for most of the population a substantial degree of economic status is transmitted directly by the intergenerational transfer of property or financial wealth.

It thus seems likely that the intergenerational persistence of wealth reflects, at least in part, parent-offspring similarities in traits influencing wealth accumulation, such as orientation toward the future, sense of personal efficacy, work ethic, schooling attainment, and risk-taking. Some of these traits covary with the level of wealth: for example, less well-off people are more likely to be risk averse, to discount the future, and to have a low sense of efficacy. Because of this correlation of wealth with the traits conducive to wealth accumulation, parent-offspring similarity in wealth may arise from sources independent of any bequests or transfers.

Whatever their source, for families with significant income from wealth, parent-offspring wealth similarities can contribute a substantial fraction to the intergenerational persistence of incomes. Using the same decomposition methods as described earlier, this contribution is the correlation of parent income and child wealth times the normalized regression coefficient of wealth in an income equation. We use data from the Panel Study of Income Dynamics (PSID) analyzed by Charles and Hurst (2003). The correlation between parent income and child wealth (both in natural logarithms) in this data set is 0.24. The average age of the children is only thirty-seven years, and so this correlation does not capture inheritance of wealth at death of the parents. To get a rough idea of the normalized regression coefficient, one way to proceed is by starting with the percentage change in income associated with a 1 percent change in wealth; this elasticity will range from virtually zero (for those with little or no wealth) to one (for those with no source of income other than wealth). A plausible mean value (based on average factor income shares) for the U.S. population is 0.20. We convert this to a normalized regression coefficient by multiplying by the ratio of the standard deviation of log wealth to the standard deviation of log income, also from the PSID data set provided by Charles and Hurst (forthcoming). This calculation suggests that higher-income parents' tendency to have wealthier children contributes 0.12 to the intergenerational correlation of incomes.

This figure, while substantial, may be an underestimate, as it is based on data that, for the reasons already mentioned, does not capture a key transmission process, namely inheritance of wealth upon the death of one's parents. Moreover, the estimate should be adjusted upward to take account of the tendency for those with greater wealth to have higher average returns on their wealth (Bardhan et al. 2000; Yitzhaki 1987). Greater parental or personal wealth may also raise the rate of return on schooling and other human investments, but we have no way to take account of this empirically. For a sample of very rich parents, the contribution of wealth to the intergenerational correlation would be much higher, of course. For a sample of families with very limited wealth, the contribution would be nearly zero. The difference in the contribution of wealth-effects across the income distribution is a reflection of the heterogeneous nature of the transmission process mentioned earlier. Because of the very skewed distribution of wealth, the family with the mean level of wealth (to which our estimates apply) is considerably wealthier than the median family.

CONCLUSION

In chapter 3, David Harding, Christopher Jencks, Leonard Lopoo, and Susan Mayer present data showing that parent-child family income correlations fell somewhat between 1961 and 1999, as did the income gap between nonwhites and whites. Moreover, they find that the income gap between those raised by advantaged and disadvantaged parents narrowed during the 1960s but has shown no trend since. This moderately egalitarian trend is more promising than recent evidence that points to a much higher level of intergenerational transmission of economic position than was previously thought to be the case. Our main objective in this book has been to assess this historically persistent process of intergenerational transmission and the apparently robust mechanisms accounting for it. Table I.3 summarizes our best estimates of the

Table I.3
The Main Causal Channels of Intergenerational
Status Transmission in the United States

Channel	Earnings	Income
IQ (conditioned on schooling)	0.05	0.04
Schooling (conditioned on IQ)	0.10	0.07
Wealth		0.12
Personality (fatalism)	0.03	0.02
Race	0.07	0.07
Total Intergenerational Correlation Accounted For	0.25	0.32

Notes: For each channel, the entry is the correlation of parent income with the indicated predictor of offspring income, multiplied by its normalized regression coefficient in an earnings or income equation. The total is the intergenerational correlation resulting from these channels, in the absence of a direct effect of parents' status on offspring status.
Source: Calculations described in Bowles and Gintis (2001).

relative importance of the main causal channels we have been able to identify. The only entry not previously explained is the first, which is an estimate of the correlation between parental income and child IQ multiplied by our estimate of the normalized effect of IQ on earnings, conditioned on, among other things, years of schooling. The estimates for IQ, schooling, and personality in the income column are simply those in the earnings column adjusted to take account of the effect of earnings differences on income differences, suitably normalized as described in Bowles and Gintis (2002). Thus, we do not take account of the way that these earnings determinants may affect the rate of return to one's wealth. By contrast, we assume that the race effect is of the same magnitude in determining the returns to both human capital and conventional wealth (if the race effect on incomes worked solely via an effect on earnings, its contribution to the intergenerational earnings correlation would be significantly greater).

While the estimates in table I.3 are quite imprecise, the qualitative results are not likely to be affected by reasonable alternative methods. The results are somewhat surprising: wealth, race, and schooling are important to the inheritance of economic status, but IQ is a less important contributor and, as we have seen above, the genetic transmission of IQ is even less important.

A policymaker who is concerned about intergenerational transmission of economic status will face two difficult sets of issues. First, many of the policies that might affect the intergenerational transmission of economic status are controversial. Eliminating racial discrimination would reduce one component of the heritability of income, but achieving this goal is difficult. Improving educational achievement, especially for those whose parents have relatively low levels of schooling, would reduce intergenerational transmission both directly, because of the impact of schooling, and perhaps also indirectly by providing a more open network of group memberships and mating choices that are less homogeneous by income class. But improving educational achievement is another goal that is easier stated than accomplished.

A second broad set of problems is normative. As Adam Swift argues in chapter 9, a zero correlation between parental and child incomes is not a morally desirable goal because there are important values of family life and privacy that would be compromised by any serious attempt to disconnect completely the fortunes of parents and children. Moreover, as dramatized by Marcus Feldman, Shuzhuo Li, Nan Li, Shripad Tuljapurkar, and Xiaoyi Jin in chapter 8, parental self-interest as well as parental altruism leads families to maintain a strong and culturally justified interest in the economic futures of their children. Thus, rather than pursuing an abstract (and to our minds unattractive) objective of zero intergenerational correlation, a better approach might be to ask which mechanisms of intergenerational transmission are unfair, and to direct policies accordingly. The role of race in transmitting status from generation to generation is clearly unfair. Many people regard the strong correlation between parental income and child health as morally suspect, and many feel the same way about high levels of wealth inheritance. Large majorities favor policies to compensate for inherited disabilities. Other mechanisms of persistence—the genetic inheritance of good looks, for example—strike most people as unobjectionable and not an appropriate target for compensatory policy interventions. Even if some consensus could be formed on which of these mechanisms are morally suspect, the policy implications would be far from clear. For example, the possible incentive effects on parental behaviors of reduced parental influence on child success would have to be estimated and considered.

Addressing the policy challenge will require not only moral clarity about these and related issues, but a better accounting of which causal mechanisms are at work in producing the substantial levels of intergenerational persistence of economic differences. We hope the research presented in this book will contribute to a renewed commitment to dealing with this pressing social issue.

NOTES

1. The analysis presented below is drawn from Bowles and Gintis (2002).

2. This decomposition can be found in Blalock (1964) and is described in the Appendix in Bowles and Gintis (2002). Goldberger (1991) describes the standard regression model with normalized (mean zero, unit standard deviation) variables on which it is based.

3. It is also true that we *can* usually account statistically for less than half of the variance of the earnings or income using the conventional variables described earlier. But this fact does not explain our limited success in accounting for the intergenerational correlation, as this correlation measures only that part of the variation of earnings that we can explain statistically by parental economic status.

Chapter One

THE APPLE DOES NOT FALL FAR FROM THE TREE

Greg Duncan, Ariel Kalil, Susan E. Mayer, Robin Tepper, and Monique R. Payne

DECADES of social science research have documented correlations between the social, educational, behavioral, and economic outcomes of parents and children. For example, children of more highly educated and economically successful parents tend themselves to complete more schooling and earn more, although the intergenerational correlations are well below unity.

Children of parents who smoke, take drugs, commit crimes, and engage in early sex are more likely to do the same compared with children whose parents do not engage in these activities. Positive correlations have also been established for social-psychological dispositions such as depression, emotional withdrawal, and locus of control. Here too the intergenerational correlations are often significant in a statistical sense but far from unity.

One common interpretation of the intergenerational correlation of behaviors is that parents pass on *general* competencies to their children— "good" or "successful" parents tend to produce "good" or "successful" children, and likewise for "bad" or "unsuccessful" parents and children. Model 1 of figure 1.1 depicts this process by showing a set of parental characteristics $(P_1, \ldots, P_n)$ that combine to form a single parental characteristic (P_z), which in turn affects many child outcomes $(C_1, \ldots, C_n)$. For example, maternal traits and behaviors might determine a mother's parenting style, which in turn influences a whole range of her child's outcomes. In this model, P_z could be parents' socioeconomic status, parenting style or any other characteristic that affects many child outcomes.

In contrast, parents could pass along *specific* traits and competencies to their children (Model 2). In this case a parent who is consistent, caring, and otherwise a "good" parent but who has a problem with alcohol will be more likely to have a child who has a problem with alcohol, but no more likely to have a child who does badly in school or suffers from depression, apart from the extent that using alcohol contributes to these other problems. Trait-specific genetic influences are one way in which this might happen. Children's modeling of a specific parental behavior

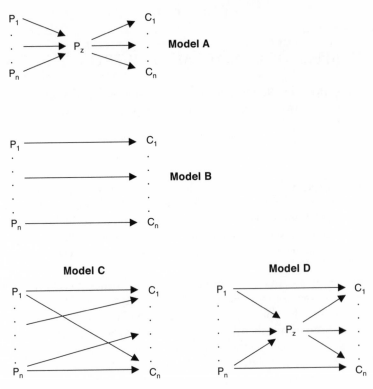

Figure 1.1 Models of intergenerational transmission process.

is another, more psychological process that could produce trait-specific intergenerational correlations.

If parents' general competencies matter most (as in Model 1), then interventions that alter P_z would improve many dimensions of their children's well-being. But if parents pass on specific competencies to their children, then such interventions might not work very well.

Of course the process of intergenerational transmission is not likely to be entirely specific or general. Models 3 and 4 in figure 1.1 show mixed processes. In Model 3 each parental characteristic affects several child characteristics. For example, parents' cognitive skills may affect the child's cognitive skills and social skills. In Model 4, parents' characteristics affect a latent parental characteristic (e.g., their income or parenting style) that affects many child characteristics, but specific parental characteristics also affect specific child characteristics. For example, parents' cognitive skills may affect children's cognitive skills directly but also affect parental income or parenting style, which then affects many other child outcomes.

An unpublished paper by Case and Katz (1991) supports the hypothesis that parents pass on specific competencies. The authors estimate five regressions, each of which relates a specific child behavior to the corresponding behaviors of the child's parents. Their results, reproduced in table 1.1, suggest that specific behaviors of parents predict the same but not other behaviors of their children. The Case and Katz study has important limitations: the sample is confined to youth residing in relatively low-income neighborhoods of Boston; parents and youth were interviewed concurrently; and the measures cover an important but limited set of child outcomes.

Our own look at intergenerational patterns avoids these problems by using two different data sets. The National Longitudinal Survey of Youth (NLSY) is nationally representative and provides identical maternal and child measures taken at roughly the same point in the life cycle (middle-to-late adolescence). The Prince Georges County study (PGC) provides data on parental characteristics from fathers as well as mothers in one county in Maryland. In total, our two data sets measure seventeen outcomes in seven domains: (1) cognitive skills, including both math and reading achievement; (2) psychological well-being, including depression,

TABLE 1.1

OLS Regressions Relating Children's Outcomes to Parental Characteristics Using Data from the Boston Inner City Youth Survey

	Children Behaviors				
Parent Behaviors	Crime in Last Year	Use Illegal Drug	Single Parent	Attends Church Often	Highest Grade Completed
Family member in jail	.08 (.03)	.03 (.03)	.03 (.03)	−.02 (.03)	−.19 (.10)
Family member w/drug, alcohol problem	.08 (.02)	.15 (.03)	.04 (.03)	−.02 (.03)	−.03 (.10)
Parents not married	.02 (.03)	.02 (.04)	.11 (.03)	−.03 (.04)	−.01 (.12)
Parents attend church often	−.02 (.02)	−.04 (.03)	.01 (.03)	.19 (.03)	−.04 (.09)
Parent's years of schooling	.00 (.01)	.02 (.01)	−.01 (.01)	.01 (.01)	.10 (.02)

Notes: Standard errors are shown in parentheses.

Source: Case and Katz (1991), table 6. Regressions also control for race, gender, and child's age.

anger, and shyness; (3) "outwardly directed" negative behaviors such as fighting; (4) "inwardly directed" negative behaviors such as taking drugs; (5) getting caught by authorities, measured by such events as school suspensions and arrests; (6) social activities such as church attendance; and (7) gender role attitudes.

We interpret the patterns that we observe in light of socioeconomic resource, parenting, role-model / identity formation, and genetic mechanisms. In general, we find much more evidence of a specific than general transmission process. Neither socioeconomic status nor parenting behaviors appear very important to the intergenerational transmission process. Our results are more consistent with genetic explanations for some traits and behaviors, and with role-model / identity formation explanations for attitudes and some behaviors, although our tests of these mechanisms are decidedly indirect.

PREVIOUS RESEARCH ON INTERGENERATIONAL CORRELATIONS

Schooling, Earnings, and Occupation.   The completed schooling of fathers correlates on average .35 with the completed schooling of sons in U.S. studies and somewhat less in most studies of other Western countries (Mulligan 1999).

Intergenerational correlations between fathers' and sons' earnings range widely, from about .10 to .50, but for predictable and important methodological reasons (Solon 1999). A major source of difference is whether earnings are measured in a single year or over a number of adjacent years. Since earnings vary from one year to the next, correlations based on single-year earnings are considerably lower (e.g., in the .2 to .3 range) than correlations based on multiyear approximations of "permanent" earnings (.4 to .5; Solon 1999). To the extent possible, our own work on intergenerational correlations of traits, behaviors, and achievement incorporates adjustments for the measurement errors stemming from intertemporal instability in measurement.

A second important consideration is when in the life cycle the two-generation measurements are taken. Correlations with fathers' middle-age earnings are between .20 and .30 if sons' earnings are measured when sons are in their twenties, but approach .50 if measured when the sons are in their thirties (Solon 1999). However, Hauser (1998) finds that the correlation between the educational level of fathers' and sons' occupations does not depend on when in the life cycle they are measured. This correlation ranges between .30 and .35. The NLSY data usually allow us to assess parent and child characteristics measured at the same stage in the life cycle.

Solon (1999) reports that father-daughter earnings correlations are similar to father-son correlations. However, Hauser (1998) finds that father-daughter correlations in the educational level of occupations are significantly lower than father-son correlations and generally range between .2 and .30. In both of our data sets, we examine parent-child correlations separately for sons and daughters.

IQ. Interest in the inheritance of IQ has generated hundreds of estimates of parent-child IQ correlations. Daniels et al. (1997) gathered data from 212 such studies, and they report average correlations of .50 between biological children and their two-parent average, and .41 between single parents and their biological children. In both cases, parents and children lived together. The difference in the two correlations points to the utility of measuring traits of both parents, a feature present in only one of the two data sets we use in our own analysis.

Psychological Characteristics. Research finds positive correlations between parents' and children's personality traits and attitudes. Loehlin (this volume) reports average correlations of modest size (.13) for personality characteristics and more substantial size (.32) for attitudes and interests between biological parents and their children. His data suggest that the parent-child resemblance in personality is mostly due to genes, whereas environments play a larger role in the similarity of attitudes. The correlations between parents and children for personality characteristics were similar whether or not the parents and children took the same questionnaire at the same age. Cunningham (2001) reported that mothers' gender role attitudes when their children were newborns are correlated .14 with offsprings' gender role attitudes at age 18; however, the correlation was larger (.27) between later assessments of maternal attitudes (when children were 15) and children's attitudes at 18. Further, in Loehlin's summary, mother-daughter correlations on personality traits were modestly higher, on average (.16) than father-son correlations (.11) but not different from mother-son similarities (.15).

Others have suggested that correlations are likely to be modest when parent and offspring characteristics are measured at different developmental stages; this may be due to the specific outcome measure. In one study, the correlation of aggression across two generations when measured at comparable ages was higher than the stability across a twenty-two-year span within one generation (Cohen et al. 1998). The correlations are also higher when the measures are based on large and representative population samples. Studies that rely on fairly homogeneous subamples (e.g., inner city or predominantly minority populations; see Hardy et al. 1998; Serbin et al. 1998) risk attenuating correlations.[1] Attrition in longitudinal studies is almost always most severe for the least advantaged sample members and can bias intergenerational correlations. A final problem with most psychological studies is that virtually all of the "parent" data reflect maternal (not paternal) characteristics. The PGC data provide measures of both.

Psychological studies focusing on the transmission of risk behaviors have also found positive correlations between mothers and children for early pregnancy, smoking, antisocial behavior, inhibited behavior, academic failure, interpersonal violence, and negative parenting practices (Patterson 1998; Serbin and Stack 1998).

Cairns et al. (1998) found a correlation of .36 between mothers' early school failure and young children's (ages 4, 5, and 6) low cognitive competence. The correlation between mothers and sons was higher (.48) and significant compared with the insignificant correlation for girls (.28). In contrast, Cairns et al. found no intergenerational correlation of aggressive behavior. Cigarette smoking has been linked across two generations (grandparent-to-parent and parent-to-adolescent); the correlation between grandparent and grandchild smoking was .16 and that between parent smoking (during adolescence) and child smoking was .32 in one study (Chassin et al. 1998). Cohen et al. (1998) found significant intergenerational similarity (.27) for a latent variable representing inhibited behavior (e.g., shy, fearful; parents were assessed at age seven, and offspring were assessed at age two), but found no statistically significant intergenerational correlation for a composite measure of difficult behavior (e.g., anger intensity, negative mood, attention seeking). In another study, mothers' childhood aggression predicted (.20) their children's aggression (observed by independent raters) when the children were approximately the same age (Serbin et al. 1998). Age at first birth appears to correlate across generations (odds ratio = 1.7) and holds for the mother-daughter link as well as the mother-son link (Hardy et al. 1998).

DATA

We use data from the National Longitudinal Survey of Youth, the Children of the National Longitudinal Survey of Youth, and the Prince Georges County Survey. The NLSY is a multistage stratified random sample of 12,686 individuals aged fourteen to twenty-one in 1979.[2]

Most of our measures of maternal outcomes are from the 1979 survey, when the mothers were between 14 and 21 years old. Thus, maternal outcomes are measured when mothers were adolescents or very young adults and before their children were born. The exceptions include a retrospective question about age at first sex that was asked in 1983, 1984, and 1985, a question about participation in high school clubs asked in 1984, and a retrospective measure of shyness—a 1985 question asking respondents to indicate how shy they were at age 6. Frequency of religious attendance was asked in 1982. Finally, two of the measures, the Pearlin Mastery scale and the depression scale, were administered to respondents as adults, in 1992, when they would have been between the ages of 27 and 34.

We measure maternal characteristics during adolescence for two reasons. First, measuring maternal characteristics before the child was born avoids potential problems of reverse causality. A child's characteristics cannot influence a parent's characteristic measured before the child was born. This is especially important when we estimate the effect of parental characteristics on later parenting behaviors. Second, we are interested in the extent to which maternal behaviors correspond to the same behavior in their children, and because some of the behaviors are age- or developmentally stage-specific, we need to measure them at approximately the same age. However, as detailed later, there is also analytic power in being able to compare intergenerational correlations for maternal behaviors and attitudes measured both concurrently and in adolescence. Thus, we also estimate the impact of differential timing of maternal measurement for a limited number of behaviors and attitudes.

Beginning in 1986, women in the original NLSY sample who had become mothers were given the mother-child supplement to the NLSY, and their children were given cognitive and other assessments creating the Children of the NLSY (CNLSY) data set. In 1986, 3,053 women from the original NLSY survey had 5,236 children.[3] Mothers and children have been interviewed repeatedly since 1984. Most of our measures of children's outcomes are from the year the child was 14 years old.[4] The number of cases in analyses using the combined NLSY and CNLSY data varies somewhat with the outcome being measured. For most models in which we predict children's outcomes from parental characteristics, the number of cases is about 1,200. The number declines to about 900 cases in models that control either parenting practices or family background. The NLSY data provide seventeen traits and behaviors of mothers and their children. Variable descriptions, means, standard deviations, ranges and cross-year reliabilities (when available) are provided in the appendix.

The PGC data were gathered in 1991 via face-to-face interviews with 7th grade children and their primary caregivers (usually their mothers) and self-administered surveys with secondary caregivers. The original sample consisted of 1,501 families in one school district (consisting of 23 middle schools) in Prince Georges County, Maryland. We imposed two restrictions on this sample. First, the youths had to come from two-parent families, either intact or step-families, because we were interested in the effect of resident fathers' characteristics on their children. This limited our sample to 900 cases. Second, the primary caregiver had to be the youth's mother or stepmother. This reduced the sample size to 897. Data are available for 462 girls and 435 boys. Approximately two-thirds of the sample is black and one-third is white. Although this sample is not representative of all young adolescents, it allows us to explore the separate effects of mothers and fathers and it provides high-quality measures of some important outcomes, including anger, depression, and gender role attitudes. Each of the three measures is based on a composite of questions and is coded so that a high score references greater anger and depression, and more liberal gender role beliefs. The mother and father measures are coded in the same fashion and are identical to the youth measures. The appendix provides descriptions and descriptive statistics for the PGC adolescent and parent measures.

Our basic empirical strategy with the larger NLSY data is to estimate unadjusted and regression-adjusted correlations (and, in the case of dichotomous measures, odds ratios) between the seventeen maternal traits measured during adolescence and each of the same seventeen characteristics of children, also measured in adolescence. Our regressions control only for the mother's race and age, and are estimated separately for sons and daughters. Thus we estimate seventeen models, each regressing a single-child outcome on seventeen maternal characteristics plus age and race. This allows us to assess the extent to which maternal characteristics have general or specific effects on children's outcomes and whether the effects differ for sons and daughters.

RESULTS

Mother-Daughter Correlations in the NLSY. Table 1.2 shows the bivariate and regression-adjusted associations between mothers' and daughters' traits and behaviors that are measured dichotomously. We used logistic regression, so entries in the table are odds ratios.[5] Table 1.3 shows corresponding associations for mother-daughter traits and behaviors that are measured on continuous scales. These entries are Pearson correlations and standardized OLS regression coefficients.[6] Together, tables 1.2 and 1.3 show the effect of seventeen characteristics of mothers on each of the seventeen corresponding outcomes for daughters.

TABLE 1.2
Odds Ratios from Multivariate and Bivariate Logistic Regressions for Dichotomous Outcomes for Mothers and Daughters

Maternal Traits and Behaviors (independent variables)		Daughter Traits and Behaviors (dependent variables)								
		Pro-Social Behavior	Substance Use				Delinquent Behavior			
		Particip. in School Clubs	Used Marijuana	Used Other Drugs	Sex Before Age 15	Damaged Property in Last Year	Fought at School/Work Last Year	Hit Someone Last Year	Ever Suspended	Ever Convicted
Participation in school clubs	odds ratio	1.39	.84	2.47	1.16	.79	.92	.96	1.10	1.20
	(z-ratio)	(2.44)	(-.77)	(1.24)	(.92)	(-1.13)	(-.48)	(-.25)	(.50)	(.45)
	bivariate odds	1.85	0.62	1.36	0.87	0.69	0.78	0.89	0.99	0.85
Used marijuana	odds ratio	.88	1.72	6.11	1.16	1.18	.95	1.59	1.34	2.56
	(z-ratio)	(-.85)	(2.06)	(2.74)	(.86)	(.72)	(-.26)	(2.50)	(1.46)	(2.41)
	bivariate odds	0.90	1.78	4.10	1.35	1.40	0.84	1.51	1.26	1.93
Used other drugs	odds ratio	.60	1.08	5.39	1.18	1.63	.97	.90	.96	.60
	(z-ratio)	(-2.54)	(.28)	(2.12)	(.74)	(1.84)	(-.10)	(-.43)	(-.15)	(-1.03)
	bivariate odds	0.68	1.88	5.62	1.55	1.87	1.01	1.30	1.26	1.21
Sex before age 15	odds ratio	.76	1.54	1.59	1.86	.92	1.37	1.37	1.50	.90
	(z-ratio)	(-1.99)	(1.80)	(.61)	(3.87)	(-.40)	(1.76)	(1.71)	(2.06)	(-.23)
	bivariate odds	0.61	1.65	1.15	2.89	1.12	1.57	1.38	2.01	1.33
Damaged property last year	odds ratio	.81	2.78	2.48	1.20	1.09	1.12	.82	.85	1.94
	(z-ratio)	(-.96)	(2.81)	(.88)	(.60)	(.25)	(.37)	(-.61)	(-.59)	(1.17)
	bivariate odds	0.70	2.65	1.55	1.47	1.11	1.52	1.07	1.52	2.75

TABLE 1.2 (cont.)

		Daughter Traits and Behaviors (dependent variables)								
		Pro-Social Behavior	Substance Use				Delinquent Behavior			
Maternal Traits and Behaviors (independent variables)		Particip. in School Clubs	Used Marijuana	Used Other Drugs	Sex Before Age 15	Damaged Property in Last Year	Fought at School / Work Last Year	Hit Someone Last Year	Ever Suspended	Ever Convicted
Fought at school / work last year	odds ratio	.85	.80	.48	0.95	1.47	1.34	1.06	1.23	1.93
	(z-ratio)	(-1.01)	(-.75)	(-.95)	(-.26)	(1.63)	(1.44)	(.30)	(1.01)	(1.60)
	bivariate odds	0.71	1.24	1.73	1.09	1.36	1.77	1.31	2.15	1.81
Hit someone last year	odds ratio	1.06	1.45	.93	1.04	1.01	1.24	1.64	1.91	.82
	(z-ratio)	(.36)	(1.45)	(-.10)	(.24)	(.04)	(1.14)	(2.79)	(3.30)	(-.50)
	bivariate odds	0.89	1.32	1.02	1.15	1.23	1.45	1.64	2.40	1.57
Ever suspended	odds ratio	.95	1.26	.49	1.26	.99	1.16	1.05	1.61	.98
	(z-ratio)	(-.36)	(.88)	(-.90)	(1.35)	(-.04)	(.79)	(.27)	(2.49)	(-.05)
	bivariate odds	0.72	1.55	1.03	1.46	1.17	1.55	1.22	2.74	1.42
Ever convicted	odds ratio	.57	1.89		1.72	1.88	1.34	.69	3.75	5.12
	(z-ratio)	(-1.22)	(1.29)		(1.16)	(1.43)	(.62)	(-.76)	(3.39)	(1.95)
	bivariate odds	0.51	3.17	1.82	2.29	2.32	2.07	1.32	3.97	5.10
Math test score	odds ratio	1.03	.98	1.03	0.98	.99	.99	1.02	.99	.93
	(z-ratio)	(3.19)	(-.89)	(.43)	(-1.43)	(-.62)	(-.93)	(1.42)	(-.53)	(-2.63)
	bivariate odds	1.05	0.99	1.00	0.98	0.98	0.96	1.00	0.95	0.95
Reading test score	odds ratio	1.02	1.01	.94	1.00	1.01	.99	.99	.98	1.03
	(z-ratio)	(2.01)	(1.07)	(-1.30)	(-.10)	(.71)	(-1.28)	(-.96)	(-1.32)	(1.12)
	bivariate odds	1.03	1.01	0.99	0.99	1.00	0.98	1.00	0.97	1.00

Pearlin mastery scale	odds ratio	1.02	.99	.95	0.98	.99	1.00	.97	.95	.90
	(z-ratio)	(.98)	(−.26)	(−.55)	(−.86)	(−.20)	(.00)	(−1.29)	(−1.51)	(−1.93)
	bivariate odds	1.05	0.97	0.97	0.96	0.98	0.96	0.95	0.95	0.89
Self-esteem scale	odds ratio	1.01	1.00	1.02	1.00	1.00	1.02	1.03	1.02	1.00
	(z-ratio)	(.69)	(−.04)	(.23)	(−.20)	(.02)	(1.03)	(1.08)	(.75)	(−.06)
	bivariate odds	1.06	0.98	0.99	0.97	0.98	0.98	1.00	0.98	0.94
Depression scale	odds ratio	1.02	1.00	.96	1.04	1.01	1.03	1.06	1.04	1.04
	(z-ratio)	(1.15)	(−.04)	(−.46)	(2.33)	(.38)	(1.92)	(3.48)	(2.03)	(1.15)
	bivariate odds	0.97	1.02	1.00	1.05	1.03	1.05	1.06	1.07	1.09
Shyness at age 6[a]	odds ratio	.85	1.16	1.20	1.00	.98	.91	.97	1.16	1.26
	(z-ratio)	(−2.46)	(1.20)	(.45)	(−.03)	(−.20)	(−1.13)	(−.32)	(1.71)	(1.30)
	bivariate odds	0.84	1.03	0.92	1.05	0.97	0.94	1.00	1.13	1.30
Traditional gender-role attitudes	odds ratio	1.01	1.00	1.05	1.01	.97	.99	.99	.93	1.00
	(z-ratio)	(.71)	(−.01)	(.47)	(.62)	(−1.28)	(−.44)	(−.31)	(−2.78)	(−.06)
	bivariate odds	0.99	1.00	0.98	1.01	0.97	0.99	0.98	0.96	1.01
Frequency attend religious services	odds ratio	1.05	1.18	1.31	0.94	1.01	.89	1.02	.96	1.16
	(z-ratio)	(1.40)	(2.29)	(1.30)	(−1.41)	(.19)	(−2.29)	(.45)	(−.71)	(1.06)
	bivariate odds	1.12	1.01	1.25	0.87	0.95	0.88	0.94	0.90	1.00
Black	odds ratio	1.14	.55	.74	0.68	1.27	1.24	1.29	3.02	.62
	(z-ratio)	(.79)	(−1.98)	(−.36)	(−1.90)	(.91)	(.93)	(1.14)	(4.55)	(−1.11)
	bivariate odds									
Hispanic	odds ratio	.81	1.38	3.50	0.81	1.74	1.35	1.42	1.86	.70
	(z-ratio)	(−1.16)	(1.16)	(1.52)	(−1.01)	(2.20)	(1.25)	(1.55)	(2.33)	(−.66)
	bivariate odds									
Age	odds ratio	1.01	1.45	2.94	1.16	1.16	.88	.84	1.27	1.02
	(z-ratio)	(.13)	(4.53)	(5.11)	(2.28)	(1.57)	(−1.09)	(−1.42)	(1.66)	(.10)
	bivariate odds									
Number of observations		1246	929	1051	964	1363	880	880	1346	848

Notes: [a] Mothers were asked as adults to indicate how shy they were at age six.

Source: National Longitudinal Survey of Youth 1979 Cohort and Children of the NLSY79.

TABLE 1.3

OLS Standardized Regression Coefficients and Pearson Correlations for Continuous Outcomes for Mothers and Daughters

Maternal Traits and Behaviors (independent variables)		Daughter Traits and Behaviors (dependent variables)							
		Cognitive Skills		Personality Traits				Other / Pro-Social Behavior	
		Math Test Score	Reading Test Score	Pearlin Mastery Scale	Self-esteem Scale	Depression Scale	Shyness at Age 6[a]	Traditional Gender-role Attitudes	Frequency Attend Religious Services
Math test score	Beta	**.22**	.16	-.05	.04	.02	-.02	-.04	.06
	(t-ratio)	(6.37)	(4.51)	(-.99)	(.79)	(.51)	(-.86)	(-.94)	(1.69)
	reliability adj.	.27	.14	-.13	.02	.08	-.04	-.02	.09
	correlation	.39	.37	.07	.07	-.03	.01	-.11	.04
Reading test score	Beta	.12	**.24**	.17	.04	-.06	-.03	-.10	-.08
	(t-ratio)	(3.45)	(6.32)	(3.58)	(.74)	(-1.24)	(-.98)	(-2.24)	(-2.09)
	reliability adj.	.13	.32	.25	.02	-.11	-.01	-.16	-.15
	correlation	.37	.40	.14	.09	-.05	-.01	-.14	-.01
Pearlin mastery scale	Beta	.04	.05	**.07**	.08	.03	.01	-.02	-.05
	(t-ratio)	(1.30)	(1.77)	(1.76)	(2.02)	(.66)	(.41)	(-.52)	(-1.49)
	reliability adj.	.03	.06	.07	.08	.07	.03	.02	-.13
	correlation	.14	.16	.13	.13	-.01	-.02	-.08	.00
Self-esteem scale	Beta	-.04	-.02	.03	**.09**	-.01	.00	.07	.03
	(t-ratio)	(-1.57)	(-.77)	(.79)	(2.46)	(-.30)	(-.13)	(1.88)	(1.16)
	reliability adj.	-.09	-.07	.02	.13	-.01	.02	.13	.08
	correlation	.13	.15	.09	.16	-.07	-.01	-.01	.05

TABLE 1.3 (*cont.*)

		Cognitive Skills			Personality Traits			Other / Pro-Social Behavior	
Maternal Traits and Behaviors (*independent variables*)		Math Test Score	Reading Test Score	Pearlin Mastery Scale	Self-esteem Scale	Depression Scale	Shyness at Age 6[a]	Traditional Gender-role Attitudes	Frequency Attend Religious Services
Depression scale	Beta	-.06	-.04	-.08	-.06	**.07**	.01	.08	-.08
	(t-ratio)	(-2.38)	(-1.58)	(-2.48)	(-1.75)	**(1.79)**	(.46)	(2.23)	(-2.84)
	reliability adj.	-.10	-.06	-.15	-.11	.14	.03	.15	-.18
	correlation	-.15	-.14	-.12	-.10	**.08**	.00	.10	-.09
Shyness at age 6[a]	Beta	-.05	-.08	-.02	-.05	.05	**.10**	.04	-.05
	(t-ratio)	(-2.14)	(-2.93)	(-.70)	(-1.69)	(1.39)	**(5.31)**	(1.15)	(-1.79)
	reliability adj.	-.11	-.17	-.04	-.11	.11	.22	.11	-.10
	correlation	-.12	-.13	-.03	-.05	.06	**.10**	.05	-.03
Traditional gender-role attitudes	Beta	.03	.00	.08	.04	.03	-.01	**.04**	-.02
	(t-ratio)	(1.18)	(.04)	(2.11)	(1.02)	(.65)	(-.31)	**(.95)**	(-.63)
	reliability adj.	n/a	n/a	n/a	n/a	n/a	n/a	n/a	n/a
	correlation	-.04	-.09	.01	-.03	.02	.02	**.10**	.01
Frequency attend religious services	Beta	.04	-.01	.00	.00	-.02	.01	.03	**.15**
	(t-ratio)	(1.48)	(-.46)	(-.10)	(.00)	(-.49)	(.48)	(.80)	**(5.11)**
	reliability adj.	.04	-.03	-.01	.00	-.01	.02	.05	.21
	correlation	.05	.01	.00	.01	-.04	.01	.02	**.16**
Participation in school clubs	Beta	.05	.01	.00	-.01	-.01	-.02	.03	.02
	(t-ratio)	(1.83)	(.27)	(.14)	(-.18)	(-.36)	(-.86)	(.94)	(.68)
	reliability adj.	.07	-.03	.00	-.04	-.01	-.02	.08	.02
	correlation	.15	.11	.09	.08	-.05	-.03	-.03	.07

Used marijuana	Beta	.01	-.02	.05	.05	.02	-.03	-.07	-.02
	(t-ratio)	(.31)	(-.65)	(1.37)	(1.34)	(.50)	(-1.17)	(-2.10)	(-.61)
	reliability adj.	.02	-.05	.08	.07	.04	-.04	-.10	-.01
	correlation	.07	.07	.05	.05	.03	-.02	-.09	-.06
Used other drugs	Beta	-.02	-.01	-.02	.02	.02	.01	-.03	.00
	(t-ratio)	(-.87)	(-.54)	(-.41)	(.63)	(.42)	(.23)	(-.88)	(-.02)
	reliability adj.	-.04	-.01	-.03	.03	-.02	.03	-.04	.02
	correlation	.05	.04	-.02	.00	.04	-.01	-.04	-.05
Sex before age 15	Beta	-.08	-.05	-.04	-.02	.01	-.01	.03	-.02
	(t-ratio)	(-3.21)	(-1.97)	(-1.16)	(-.47)	(.21)	(-.34)	(1.00)	(-.63)
	reliability adj.	n/a	n/a	n/a	n/a	n/a	n/a	n/a	n/a
	correlation	-.14	-.13	-.06	-.03	.03	-.02	.03	-.03
Damaged property in last year	Beta	.01	.01	-.02	-.03	.04	.01	.01	-.03
	(t-ratio)	(.50)	(.50)	(-.66)	(-.92)	(1.39)	(.28)	(.20)	(-.91)
	reliability adj.	.03	.04	-.05	-.06	.11	.02	-.04	-.07
	correlation	-.04	-.03	-.03	-.03	.05	.01	.04	-.03
Fought at school / work last year	Beta	.00	-.01	-.01	.00	-.03	.01	.05	.01
	(t-ratio)	(.01)	(-.50)	(-.20)	(-.07)	(-.77)	(.61)	(1.38)	(.36)
	reliability adj.	.00	-.03	-.04	-.05	-.10	.12	.19	.06
	correlation	-.12	-.12	-.04	-.03	.01	-.01	.09	.00
Hit someone last year	Beta	-.01	.00	.03	.04	.00	-.04	.00	-.02
	(t-ratio)	(-.22)	(.01)	(.87)	(1.20)	(-.05)	(-1.74)	(-.10)	(-.60)
	reliability adj.	-.01	.01	.10	.14	.02	-.15	-.09	-.03
	correlation	-.05	-.06	.03	.05	.04	-.04	.02	-.04
Ever suspended	Beta	-.03	-.06	-.03	-.05	.00	-.01	.08	-.02
	(t-ratio)	(-1.21)	(-2.26)	(-.86)	(-1.57)	(-.03)	(-.61)	(2.26)	(-.65)
	reliability adj.	-.03	-.07	-.05	-.08	.00	-.04	.10	-.03
	correlation	-.15	-.16	-.03	-.05	.04	-.04	.07	-.03

Table 1.3 (cont.)

| | Daughter Traits and Behaviors (dependent variables) | | | | | | | |
| | Cognitive Skills | | Personality Traits | | | | Other / Pro-Social Behavior | |
Maternal Traits and Behaviors (independent variables)	Math Test Score	Reading Test Score	Pearlin Mastery Scale	Self-esteem Scale	Depression Scale	Shyness at Age 6[a]	Traditional Gender-role Attitudes	Frequency Attend Religious Services
Ever convicted								
Beta	-.02	-.05	.04	-.01	.04	.01	0.02	.00
(t-ratio)	(-1.17)	(-2.62)	(.95)	(-.28)	(1.05)	(.34)	(.51)	(-.07)
reliability adj.	-.04	-.12	.06	-.04	.07	.01	.07	.02
correlation	-.04	-.05	.00	-.04	.05	-.01	.02	-.03
Black								
Beta	-.14	-.11	.10	.20	-.01	-.08	-0.11	.03
(t-ratio)	(-4.27)	(-3.43)	(2.34)	(4.38)	(-.24)	(-3.33)	(-2.62)	(.87)
reliability adj.	-.11	-.07	.12	.20	.01	-.10	-.17	.02
correlation								
Hispanic								
Beta	-.11	-.04	.02	.00	.02	-.01	-0.01	-.01
(t-ratio)	(-3.66)	(-1.20)	(.42)	(.01)	(.38)	(-.60)	(-.29)	(-.30)
reliability adj.	-.09	-.01	.03	.01	.03	-.03	-.04	-.02
correlation								
Age								
Beta	-.02	-.01	.02	.05	.04	-.12	-0.08	.00
(t-ratio)	(-.76)	(-.44)	(.47)	(1.42)	(1.25)	(-6.07)	(-2.48)	(-.04)
reliability adj.	-.02	-.02	.01	.04	.05	-.11	-.08	.00
correlation								
R-squared	.21	.24	.05	.08	.02	.03	.06	.04
Number of observations	1278	1272	919	920	922	2717	901	1350

Notes: [a] Mothers were asked as adults to indicate how shy they were at age six. Daughters' shyness was assessed by mothers and interviewers when the child was six years old.

Source: National Longitudinal Survey of Youth 1979 Cohort and Children of the NLSY79.

Of the 289 coefficients in tables 1.2 and 1.3, only 19 percent are statistically significant at the .05 level. However, almost all maternal characteristics predict the corresponding characteristic in daughters. Tables 1.2 and 1.3 show that 14 (82%) of the 17 maternal traits and behaviors significantly predict the corresponding trait or behavior in daughters at the .10 level and 11 of 17 are predictive at the .05 level. (These are the coefficients on the diagonal.) In nearly every case the associations for the matched pair of characteristics are stronger than all others in the row. Of the 272 off-diagonal coefficients, only 38 (13%) are statistically significant at the .05 level, a higher fraction than one would expect by chance but still many lower than on the diagonal.

Thus it appears that there is a great deal of trait specificity to these patterns of correlations. This impression is reinforced by the fact that some of the off-diagonal correlations may arise because the outcomes are correlated with the on-diagonal relationship. For example, if the tendency to take drugs other than marijuana has a large genetic component and the tendency to use marijuana is correlated with the tendency to use other drugs, then parental use of other drugs is likely to be correlated with daughters' use of both marijuana and other drugs. In fact, mothers who used marijuana when they were teens are more likely to have daughters who use both marijuana and other drugs. Similarly mothers' math scores predict daughters' math scores and their participation in school clubs. This would not be surprising if smarter girls are more likely to participate in school clubs. We have not tried to specify which of the child outcomes are causally prior to others, and so we do not control any child outcomes in these models. This leaves open the possibility that some off-diagonal effects reflect on-diagonal influences.

On the other hand, other aspects of tables 1.2 and 1.3 suggest less than universal support for a trait-specific view. Suppose we look across the rows of these tables. Row values tell us how many outcomes of daughters are predicted by a particular maternal characteristic. Maternal characteristics that predict many outcomes suggest general rather than specific influence on daughters' outcomes and would support the kind of model depicted in Model 1 of figure 1.1. Maternal characteristics most predictive of daughters' outcomes are her reading scores (six significant coefficients) and having had sex before the age of fifteen (five significant coefficients). This could be taken as evidence of general effects. However, it also might reflect specific effects. Suppose, for example, that mothers who engage in early sex have daughters who engage in early sex. If early sex reduces girls' school participation and increases suspensions, then a mother's early sex would reduce her daughter's chances of joining clubs and increase her chances of getting suspended.

Now suppose we look at the columns of tables 1.2 and 1.3, which, by showing how many daughter traits have multiple determinants, provide a kind of test of Model 3 in figure 1.1. Each daughter trait has 16 possible off-diagonal coefficients in each column. By chance (at the 5 percent level) we would expect about one off-diagonal coefficient to be statistically significant for most traits. For seven (44 percent) of the daughters' outcomes one or fewer off-diagonal maternal traits has a coefficient on a daughter's characteristic with a t-statistic of at least 2. Thus, only about half of the daughter outcomes demonstrate the single-trait pattern, unless you believe that the off-diagonal maternal traits are related to daughters' traits because of the on-diagonal relationship. A column-based look at the data is thus at least as supportive of Model 3 or 4 as it is of the pure trait-specific Model 2.

Mother-Son Correlations in the NLSY.   Tables 1.4 and 1.5 show the associations between the characteristics of mothers and sons. Of the 289 coefficients in these two tables, 19 percent are significant. By this accounting, maternal characteristics appear to have a similar pattern of effects for sons and daughters. But only 8 of the 17 (47 percent) on-diagonal effects of maternal characteristics on sons' outcomes are statistically significant. This is considerably fewer than the 84 percent of on-diagonal effects that were significant for daughters. In addition, most of the on-diagonal effects of mothers on daughters are larger than the on-diagonal effects of mothers on sons. This suggests more specific effects of maternal characteristics on daughters than on sons.

Some of the gender difference in the off-diagonal effects may reflect different consequences of behavior for boys and girls rather than different transmission processes. For example, mothers who had sex before the age of 15 are more likely to have both sons and daughters who have sex before age 15. Their daughters but not their sons are also less likely to participate in school clubs and more likely to be suspended from school. If daughters who have sex before the age of 15 get pregnant, it would not be surprising that they do not participate in clubs and are suspended due to their pregnancy. Since the sons who have sex before age fifteen do not get pregnant, this will not curtail their school activities.

Four maternal characteristics are statistically significantly predictors of at least four outcomes for sons: participation in school clubs, ever suspended, reading test score, and frequency of attending religious services. These patterns are similar to those found for mothers and daughters. All in all, there appear to be few differences in the way maternal characteristics affect sons and daughters.

Parent-Child Correlations in the PGC.   The PGC data include information on fathers who reside with their children. Using these data we can compare the effect of fathers' and mothers' characteristics on sons and daughters. Unfortunately, we are able to do this for only three mea-

TABLE 1.4

Odds Ratios from Multivariate and Bivariate Logistic Regressions for Dichotomous Outcomes for Mothers and Sons

Maternal Traits and Behaviors (independent variables)		Son Traits and Behaviors (dependent variables)								
		Pro-Social Behavior	Substance Use		Sex Before Age 15	Delinquent Behavior				
		Particip. in School Clubs	Used Marijuana	Used Other Drugs		Damaged Property Last Year	Fought at School/Work Last Year	Hit Someone Last Year	Ever Suspended	Ever convicted
Participation in school cubs	odds ratio	1.29	.87	1.44	.97	.91	1.82	1.47	.96	1.26
	(z-ratio)	(1.93)	(-.67)	(.94)	(-.17)	(-.60)	(3.44)	(2.15)	(-.33)	(.84)
	bivariate odds	1.50	0.68	0.96	0.72	0.76	1.07	1.26	0.80	1.01
Used marijuana	odds ratio	1.18	1.75	1.38	1.29	1.44	1.12	1.49	1.04	1.23
	(z-ratio)	(1.13)	(2.54)	(.73)	(1.49)	(2.10)	(.61)	(2.16)	(.26)	(.70)
	bivariate odds	1.10	1.87	1.77	1.43	1.43	1.24	1.83	1.22	1.43
Used other drugs	odds ratio	.55	1.42	1.64	1.30	1.04	1.18	.86	1.53	1.31
	(z-ratio)	(-2.81)	(1.27)	(.97)	(1.12)	(.16)	(.66)	(-.60)	(2.00)	(.74)
	bivariate odds	0.72	2.13	2.26	1.34	1.22	1.19	1.50	1.38	1.39
Sex before age 15	odds ratio	.94	1.27	.78	2.01	1.20	1.30	1.29	1.26	2.90
	(z-ratio)	(-.44)	(1.11)	(-.68)	(4.49)	(1.09)	(1.52)	(1.41)	(1.62)	(4.13)
	bivariate odds	0.87	1.60	1.60	2.64	1.46	1.68	1.34	1.87	2.57
Damaged property last year	odds ratio	.79	1.13	2.63	.78	.77	.89	1.19	.84	.49
	(z-ratio)	(-.93)	(.32)	(1.74)	(-.88)	(-.88)	(-.38)	(.55)	(-.71)	(-1.10)
	bivariate odds	0.88	1.15	1.66	1.32	1.04	1.14	1.22	1.46	0.40
Fought at school / work last year	odds ratio	1.26	.63	.25	.90	.92	.71	1.11	1.16	.63
	(z-ratio)	(1.37)	(-1.82)	(-2.08)	(-.57)	(-.42)	(-1.71)	(.53)	(.84)	(-1.24)
	bivariate odds	0.95	0.93	0.52	1.54	1.29	1.13	1.18	1.43	0.56

Measure		(1)	(2)	(3)	(4)	(5)	(6)	(7)	(8)	(9)
Hit someone last year	odds ratio	.99	.95	1.03	1.19	1.17	1.47	**1.23**	1.09	.58
	(z-ratio)	(−.06)	(−.22)	(.07)	(1.03)	(.90)	(2.18)	**(1.16)**	(.59)	(−1.85)
	bivariate odds	1.04	0.97	1.09	1.43	1.34	1.40	**1.38**	1.42	0.55
Ever suspended	odds ratio	1.14	1.54	2.07	1.60	1.41	1.31	.96	**1.52**	1.26
	(z-ratio)	(.89)	(2.11)	(1.90)	(2.92)	(2.02)	(1.49)	(−.22)	**(2.89)**	(.87)
	bivariate odds	0.98	1.80	2.44	2.45	1.54	1.69	1.11	**1.98**	1.27
Ever convicted	odds ratio	1.33			1.22	1.23	.99	.47	2.37	**1.19**
	(z-ratio)	(.61)			(.31)	(.38)	(−.02)	(−.85)	(1.90)	**(.16)**
	bivariate odds	0.59	0.68	1.41	1.05	1.53	1.46	0.83	1.67	**0.56**
Math test score	odds ratio	1.01	.99	1.02	.98	1.01	1.00	1.00	.98	1.02
	(z-ratio)	(1.12)	(−.60)	(.68)	(−1.35)	(.76)	(−.11)	(.03)	(−2.03)	(1.05)
	bivariate odds	1.03	0.99	1.00	0.96	0.98	0.98	1.02	0.96	1.00
Reading test score	odds ratio	1.01	1.00	.95	.99	.99	.96	1.00	1.01	.98
	(z-ratio)	(1.20)	(−.24)	(−2.25)	(−.79)	(−1.00)	(−3.69)	(.33)	(1.65)	(−1.14)
	bivariate odds	1.02	1.00	0.97	0.97	0.98	0.98	1.02	0.98	1.00
Pearlin mastery scale	odds ratio	1.02	.99	.93	1.00	.98	.99	1.03	1.01	1.02
	(z-ratio)	(1.21)	(−.43)	(−1.20)	(.10)	(−.80)	(−.48)	(1.25)	(.58)	(.56)
	bivariate odds	1.05	1.00	0.96	0.95	0.97	0.97	1.03	0.98	1.02
Self-esteem scale	odds ratio	.98	1.05	.89	.98	.96	1.03	1.01	.96	1.00
	(z-ratio)	(−.91)	(1.70)	(−2.64)	(−1.26)	(−1.85)	(1.52)	(.62)	(−2.16)	(−.04)
	bivariate odds	1.04	1.00	0.86	0.96	0.94	0.98	1.01	0.96	1.00
Depression scale	odds ratio	.98	1.02	.88	1.03	.99	1.02	1.03	1.04	1.03
	(z-ratio)	(−1.80)	(.76)	(−2.19)	(1.83)	(−.74)	(1.09)	(1.59)	(2.90)	(1.05)
	bivariate odds	0.97	1.02	0.94	1.05	1.01	1.03	1.02	1.05	1.01
Shyness at age 6[a]	odds ratio	.98	1.17	1.43	1.04	1.10	.99	1.06	1.07	.97
	(z-ratio)	(−.32)	(1.42)	(1.53)	(.48)	(1.20)	(−.12)	(.63)	(.89)	(−.24)
	bivariate odds	0.91	1.16	1.54	1.02	1.12	1.00	1.04	1.08	0.95

TABLE 1.4 (cont.)

Son Traits and Behaviors (dependent variables)

Maternal Traits and Behaviors (independent variables)		Pro-Social Behavior	Substance Use		Delinquent Behavior					
		Particip. in School Clubs	Used Marijuana	Used Other Drugs	Sex Before Age 15	Damaged Property Last Year	Fought at School/Work Last Year	Hit Someone Last Year	Ever Suspended	Ever convicted
Traditional gender-role attitudes	odds ratio	.99	1.01	.99	.97	1.03	1.02	1.02	.98	.92
	(z-ratio)	(−.85)	(.19)	(−.26)	(−1.43)	(1.23)	(.90)	(.87)	(−1.09)	(−2.45)
	bivariate odds	0.96	1.00	0.99	0.97	1.03	1.01	0.97	0.99	0.93
Frequency attend religious services	odds ratio	.99	.91	.85	.88	.95	.86	.85	.94	.93
	(z-ratio)	(−.34)	(−1.63)	(−1.26)	(−2.87)	(−1.03)	(−3.18)	(−3.15)	(−1.45)	(−.90)
	bivariate odds	1.04	0.87	0.73	0.85	0.94	0.88	0.86	0.92	0.86
Black	odds ratio	.82	1.08	.80	2.62	1.17	1.05	.74	2.62	.96
	(z-ratio)	(−1.23)	(.28)	(−.44)	(5.27)	(.77)	(.26)	(−1.42)	(5.46)	(−.14)
	bivariate odds									
Hispanic	odds ratio	.62	2.37	.48	1.30	1.11	1.02	.95	.90	1.47
	(z-ratio)	(−2.83)	(3.30)	(−1.19)	(1.29)	(.50)	(.08)	(−.22)	(−.50)	(1.21)
	bivariate odds									
Age	odds ratio	1.07	1.37	1.42	1.01	1.22	1.05	1.22	1.24	1.39
	(z-ratio)	(.72)	(4.15)	(1.88)	(.11)	(2.51)	(.42)	(1.71)	(2.00)	(1.98)
	bivariate odds									
Number of observations		1270	924	1059	998	1400	872	875	1403	833

Notes: [a] Respondents were asked as adults to indicate how shy they were at age six.

Source: National Longitudinal Survey of Youth 1979 Cohort and Children of the NLSY79.

TABLE 1.5
OLS Standardized Regression Coefficients and Pearson Correlations for Continuous Outcomes for Mothers and Sons

Maternal Traits and Behaviors (independent variables)		Cognitive Skills		Personality Traits			Other/Pro-Social Behavior		
		Math Test Score	Reading Test Score	Pearlin Mastery Scale	Self-esteem Scale	Depression Scale	Shyness at Age 6[a]	Traditional Gender-role Attitudes	Frequency Attend Religious Services
Math test score	Beta	.15	.09	.07	.00	.00	.05	-.03	.05
	(t-ratio)	(4.27)	(2.59)	(1.58)	(.11)	(.07)	(1.82)	(-.57)	(1.38)
	reliability adj.	.19	.07	.08	-.04	.01	.08	.00	.06
	correlation	0.38	0.35	0.11	0.10	0.01	0.01	-0.11	0.03
Reading test score	Beta	.15	.20	.07	.12	-.08	-.03	-.09	-.04
	(t-ratio)	(4.11)	(5.33)	(1.47)	(2.37)	(-1.67)	(-1.04)	(-1.90)	(-1.14)
	reliability adj.	.16	.25	.10	.18	-.11	-.05	-.12	-.08
	correlation	0.38	0.39	0.13	0.15	-0.02	-0.03	-0.17	-0.08
Pearlin mastery scale	Beta	.04	.05	.06	.11	.04	-.02	-.11	-.07
	(t-ratio)	(1.47)	(1.81)	(1.59)	(3.04)	(.99)	(-.88)	(-3.07)	(-2.51)
	reliability adj.	.04	.07	.05	.20	.10	.00	-.20	-.17
	correlation	0.17	0.18	0.12	0.15	-0.01	-0.06	-0.14	-0.02
Self-esteem scale	Beta	-.01	.04	-.03	-.02	.00	-.02	.02	.04
	(t-ratio)	(-.36)	(1.46)	(-.76)	(-.56)	(-.07)	(-1.14)	(.59)	(1.28)
	reliability adj.	-.06	.03	-.07	-.05	.00	-.01	.06	.08
	correlation	0.14	0.18	0.08	0.10	-0.02	-0.05	-0.10	0.04
Depression scale	Beta	-.05	-.03	-.07	.01	.05	.03	.02	-.08
	(t-ratio)	(-1.86)	(-1.23)	(-1.93)	(.24)	(1.25)	(1.60)	(.49)	(-2.80)
	reliability adj.	-.09	-.05	-.13	.06	.13	.07	-.01	-.16
	correlation	-0.11	-0.11	-0.07	-0.04	0.05	0.04	0.05	-0.08

TABLE 1.5 (*cont.*)

Maternal Traits and Behaviors (*independent variables*)		Cognitive Skills			Personality Traits			Other/Pro-Social Behavior	
		Math Test Score	Reading Test Score	Pearlin Mastery Scale	Self-esteem Scale	Depression Scale	Shyness at Age 6[a]	Traditional Gender-role Attitudes	Frequency Attend Religious Services
Shyness at age 6[a]	Beta	−.04	−.02	−.02	−.03	.01	.10	.01	.02
	(t-ratio)	(−1.48)	(−.95)	(−.76)	(−.81)	(.36)	(5.32)	(.32)	(.77)
	reliability adj.	−.09	−.04	−.07	−.05	.04	.20	.00	.05
	correlation	−.09	−.08	−.04	−.03	.01	.10	.04	.02
Traditional gender-role attitudes	Beta	−.01	.00	−.02	−.08	−.03	.01	.15	.03
	(t-ratio)	(−.49)	(.13)	(−.47)	(−2.00)	(−.81)	(.52)	(3.88)	(.99)
	reliability adj.	.00	.02	−.02	−.08	−.02	.00	.14	.01
	correlation	−.11	−.11	−.05	−.12	.00	.03	.16	.05
Frequency attend religious services	Beta	.03	.02	.03	.00	−.03	.00	.02	.16
	(t-ratio)	(1.24)	(.73)	(.82)	(−.02)	(−.95)	(−.24)	(.62)	(5.92)
	reliability adj.	.03	.02	.05	.00	−.05	.00	.04	.21
	correlation	.05	.04	.03	.00	−.04	0.00	.02	.17
Participation in school clubs	Beta	.07	.05	−.04	−.05	.02	−.03	−.04	.07
	(t-ratio)	(2.54)	(1.85)	(−1.03)	(−1.54)	(.48)	(−1.70)	(−1.14)	(2.49)
	reliability adj.	.12	.07	−.09	−.12	.04	−.06	−.08	.12
	correlation	.17	.14	−.01	−.01	.00	−.04	−.05	.09
Used marijuana	Beta	.05	.01	.05	−.06	.02	−.03	.02	−.03
	(t-ratio)	(1.74)	(.43)	(1.21)	(−1.47)	(.50)	(−1.54)	(.49)	(−.96)
	reliability adj.	.09	.01	.09	−.12	.02	−.05	.06	−.02
	correlation	0.09	0.08	0.03	−0.01	0.06	−0.04	−0.04	−0.08

Used other drugs								
Beta	-.03	.02	-.04	.02	.04	-.02	-.01	.01
(t-ratio)	(-.95)	(.64)	(-1.09)	(.59)	(1.05)	(-1.08)	(-.33)	(.18)
reliability adj.	-.08	.02	-.09	.06	.05	-.02	-.05	.03
correlation	0.06	0.08	-0.01	0.02	0.08	-0.03	-0.03	-0.04
Sex before age 15								
Beta	-.04	-.05	-.05	-.06	.04	.00	.03	-.05
(t-ratio)	(-1.48)	(-1.71)	(-1.57)	(-1.71)	(1.14)	(.22)	(.97)	(-1.77)
reliability adj.	-.03	-.04	-.05	-.05	.04	.00	.02	-.03
correlation	-0.13	-0.14	-0.09	-0.07	0.04	0.01	0.07	-0.07
Damaged property in last year								
Beta	.03	.01	-.05	-.02	.10	.01	.02	-.01
(t-ratio)	(.96)	(.48)	(-1.51)	(-.63)	(2.68)	(.56)	(.49)	(-.23)
reliability adj.	.07	.03	-.09	-.04	.18	.03	.06	-.05
correlation	0.01	0.00	-0.06	-0.03	0.09	0.00	0.00	0.00
Fought at school / work last year								
Beta	-.02	-.02	.02	.03	.00	.00	-.06	.04
(t-ratio)	(-.81)	(-.65)	(.67)	(.79)	(-.05)	(-.11)	(-1.60)	(1.46)
reliability adj.	-.11	-.04	.03	.11	.02	.00	-.16	.13
correlation	-0.08	-0.10	-0.01	0.00	0.03	-0.01	-0.01	0.01
Hit someone last year								
Beta	.02	.01	.02	.00	-.04	.00	-.02	.00
(t-ratio)	(.72)	(.24)	(.52)	(-.14)	(-1.19)	(-.21)	(-.46)	(.11)
reliability adj.	.10	.01	.07	-.05	-.13	-.01	.01	-.03
correlation	0.00	0.00	-0.02	-0.01	-0.02	-0.02	-0.02	-0.02
Ever suspended								
Beta	.00	-.04	.00	-.03	-.02	-.01	.02	-.01
(t-ratio)	(.04)	(-1.34)	(.06)	(-.75)	(-.44)	(-.32)	(.54)	(-.43)
reliability adj.	.03	-.05	.01	-.07	-.04	-.01	.07	-.04
correlation	-0.11	-0.14	-0.05	-0.05	0.02	-0.02	0.02	-0.02
Ever convicted								
Beta	-.02	.01	-.07	-.04	.00	.01	-.01	.02
(t-ratio)	(-.91)	(.47)	(-3.23)	(-3.35)	(.01)	(.27)	(-.35)	(.73)
reliability adj.	-.07	.01	-.14	-.06	.01	.01	-.05	.07
correlation	-0.04	-0.02	-0.08	-0.03	0.01	0.00	0.00	-0.02

TABLE 1.5 (cont.)

Maternal Traits and Behaviors (independent variables)		Cognitive Skills		Personality Traits				Other/Pro-Social Behavior	
		Math Test Score	Reading Test Score	Pearlin Mastery Scale	Self-esteem Scale	Depression Scale	Shyness at Age 6[a]	Traditional Gender-role Attitudes	Frequency Attend Religious Services
Black	Beta	-.20	-.18	.02	.06	-.08	-.03	-.03	.05
	(t-ratio)	(-5.76)	(-5.26)	(.45)	(1.33)	(-1.84)	(-1.40)	(-.66)	(1.45)
	reliability adj. correlation	-.17	-.16	.03	.06	-.09	-.04	-.03	.03
Hispanic	Beta	-.08	-.03	.02	.00	-.02	.00	-.05	.04
	(t-ratio)	(-2.51)	(-1.13)	(.55)	(-.05)	(-.41)	(.11)	(-1.25)	(1.13)
	reliability adj. correlation	-.05	-.02	.04	-.02	-.03	-.01	-.05	.04
Age	Beta	-.10	-.02	.04	.05	-.02	-.07	-.06	.07
	(t-ratio)	(-4.12)	(-.99)	(1.19)	(1.41)	(-.64)	(-3.81)	(-1.96)	(2.56)
	reliability adj. correlation	-.10	-.02	.04	.05	-.03	-.07	-.06	.06
R-squared		.22	.21	.05	.05	.03	.03	.07	.07
Number of observations		1325	1308	932	934	933	2906	875	1407

Notes: [a] Mothers were asked as adults to indicate how shy they were at age six. Daughters' shyness was assessed by mothers and interviewers when the child was six years old.

Source: National Longitudinal Survey of Youth 1979 Cohort and Children of the NLSY79.

sures—anger, depression, and gender role attitudes. Table 1.6 shows that mothers' but not fathers' gender role attitudes have a significant effect on daughters' gender role attitudes, while table 1.7 shows that fathers' depression also has a larger effect than mothers' depression on sons' depression. This suggests that same-sex intergenerational linkages

TABLE 1.6

OLS Standardized Regression Coefficients and Pearson Correlations for Scales for Mothers, Fathers, and Daughters

Maternal / Paternal Traits and Behaviors (independent variables)		Daughter Traits and Behaviors (dependent variables)		
		Anger Scale	Depression Scale	Gender-role Attitudes
Mother: Anger scale	Beta	.11	.11	−.05
	(t-ratio)	(1.61)	(1.60)	(−.70)
	correlation	.13	.15	−.06
Mother: Depression scale	Beta	.01	.05	.02
	(t-ratio)	(.17)	(.69)	(.33)
	correlation	.10	.12	−.06
Mother: Gender-role attitudes	Beta	−.08	.00	.13
	(t-ratio)	(−1.18)	(−.05)	(2.05)
	correlation	−.08	−.03	.14
Father: Anger scale	Beta	−.01	−.11	.09
	(t-ratio)	(−.15)	(−1.50)	(1.19)
	correlation	.05	−.02	−.02
Father: Depression scale	Beta	.06	.15	−.13
	(t-ratio)	(.87)	(1.97)	(−1.73)
	correlation	.08	.10	−.09
Father: Gender-role attitudes	Beta	.01	−.03	−.01
	(t-ratio)	(.22)	(−.48)	(−.09)
	correlation	−.03	−.04	.08
Average parental age at birth of child	Beta	.03	.06	.02
	(t-ratio)	(.45)	(.96)	(.24)
	correlation	−.03	.05	.08
Average parental education	Beta	−.12	.00	.19
	(t-ratio)	(−1.86)	(−.05)	(2.89)
	correlation	−.14	.01	.18
Youth Black	Beta	.11	.01	.09
	(t-ratio)	(1.87)	(.24)	(1.62)
	correlation	.13	.01	.07
R-squared		.056	.042	.071
Number of observations		289	289	289

Source: Prince Georges County data.

CHAPTER ONE

TABLE 1.7
OLS Standardized Regression Coefficients and Pearson Correlations
for Scale for Mothers, Fathers, and Sons

Maternal / Paternal Traits and Behaviors (independent variables)		Son Traits and Behaviors (dependent variables)		
		Anger Scale	Depression Scale	Gender-role Attitudes
Mother: Anger scale	Beta	.05	.02	−.04
	(t-ratio)	(.69)	(.28)	(−.58)
	correlation	.11	.09	−.03
Mother: Depression scale	Beta	.07	.12	.01
	(t-ratio)	(.07)	(1.68)	(.09)
	correlation	.12	.14	−.04
Mother: Gender-role attitudes	Beta	.06	.07	.10
	(t-ratio)	(.87)	(.99)	(1.43)
	correlation	.03	.05	.17
Father: Anger scale	Beta	−.01	−.09	.09
	(t-ratio)	(−.10)	(−1.15)	(1.19)
	correlation	.06	.02	.02
Father: Depression scale	Beta	.09	.16	−.09
	(t-ratio)	(1.22)	(2.10)	(−1.23)
	correlation	.11	.13	−.07
Father: Gender-role attitudes	Beta	−.03	−.06	.09
	(t-ratio)	(−.46)	(−.86)	(1.32)
	correlation	−.03	−.04	.17
Average parental age at birth of child	Beta	−.01	.02	−.06
	(t-ratio)	(−.16)	(.33)	(−.91)
	correlation	−.07	.00	.00
Average parental education	Beta	−.12	.00	.16
	(t-ratio)	(−1.76)	(−.01)	(2.40)
	correlation	.13	.14	−.06
Youth Black	Beta	.02	.11	.12
	(t-ratio)	(.25)	(1.83)	(1.92)
	correlation	.03	.11	.12
R-squared		.046	.058	.080
Number of observations		270	270	270

Source: Prince Georges County data.

may be especially important. But fathers' depression has a much larger effect than mothers' depression on daughters' depression, which is inconsistent with the role model hypothesis. Thus these PGC results provide contradictory evidence regarding same vs. opposite-sex linkages.

Reliability Adjustments.   Measurement error in maternal traits and behaviors would tend to downwardly bias their estimated impacts on their children's traits and behaviors. Some of the measures of maternal characteristics that we use have been carefully developed in ways that increase their reliability. For example, the AFQT assessments of math and reading skills have been constructed to be highly reliable. In contrast, parents and children may be disinclined to accurately report their drug use or whether they got in fights, leading to considerable measurement error. Differential reliability of our measures could account for some of the differences in their effect on children's outcomes.

One way to estimate the reliability of a measure is to gauge its consistency over time. If, say, a son accurately reports his mother's unchanging completed schooling, he will provide the same answer each time he is asked about his mother's education. If he provides a different answer every time he is asked, the reliability of any one answer is low. While the NLSY does not include repeated measures of most parental characteristics, the CNLSY does include repeated measures of many child characteristics. If we assume that a mother's characteristics are about as reliably reported as the same characteristics measured among children, we can use the repeated child measures to approximate the reliabilities of mothers' characteristics.

Appendix Table 1.A1 shows the alphas for children's characteristics that were measured at different ages.[7] We use these alphas to correct our regression estimates for differences in reliability.[8] The rows labeled "reliability adj." in tables 1.3 and 1.5 show the measurement-error-adjusted unstandardized regression coefficients for our continuous outcomes. Correcting for reliability in this way increases many of the coefficients. In some cases, coefficients more than double. But this correction also raises the standard errors (not shown). No coefficient becomes statistically significant because of this correction, and none of our conclusions change as a result of it. Reliability adjustments may indeed matter, but our data are not up to the task of showing how.[9]

All in all the results in these tables suggest that most maternal traits and behaviors affect the same traits and behaviors of sons and daughters but not many other characteristics of their children. Maternal traits and behaviors seem to have a stronger and more consistent relationship with the corresponding traits and behaviors of daughters than with the corresponding traits and behaviors of sons. We now turn to possible explanations for the rather specific patterns of associations between characteristics of mothers and their children.

Explaining the Intergenerational Correlations

At least four hypotheses could explain the intergenerational transmission of characteristics: socioeconomic resources, parenting, genetic inheritance, and role model / identity formation. Each makes different predictions about which behaviors of parents and children are likely to be correlated and whether the correlation is likely to be higher with same-sex parent-child pairs.

Parental Socioeconomic Resources.   Parents' and children's traits and behaviors might be linked through parental socioeconomic resources. Suppose that "good" parental traits and behaviors (e.g., cognitive skills, motivation, conscientiousness) are rewarded handsomely in the labor market. Higher earnings increase family incomes, which enables parents to provide better childcare and more stimulating home environments for their preschoolers; live in safer, more affluent neighborhoods with better schools; and provide their misbehaving adolescents with second and third chances to avoid the stigma of a criminal record. If these environmental advantages lead children to acquire more positive traits, behaviors, and attainments, then economic resources are a key mediator in accounting for intergenerational correlations in the parental traits and behaviors that increase economic resources.

Other socioeconomic resources such as parents' schooling may influence children's well-being. Highly educated parents may produce more cognitively stimulating home learning environments and more verbal and supportive teaching styles (Harris, Terrel, and Allen 1999). Skills acquired through schooling may enhance parents' abilities to organize their daily routines and resources in a way that enables them to accomplish their parenting goals effectively (Michael 1972).

This SES hypothesis predicts that the maternal traits and behaviors that are correlated with a woman's eventual socioeconomic status (SES) would have general rather than specific effects on her daughter's outcomes. If SES is the only mechanism linking mothers' and daughters' characteristics, maternal adolescent traits and behaviors that are uncorrelated with maternal SES should have little effect on daughter's outcomes. To investigate these ideas, we performed an auxiliary analysis regressing mother's eventual family income on our seventeen maternal characteristics, almost all of which were measured during adolescence. We use a sample of NLSY females who were present in the study between 1979 (when they were between the ages of 14 and 21) and at least age 30. We averaged family income when the women were ages 30 to 34, using as many years of data in this interval as possible.

The first column of table 1.8 shows the bivariate correlations and regression-adjusted standardized effects of the 17 maternal adolescent traits and behaviors on her own eventual family income, controlling her birth cohort and race / ethnicity. Math scores, self-esteem, mastery, participation in school clubs, having sex before age 15 and getting suspended from school are the strongest predictors of mothers' future income. There is considerable cross-time instability in all of these measures of psychological well-being (alphas range from .5 to .7), and so table 1.8 likely understates "true" effect of these traits and behaviors measured in adolescence on mothers' eventual income.

Given these relationships, the SES hypothesis would suggest that a mother's math scores, self-esteem, mastery, participation in school clubs, having sex before age 15, and getting suspended from school will have a general effect on a child's outcome. Turning back to tables 1.2 through 1.5, we see that having had sex before the age of 15 has a relatively general effect on daughter's outcomes (5 of 17) but not son's outcomes (2 of 17). Mothers' AFQT math score has a statistically significant effect on 4 of 17 outcomes for daughters and 3 of 17 for sons. Having been suspended from school has a statistically significant effect on 4 outcomes of sons and 3 of daughters. Maternal mastery and self-esteem affect few outcomes for sons or daughters.

The second column of table 1.8 shows that 13 of the 17 traits of mothers' measured during adolescence have a statistically significant relationship to her educational attainment. The SES explanation suggests that these traits would have a general affect on her children's outcomes. But, as we have already discussed, most do not.

The SES explanation would also suggest that the effect of mother's math scores, Pearlin Mastery Scale, self-esteem, participation in school clubs, having sex before age fifteen, and being suspended should decline when SES is controlled, because these were strongly related to mothers' eventual income. Tables 1.9 and 1.10 show how the effects of maternal traits change when we control mothers' schooling, age at the birth of the child, family income averaged when the child was twelve to fourteen years old, family size, and the mother's marital status.

Remarkably, the effect of the maternal characteristics on son and daughter outcomes is reduced very little by this extensive set of SES controls. In addition, when we control all the maternal characteristics measured in adolescence, none of the measures of family background was statistically significant for 11 of the 17 outcomes of daughters, and no measure of family background had a statistically significant effect on

TABLE 1.8
OLS Standardized Regression Coefficients and Pearson Correlations
Relating Mothers' Family Income and Years of Schooling to
Her Adolescent Traits and Behaviors

Traits and Behaviors in Adolescence (independent variables)	Total Avg. Family Income (age 30–34)		Total Years of Schooling	
Math test score	Beta	.18	Beta	.31
	(t-ratio)	(7.57)	(t-ratio)	(16.57)
	correlation	.25	correlation	0.53
Reading test score	Beta	.00	Beta	.24
	(t-ratio)	(−.11)	(t-ratio)	(12.54)
	correlation	.21	correlation	0.52
Pearlin mastery scale	Beta	.05	Beta	.06
	(t-ratio)	(2.32)	(t-ratio)	(3.91)
	correlation	.14	correlation	0.26
Self-esteem scale	Beta	0.08	Beta	.09
	(t-ratio)	(4.80)	(t-ratio)	(6.25)
	correlation	.15	correlation	0.33
Depression scale	Beta	−.02	Beta	.01
	(t-ratio)	(−1.22)	(t-ratio)	(.43)
	correlation	−.10	correlation	−0.16
Shyness at age 6[a]	Beta	−.03	Beta	−.03
	(t-ratio)	(−1.66)	(t-ratio)	(−2.52)
	correlation	−.07	correlation	−0.10
Traditional gender-role attitudes	Beta	−.02	Beta	−.07
	(t-ratio)	(−.94)	(t-ratio)	(−5.11)
	correlation	−.07	correlation	−0.25
Frequency attend religious services	Beta	.01	Beta	.10
	(t-ratio)	(.84)	(t-ratio)	(7.40)
	correlation	.02	correlation	0.14
Participation in school clubs	Beta	.03	Beta	.07
	(t-ratio)	(2.38)	(t-ratio)	(5.46)
	correlation	.12	correlation	0.29
Used marijuana	Beta	−.01	Beta	−.03
	(t-ratio)	(−.60)	(t-ratio)	(−2.07)
	correlation	.01	correlation	0.03
Used other drugs	Beta	.02	Beta	.01
	(t-ratio)	(.85)	(t-ratio)	(1.03)
	correlation	.02	correlation	0.02
Sex before age 15	Beta	−.04	Beta	−.11
	(t-ratio)	(−2.88)	(t-ratio)	(−8.34)
	correlation	−.07	correlation	−0.21
Damaged property in last year	Beta	.00	Beta	.04
	(t-ratio)	(.32)	(t-ratio)	(2.83)
	correlation	−.01	correlation	−0.01

TABLE 1.8 (*cont.*)

Traits and Behaviors in Adolescence (independent variables)	Total Avg. Family Income (age 30–34)		Total Years of Schooling	
Fought at school / work	Beta	−.01	Beta	−.01
last year	(t-ratio)	(−.76)	(t-ratio)	(−.70)
	correlation	−.06	correlation	−0.16
Hit someone last year	Beta	−.01	Beta	−.05
	(t-ratio)	(−.48)	(t-ratio)	(−3.53)
	correlation	−.05	correlation	−0.09
Ever suspended	Beta	−.04	Beta	−.08
	(t-ratio)	(−2.40)	(t-ratio)	(−6.12)
	correlation	−.10	correlation	−0.20
Ever convicted	Beta	−.01	Beta	−.01
	(t-ratio)	(−.38)	(t-ratio)	(−.69)
	correlation	−.02	correlation	−0.07
Black	Beta	−.07	Beta	.17
	(t-ratio)	(−4.22)	(t-ratio)	(10.63)
	correlation	−.12	correlation	−0.04
Hispanic	Beta	−.02	Beta	.01
	(t-ratio)	(−1.40)	(t-ratio)	(.54)
	correlation	−.04	correlation	−0.15
Age	Beta	−.04	Beta	−.08
	(t-ratio)	(−2.31)	(t-ratio)	(−5.60)
	correlation	−.02	correlation	0.00
R-squared		.10		0.41
Number of observations		3582		3679

Notes: [a] Respondents were asked as adults to indicate how shy they were at age six.
Source: National Longitudinal Survey of Youth 1979 Cohort.

more than two of the daughters' outcomes. The pattern of effects is similar for sons. Controlling income in the PGC also does not change the effect of mothers' or fathers' anger, depression, or gender-role attitudes on these same traits in sons or daughters (results not shown). Thus, although some maternal adolescent characteristics are associated with mothers' later income, family income does not appear to be the main mechanism through which these maternal characteristics affect children's outcomes. Previous research showing a sizable effect of family background on these child outcomes may have been biased because some important maternal characteristics were omitted.

TABLE 1.9

Standardized Regression Coefficients for Daughters and Sons, with and without SES and Parenting Style Controls

Maternal Traits and Behaviors (independent variables)		Daughters' Traits and Behaviors (dependent variables)							
		Math Test Score	Reading Test Score	Pearlin Mastery Scale	Self-esteem Scale	Depression Scale	Shyness at Age 6[d]	Traditional Gender-role Attitudes	Frequency Attend Religious Services
Math test score	no controls[a]	.23	.17	-.06	.04	.00	-.08	-.02	.10
	parenting only[b]	.21	.15	-.07	.03	.01	-.07	-.01	.09
	SES only[c]	.22	.15	-.06	.04	.01	-.08	.00	.07
Pearlin mastery scale	no controls	.03	.06	.12	.14	.03	.03	-.06	-.02
	parenting only	.03	.05	.13	.14	.03	.03	-.06	-.01
	SES only	.04	.06	.11	.13	.03	.03	-.05	-.02
Self-esteem scale	no controls	-.07	-.02	.00	.06	.05	.04	.12	-.01
	parenting only	-.08	-.04	.00	.06	.05	.06	.11	-.04
	SES only	-.08	-.03	.00	.06	.07	.04	.13	-.03
Shyness at age 6[d]	no controls	-.08	-.05	.01	-.05	.07	.14	.07	-.02
	parenting only	-.07	-.03	.00	-.05	.06	.13	.07	.00
	SES only	-.09	-.04	.01	-.05	.07	.13	.06	-.01
Traditional gender-role attitudes	no controls	.06	.00	.12	.06	.00	-.08	.02	-.02
	parenting only	.06	.00	.13	.07	.00	-.07	.03	-.01
	SES only	.06	.01	.12	.06	.00	-.08	.02	-.02
Frequency attend religious services	no controls	.04	-.05	.01	-.01	-.06	.05	.08	.16
	parenting only	.04	-.05	.00	-.03	-.06	.06	.07	.13
	SES only	.03	-.05	.02	-.01	-.05	.04	.07	.15

Maternal Traits and Behaviors (independent variables)		Math Test Score	Reading Test Score	Pearlin Mastery Scale	Self-esteem Scale	Depression Scale	Shyness at Age 6	Traditional Gender-role Attitudes	Frequency Attend Religious Services
Sex before age 15	no controls	-.09	-.04	-.09	-.10	.03	.01	.05	-.04
	parenting only	-.08	-.02	-.09	-.09	.03	.01	.03	-.02
	SES only	-.07	-.02	-.09	-.10	.03	.00	.03	-.04
Ever suspended	no controls	-.04	-.06	-.06	-.09	.03	.01	.08	-.02
	parenting only	-.04	-.05	-.06	-.09	.03	.01	.09	.00
	SES only	-.03	-.05	-.06	-.08	.02	.01	.06	-.01

Sons' Traits and Behaviors (dependent variables)

Maternal Traits and Behaviors (independent variables)		Math Test Score	Reading Test Score	Pearlin Mastery Scale	Self-esteem Scale	Depression Scale	Shyness at Age 6	Traditional Gender-role Attitudes	Frequency Attend Religious Services
Math test score	no controls[a]	.15	.12	.08	.00	-.02	.06	.00	.03
	parenting only[b]	.15	.11	.08	.01	-.01	.06	.00	.04
	SES only[c]	.13	.10	.08	-.01	-.02	.07	.02	.02
Pearlin mastery scale	no controls	.02	.03	.05	.10	.02	.00	-.15	-.04
	parenting only	.01	.02	.04	.08	.04	.00	-.14	-.05
	SES only	.01	.02	.04	.10	.02	.00	-.13	-.04
Self-esteem scale	no controls	-.03	.01	-.08	-.07	.05	.03	.08	.06
	parenting only	-.03	.02	-.09	-.08	.04	.03	.08	.05
	SES only	-.04	.00	-.08	-.08	.05	.04	.09	.05
Shyness at age 6[d]	no controls	-.02	-.03	-.02	-.03	.04	.14	.04	.04
	parenting only	-.02	-.02	-.02	-.02	.03	.14	.03	.05
	SES only	-.01	-.02	-.01	-.02	.04	.13	.03	.04
Traditional gender-role attitudes	no controls	-.02	-.04	-.02	-.05	.01	.01	.15	.04
	parenting only	-.02	-.04	-.02	-.06	.01	.01	.15	.03
	SES only	-.01	-.03	-.02	-.05	.01	.01	.14	.03

TABLE 1.9 (cont.)

		Sons' Traits and Behaviors (dependent variables)							
Maternal Traits and Behaviors (independent variables)		Math Test Score	Reading Test Score	Pearlin Mastery Scale	Self-esteem Scale	Depression Scale	Shyness at Age 6	Traditional Gender-role Attitudes	Frequency Attend Religious Services
Frequency attend religious services	no controls	.02	.02	.00	−.03	−.02	−.01	.02	.20
	parenting only	.02	.02	−.01	−.04	−.02	−.01	.02	.18
	SES only	.01	.01	.01	−.03	−.01	−.01	.01	.19
Sex before age 15	no controls	−.06	−.05	−.06	−.05	.09	.03	.07	−.08
	parenting only	−.06	−.05	−.04	−.03	.08	.03	.05	−.08
	SES only	−.04	−.04	−.07	−.03	.08	.02	.06	−.08
Ever suspended	no controls	.02	−.02	.02	−.03	.05	−.01	.01	−.01
	parenting only	.01	−.02	.02	−.03	.05	−.01	.01	−.01
	SES only	.02	−.02	.01	−.02	.05	−.01	.01	.00

Notes: [a] All regressions include controls for all mothers' traits and behaviors, children's age, and race. Only selected variables are shown.
[b] Parenting stimulation style controls include measures of parental involvement, degree of parental monitoring, child autonomy, emotional warmth, and cognitive stimulation in the home.
[c] SES controls include mother's age at birth of the child, highest level of education received, average total net family income when the child was 12–14 years old, whether the mother had ever divorced and whether the mother was married when the child was fourteen.
[d] Mothers were asked as adults to indicate how shy they were at age six. Daughters' shyness was assessed by mothers and interviewers when the child was six years old.

Source: National Longitudinal Survey of Youth 1979 Cohort and Children of the NLSY79.

TABLE 1.10

Logistic Regression Odds Ratios for Daughters and Sons, with and without SES and Parenting Style

Maternal Traits and Behaviors (independent variables)		Daughters' Traits and Behaviors (dependent variables)								
		Particip. in School Clubs	Used Marijuana	Used Other Drugs	Sex Before Age 15	Damaged Property in Last Year	Fought at School/ Work Last Year	Hit Someone Last Year	Ever Suspended	Ever Convicted
Math test score	no controls[a]	1.04	1.00	1.04	.98	.98	.97	1.02	1.00	.88
	parenting only[b]	1.03	1.00	.99	.99	.98	.98	1.02	1.00	.88
	SES only[c]	1.03	1.01	na	.99	.97	.97	1.03	1.00	.89
Pearlin mastery scale	no controls	1.03	.95	1.04	.97	.91	.98	.93	.99	.89
	parenting only	1.03	.96	.69	.97	.92	.99	.93	.99	.89
	SES only	1.03	.93	na	.96	.90	.98	.94	.99	.88
Self-esteem scale	no controls	.99	1.04	1.19	1.00	1.01	1.07	1.06	1.03	1.02
	parenting only	.98	1.04	1.16	1.00	1.01	1.07	1.06	1.03	1.04
	SES only	.98	1.07	na	1.01	1.00	1.43	1.07	1.03	1.07
Shyness at age 6[d]	no controls	.77	1.20	3.93	1.06	.86	.94	.99	1.30	1.03
	parenting only	.79	1.19	10.82	1.05	.85	.93	1.00	1.30	1.02
	SES only	.77	1.37	na	1.09	.88	.92	.98	1.28	1.01
Traditional gender-role attitudes	no controls	1.02	1.03	1.26	1.01	.99	.99	.99	.97	.97
	parenting only	1.01	1.02	1.11	1.01	.99	.99	.98	.97	.96
	SES only	1.02	1.04	ba	1.02	.99	.98	.98	.97	.97
Frequency attend religious services	no controls	1.01	1.29	2.04	.97	.93	.88	1.08	1.11	1.13
	parenting only	.98	1.31	4.02	1.00	.92	.88	1.08	1.11	1.14
	SES only	1.01	1.39	na	.99	.94	.89	1.09	1.15	1.12

TABLE 1.10 (cont.)

Daughters' Traits and Behaviors (dependent variables)

Maternal Traits and Behaviors (independent variables)		Particip. in School Clubs	Used Marijuana	Used Other Drugs	Sex Before Age 15	Damaged Property in Last Year	Fought at School/Work Last Year	Hit Someone Last Year	Ever Suspended	Ever Convicted
Sex before age 15	no controls	.78	1.67	.70	2.07	.91	1.86	1.90	1.78	.55
	parenting only	.89	1.61	1.49	1.93	.93	1.86	1.94	1.81	.61
	SES only	.91	1.53	na	2.11	1.02	1.79	1.82	1.75	.30
Ever suspended	no controls	1.07	1.33	.03	1.34	.91	1.20	.88	1.70	.47
	parenting only	1.11	1.29	.00	1.36	.87	1.21	.91	1.69	.43
	SES only	1.15	1.37	na	1.41	.92	1.13	.83	1.69	.38

Sons' Traits and Behaviors (dependent variables)

Maternal Traits and Behaviors (independent variables)		Particip. in School Clubs	Used Marijuana	Used Other Drugs	Sex Before Age 15	Damaged Property in Last Year	Fought at School/Work Last Year	Hit Someone Last Year	Ever Suspended	Ever Convicted
Math test score	no controls[a]	1.01	.96	.99	.98	1.02	.99	1.00	.98	1.03
	parenting only[b]	1.01	.96	1.01	.99	1.02	.99	1.00	.98	1.03
	SES only[c]	1.01	.96	1.02	1.00	1.03	.99	1.01	.98	1.03
Pearlin mastery scale	no controls	1.05	.98	.99	.97	.98	1.02	1.05	1.02	1.13
	parenting only	1.04	.97	1.02	.98	.99	1.03	1.05	1.02	1.16
	SES only	1.04	.98	1.15	.97	.99	1.03	1.06	1.03	1.14

Self-esteem scale	no controls	.98	1.06	.81	1.01	.96	1.04	.99	.95	.93
	parenting only	.96	1.06	.83	1.01	.96	1.03	.99	.95	.92
	SES only	.98	1.06	.74	1.02	.96	1.05	.99	.95	.92
Shyness at age 6[d]	no controls	.98	1.12	1.16	.91	1.02	.87	1.10	1.07	.99
	parenting only	1.04	1.12	1.20	.89	1.00	.84	1.08	1.06	.93
	SES only	1.00	1.07	.91	.91	1.00	.88	1.07	1.07	.95
Traditional gender-role attitudes	no controls	.99	1.05	.92	1.00	1.02	1.05	1.03	.98	.87
	parenting only	.99	1.05	.89	1.00	1.03	1.05	1.02	.98	.85
	SES only	.99	1.05	.94	1.00	1.02	1.05	1.02	.98	.86
Frequency attend religious services	no controls	1.02	.94	.84	.97	.98	.92	.85	.92	.94
	parenting only	.98	.95	.88	.97	.98	.89	.84	.92	.92
	SES only	1.02	.94	.92	.99	.99	.92	.86	.93	.94
Sex before age 15	no controls	.98	1.56	1.37	2.01	1.49	1.39	1.16	1.92	2.68
	parenting only	1.09	1.56	1.24	1.95	1.43	1.37	1.10	1.92	2.16
	SES only	1.00	1.65	1.51	1.82	1.51	1.31	1.15	2.00	2.67
Ever suspended	no controls	1.44	1.78	1.01	1.84	1.69	1.41	.84	1.64	1.05
	parenting only	1.56	1.81	.64	1.74	1.65	1.37	.82	1.66	.99
	SES only	1.45	1.71	1.00	1.72	1.66	1.41	.79	1.61	.96

Notes: [a] All regressions include controls for all mothers' traits and behaviors, children's age, and race. Only selected variables are shown.
[b] Parenting style controls include measures of parental involvement, degree of parental monitoring, child autonomy, emotional warmth, and cognitive stimulation in the home.
[c] SES controls include mother's age at birth of the child, highest level of education received, average total net family income when the child was 12–14 years old, whether the mother had ever divorced and whether the mother was married when the child was fourteen.
[d] Mothers were asked as adults to indicate how shy they were at age six. Daughters' shyness was assessed by mothers and interviewers when the child was six years old.

Source: National Longitudinal Survey of Youth 1979 Cohort and Children of the NLSY79.

The SES hypothesis implies that the intergenerational correlation of outcomes ought to be gender neutral if the benefits of higher SES should accrue to both sons and daughters from the resource-enhancing characteristics of either the father or the mother. Since the pattern of effects of maternal characteristics appears to be generally gender-neutral, this would be consistent with the SES hypothesis.

Taken together, however, these results are not supportive of the SES hypothesis. Mothers' income appears to affect children's income mainly because specific behaviors of mothers result in low income and children are likely to engage in these same behaviors, which in turn lowers their own income.

Parenting Style and the Home Environment. The underlying assumption in developmental psychology is that parents have a powerful impact on children. Parenting style, assessed in terms of parental involvement and control, is often seen as the main mechanism for the transfer of parental characteristics to children. Researchers (e.g., Baumrind 1967) commonly identify four parenting styles based on the warmth and control dimensions of parenting. Authoritative parents demonstrate high levels of both warmth and control, authoritarian parents display high control but low warmth, permissive parents share high warmth but low control, and disengaged parents demonstrate both low warmth and low control. Many studies have shown that children raised by authoritative parents demonstrate higher levels of competence, achievement, and social development, and have higher self-esteem and fewer mental health problems (Maccoby and Martin 1983). Some studies report correlations of .50 or higher (Hetherington et al. 1999).

Theories of parenting tend not to match specific parenting styles to specific child outcomes. Rather, "good" parenting is expected to relate broadly to "good" child outcomes. There is no reason to expect gender-specific associations, not only because "good" parenting is similar for boys and girls but also because, on average, parents tend to treat their daughters and sons similarly. Some have suggested, however, that optimal parenting is dependent on the social context. In Kohn's work on families headed by fathers in blue-collar jobs, an authoritarian parenting style was viewed as optimal because it socialized children for the world in which they lived.

In addition, many studies have highlighted the role of the emotional warmth and cognitive stimulation that parents provide. Together, these two aspects of parental socialization represent key aspects of the "home environment," which have been widely linked to positive outcomes for children (Bradley and Corwyn 2003).

One theory proposes that parenting style, in particular, "unskilled parenting" (i.e., ineffective and coercive discipline practices, lack of monitoring) plays a key role in linking parents' and children's antisocial behavior (see Patterson 1998). According to the theory, children whose parents practice "unskilled parenting" develop antisocial behavior, which persists into adulthood when their own antisocial behavior is transferred to their children. The model does not posit a direct correspondence between specific dimensions of antisocial behavior. Rather, the antisocial behavior that children develop early in life (resulting from ineffective parenting practices) is thought to be broadly linked to a host of negative outcomes in later life, including economic outcomes, substance use, and mental health problems (Capaldi and Clark 1998).

The theory that parenting styles link parents and children's behavior, however, has only rarely been tested. Only one of the studies cited earlier as having obtained an intergenerational correlation in behavior tested this hypothesis (Cairns et al. 1998). It examined the mediating role of "high-literacy environments," indexed by frequency of mother reading to child, the HOME score, and observed parental responsiveness, and found only a small correlation between mothers' childhood characteristics and her later parenting behavior. Thus, even though many studies show substantial concurrent correlations between mothers' parenting behavior and children's outcomes, they have not yet provided support for the idea that parenting behaviors play a key role in linking behavior across generations.

The CNLSY measures five parenting practices of sample females who eventually become mothers: parental involvement, parental monitoring, child autonomy, emotional warmth, and cognitive stimulation. Maternal adolescent characteristics that are associated with the mother's future parenting behaviors ought to have a general effect on children's outcomes. When we regressed each of the parenting measures on the mother's adolescent traits and behaviors (data not shown in tables), we found that no single maternal adolescent characteristic significantly affects all five parenting practices. This is not surprising because the parenting practices themselves are not strongly correlated.[10] About half of the maternal characteristics (depression, using marijuana, using other drugs, damaging property, fighting, hitting, and having been convicted) are statistically significantly associated with either no or only one parenting practice. Only one maternal adolescent characteristic (attending religious services) is significantly related to three of the five parenting practices. Two additional maternal characteristics, having sex before age 15 and having been suspended from school, are significantly related to three parenting practices at the .10 level.

If parental involvement, monitoring, autonomy-granting, emotional warmth, and cognitive stimulation are the mechanisms through which parents influence their children, we might expect the effect of attending religious services, having sex before age 15, and having been suspended from school to decline when we control these indicators of parental behaviors, because these characteristics of mothers were associated with three of the five behaviors. But tables 1.9 and 1.10 show that controlling the five measures of parenting practices hardly changes the effect of these maternal characteristics on children's outcomes. Furthermore, for 12 of the 17 outcomes of daughters, none of the parenting practices has a statistically significant effect when all the maternal adolescent characteristics are controlled. No parental behavior has a significant effect on more than two outcomes for daughters. Thus, none of the five parenting behaviors we measure is likely to be the main mechanism through which parents transmit characteristics to their children. This same conclusion holds in the PGC data (not shown; a description of the parenting measures examined in the PGC is in the appendix).

It is somewhat surprising that the majority of the parenting practices measures have no statistically significant effect on any child outcome, since a considerable body of research claims that parenting practices are key to children's outcomes. Our analysis suggests that previous studies may have omitted important background characteristics, including parental traits and behaviors before they become parents. Other possible explanations for our results include the following: (1) the aspects of parenting that we measure do not matter but something else does, (2) these aspects of parenting matter but we have mismeasured them, or (3) parenting really does not matter.

We do not find the first explanation to be very plausible because, taken together, our parenting measures cover the major dimensions (e.g., warmth, control, and cognitive stimulation) that developmental psychologists have claimed are important. (One noteworthy exception is harsh discipline practices, which have been highlighted in studies of parenting effects: Dodge et al. 1994; McLoyd et al. 1994). It is also likely that other parenting practices would be correlated with the five we do measure.

Poor measurement is unlikely since the measures we employ were developed and field-tested for the CNLSY by a leading panel of experts in developmental psychology. In recent work using the CNLSY (e.g., Carlson and Corcoran 2001), a composite measure of the HOME score (one that combined the emotional warmth and cognitive stimulation subscales) was a significant predictor of behavior problems, PIAT math, and PIAT reading among children ages 7 to 10. Carlson (1999) also linked a seven-item measure of father involvement for kids 10 to 14 years old to BPI internalizing and externalizing scores, delinquency, and substance use. The parenting measures in the NLSY may be better predictors of the outcomes of young children than of adolescent outcomes. But if parenting behaviors affect the outcomes of young but not older children, they cannot be the mechanism through which the intergenerational correlation of adolescent or adult psychological, educational, or economic outcomes operate.

The third explanation—that parents do not matter much for their children's development—has been proposed in a controversial book by Judith Rich Harris (1998), which argued that peer rather than parental influences are key. Much of Harris's argument rests on the observation that, net of genetic similarities, siblings sharing the same family environment develop almost as differently as children raised in different families. Harris argued that children's "groups" are the active agents of socialization; peers are the primary influence because it is peers with whom children identify. Our results shed no light on peer influence, but they do suggest a substantially smaller role for parental monitoring, involvement, autonomy-granting, emotional warmth, and cognitive stimulation than previously assumed. This is an important, but not exhaustive, list of what parents do. However, as discussed below, our results also provide some support for the role model hypothesis, which would be contrary to Harris's argument that parents do not matter.

Inheritance. Behavioral geneticists believe that a large portion of parent-child correlations in many traits and behaviors but not social attitudes can be attributed to genetic inheritance (Loehlin, this volume; Rowe 1994).

The debate over the heritability of IQ has raged for decades, with Herrnstein and Murray (1994) suggesting that .60 is a "middling value." Critics who accept the basic logic of behavioral genetics models still argue for a substantial role of inheritance, in one recent case ranging between 27 and 54 percent (Daniels et al. 1997). Loehlin and Rowe (1992) estimate "broad sense" heritability of the so-called "Big Five" personality characteristics (extroversion, agreeableness, conscientiousness, emotional stability, and intellectual openness) ranging from about .34 to .54. Goodman and Stevenson (1989) estimate high heritability in hyperactivity and inattentiveness. The behavioral genetics literature also suggests heritability in criminal, especially adult criminal, behavior (Cloninger and Gottesman 1987) as well as in smoking and substance use (Chassin et al. 1998).

Behavioral genetics models also yield miniscule estimates of the contributions of the environments shared by siblings who grow up together. The most direct assessment of shared environmental influences comes from comparisons of twins reared together and apart, which show remarkably similar twin correlations for personality inventories and vocational interests (Bouchard et al. 1990). More formal models suggest that less than 5 percent of the sibling variance is attributable to shared environmental influences, a figure that is often found in a broader set of behavioral genetics studies.

There are many reasons to doubt the precision of the estimates from behavioral genetic models (e.g., Daniels et al. 1997). Particularly problematic is the task of accounting for the complex interactions between genetically transmitted attributes and environmental influences. Nonetheless, cognitive skills have a large genetic component, and recent research suggests that shyness and depression may also have a significant genetic component.[11] Some behavioral geneticists claim that crime and substance abuse also have high heritability, while none appears to claim that social attitudes do. Little research has tried to assess the genetic component of the other outcomes that we measure, and so other characteristics could also be associated because of genetic links.

If child behavior were inherited from parents in the same way as eye color or high blood pressure, we would expect to observe a strong correlation between specific outcomes, such as cognitive skill, substance use, and shyness (all outcomes for which there is evidence of a genetic link), of parents and their children. If this were the only reason children resembled their parents, we would expect that, say, parental use of alcohol would affect their children's use of alcohol but it would have little effect on other outcomes of children except through the correlation of those outcomes with alcohol use. These correlations, however, could produce very general effects of a maternal trait or behavior. For example, race is genetically transmitted, but it has wide-ranging consequences for nearly all child outcomes. If some characteristics such as social attitudes are not genetically transmitted and genetic transmission is the only mechanism linking parents' and children's outcomes, we should not observe specific correlations for social attitudes.

Tables 1.2 through 1.5 show that daughters' and sons' traits and behaviors known to have a significant genetic component (cognitive skill, shyness, and substance use) are all predicted by their corresponding maternal trait or behavior. Our measure of maternal depression, however, does not have a statistically significant effect on either sons' or daughters' depression in either the NLSY or the PGC. Fighting, hitting, and being convicted of a crime may be signs of criminal behavior. But none of these maternal behaviors has an effect on the corresponding behavior of sons and only maternal hitting or being convicted affect the corresponding behavior of daughters. Our one measure of maternal social attitudes, traditional gender-role attitudes, has a statistically significant effect on sons' but not daughters' gender-role attitudes.

Maternal math and reading skills have relatively general affects on their children. Mothers' reading scores have a statistically significant effect on five outcomes for daughters and four for sons. Mothers' math scores have a statistically significant effect on four outcomes of daughters and three outcomes of sons. Maternal shyness and marijuana use also have relatively general effects on daughters but not sons.

Sex-linked inheritance (as with color-blindness) would be expected to produce gender-specific correlations, although the number of traits for which sex linkages have been established is relatively small. Gender-of-child differences in parent-child correlations could also result if environments cause the same genes to express themselves differently in boys and girls. Suppose, for example, that aggression is genetically determined but that it manifests itself as fighting in boys and aggressive social interactions among girls. Fighting in fathers would be correlated with fighting in sons but not daughters, while aggressive social interactions would be correlated in mother-daughter but not mother-son pairs. All in all, it is difficult to judge whether gender-specific intergenerational correlations are consistent or inconsistent with a genetic explanation.

Role Modeling. Social learning models of the intergenerational transmission of behavior posit that parental behavior is observed and directly modeled in concurrent or later behaviors or relationships (Capaldi and Clark 1998). For example, observation of parental use of illicit substances may "legitimate" these behaviors in children's eyes. Or, children may learn that certain modes of behavior, such as aggression toward a relationship partner, are tactics one should use to gain power in family relationships. This mechanism is likely to produce behavior-specific associations as children mimic particular behaviors of parents. Resulting intergenerational correlations are likely to be higher for social attitudes, which are more likely the product of social learning, than more basic traits such as cognitive skill and mental health.

If adolescents model the behaviors of valued individuals, then they are more likely to model the behavior of a parent with whom they have a good relationship. This theory further suggest that same-sex modeling may be more common than opposite sex modeling because children may see same-sex parents as exemplars of appropriate social behavior for each gender and, from these, form gender-role schemas to guide their behavior. Cognitive learning theory holds that same-sex modeling is more likely because the same-sex parent is more influential on the child (but see Kandel and Wu [1995], who report that maternal smoking is a more powerful influence on adolescent smoking than is paternal smoking). Sex-role identification may take place by modeling or reinforcement. Thus, we might expect in particular to see gender-specific associations in sex role attitudes.

The role model hypothesis suggests that fathers should have a greater influence on sons and mothers should have a greater influence on daughters. The genetic hypothesis makes similar predictions for characteristics transmitted by sex-linked genes or gender-specific expression of genes. Neither SES nor parenting hypotheses predict gender-specific parent-child associations. The NLSY data do not suggest that mothers' characteristics are much less important to sons than daughters. But these data include no information on fathers. Mothers' characteristics may be important to sons because her characteristics are correlated with the fathers' characteristics.

The PGC study provides information on fathers who reside with their children. Using these data we can compare the effect of fathers' and mothers' characteristics on sons and daughters. Unfortunately, we are able to do this for only three measures—anger, depression, and gender-role attitudes. Table 1.6 shows that mothers' but not fathers' gender-role attitudes have a significant effect on daughters' gender-role attitudes. Table 1.7 shows that fathers' depression also has a larger effect than mothers' depression on sons' depression. Both of these results are consistent with the role model hypothesis. But fathers' depression has a much larger effect than mothers' depression on daughters' depression, which is inconsistent with the hypothesis. Thus these PGC results provide contradictory evidence regarding the role model and genetic hypothesis.

The role model hypothesis also predicts that children's behavior should be more like parents' behavior when children strongly identify with their parents. We test this hypothesis by interacting fathers' traits with a variable that measures the extent to which a child reports having a negative relationship with the father. The results (not shown) show that daughters are angrier when their fathers are angrier and when they have a more negative relationship with their father. But the more negative the relationship with the father the less the father's anger increases the daughters' anger. Put another way, daughters with more positive relationships with their fathers are more prone to be angry if their father is angry. The same pattern arises for the relationship between fathers' and daughters' depression, fathers' and sons' anger, and fathers' and sons' gender-role attitudes. This supports the role model hypothesis.[12] We do not replicate these results, however, when we test the interactions between mothers' traits and children's identification with mothers. In sum, interaction results support the role model hypothesis in four of six possible interactions with fathers, but none with mothers. This evidence on gender-specific associations provides somewhat contradictory conclusions about the role model hypotheses.

We lack direct measures of role modeling or genetic mechanisms. We can, however, conduct an additional indirect test. The most plausible way in which a child models a parent's behavior is to see the parent engage in the behavior. But thus far we have measured maternal characteristics during adolescence, well before most children were born. For those characteristics to be transmitted through role modeling they have to be correlated with the mother's behavior after the child is born. If a characteristic is transmitted genetically, on the other hand, it should not matter when the trait is measured as long as it is measured accurately.

Thus, if we regress children's outcomes on maternal traits measured in adolescence and in adulthood and find that the effect of the latter measure is greater than the effect of the former, it suggests role modeling rather than genetic transmission of that characteristic. If both measures are equally predictive of the children's outcomes, it is evidence of a genetic mechanism. If traits and behaviors were highly correlated between adolescence and adulthood, then we would be unable to distinguish between their separate effects. But the traits and behaviors for which we have both concurrent and adolescent measurement never correlate more than .50 between these two times, and most correlations are in the .2 to .4 range.

Ideally, we would measure each maternal characteristic during adolescence and at the same time that we measure the child outcome. Unfortunately, the NLSY includes only three maternal characteristics measured at both these times: depression, use of drugs, and use of marijuana. When we regress both maternal measures of drug use on children's drug use, we find that all seventy-one mothers who used drugs as adults had children who also reported using drugs. So we cannot separate the effect of mother's adolescent and adult drug use on her child's drug use. Table 1.11 shows that when we regress both measures of maternal marijuana use on child's marijuana use, the coefficients are very similar. The same is true for mothers' depression.[13]

Two additional maternal traits are measured both during adolescence and adulthood but not contemporaneously with the child outcome. These are self-esteem and gender-role attitudes. We estimate a model in which we control both measures of maternal traits on the corresponding outcome of children who were are least six years old when the second maternal trait was measured. These children were probably old enough to learn from observing their mothers' behavior. Table 1.11 presents standardized regression coefficients and t-ratios from these four regressions.[14] There is little difference in the effect of the two measures of

TABLE 1.11
Odds Ratios and Standardized Regression Coefficients for Models
Regressing Children's Behaviors and Attitudes on Corresponding Adolescent
and Adult Measurements of Mothers' Behaviors and Attitude

	Use of Marijuana (Odds Ratio)	Depression (OLS regression coefficient)	Self-esteem (OLS regression coefficient)	Gender-role Attitude (OLS regression coefficient)
Mothers' adolescent characteristic	1.76 (2.90)	.05 (1.52)	.09 (2.58)	.06 (2.02)
Mothers' adult characteristic	1.64 (1.83)	.06 (1.86)	.11 (3.72)	.17 (6.43)
N	721	554	648	554

Notes: t- and z-ratios are given in parentheses. Regression models include both maternal measures.
Source: NLSY.

maternal self-esteem on the child's self-esteem, but the more recent measure of mothers' gender-role attitudes has a much greater effect than the measure of mothers' adolescent gender-role attitude.

These results are consistent with a large genetic component to self-esteem, depression, and use of marijuana, but with role modeling for gender-role attitudes. These patterns are similar to those in the behavioral genetics research, which have also found weak genetic links for attitudes but stronger genetic links for personality attributes (Loehlin this volume; Rowe 1994). The results for drug use are somewhat ambiguous. A mother's current drug use is a perfect predictor of her children's drug use, and this is a much greater effect than her drug use as an adolescent. Since only a small number of mothers report using drugs in adulthood, we caution against making too much of this difference. A final, more general caution is that while these patterns appear consistent with genetic explanations, the nature of the evidence is extremely indirect.

DISCUSSION

We have used patterns of correlations in two data sets to describe the relationship between the characteristics of parents and their children. We have found evidence of many more specific than general intergenerational associations. We next discuss four possible explanations of similarities in parents and children. We begin with a summary of evidence on each explanation, followed by some caveats and general conclusions.

Socioeconomic Status. Our results provide little support for the idea that parental SES is the key cause of similarities in parents and children. Only a few maternal adolescent characteristics are related to future income, and the effect of these characteristics on children's outcomes does not decline when direct measures of parental SES are controlled. Also inconsistent with an SES-based explanation is our evidence of many more specific than general effects of maternal traits and behaviors on children.

Parenting Styles and the Home Environment. Given the strong presumption by developmental psychologists of the key role played by parenting behaviors such as warmth and control, we were most surprised by the weak support accorded this hypothesis by our data. Most maternal characteristics were related to either none, one, or at most two of the parenting practices that we can measure, and these maternal characteristics did not display the pattern of general effects on daughters' outcomes predicted by the parenting explanation. Most telling is that direct controls for five measures of parenting practices accounted for none of the many strong intergenerational correlations observed in our data. To our knowledge, ours is the first to test this hypothesis in a nationally representative sample.

Genetic Influence. According to this hypothesis, each of a parent's genetically determined traits and behaviors should predict its counterpart trait or behavior in children. A genetic explanation would also lead us to expect that a given trait or behavior would not be closely linked to other child traits and behaviors. Although hampered by a lack of data on fathers, our results are generally consistent with this prediction. Most maternal characteristics are associated with only the same characteristic in their children. But certain maternal traits (e.g., AFQT math and reading score as well as depression) predict several other outcomes, which may be inconsistent with the genetic explanation. Consistent with a genetic explanation is the fact that traits do not appear to be gender specific, and that neither family background nor parenting practices have much effect on child outcomes once all maternal characteristics are controlled. Finally, measures of maternal depression, self-esteem, and marijuana use in adolescence are as good as adult measures of the same characteristic at predicting the corresponding outcome in children, and this fact is consistent with a genetic link for these outcomes. All in all, we find considerable indirect support for the genetic explanation.

Role Modeling. The pattern of trait and behavior-specific correlations across generations that we observe in our data supports key predictions of both the genetic and role-modeling hypotheses. But it proved difficult to develop competing predictions between the role model and genetic explanations. One possible exception is that the role model but not the genetic explanation predicts gender-specific effects. We find some evidence that mothers' characteristics more often predict the same characteristics in daughters than in sons, and that the effects are greater for daughters than for sons. Some characteristics of fathers also seem to have a greater effect when children report a positive relationship with their father. Evidence of a differential effect of fathers on sons and daughters, however, is weak. Maternal gender-role attitudes measured in adulthood have a much greater effect on those of children than do maternal gender role attitudes measured in adolescence, indicating that role modeling is important for this outcome.

All told, we are left with suggestive evidence that genetic and / or identity formation influences figure prominently in explaining the resemblance between parents and their children. Our evidence suggests that Models 1 and 4 in figure 1.1 are not likely to represent the intergenerational transmission process, at least if P_z is either parental SES or the parenting behaviors that we are able to measure. Because many of the children's outcomes that we measure are related to their future economic success, our results also provide suggestive evidence of the importance of genetic and role-modeling influences on the intergenerational transmission of economic success. In contrast, little of the evidence we gathered supported the idea that either parenting practices or parental economic resources account for intergenerational linkages.

At the same time, we have not tested the well-accepted proposition that behavioral traits are the result of not only environmental and genetic influences but also the interactions between environment and genetics. In other words, social conditions, such as parental SES or the socialization environment created by parenting practices, can moderate the expression of biological or genetic predispositions. Guo and Stearns (1999) suggest that individuals living under greater societal constraint have more difficulty realizing their genetic potential and provide evidence that low-SES environments decrease the heritability of cognitive skills. A similar point is made by Maccoby (2000), who summarized evidence that the cross-generational transmission of psychiatric disorders is moderated by the socialization environment provided by parents. In studies of adopted children, for example, children with a schizophrenic biological parent were more likely to develop a range of psychiatric problems, but only if they were adopted into a dysfunctional adoptive family (Maccoby 2000). Well-functioning parents may buffer children against the emergence of negative genetic potentials. Future studies should examine intergenerational correlations of traits and behaviors in different subgroups defined by levels of SES and in a variety of socialization environments.

Furthermore, recent welfare-to-work interventions that have experimentally changed the economic context of low-income families appear to affect children's adjustment (Morris et al. 2001). Interestingly, these same interventions did not appear to affect the specific parenting behaviors deemed key by developmentalists (e.g., emotional warmth, monitoring, involvement). Nevertheless, these experimental findings support the contention that social environments do matter for children's development, but perhaps also demonstrate that certain dimensions of parental behavior matter less than previously thought.

Our list of methodological concerns is long. We lack direct evidence on the genetic makeup of our parents and children. Our list of available traits and behaviors, although long, is dictated by data availability rather than theory. Most measures in our key data set (the NLSY) have dubious reliability, and our attempts to adjust for measurement error reduced the precision of our estimates to the point that we were uncertain about the consequences of measurement error for our main conclusions.

Despite these concerns, we do have confidence in several stylized facts for which future work on intergenerational processes must account. Above all, as with Case and Katz (1991), we find striking evidence that "like begets like" across generations. Many more specific than general competencies appear to be passed down from one generation to the next. This is perhaps unfortunate from a policy perspective, since necessarily blunt policy instruments are better suited for addressing general than specific competencies.

APPENDIX TABLE 1.A1
Variable Descriptions and Descriptive Statistics for Mothers', Daughters', and Sons' Traits and Behaviors

Variable Name	Variable Description	Mothers[a] Mean (St. Dev.)	Daughters Mean (St. Dev.)	Sons Mean (St. Dev.)	Range	Reliability[b]
Math test score	Standardized AFQT/PIAT math score[c]	43.17 (8.31)	96.90 (12.92)	97.53 (13.65)	(20,66) AFQT (65,135) PIAT	.87
Reading test score	Standardized AFQT/PIAT reading score[c]	44.48 (11.28)	95.83 (12.80)	94.88 (13.54)	(20,66) AFQT (65,135) PIAT	.86
Pearlin mastery scale	Pearlin mastery scale (higher score = greater mastery)	21.28 (3.34)	21.44 (2.99)	21.59 (2.91)	(7,28)	.70
Self-esteem scale	Self-esteem scale (higher score = higher self-esteem)	31.69 (4.02)	31.74 (4.11)	32.01 (4.02)	(10,40)	.73
Depression scale	Depression scale (higher score = more depressed)	5.22 (4.55)	5.57 (3.88)	4.53 (3.29)	(0,21)	.61
Shyness at age 6	How shy at age 6 (higher score = more shy)[d]	2.79 (.91)	2.26 (.95)	2.18 (.94)	(1,5)	.51
Traditional gender-role attitudes	Gender-role attitudes scale (higher score = more conservative attitudes)	17.09 (3.58)	14.97 (3.05)	16.82 (2.94)	(8,32)	N/A
Frequency attend religious services	How often attend religious services (1 = never, 6 = more than 1× week)	3.07 (1.66)	3.74 (1.79)	3.48 (1.84)	(1,6)	.74
Participation in school clubs	Participated in high school clubs/ organizations	.66 (.47)	.60 (.49)	.61 (.49)	(0,1)	.57
Used marijuana	Smoked marijuana more than once	.32 (.47)	.12 (.32)	.17 (.37)	(0,1)	.72

Variable	Description				Range	
Used other drugs	Ever used drugs other than marijuana	.13 (.34)	.01 (.11)	.03 (.17)	(0,1)	.77
Sex before age 15		.28 (.45)	0.35 (.48)	0.42 (.49)	(0,1)	N/A
Damaged property in last year	Damaged property in last year	.07 (.25)	.10 (.30)	.17 (.38)	(0,1)	.58
Fought at school / work last year	Fought at school/work in last year	.20 (.40)	.27 (.44)	.35 (.48)	(0,1)	.53
Hit someone last year	Hit or seriously threatened to hit someone in the last year	.26 (.44)	.28 (.45)	.28 (.45)	(0,1)	.49
Ever suspended	Ever suspended from school	.27 (.44)	.14 (.35)	.27 (.44)	(0,1)	.68
Ever convicted	Ever convicted of a crime	.01 (.12)	.05 (.21)	.11 (.31)	(0,1)	.57
Average family income	Average total family income when the child was 12–14 years old	N/A	37949 (56407)	36122 (48190)	(0 , 974,100)	N/A
Mother's education	Highest level of education mother had received when child was 14 years old	N/A	11.64 (2.23)	11.63	(1, 20)	N/A
Family size	Total family size when the child was 14 years old	N/A	4.46 (1.55)	4.42 (1.49)	(2, 13)	N/A
Divorced	Mother had ever been divorced	N/A	.30 (.46)	.29 (.45)	(0, 1)	N/A
Two-parent home	Mother was married when child was 14 years old	N/A	.54 (.50)	.54 (.50)	(0, 1)	N/A
Parental monitoring	Higher score indicates more parental monitoring of child's activities	N/A	3.05 (.85)	2.92 (.92)	(0, 4)	N/A

APPENDIX TABLE 1.A1 *(cont.)*

Variable Name	Variable Description	Mothers[a] Mean (St. Dev.)	Daughters Mean (St. Dev.)	Sons Mean (St. Dev.)	Range	Reliability[b]
Parental involvement	Higher score indicates more active engagement with parent	N/A N/A	4.26 (1.89)	4.28 (1.99)	(0, 8)	N/A N/A
Child autonomy	Higher score indicates child has input on important household decisions	N/A N/A	13.64 (3.58)	13.67 (3.35)	(6, 22)	N/A N/A
Cognitive stimulation	Percentile cognitive stimulation score from the HOME inventory	N/A N/A	49.03 (29.26)	44.78 (29.52)	(0,100)	N/A N/A
Emotional warmth	Percentile emotional warmth score from the HOME inventory	N/A N/A	47.52 (30.07)	47.78 (29.63)	(0,100)	N/A N/A

Notes: [a] Variable reliabilities were calculated using multiple observations over time for children. Child reliabilities were then used as proxies for the reliabilities of the mothers in the analysis.
[b] The sample sized used in each regression differs depending on the dependent variable being analyzed, thus means and standard deviations for mothers change across analyses. The means and standard deviations presented here are meant to be representative.
[c] Mothers were administered the AFQT, while daughters and sons were administered the PIAT.
[d] Mothers were asked as adults to indicate how shy they were at age six. Daughters' shyness was assessed by mothers and interviewers when the child was six years old.

Descriptive Statistics of Variables by Gender, Prince Georges's County Data

Variable	Variable Description	Females Mean (Std. Dev.)	Males Mean (Std. Dev.)
Youth: Anger scale	Continuous variable averaging frequency youth felt very angry, felt so angry wanted to hit someone / something, and couldn't control temper. Range 1 to 5.	2.19 (.86)	2.32 (.84)
Youth: Depression scale	Continuous variable averaging frequency youth felt hopeless, lonely, sad, depressed, didn't care anymore and suicidal. Range 1 to 5.	1.86 (.67)	1.77 (.67)
Youth: Gender-role attitudes	Continuous variable averaging youth belief that male should be breadwinner and children suffer when mother works. Range 1 to 7.	5.26 (1.50)	4.56 (1.50)
Youth: Black	Dummy variable with 1 = black, 0 = nonblack.	.57 (0.50)	.60 (0.49)
Mother: Anger scale	Continuous variable averaging frequency mother felt very angry, felt so angry wanted to hit someone / something, and couldn't control temper. Range 1 to 5.	1.52 (.56)	1.55 (.52)
Mother: Depression scale	Continuous variable averaging frequency mother felt hopeless, lonely, sad, depressed, and didn't care anymore. Range 1 to 5.	1.60 (.63)	1.66 (.64)
Mother: Gender-role attitudes	Continuous variable averaging mother belief that male should be breadwinner and children suffer when mother works. Range 1 to 4.	2.83 (.79)	2.80 (.81)
Father: Anger scale	Continuous variable averaging frequency father felt very angry, felt so angry wanted to hit someone / something, and couldn't control temper. Range 1 to 5.	1.52 (.55)	1.48 (.52)

APPENDIX TABLE 1.A2 (cont.)

Variable	Variable Description	Females Mean (Std. Dev.)	Males Mean (Std. Dev.)
Father: Depression scale	Continuous variable averaging frequency father felt hopeless, lonely, sad, depressed, and didn't care anymore. Range 1 to 5.	1.53 (.65)	1.51 (.61)
Father: Gender-role attitudes	Continuous variable averaging father belief that male should be breadwinner and children suffer when mother works. Range 1 to 4.	2.62 (.85)	2.68 (.80)
Mother: Age at birth of child	Continuous variable composed of mother's current age minus youth's current age.	26.80 (5.44)	26.83 (5.51)
Mother: Education	Continuous variable of self-reported educational attainment. (Q: What is the highest grade of school you have completed?)	13.96 (2.35)	14.21 (2.43)
Father: Age at birth of child	Continuous measure of father's current age minus youth's current age. For missing cases, mother's age plus mean difference of reported ages was substituted.	29.37 (5.99)	29.46 (5.87)
Father: Education	Categorical variable from 8th or less to professional degree, recoded as a continuous variable assigning years to each category.	14.66 (2.59)	14.65 (2.61)
Average Parental Age at Birth of Child	Continuous variable composed of the average of mother's and father's age.	28.08 (5.45)	28.12 (5.47)
Average Parental Education	Continuous variable composed of the average educational level of mother and father.	14.35 (2.11)	14.49 (2.24)

APPENDIX TABLE 1.A2 (*cont.*)

Variable	Variable Description	Females Mean (Std. Dev.)	Males Mean (Std. Dev.)
Total Family Income	Categorical variable of income ranges, recoded as continuous variable w/each category assigned midpoint. (Mother's report of total family income.)	54,335.23 (17,776.41)	55,382.21 (17,862.22)
Mother: Authoritarianism	Continuous variable averaging mother's belief that youth should follow directions, ask permission to do things, and not disagree in front of others. Range 1 to 5.	3.99 (.67)	4.00 (.67)
Mother: Youth involvement in decision-making	Continuous variable averaging mother's report of youth involvement in decisions affecting him / her and respect of youth's opinion. Range 1 to 5.	3.97 (.68)	3.97 (.64)
Father: Authoritarianism	Continuous variable averaging father's belief that youth should follow directions, ask permission to do things, and not disagree in front of others. Range 1 to 5.	3.75 (.78)	3.66 (.79)
Father: Youth involvement in decision-making	Continuous variable averaging father's report of youth involvement in decisions affecting him / her and respect of youth's opinion. Range 1 to 5.	3.75 (.72)	3.76 (.75)
Youth identification w / mother	Continuous variable averaging how much youth likes, respects, and feels close to mother. Range 1 to 4.	3.37 (.54)	3.36 (.49)
Youth negative relationship w / father	Continuous variable averaging youth's perception of frequency father criticizes, hits, yells at, or puts his needs above youth. Range 1 to 5.	1.58 (.55)	1.60 (.60)

Notes

Corresponding author is Greg J. Duncan, Institute for Policy Research, Northwestern University, 2040 Sheridan Road, Evanston, IL 60208, e-mail: greg-duncan@northwestern.edu. We are grateful for financial support from the National Institute on Aging (George Kaplan, PI, grant P50-HD38986 Michigan Interdisciplinary Center on Social Inequalities, Mind and Body) for supporting Duncan's time. The first three authors made equal contributions to the paper and are listed in alphabetical order. We are grateful for very helpful comments from Paula England, Christopher Jencks, James Rosenbaum, Sam Bowles, Melissa Osborne-Groves, and other conference participants.

1. This is a problem in intergenerational studies of earnings correlations as well. Studies based on homogeneous samples such as Mormon men or Air Force veterans produce lower correlations than studies based on broader, more representative samples.

2. Black, Hispanic, and low-income youth were oversampled in the NLSY; our regression results do not change in important ways depending on whether or not we weight the data for oversampling and differential nonresponse.

3. Interviews about and assessments of the children were conducted every other year after 1986, with the most current data available for 1998. Early cohorts of the CNLSY disproportionately sampled children born to young mothers. With each additional cohort the children become more representative of all children. NLSY children up to about age 15 in 1999 share many demographic characteristics of their broader set of age mates, although none was born to a mother older than 26. While this is a noteable sample restriction, it is unlikely to seriously bias our results. In 1980 half of all births were to women under the age of 24 and 80 percent were to mothers under the age of 29. By 1990, 39 percent of births were to mothers under the age of 24 with 70 percent to mothers under the age of 29 (U.S. Statistical Abstract of the United States, 2000, http://www.census.gov/prod/2001pubs/statab/sec02.pdf).

4. When an age 14 measure was not available, we first took an age 13 measure; and if that wasn't available, we took an age 15 measure. Some youth measures were asked only of those 15 and older; we first took the age 15 measure, then 16 or 17 if the age 15 measure was not available. We control for the child's age at interview in all analyses.

5. Taking the first cell in table 1.2 as an example, the odds of a daughter participating in school clubs in adolescence are 1.85 times higher if her mother reported participating in such clubs in adolescence than if her mother reported *not* participating, and no other regression controls are included. Adjusting for the effects of sixteen other traits and behaviors, as well as age in 1979 and race / ethnicity, reduces this odds ratio to a statistically significant (z-ratio = 2.44) 1.39.

6. The bivariate correlations and standardized regression coefficients would be identical if the given trait or behavior were uncorrelated with other regressors. This table also includes entries for measurement-error-adjusted regression coefficients, which are explained later.

7. PIAT scores have the highest alphas and the personality variables have the second highest alphas. This is not surprising, because these are the variables that have been constructed to be highly reliable. Nonetheless, even these variables show considerable fluctuation over time. These alphas tend to increase in adolescence and young adulthood in the NLSY data.

8. We do this using the "eivreg" (errors-in-variables) procedure in STATA.

9. Correcting for reliability in this way raises some potential problems. First, we do not expect intertemporal consistency in many child characteristics. If depression at age 10 and at age 14 are weakly correlated, it could be because of measurement error or because the child was depressed at age 14 but not at age 10. In addition, the age at which behaviors occur may be important. If a young child damages property he may get in less trouble than an older child who does the same thing. Thus, damaging property in adolescence may be more important than damaging property at age 10. In this case we may not be interested in a child's lifetime propensity to damage property, but only in whether he damaged property when he was a teenager. On the other hand, if we mean to measure some underlying attribute of children, the reliabilities may be helpful. Imagine that, as with family incomes, children's depression has both a transitory and a permanent component. Children's feelings of depression fluctuate, so that many children have bouts of depression but truly depressed children have more consistent depressive symptoms, and these are the children for whom depression interferes with life chances. A one-time measure of depression in adolescence (such as we have for mothers) is at best a moderate predictor of the permanent and more harmful aspect of depression.

10. The largest correlation among the parenting practices is between cognitive stimulation and parental warmth (r = .33), and the next largest correlation is between parental involvement and parental autonomy (r = .23). Only two other correlations are greater than .10.

11. Because children get half their genes from each parent, and these genes constitute a roughly random sample of each parent's total genetic endowment, the expected parent-child correlation for a trait that is entirely genetically transmitted would probably be between 0.4 and 0.6. Assortative mating raises this expected value. Dominant and recessive genes depress it. If genes express themselves differently under different environmental conditions, and if these environmental conditions vary, the parent-child correlation is further depressed. None of our correlations approach this size.

12. Because fathers and children's outcomes are measured at the same time, it is possible that children's psychological attributes affect fathers' attributes rather than the other way around. But the NLSY data suggest that this is not the case.

13. Although we do not show it, the results are similar when we estimate these models separately for boys and girls.

14. We also estimated these models for children who were at least 4 years old or at least 6 years old when the second maternal trait was measured. The results were substantively similar to the models for children who were at least 6 years old.

Chapter Two

THE APPLE FALLS EVEN CLOSER
TO THE TREE THAN WE THOUGHT

New and Revised Estimates of the

Intergenerational Inheritance of Earnings

Bhashkar Mazumder

PREVIOUS estimates of the intergenerational elasticity in earnings between fathers and sons in the United States that have been based on the Panel Study of Income Dynamics (PSID) and National Longitudinal Surveys (NLS) have underestimated the degree of persistence in earnings. These studies have typically used short-term averages of fathers' earnings as a proxy for lifetime economic status and have not fully adjusted for the potential bias due to serially correlated transitory shocks and the age at which fathers' earnings are observed. New empirical evidence using the long-term earnings histories of fathers and sons and the use of a new technique to correct for the bias suggest that the intergenerational elasticity may be close to 0.6. This suggests that earnings gaps in society may persist for many decades more than previously thought. New results using transition matrices also point to an especially high degree of rigidity at the bottom and top of the earnings distribution. These findings may have important policy implications, especially with respect to borrowing constraints, and are an important area for further research.

INTRODUCTION

During the 1990s several studies found a relatively high degree of transmission of economic status in the United States from fathers to their sons (e.g., Solon 1992; Zimmerman 1992). These studies used substantially better sources of data than previous research and estimated the intergenerational elasticity in earnings to be about 0.4, suggesting a relatively high degree of similarity between the income of fathers and sons. The results seemed to confirm the old German proverb "The apple does not fall far from the tree." The implication of these results also suggests that income inequality among families is fairly persistent and may linger for several generations. The results also clearly challenge the ideal of America as a highly mobile society where individuals succeed or fail irrespective of their initial circumstances at birth. Moreover, given the well-documented trend toward higher income inequality during the 1980s and the early 1990s, intergenerational inequality would appear to be a particularly important issue that policymakers will have to confront in the coming decades.

Yet, despite the ramifications of this issue, we still have very limited knowledge about the extent of intergenerational inequality and its underlying causes. This stands in stark contrast to the literature on cross-sectional income inequality, where there is an abundance of data and measurement tools to describe the income distribution and ways to test various theories concerning changes in inequality over time. One major problem is that constructing meaningful measures of intergenerational inequality requires reliable data on income for *two* generations of individuals from the same families for a nationally representative sample. All of the more recent studies on intergenerational income inequality in the United States therefore have had to rely exclusively on two sources of data: the Panel Study of Income Dynamics (PSID) and the National Longitudinal Surveys (NLS).

While these longitudinal data sets have dramatically improved the estimates of intergenerational inheritance of earnings compared to earlier research, they have some important limitations that have hindered accurate measurement. In particular, due to sample attrition, the intergenerational samples that may be constructed from these data sets are quite small and measure economic status over relatively short time spans. Various studies of earnings dynamics, however, have well established that measures of earnings over short periods of time may contain a large "transitory" component that make them an unreliable gauge of "permanent" or lifetime economic status. In addition, several studies have shown that there may be substantial differences in the size of transitory fluctuations in earnings over the life cycle. In particular, the income of fathers who are especially young or especially old is not likely to be an accurate proxy for long-term economic status.

In this chapter, I review evidence from some recent studies that incorporate these fairly noncontroversial ideas into the analysis of intergenerational mobility. These studies using different approaches all strongly suggest that the intergenerational elasticity in earnings in the United States is substantially higher than the consensus estimate of 0.4 that was based on the PSID and NLS. First, evidence is reviewed from a recent study by Mazumder (2001a), who runs simulations that incorporate the time-series properties of earnings to identify the likely degree of mismeasurement when short-term averages of earnings are used as a proxy for lifetime status. Second, new empirical results from Mazumder (2001a) are described. The study uses a data set that contains the long-term social security earnings histories of fathers and children and, therefore, largely overcomes the measurement problems that are encountered in other data sets. Third, Mazumder (2003) reconsiders the results from Solon (1992) by using a new econometric technique developed by Sullivan (2001). This procedure is able to address both serially correlated transitory shocks and age-related bias by utilizing information about the reliability of each data point directly into the estimation process. The results from each of these approaches suggest that the intergenerational elasticity in earnings in the United States is likely to be about 0.6.

An intergenerational elasticity of 0.6 compared to 0.4 paints a dramatically different picture of mobility in American society. For example, it implies that a family whose earnings are half the national average would require five generations instead of three before it substantially closed the gap. Obviously a difference of two generations, or about fifty years, is quite substantial and suggests the need to examine policies that foster greater mobility.

One important limitation of studies that focus on only a single parameter to measure intergenerational inequality, however, is that they miss out on possible differences in the rate of transmission of status over the earnings distribution. An attempt is made here to identify these differences by using a transition matrix to characterize differences in the rate of mobility across quartiles and deciles of the distribution using social security earnings data. The results support findings from other studies that show that there is a large degree of immobility at both the bottom and top of the earnings distribution. The rigidities, however, are more striking using this data. For example, for those sons whose fathers' earnings are in the bottom decile, more than 80 percent will have earnings below the sixtieth percentile. This provides evidence that poverty appears to be an especially persistent problem even if there is a reasonable degree of economic mobility for many individuals in the middle of the distribution. The finding is also consistent with theoretical models that suggest that borrowing constraints among poor families might induce a sizable intergenerational elasticity. This suggests that greater attention should be focused on measuring and explaining nonlinearities in the intergenerational transmission process.

The next section reviews the basic methodology that has been used by researchers to measure the intergenerational elasticity. This section also discusses some of the key measurement problems and reviews new empirical findings from Mazumder (2001a). The results from Mazumder

(2003) that reestimates the intergenerational elasticity in earnings on the same PSID sample used by Solon (1992) are reviewed next, followed by the results from using transition matrices. The main findings of the research and its potential implications are summarized in the concluding section.

EVOLUTION IN THE MEASUREMENT OF
THE INTERGENERATIONAL ELASTICITY

Intergenerational Elasticity as a Measure of Rigidity

Beginning with Sir Francis Galton in the nineteenth century, researchers have tried to measure the rate of regression to the mean of particular characteristics across generations. In a famous example, Galton (1889) plotted the heights of adults against their parents' heights and calculated the slope of the line that best fit the data. Galton found that, on average, the height of children was about two-thirds closer to the mean than the height of their parents. Sociologists were the first to apply this type of statistical model to characterize intergenerational inequality by calculating the correlation of various measures of socioeconomic status across generations.[1] Economists in recent decades have begun to use the Galton model on more traditional economic measures such as wages and annual earnings. Typically, the following regression model is used to measure the intergenerational persistence in economic status between fathers and sons:

$$y_{1i} = \alpha + \rho y_{0i} + \beta_1 Age_{0i} + \beta_2 Age^2_{0i} + \beta_3 Age_{1i} + \beta_4 Age^2_{1i} + \varepsilon_i \qquad (1)$$

Here y_{1i} represents a measure of economic status such as the log of annual earnings of the son in family i, while y_{0i} is the corresponding measure for the father, often averaged over several years. The only additional right-hand side variables that are generally included are age and age squared, in order to account for the effects of the lifetime profile of earnings for both the father and son.[2] Ordinary least squares (OLS) is then used to estimate the equation. The coefficient of interest, of course, is ρ, which measures the intergenerational elasticity.[3] While theoretically this measure can take on a wide range of values, in practice virtually all estimates will fall between 0 and 1.

An intergenerational elasticity of 1 would imply an extremely rigid society, where the son's position in the earnings distribution would typically replicate his father's position in the previous generation. In contrast, an intergenerational elasticity of 0 suggests an extremely mobile society in which the son's earnings is essentially unrelated to his father's earnings. Values between 0 and 1 provide a useful gauge of the degree of economic rigidity in society.[4] One minus ρ, on the other hand, provides a measure of the degree to which earnings "regress" toward the mean and can be viewed as a measure of mobility. Therefore, a society with a high ρ may be seen as a less mobile society than one with a low ρ.

One useful way to illustrate the significance of this measure is to imagine what it implies about the evolution of the black-white wage gap in the United States under a set of simplifying assumptions. An intergenerational elasticity of 0.2, for instance, implies that only 20 percent of any earnings gap between groups would remain after a generation (say twenty-five years).[5] Using this logic, the black-white weekly wage differential that stood at about 25 percent for men of age twenty-five to forty in 1980[6] would be reduced to just 5 percent by 2005 for similarly aged men if all other shocks were ignored. If instead, the intergenerational coefficient were 0.6, then the black-white wage gap would still be a sizable 15 percent in 2005.

Mismeasurement of Long-Run Status in Previous Studies

A review of the economic studies shows a gradual evolution in the quality of data used to measure the intergenerational transmission of economic status and a gradual increase in the size of the estimates. Some of the first attempts at this type of analysis used data from peculiar samples that happened to have information on income for both parents and children.[7] These studies used only single-year measures of fathers' income or earnings and found the intergenerational correlation to be less than 0.2. On the basis of these early results, some observers such as Becker (1988) concluded that there appeared to be substantial economic mobility.

The use of only a single year of income for the fathers posed significant measurement problems as noted by Bowles (1972) and Solon (1989, 1992). Solon pointed out that using single-year measures of income as a proxy for permanent income adds considerable noise to the problem, thereby resulting in a regression coefficient that is attenuated. In addition, he shows that the use of a homogeneous sample would tend to exacerbate this bias—suggesting the importance of using a nationally representative sample. Solon then demonstrates how taking a multiyear average of fathers' income should very quickly average away the noise. Using the PSID, a nationally representative longitudinal survey, Solon was able to overcome both these problems. Solon averaged fathers' earnings over as many as five years and estimated ρ to be in the neighborhood of 0.4. Zimmerman (1992) conducted a similar analysis matching fathers and sons in the original NLS cohorts using up to four-year averages of fathers' earnings, and found slightly higher results.

These studies, however, emphasized a fairly simple model of the earnings process. Here, earnings simply consisted of a "permanent" component that reflected the individual's true long-term earnings capacity, and a second component that reflected all other factors that might cause an individual's earnings to deviate from this permanent level *in that particular year*.[8] This would include both simple measurement error and "transitory" shocks that would, for whatever reason, cause earnings in that particular year to be higher or lower. Examples include a new job, promotion, or spell of unemployment. In this framework it was assumed that such factors had no *persistent* effect that carried over into future years. In this case, averaging earnings over a few years would, in fact, tend to average out both the measurement error *and* transitory fluctuations.

As far back as the 1970s labor economists, however, have studied the process by which earnings fluctuate from year to year in a more refined way (e.g., Lillard and Willis 1978). As part of the analysis, these studies of "earnings dynamics" typically modeled the transitory component of earnings as following an autoregressive process, whereby any shocks to earnings in one year would continue to be felt in future years, though the size of the effect would decay exponentially. In this framework, adjacent years of earnings for the same individual might be very similar not only because of the permanent component, but also because a transitory shock that took place in the first year continued to influence the level of earnings in the second year. Depending on the size of the transitory shock and the degree to which such shocks persist over time, it is easy to imagine how a two- or three-year average of earnings might actually give a very poor read of an individual's lifetime economic status. These studies would typically estimate the size of the transitory variance relative to the overall earnings variance and measure the auto correlation coefficient using a longitudinal data set such as the PSID.

In order to account for the effect of the persistence of transitory fluctuations on estimates of the intergenerational earnings elasticity, Mazumder (2001a) runs simulations that calculate the amount of bias that would result from using averages of fathers' earnings over various lengths as a proxy for fathers' lifetime economic status.[9] Figure 2.1 plots the percent of attenuation bias as earnings are progressively averaged over more years. So, for example, using just one year of fathers' earnings as a proxy for lifetime earnings results in an estimate of ρ that is biased down by about 45 percent, while using a thirty-year average would lead to an estimate that is biased down by just 4 percent. The results imply that even a five-year average would lead to estimates that are biased down by nearly 30 percent. This implies that if a five-year average of fathers' earnings resulted in an estimate of ρ of about 0.4, then the true value of ρ might, in fact, be close to 0.6.

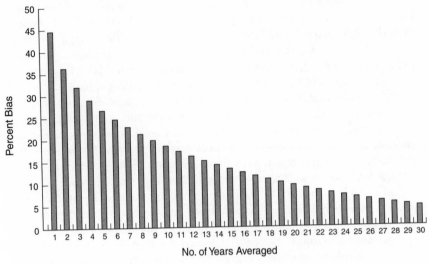

Figure 2.1 Implied attenuation bias by number of years used in average.

A possible criticism of this exercise is that the earnings process might be considerably more complicated than what is considered in the simulation, and that the omission of other factors might affect the results.[10] Until recently, economists have not had adequate data to test more structured models of earnings dynamics. However, a recent study by Mazumder (2001b) has shown that even a highly structured model still implies that short-term averages of earnings are poor proxies for permanent economic status. The degree of attenuation bias for a five-year average of earnings for a typical cohort is estimated to be more than 32 percent.[11]

Lifecycle Bias

Estimates of the intergenerational elasticity may also be sensitive to the age at which fathers' earnings are measured. If the variance of the transitory component of earnings changes considerably over the course of the life cycle, then short-term averages of earnings taken at a time when earnings are considerably noisy may compound the degree of bias. Intuitively, it makes sense to measure earnings of the parents at an age at which their earnings more accurately reflect their lifetime economic status. Researchers using the PSID or NLS, however, don't have access to earnings information from *before* the starting point of these longitudinal surveys, thereby restricting the range of ages at which fathers' earnings may be measured.[12] Several studies have found that the transitory component of earnings follows a "U-shaped" pattern over the lifecycle.[13] Figure 2.2, taken from Mazumder (2001b), shows estimates of the life-cycle profile of transitory innovations to earnings. As the figure demonstrates, measures of earnings around age 40 may be much less noisy than those taken at age 25 and significantly less noisy than those taken when fathers' are in their 50s. Solon's (1992) sample, for example, includes fathers as young as 27 and as old as 68, though the average age is 42. The implication of this bias on Solon's estimate is discussed in more detail in the next section.

New Estimates Using Social Security Earnings Data

Mazumder (2001a) also presents new empirical results using a new data set that largely overcomes the measurement problems that have been discussed.[14] Specifically, individuals in the 1984 Survey of Income and Program Participation (SIPP) were matched to the Social Security Administration's (SSA) summary earnings records (SER) via their social security numbers. The 1984 SIPP was a nationally representative longitudinal survey conducted by the Census Bureau containing a large range of demographic, employment, and income variables. The SER data pro-

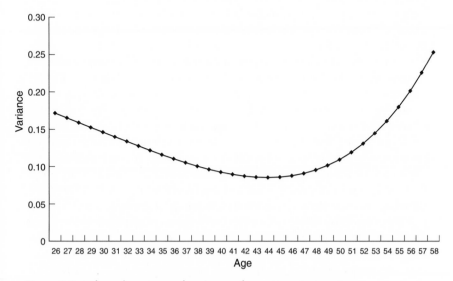

Figure 2.2 Life-cycle pattern of variance of transitory innovation.

vides the earnings histories of individuals between the years 1951 and 1998. The matched file allows for intergenerational analysis of families where children were living with their parents at the time of the survey and where the parents and children had social security numbers that were provided to SIPP interviewers.[15] The universe selected for analysis included children born between 1963 and 1968. Children's earnings are then measured over the period covering 1995 to 1998 when they are between 27 and 35. In principle, fathers' earnings may be measured as far back as 1951.

There are several clear advantages to this data set. First, the sample size is several times larger than what has been used in most other studies. This is due to both a larger initial survey base and the lack of attrition when using administrative data. Second many more years of earnings for the fathers are available for analysis. Third, because lifetime earnings histories are available, the effects of age-related bias may be mitigated. On the other hand, there are problems with using social security earnings data that do present estimation problems.[16]

In the first part of the analysis, Mazumder shows that estimates of the intergenerational elasticity, when using a two-year average of fathers' earnings and the *survey* data from the SIPP, closely match the results in the existing literature. Estimates for sons and daughters are about 0.35. In the second part of the analysis, social security earnings data for the fathers are averaged over progressively longer time periods. The estimates for the sons are below 0.3 when using only two-year averages but increase to just over 0.6 when fathers' earnings are averaged over as many as sixteen years. These are shown in figure 2.3. The estimates for daughters (not shown) follow a similar pattern but are less precise.

In addition, Mazumder uses broader measures of parental economic status such as *family income* culled from highly detailed data in the SIPP covering 1984 and 1985 and finds that the elasticity is sharply higher than when using two years of data on *fathers' earnings*. The SIPP interviews families every four months and collects information on income from over thirty specific categories. Both the detail of the data and the frequency at which it is collected is far superior to that found in the PSID and the NLS. Estimates of the intergenerational elasticity are about 0.55 when using two-parent income compared to just 0.35 when using only fathers' earnings. Using family income is arguably a good alternative way of eliminating much of the noise that is present in earnings data since families can use nonearnings forms of income such as asset income or government transfers to smooth consumption in periods when earnings are especially low. This approach provides additional evidence that studies that focused on short-term proxies of permanent earnings may have understated the degree of inheritance of economic status.

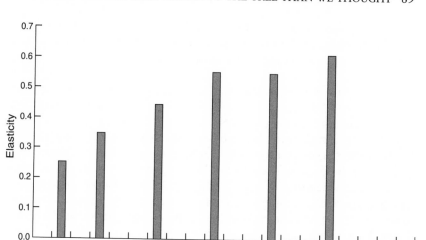

Figure 2.3 Estimated intergenerational elasticity as father's earnings are averaged over more years.

REVISED ESTIMATES USING THE PSID

Given the measurement problems that result from persistent transitory shocks to earnings and age-related bias, it seems appropriate to reconsider earlier estimates to see if they can be reconciled by taking into account these issues. As Solon (1992) noted, "If the process governing earnings dynamics were known, that knowledge could be exploited to achieve consistent estimation of the intergenerational correlation in long-run earnings . . . because considerable uncertainty still clouds the current understanding of earnings dynamics and because the data set used in the present study could not possibly resolve the issues, the present study settles for inconsistent estimators and discussing the likely direction of the inconsistency."

While it is clear that the definitive word on how the earnings process works is still far from settled there have been some substantial improvements in our understanding of earnings dynamics, since Solon's paper, that might be applied to this question. A recent study by Baker and Solon (2003) using the tax records of an extraordinarily large sample of Canadians has estimated a highly structured earnings dynamics model. This study was able to distinguish many different effects that contribute to the overall variance of earnings that were impossible with other data sets such as the PSID due to the limited sample size.[17]

Of particular relevance to the research on intergenerational mobility was their ability, in their Canadian sample, to estimate how the transitory variance changed over the life cycle. Ideally this kind of information could be used to address the issue of age-related bias and provide better estimates of the intergenerational elasticity.[18] The only problem is that it is unlikely that Baker and Solon's results are appropriate to measuring earnings dynamics in the United States.

In fact, as noted in the last section, Mazumder (2001b) has applied the Baker and Solon methodology to a large sample of men in the United States who were surveyed in the 1984, 1990, and 1996 SIPPs and who were also matched to their social security earnings histories. Specifically, an earnings dynamics model is estimated over the time period spanning 1983 to 1997 for eighteen two-year cohorts born between 1931 and 1966. As noted in the last section, Mazumder (2001b) then applies the parameter estimates from the model for one representative cohort and argues that previous estimates of the intergenerational elasticity based on five-year averages of fathers' earnings are probably biased down by about 30 percent. This implies that such estimates should be scaled up by a factor of about 1.4.

While this gives a rough idea of the bias and allows us to correct previous estimates by using an *overall* correction factor, it would be even more efficient actually to correct *each data point* using known information about its reliability, and then estimate the intergenerational elasticity with this corrected data. For example, it is clear that observations with very old fathers should be deemed less reliable and downweighted, compared to observations where the fathers are in their prime earning years. Such an approach would allow information about each father's age to influence how the estimation process treats the data point.

Mazumder (2003) uses exactly this approach on Solon's PSID sample by using Sullivan's (2001) heteroskedastic errors in variables (HEIV) estimator. To implement this estimator, an estimate of the "reliability ratio" of each observation is needed.[19] Sullivan runs Monte Carlo experiments to show that this new estimator provides a significant efficiency gain over simply using one overall correction factor for all the observations. To construct these observation-specific reliability ratios, a simplified earnings dynamics model utilizing the same data from Mazumder (2001b) is estimated and the parameter estimates are then used as inputs.[20] In this exercise, the reliability ratios for each observation will differ only by the fathers' age.

To see what this new estimator implies about previous estimates of the intergenerational elasticity, the analysis attempts to use the identical PSID sample used by Solon (1992).[21] As a result of sample selection rules, Solon's sample size when using five-year averages for father's in-

TABLE 2.1
"Revised" Estimate of Solon (1992)

	Elasticity	(Std. Error)	N
Solon (1992)	0.413	(0.093)	290
Replication	0.415	(0.095)	287
Fathers Aged < 59	0.426	(0.096)	281
HEIV Estimator	0.620	(0.168)	281

Notes: Results from Solon (1992) are from table 2.

come is 290. In the replication exercise undertaken here, there are a total of 287 pairs. Using the same specification, the intergenerational elasticity is estimated to be 0.415 compared to Solon's reported result of 0.413 (see table 2.1).

Since observation specific reliability ratios are only calculated for individuals between the ages of 26 and 58, the sample of fathers in the PSID is also restricted to this age range. This has the effect of removing six fathers who are over the age of 58 and increases the estimated intergenerational elasticity to 0.426.[22] Reestimating the intergenerational elasticity with the HEIV estimator sharply increases the estimate to 0.620. This provides further evidence that the rate of inheritance of economic status may be closer to 0.6 than to 0.4.

TRANSITION MATRIX RESULTS

Finally, transition matrices that track movements across specific parts of the distribution are used to identify any nonlinearities in the rate of intergenerational earnings mobility. The earnings distribution in both generations is broken into equally divided sections such as quartiles or deciles, and transitions of families across these sections over time are tabulated. The advantage of this approach is that rather than summarizing intergenerational inequality into one parameter, it enables one to see where the rigidities might exist along the earnings distribution. This might have important policy ramifications or explain the apparent cross-country differences in intergenerational mobility. For example, is the low level of mobility in the United States primarily due to a poverty trap that affects primarily the lowest strata of society?

On the other hand, this type of methodology has its limitations as well. Mobility rates for the very top and bottom parts of the distribution will always be constrained by the "floor" and "ceiling" imposed by the exercise.[23] In addition, rates of mobility very quickly become imprecise as one attempts to make finer grids when there are small samples. Even with the relatively large sample used here, the analysis does not attempt to use bins smaller than deciles.

The data used here is from the 1984 SIPP matched to social security earnings briefly described earlier.[24] Fathers' earnings are averaged over the period from 1979 to 1985, and son's earnings are averaged over 1995 to 1998. Initially, the sample is sorted into quartiles of both the fathers' earnings distribution and the son's earnings distribution.[25] A four-by-four matrix is then constructed where the values represent the percent of children originating in quartile a, who end up in quartile b. Under perfect mobility one would expect that all the values in the matrix would be 25 percent since the probability of ending up in any quartile would be independent of which quartile your father was in. For example, a son whose father was in the bottom quartile of the earnings distribution would be just as likely to be in the top quartile as the bottom quartile.

Table 2.2 presents the results from calculating transition probabilities. The top panel shows the results when using quartiles and clearly shows substantial evidence of immobility at the ends of the distribution. The results are very similar to those found in Zimmerman (1992). Only 32 percent of the sons whose fathers are in the bottom quartile of the distribution will end up in the top half of the distribution. Similarly, only 34 percent of the sons whose fathers are in the top quartile of the distribution will have earnings below the median.

In an effort to probe deeper into this issue, the sample was divided into deciles of the fathers and sons distributions, which has not been previously done with U.S. data. This is shown in the bottom panel of table 2.2. Here the rigidity at both tails is even more striking. For those sons whose fathers were in the bottom decile, 50 percent will have earnings below the 30th percentile and 80 percent will have earnings below the 60th percentile. More than 50 percent of the offspring of fathers in the top decile will have earnings above the 80th percentile and 68 percent will have earnings above the median.

A similar analysis using a significantly larger sample of Canadians by Corak and Heisz (1999) showed a roughly similar pattern but with less extreme values, particularly at the tails. For example, with the Canadian sample, 16 percent of the sons with fathers in the bottom decile remained in the bottom decile while about 18 percent of the sons in the top decile stayed in the top. The analogous figures for the United States, shown in table 2.2, are 22 percent and 26 percent. These results clearly imply that there is substantial rigidity in earnings status over generations in the United States and further bolster the general findings of the regression analysis.

TABLE 2.2
Transition Matrix Results

		Fathers' Earnings Quartile			
		Bottom	Second	Third	Top
Sons' Earnings Quartile	Bottom	0.38	0.26	0.21	0.15
	Second	0.30	0.25	0.26	0.19
	Third	0.19	0.29	0.30	0.22
	Top	0.13	0.21	0.24	0.43

		Fathers' Earnings Decile									
		Bottom	Second	Third	Fourth	Fifth	Sixth	Seventh	Eighth	Ninth	Top
Sons' Earnings Decile	Bottom	0.22	0.09	0.09	0.17	0.12	0.07	0.08	0.08	0.04	0.03
	Second	0.18	0.15	0.10	0.09	0.07	0.11	0.07	0.08	0.08	0.08
	Third	0.10	0.16	0.12	0.10	0.12	0.06	0.12	0.08	0.08	0.06
	Fourth	0.10	0.15	0.17	0.12	0.06	0.10	0.09	0.11	0.05	0.07
	Fifth	0.11	0.09	0.15	0.03	0.14	0.11	0.11	0.10	0.09	0.07
	Sixth	0.11	0.09	0.09	0.15	0.09	0.13	0.09	0.07	0.11	0.05
	Seventh	0.05	0.09	0.09	0.09	0.12	0.13	0.16	0.11	0.07	0.10
	Eighth	0.05	0.05	0.07	0.11	0.10	0.11	0.13	0.15	0.09	0.16
	Ninth	0.02	0.09	0.07	0.07	0.12	0.07	0.09	0.13	0.20	0.11
	Top	0.07	0.05	0.05	0.07	0.08	0.11	0.05	0.08	0.19	0.26

Notes: Deciles of fathers' earnings are based on the average earnings over 1979–85. Deciles of sons earnings are based on the average earnings over 1995–98.

Is Borrowing Constraints Important?

How might we explain this finding of substantial nonlinearity in the rate of intergenerational mobility? For economists, the well-developed theory of human capital is an obvious starting point. These theoretical models (e.g., Becker and Tomes 1979, 1986; Mulligan 1997) typically predict that under ideal market conditions the intergenerational elasticity should be quite low, since parents will optimally choose the appropriate level of "investment" in their child's schooling irrespective of their own financial conditions. Specifically, parents would purchase the amount of schooling such that the marginal benefit would equal the marginal cost. With perfect markets, parents can borrow against their future income or their children's future income to cover such expenses. In the presence of borrowing constraints, however, poor families with "high-potential" children might underinvest in their children's schooling, thereby inducing a sizable correlation in economic status across generations.

The obvious example that comes to mind is one of a poor family that cannot afford to send their child to *college*, causing the child to experience a similar lifetime earning experience as the parents. But it could be that these borrowing constraints actually operate far earlier in the child's life. For example, it could be that families with meager resources are unable to "buy into" a neighborhood with good-quality schools, thereby leading the child to lower lifetime earnings.

Intergenerational studies using the PSID and NLS have so far been largely unsuccessful in identifying whether borrowing constraints are a factor in reducing intergenerational mobility. This has been due primarily to small samples but there are also issues of the appropriate methodology.[26] Mazumder (2001a), using the larger samples from the SIPP-SER, data also incorporates measures of wealth into the analysis and finds that families with low net worth have a significantly higher intergenerational elasticity than families with high net worth. This provides some suggestive evidence that borrowing constraints might explain the high rigidity found at the bottom of the earnings distribution.[27]

This is also a potentially an important result because a number of studies have been unable to identify any *causal* effect of family income on children's future success despite the large intergenerational correlation or elasticity (e.g., Mayer 1997; Shea 2000). This has led some to argue that money itself does not matter but rather it is other family characteristics associated with income, such as motivation, that may be driving the intergenerational association in earnings. These studies, however, typically have not focused on families with little or no *wealth*. If money matters, but primarily for families that are unable to borrow against future income, then this might help explain the puzzle.

On the other hand, a high elasticity among low net-worth families doesn't explain, and might even appear, to contradict the finding from the transition matrix studies that there is a high level of rigidity at the *top* of the earnings distribution as well as the bottom. One explanation might be purely statistical in nature. It is possible that transition matrices show greater rigidity at the top of the distribution because fewer people tend to leave the top quantile due to the "ceiling" problem described earlier. At the same time the movement, or mobility, *within* the particular quantile might still be quite substantial. This might lead to low estimates of the intergenerational elasticity for that group or a similar group consisting of only high net-worth families.

While the transition matrix results provide some important new descriptive evidence of possible rigidities at the tails of the distribution, it is clear that much more research is needed before firm conclusions should be drawn about nonlinearities in the intergenerational transmission of earnings. Still, the idea that disparities in wealth in one generation may in turn cause disparities in earnings in the next generation in the presence of borrowing constraints holds some promise as an avenue to explain at least part of the low level of earnings mobility in the United States.

CONCLUSIONS

Although recent studies that have used nationally representative longitudinal surveys to measure the intergenerational elasticity in earnings are a considerable improvement over previous work, they still appear to have understated the persistence in earnings over generations. Researchers using these data sources have been forced to use relatively short-term averages of earnings as a proxy for lifetime earnings. There are two key problems with this approach. First, many studies on earnings dynamics have shown that the size and persistence of transitory fluctuations to earnings are quite large. Incorporating this insight into the statistical models of intergenerational mobility strongly suggests that short-term averages of earnings still provide a relatively poor gauge of lifetime economic status and bias down the estimates of the intergenerational elasticity by about 30 percent. Second, various studies imply that there might be a substantial bias when intergenerational samples include fathers whose earnings are observed when they are especially young or old, since their earnings might be especially noisy.

In this chapter it is argued that due to these reasons the true intergenerational elasticity in earnings may be sharply higher than the previous consensus view of 0.4. Using a new data source that contains the long-term earnings histories of fathers, Mazumder (2001a) presents new empirical results that suggest that the intergenerational elasticity in earnings between fathers and sons is about 0.6. The father-daughter elasticity also appears to be of a similar magnitude. In addition, this chapter reviews the findings from Mazumder (2003), which uses a new econometric estimator developed by Sullivan (2001) to address measurement problems when observation-specific reliability ratios are known. Applying this estimator to the same PSID sample used by Solon (1992) results in an estimated intergenerational elasticity of 0.62. These results suggest that the apple might fall even closer to the tree than we thought.

Transition matrices calculated using the SIPP-SER data also appear to bolster the general finding that there is substantial immobility in the United States. There is an especially high degree of rigidity at the bottom and top of the earnings distribution. For example, the vast majority of children born to parents in the lowest decile are likely to remain in the lower half of the earnings distribution. This finding is consistent with the hypothesis that a sizable intergenerational elasticity might be due to the inability of families to invest adequately in their children's human capital due to the lack of resources. Further research using alternative methodologies is required to examine the issue of nonlinearities in the rate of intergenerational transmission of earnings inequality.

This revised view of intergenerational mobility may have important ramifications for policymakers concerned with addressing long-term inequities in society. For example, the well-documented rise in cross-sectional inequality in recent years may linger for many decades. The black-white earnings gap may also take considerably longer to dissipate than we might have thought, suggesting that policies such as affirmative action may continue to be relevant. The evidence from the transition matrices combined with the finding of a high intergenerational elasticity among families with low net worth suggest that borrowing constraints might be an important causal channel for the transmission of inequality and one that policymakers may potentially be able to influence.

NOTES

1. An early example is Duncan (1961).

2. Other covariates have generally not been included in these studies since the goal is to obtain a summary measure of all the factors related to income that are transmitted over generations. Therefore, ρ should not be given a *causal* interpretation.

3. This is similar to but not equal to the intergenerational *correlation*, which has been emphasized in the sociology literature on intergenerational mobility. See Mazumder (2001a) for a brief discussion of the differences in the two measures.

4. Strictly speaking, the interpretation of "positional" mobility actually corresponds to the intergenerational correlation not the intergenerational elasticity. Since the two are extremely close in practice, the interpretation is reasonable. In contrast, the discussion of "regression to the mean" that follows does, in fact, correspond directly to the intergenerational elasticity and not to the intergenerational correlation.

5. This example also assumes a common intergenerational elasticity for both groups and no other group-specific effects. For example, a number of factors such as skill-biased technical change or declining unionism could affect each group differently and temporarily widen the gap further.

6. See Smith and Welch (1986).

7. For example, Behrman and Taubman (1985) used a sample of white male twins who served in the armed forces. Sewell and Hauser (1975) used a sample of high school seniors in Wisconsin who was no longer in school seven years later.

8. To be fair, both Solon (1992) and Zimmerman (1992) consider more complicated earnings processes, including serially correlated transitory shocks, but neither pursues the implications of these alternative earnings processes for their main results.

9. In this example earnings in a given year consist of a permanent component, a serially correlated transitory component, and a white noise component. It is assumed that the point of interest is the elasticity between son's earnings and fathers' *lifetime* earnings. Fathers' lifetime earnings are assumed to be earnings over the period covering ages 21 to 65. The calculation takes parameter estimates from the more recent models of earnings or wage dynamics estimated by Card (1994), Hyslop (2001), and Mazumder (2001b). Specifically the formula uses the share of earnings variance due to transitory factors (0.3), the share of earnings variance due to measurement error (0.2), and the autocorrelation coefficient of transitory shocks (0.8). Mazumder experiments with other parameter estimates, but these are viewed as the preferred values. See the appendix of Mazumder (2001a) for details on the calculations.

10. For example, there has been some debate in the literature on earnings dynamics as to whether there is also a significant random walk component to earnings or substantial heterogeneity in the age-earnings profile of individuals (e.g., Baker 1997).

11. This is the implied reliability ratio when earnings are averaged over five years for men born in 1943 / 44 (aged 39 to 40 in 1983). This is the average of column 5 in the top panel of table 5 of Mazumder (2001b). The results are robust across cohorts.

12. In practice this is less of a problem in the PSID. The average age of fathers is 42 for Solon (1992). The problem is more severe with the original NLS cohorts. The average age of fathers is 50 for Zimmerman (1992).

13. See Gordon (1984), Baker and Solon (2003), and Mazumder (2001b).

14. See Mazumder (2001a) for a detailed and technical description of the research and methodology. Special permission is required from the Census Bureau or Social Security Administration to access this data.

15. See Mazumder (2001a) for more details about the match process. Robustness checks indicated that the match process did not bias the results.

16. Some individuals may have a main job or a secondary job that is not covered by social security. In addition, the data is recorded only up to the taxable maximum for that year. A number of approaches are taken to overcome these problems. See Mazumder (2001a) for details.

17. In particular they identified a random walk component, heterogeneity in age-earnings profiles, an age-based component to the transitory variance, a time-varying permanent component, and a serially correlated transitory component.

18. For example, the various parameter estimates would allow one to calculate the fraction of the variance of a five-year average of fathers' earnings taken over a particular age range and over particular years that reflects the variance in lifetime earnings as opposed to transitory noise or measurement error. This fraction could then be used to scale up previous estimates of the intergenerational elasticity.

19. In a simple bivariate regression, the reliability ratio is the variance of the correctly measured explanatory variable divided by the variance of the mismeasured explanatory variable. This is sometimes referred to as the ratio of the "signal" to the "signal plus noise." Intuitively, it gives the fraction of the total variance in the explanatory variable that represents the true signal from the data. The HEIV estimator regresses the dependent variable on the explanatory variable multiplied by its estimated reliability ratio. See Sullivan (2001) for more detail.

20. The model assumes that there is a common permanent component, a random walk component, heterogeneous growth in experience, a serially correlated transitory component that follows a quartic in age, and a nonserially correlated white noise component. The various parameter estimates are then used to calculate the reliability ratio for using a five-year average of earnings of fathers beginning at age s, as a proxy for average lifetime earnings (average earnings between the ages of 26 and 58). See Mazumder (2003) for a detailed description.

21. Although reliability ratios derived from the SIPP-SER data covering the 1980s and 1990s are not ideal to use for data on fathers' earnings from the late 1960s and early 1970s drawn from the PSID, in practice this does not appear to be a major problem. First, Gottschalk and Moffitt (1994) have shown that the permanent and transitory components of earnings appear to have risen at the same rate from the 1970s to the 1980s. This suggests that the reliability ratio, which is roughly equivalent to the permanent component over the permanent plus transitory component, should not have changed much over this time period. Second, the results of the very simple earnings dynamics models using the SIPP-SER data in Mazumder (2001b) yield almost equivalent estimates to those using the PSID (e.g., Card 1994), even though they are from different data sets and cover different time periods.

22. The youngest age of a father in the PSID sample is 26 so no fathers are removed by the lower boundary.

23. For example, families say, in the top quartile cannot move to a higher quartile. So even if the son's earnings are sharply higher than the father's, the family will remain in the top quartile suggesting rigidity, when in fact this might be more appropriately interpreted as mobility.

24. See Mazumder (2001a) for a detailed description of the data.

25. This follows the tradition of studies such as Zimmerman (1992), Dearden, Machin, and Reed (1997), and Corak and Heisz (1999) and is useful for comparison with the earlier literature.

26. For example, Mulligan (1997) divides his sample by whether the children expect to receive an inheritance as an indicator of intergenerational borrowing constraints and finds no significant difference. Mazumder (2001a) argues that it is more appropriate to test for whether parents can borrow from *their own* future income, and he measures borrowing constraints at the time the children are still adolescents.

27. Other possible reasons might explain this result. For example, parents who have a higher tendency to save, and therefore have higher wealth, might also tend to invest more in their children's human capital, leading to greater intergenerational mobility among this group. Still, this finding at a minimum suggests that rather than dismissing the possibility of borrowing constraints it should be an issue for further exploration.

Chapter Three

THE CHANGING EFFECT OF FAMILY BACKGROUND ON THE INCOMES OF AMERICAN ADULTS

DAVID J. HARDING, CHRISTOPHER JENCKS,
LEONARD M. LOPOO, AND SUSAN E. MAYER

MOST Americans endorse the ideal of equal opportunity, and many interpret this ideal as requiring that children from different backgrounds have an equal chance of achieving economic success. Most Americans also recognize that children whose parents have "all the advantages" are more likely to prosper than children whose parents lack these advantages. Reducing the correlation between parental advantages and children's economic success has therefore become a prominent goal of liberal social policy, especially since the 1960s. This chapter investigates how the correlation of American adults' family incomes with their parents' characteristics changed between 1961 and 1999.

Our approach to measuring trends in intergenerational inheritance differs from earlier studies in two important respects. First, almost all earlier studies have focused on the determinants of individuals' labor market success, defined either in terms of occupational rank or earnings. We focus instead on an individual's total family income. This change allows us to assess the impact of family background on the economic status of individuals who are not working. It also allows us to take account of the fact that individuals' economic status often depends more on how they fare in the marriage market than on how they fare in the labor market.

Our second innovation is that we measure changes in the effect of family background in two conceptually distinct ways. Our first measure of intergenerational inheritance is the multiple correlation between adults' family income and their parents' socioeconomic rank. This measure can—and often does—remain stable even when the economic distance between rich and poor adults is changing. Our second measure of inheritance is the ratio of the income received by adults who grew up in advantaged families to the income received by adults who grew up in disadvantaged families. This measure incorporates the effect of changes in the degree of inequality in family income as well as changes in intergenerational correlations.

We concentrate on trends among men and women between the ages of 30 and 59, whom we often refer to as "mature adults." Family income prior to the age of 30 shows little relationship to either family income at later ages or the parental characteristics that predict later family income. The reason seems to be that the young make the transition to full adulthood at different ages. Individuals who are in their twenties are often still in school, childless, or both. As a result, they are more willing to work irregularly or take temporary jobs that provide little evidence about their future earnings. In addition, many are unmarried or in short-term cohabiting relationships that provide few clues about subsequent partners' likely income.

Men and women over 59 are often retired, and the likelihood of their being retired rose between 1960 and 2000. Family income in retirement is strongly related to both parental characteristics and earlier income, but we concluded that pooling retirees with working-age adults would be a mistake.

Our data come from three widely used surveys: Occupational Changes in a Generation, the General Social Survey, and the Panel Study of Income Dynamics. Unfortunately, none of these surveys covers individuals living in institutions. This omission probably leads to some downward bias in our estimates of the relationship between respondents' family income and their parents' characteristics.

Our major findings are as follows:

Intergenerational Correlations and Income Gaps. The multiple correlation between a mature man's family income and his parents' measured characteristics fell during the 1960s and then remained stable from the 1970s through the 1990s. But men's family incomes began growing more unequal in the 1970s, so the income gap between men raised by advantaged rather than disadvantaged parents widened between the 1970s and the 1990s.

We have no data on trends among women during the 1960s. In the early 1970s intergenerational correlations were higher among daughters than among sons, and daughters' family incomes were also more unequal. The economic cost of having grown up in a disadvantaged family was therefore considerably larger for daughters than for sons. But whereas the correlation between a mature man's family income and his parents' socioeconomic position was almost constant between the 1970s and the 1990s, this correlation fell among women. As a result, the economic cost of growing up in a disadvantaged family was therefore roughly constant for women, although it remained larger for women than for men.

Race, Ethnicity, and Region.   At least among those between the ages of 30 and 59, disparities in family income between blacks and whites, between Hispanics and Anglos, and between those raised in the South and North narrowed between 1961 and 1999.

Parental Education.   The effect of parental education on men's family income fell during the 1960s but rose again over the next three decades. Parental education mattered more for mature women's family income than for men's in the 1970s, but this difference had disappeared by the late 1990s.

Parental Occupation.   When we rank occupations in terms of their educational requirements and economic rewards, which we treat as a rough proxy for skill requirements, the effect of a one-point difference between two fathers' occupations on their mature sons' family income declined during the 1960s. The effect of fathers' occupation shows no clear trend after that for either men or women, but it is consistently larger for women than for men, partly because women's family incomes are more unequal than men's.

Parental Income.   The effect of parental income on thirty-year-old children's family income shows no clear trend between 1979 and 1996. We have no data on this relationship before 1979.

Although we talk about the "effect" of parental characteristics on children's eventual family income, readers should not take the term too literally. The parental characteristics that we can measure are all correlated with other characteristics that we cannot measure, so we cannot say with any confidence what would happen if we were to change any one parental characteristic while leaving all the others constant. The word "effect" is just shorthand for an association or partial correlation.

This chapter begins by briefly summarizing previous research on trends in intergenerational inheritance in the United States. The next section outlines a framework for thinking about the ways in which parental characteristics can affect a grown child's family income, after which we describe our data, and then summarize trends in inequality among parents. We next show changes in the multiple correlation between mature adults' family income and their parents' characteristics, and then show changes in the income gap among adults from different backgrounds. The final section discusses possible criteria for deciding whether the intergenerational correlations that we observe are too high, too low, or about right.

PREVIOUS RESEARCH

"Occupational Changes in a Generation" (OCG) was the first large carefully designed study of changes in intergenerational economic mobility in the United States. Featherman and Hauser (1976) compared men who were between the ages of 25 and 64 in 1962 and 1973. They found that parental advantages explained 18 percent of the variance in occupational rank in 1973, compared to 21 percent in 1962. Hauser et al. (2000) report that the bivariate correlation between fathers' and sons' occupations also fell among nonblacks, although it rose among blacks. Hauser et al. found a further decline when they compared intergenerational occupational correlations in the 1986 Survey of Income and Program Participation (SIPP) to those in the 1973 OCG.[2] Using the General Social Survey (GSS), both Hout (1988) and Grusky and DiPrete (1990) also concluded that intergenerational occupational correlations declined between 1972 and the mid-1980s.

Most assessments of change in the intergenerational earnings correlation are based on the Panel Study of Income Dynamics (PSID). Almost all of these studies also suggest that the inheritance of economic advantages has declined.[2] Mayer and Lopoo (2001) found, however, that when they added other parental characteristics to their model, the multiple correlation between parental advantages and PSID sons' wages was relatively stable.

Although the PSID usually shows a declining effect of parental earnings or family income on men's earnings, the National Longitudinal Surveys do not. Levine and Mazumder (2002) compare the twenty-eight to thirty-six-year-old men whom the National Longitudinal Survey of Youth surveyed in 1994 to men of the same age whom the National Longitudinal Survey of Young Men surveyed in 1981. Among men raised in two-parent families, the elasticity of sons' earnings with respect to their parents' income rose from 0.22 to 0.41. This means that a 10 percent difference in parental income was associated with a 4.1 percent difference in sons' earnings in 1994 compared to a 2.2 percent difference in 1981. But while focusing on two-parent families holds family structure constant, it ignores the fact that disadvantaged sons were less likely to have grown up in two-parent families. When Levine and Mazumder included sons raised by single parents, the elasticity of sons' earnings with respect to their parents' total income only rose from 0.23 to 0.33, and the change was no longer statistically significant.

All these studies focus on the intergenerational inheritance of labor market status, so they omit respondents who are not in the labor force. This restriction could easily introduce some bias, because family background affects adults' economic position partly by affecting their chances of working for pay, and this effect may well have changed over time. The studies that look at earnings are also limited to trends since around 1980, which means that they cover a relatively short window.

The existing literature also focuses largely on men and ignores the growing role that wives' earnings play in determining many families' economic position. Figure 3.1 shows changes between 1968 and 1996 in the correlation between a mature adult's own earnings in a given year and his or her total family income in the same year. Men and women without earnings are included and assigned earnings of zero. Among men the correlation between earnings and total family income fell from 0.87 in 1968 to 0.75 in 1996. Among women, the correlation rose from 0.18 in 1968 to 0.39 in 1996. Earnings are still a much better proxy for living standards among men than among women. But since family

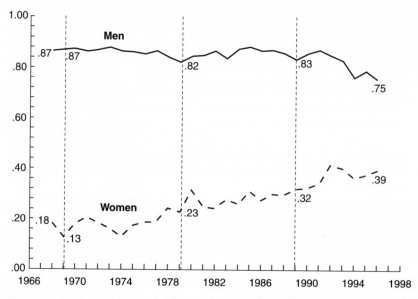

Figure 3.1 Correlation of respondents' earnings with total family income among PSID men and women ages 30 to 59 between 1968 and 1996.

Notes: Dashed vertical lines are business cycle peaks. Earnings and incomes are unlogged, and those without earnings are assigned values of zero. The data do not cover individuals who are neither household heads nor partners of heads.

Source: Family vs Individual Income-PSID.xls.

background influences an individual's chance of having a well-paid spouse, ignoring this fact is likely to bias trend estimates of how background affects economic status among either men or women.

How Parental Advantages Affect Family Income

Figure 3.2 shows some of the pathways by which parental characteristics can influence children's eventual family income. Figure 3.2 is not a complete causal model. It omits many links that are well established in the research literature, such as the reciprocal effects of spouses' earnings on one another, to highlight the links that we think most likely to have changed. It also contains several hypothetical constructs that require brief discussion.

Genetic Advantages. A growing body of evidence suggests that genetic differences can influence an individual's earnings. In some cases this is obvious. American men whose physical appearance suggests that they are of European descent earn more than those whose appearance suggests that they are of African descent, for example. But even when we focus on white males, genes still seem to matter. Monozygotic (MZ) twins have all their genes in common, while dizygotic (DZ) twins share roughly half their genes. When Taubman (1976) collected data on the 1973 earnings of white male twins who had both served in the American armed forces during World War II, MZ twins' 1973 earnings correlated 0.54, while DZ twins' earnings correlated 0.30. If genetic resemblance were the only reason for the higher correlation among MZ twins, we could infer that nearly half the variance in annual earnings was linked in some way to genetic variation.[3] Twin data collected by Orley Ashenfelter and his collaborators in the 1990s yield roughly the same estimate for hourly wages.[4] These estimates require a number of problematic assumptions (Goldberger 1978), and they should not be taken literally. They do suggest, however, that genes are likely to play a significant role in explaining parent-child earnings correlations.

Björklund, Jäntti, and Solon (this volume) report earnings correlations not just for MZ and DZ twins but also for large samples of ordinary siblings reared together and apart, as well as for half-siblings reared together and apart and for pairs of genetically unrelated siblings reared together. Their data underscore the danger of extrapolating from twin data alone. The assumptions that psychologists developed to estimate heritabilities from IQ data on MZ and DZ twins do not appear to hold for earnings. If one makes the traditional assumptions, genes appear to explain almost two-fifths of the variance in Swedish twins' earnings. But

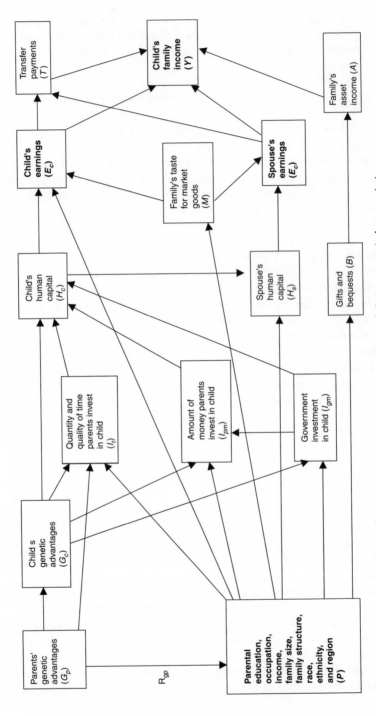

Figure 3.2 Some possible links between respondents' family incomes and their parents' characteristics.

when Björklund et al. use all their sibling data, they conclude that the figure is closer to one fifth.

If we want to estimate the role of genes in the intergenerational transmission of economic privilege, one obvious strategy is to compare father-son correlations for sons who grew up with their biological father to correlations for sons who grew up with a man who was not their biological father. We do not have such data for the United States, but Björklund and Chadwick (2002) have assembled such data for Sweden. At the mean of the distribution, the elasticity of a Swedish son's earnings with respect to his biological father's earnings is 0.28 if the son always lived with his biological father and 0.09 if he never lived with his biological father.[5]

The fact that genetic resemblance helps explain economic resemblance between fathers and sons does not mean that this source of economic resemblance operates independently of the environment. Suppose, for example, that myopia has a genetic component. Most affluent societies ensure that myopic children get glasses. As a result, myopic children can usually see almost as well as other children. In poor societies where glasses are not available to everyone, the genes that contribute to myopia have a larger impact.

People's genes also influence the environments they choose for themselves. Consider two sisters, one of whom finds reading easy and one of whom finds it difficult. The sister who finds reading easier is likely to enjoy reading more and do more of it. As a result, she is likely to score higher on vocabulary and reading tests, get higher grades, stay in school longer, and earn more when she enters the labor force.

Human Capital. Economists use the term "human capital" to describe the skills, knowledge, and character traits that influence a worker's potential earnings. If employers value the same attributes for several generations, parents with above-average human capital are likely to have children with above-average human capital. To begin with, parents with traits that employers value tend to have above-average earnings, and so they can invest more in their children's nutrition, health care, and education. Such parents also tend to live in political jurisdictions where the government invests a lot in children. In addition, while most parents want their children to develop traits that will pay off in the labor market, achieving this goal is easier for parents who have such traits than for parents who do not (Duncan et al., this volume). Finally, as we have already noted, many traits that employers value depend partly on genes, and children get half their genes from each parent.

Although economists use the term "human capital" to describe characteristics that pay off in the labor market, one can easily broaden the concept to include characteristics that pay off in the marriage market. As we shall see, parental characteristics explain slightly more of the variation in daughters' family incomes than in sons' family incomes. This difference between sons and daughters deserves a more careful analysis than we can provide here, but it suggests that parental advantages may exert even more influence on a daughter's success in the marriage market than on a son's success in the labor market.

Taste for Market Goods.   Families vary dramatically in the number of hours that their adult members spend doing paid labor. Family members also vary in the extent to which they maximize their hourly wages. Some always take the best-paid job they can find, while others settle for less money to get shorter hours, more congenial colleagues, more interesting work, or other nonmonetary advantages. Family background appears to influence how much people work (Altonji and Dunn 2000), and it probably also influences the weight that individuals assign to earnings relative to goals like short hours and interesting work. If these correlations change over time, the correlation between family income and parental characteristics is also likely to change.

Gifts and Bequests.   Dividends, interest, and rent accounted for 7 percent of all income received by individuals between the ages of 25 and 64 in 1999.[6] Wolff (2002) concludes that gifts and bequests accounted for about 19 percent of all assets in 1998. Gale and Scholz (1994), in contrast, conclude that three-quarters of all assets are inherited.[7] If Wolff is right, inherited assets probably account for about 1 percent of money income among thirty to fifty-nine year olds. If Gale and Scholz are right, the figure could be more like 5 percent.[8] We do not know how this figure has changed over time, but the age at which adults inherit their parents' assets is rising, so the relative importance of inherited assets could be falling for those under the age of 60.[9]

Rates of Change.   Figure 3.2 suggests that intergenerational correlations can change for two quite different reasons. First, the effects of various parental advantages on children's human capital can change. Second, the effects of children's human capital on their family income can change. Children's education illustrates both of these possibilities.

The correlation between parents' socioeconomic advantages and the number of years of school that their children complete declined for children completing school between World War I and the early 1970s (Hauser and Featherman 1976). As a result, educational disparities among adults from different kinds of families kept shrinking throughout the twentieth century. All else being equal, this trend should have reduced the impact of parental advantages on children's family income. But all else was not equal, because the economic value of an extra year of schooling also changed. The effect of an extra year of school on men's annual earnings fell between 1940 and 1975. This change accentuated the declining impact of parental advantages on children's educational attainment, making it doubly difficult for economically advantaged parents to pass along their advantages by keeping their children in school. But after 1975 the labor market returns to schooling rose again. The payoff to schooling also rose in the marriage market. If we compare the most educated third of all mothers to the least educated third, about 93 percent of the most educated and 87 percent of the least educated were living with a husband in both 1940 and 1960. By 1990 the proportions were 84 percent for the most educated and 70 percent for the least educated.[10] The marriage gap between the most and least educated mothers had thus risen from 6 to 14 percentage points. The net result was that while parental advantages had less impact on how much schooling young people got in the last third of the century than earlier in the century, the value of each year of school rose during the last decades of the century.

Mature adults seldom go back to school, and so the correlation between educational attainment and parental characteristics when a birth cohort is sixty is about the same as when it was thirty. The correlation does change as more recent birth cohorts replace earlier ones, but this takes a long time. In principle, we can hold changes of this kind constant by tracking the same birth cohort over time. When we do this, almost all the remaining changes in the correlation between family income and parental characteristics are attributable to changes in the way employment, marriage, and earnings are distributed among individuals with fixed characteristics. Some of these changes are predictable byproducts of aging. Adults who head families with children, for example, tend to be more concerned with maximizing their income than young people just out of school. In other cases, however, changes in employment, marriage, and earnings reflect changes over time in the character of the labor market or the marriage market. We return to this issue later.

Whereas cohort replacement is slow, the economic value of respondents' characteristics can change relatively rapidly. When job opportunities improved for black workers in the wake of the civil rights movement, for example, young blacks benefited the most, but older blacks also gained. Likewise, when the wage gap between high school and college graduates widened in the 1980s, the change was largest among younger workers but it also affected mature workers. Changes in the marriage market can also change the value of personal characteristics quite rapidly. When divorce rates rise, all women are more likely to experience sudden reductions in family income, but the change is likely to be largest among those with disadvantaged parents, because their divorce rates are likely to rise the most.

The Data

The Occupational Changes in a Generation (OCG) surveys were supplements to the Census Bureau's Current Population Survey and were conducted in 1962 and 1973. They both asked men (but not women) about their family background. Our first sample of mature OCG men was born between March 1902 and March 1932. Our second sample was born between March 1913 and March 1943.

The General Social Survey (GSS) is a smaller survey that has been conducted by the National Opinion Research Center either annually or biennially since 1972. The GSS asks both men and women about their family income and family background. We analyze the surveys conducted between 1972 and 2000, and so our samples of mature adults were born between the spring of 1912 and the spring of 1970.

The Panel Study of Income Dynamics (PSID) is a longitudinal survey conducted by the Survey Research Center at the University of Michigan. It has followed all members of about 5,000 households (including those who leave to form a new household) since 1968. Unlike OCG and GSS, the PSID has asked parents about annual income since 1968, so we can link parents' incomes to their grown children's family income at age 30. Our PSID sample includes all children born between 1949 and 1966.

Family Income. All three surveys were conducted in the spring and asked respondents about their income during the previous calendar year: 1961 and 1972 in OCG, 1971 to 1999 in GSS, and 1979 to 1996 in PSID. We adjust OCG and GSS family incomes to eliminate differences in family income based on age, gender, and survey year and analyze the effect of parental characteristics on the natural logarithm of adjusted family income.[11] Thus if a parental characteristic has a coefficient of 0.01, a one-unit change in the parental characteristic is associated with a 1 percent increase in respondents' family income. Although we refer throughout to "family" income, we include individuals who live alone or with nonrelatives, treating them as families of one. We do not adjust respondents' family income for differences in family size. If respondents did not provide any income data we drop them.

In OCG, the income data come from the March Current Population Survey (CPS). We have data on the total pretax money income from all sources for the respondent and his wife (if he was married), but not for other family members. Our measure of "family" income is therefore the sum of the respondent's income and his wife's income if he was married.[12]

In the GSS, interviewers handed respondents a card with a list of income categories, each of which was identified by a different letter, and asked respondents to say which letter best matched their family's pretax income. The card does not tell respondents how they should define their family, and so there was probably some variation in the treatment of income received by elderly parents, grown children, and partners to whom the respondent was not married. As inflation pushed up nominal incomes, the GSS added more categories at the top, raising the total number of categories from twelve in 1972 to twenty-three in 2000. Such changes were associated with increases in the estimated dispersion of income, but these "methodological" increases were small. We assigned all GSS respondents who put themselves in the top income category an amount 1.5 times the top category's lower bound. We assigned respondents who put themselves in lower categories the midpoint of their category.

To see how grouping income affected the estimated impact of parental characteristics, we tried grouping the 1972 OCG income data into the twelve GSS categories for 1972. Grouping reduced the standard deviation of logged family income by 7 percent. Contrary to what we had expected, however, grouping had no systematic effect on the coefficients of parental characteristics. As a result, parental characteristics explained slightly *more* of the variance in grouped than ungrouped OCG incomes. This finding suggests that most of the within-category variance is noise. We therefore decided to group both OCG and GSS incomes.[13] Implausibly low incomes are less common in the PSID, so we trimmed the top and bottom one percent of the distribution rather than grouping PSID incomes.

Annual Versus Permanent Income. Most families' income fluctuates from year to year. To see how much annual income varied over time we tracked PSID family heads who were between the ages of 30 and 39 in 1968. The correlations between annual incomes separated by twenty years averaged about 0.5. This finding suggests that respondents' stable characteristics are unlikely to explain more than half the variance in annual income. Thus if family background explains 15 percent of the variance in respondents' annual income, it should to explain more like 30 percent of the variance in their average income between the ages of 30 and 59.

If the correlations among family incomes measured one, five, ten, or twenty years apart were changing over time, the correlation between parental characteristics and annual income would not necessarily show the same long-term trend as the correlation between parental characteristics and long-term income. But year-to-year income fluctuations have risen at about the same rate as overall income inequality, so the year-to-year and decade-to-decade correlations among thirty to fifty-nine year olds in the PSID show no clear trend (results not shown). It follows that the correlations of parental characteristics with annual income and long-term income should move in tandem.

Parental Occupation. OCG asked respondents to describe the occupation of the individual who headed their family when they were sixteen years old. GSS asked respondents to describe the occupation of their father or stepfather when they were sixteen. If respondents did not report their father's occupation, we imputed a value based on their other characteristics using "best subset" regression (Little and Rubin 1987).

Both OCG and GSS assign fathers to a three-digit Census occupational category using the same categories for fathers as for sons.[14] We used updated versions of Duncan's "socioeconomic index" (SEI) to rank these occupations.[15] These SEI scores give roughly equal weight to the educational attainment and income of workers in a given occupation. We interpret these scores as estimates of the occupation's skill requirements. Hauser and Warren (1997) have shown that fathers' SEI scores predict children's life chances more accurately than an occupational ranking based solely on the mean earnings of those who worked in the occupation.

We transformed all our SEI scores so that they had means of zero and standard deviations of one in the full sample of OCG or GSS fathers. Since the OCG and GSS standardizations differ, differences between OCG and GSS have no substantive meaning. Changes in dispersion *within* OCG should, however, reflect changes in the distribution of fathers across occupations, since OCG occupations were assigned the same score in all years. Because GSS switched from the 1970 to the 1980 occupational classification in 1988, occupations got new SEI scores at that time, but this switch did not change the dispersion of fathers' SEI scores. Trends in the dispersion of GSS fathers' scores are therefore real.

Parental Education. Once again, OCG asked about the educational attainment of the person who headed the respondent's family at age sixteen, while GSS asked about the respondent's father or stepfather. When GSS respondents did not report their father's or stepfather's education, we substituted the mother's education. The coefficients of father's and mother's education do not differ in any consistent way. We assigned all OCG and GSS parents in a given educational category the estimated mean of the interval, measured in years. In the PSID, parental education is the number of years of school completed by the respondent's mother, with the father's education substituted when the mother's education was not available.

Siblings.   This is the number of siblings reported by the respondent, top coded at nine in OCG and ten in GSS.

Black.   This is a dichotomous variable, with a value of one for blacks and zero for nonblacks. In almost all cases this measure is based on the interviewer's judgment rather than the respondent's self-identification.

Hispanic.   The 1973 OCG included a question about "original nationality." This question is roughly (though not exactly) comparable to the question that the Census Bureau uses today. It allows anyone with any Latin American ancestors, no matter how remote, to identify themselves as Hispanic if they wish to do so. Those with ancestors from many places can choose their own ethnicity. The 1962 OCG did not include a question of this kind, and so we classified men as Hispanic on the basis of their place of birth and their parents' place of birth. This definition excludes Hispanics whose parents were both born in the United States, and it presumably yields a poorer Hispanic population than the 1973 definition. The GSS asked respondents if they had ancestors from Latin America, but since the GSS only interviews in English, it probably underrepresents first-generation immigrants. The PSID is limited to families who lived in the United States in 1968, and so it does not include many immigrants. These definitional difficulties mean that our data cannot tell us much about changes in the economic status of Hispanics.

Southern Origins.   In OCG this measure is the respondent's region of birth. In GSS and PSID it is the region where the respondent lived as a teenager.

Intact Family.   OCG asked respondents whether they were living with both parents "most of the time" up to age 16. GSS asked respondents whether they were living with both parents *at* age 16. The PSID measure is for the year when the respondent was 19 rather than 16, even if the respondent no longer lived at home.

Parental Income.   The PSID is our only source of reliable data on parental income. We calculated PSID parents' average income when a child was between the ages of 19 and 25. Most readers would probably prefer a measure of parental income when the child was younger, but since the

PSID did not begin until 1968, children born in the late 1940s and early 1950s were already in their middle or late teens when the first data on parental income was collected. Eliminating these children would shrink both our sample and the time interval over which we could calculate trends.

To see if measuring parental income when children were aged 19 to 26 biased our results, we also calculated average parental income during adolescence for respondents who had such data. Average parental income when children were adolescents was highly correlated with average parental income when children were young adults, and when Mayer and Lopoo (2001) used both measures to predict children's incomes they could not reject the hypothesis that the coefficients were equal.

Changes in Inequality among Parents

Suppose that a 10 percent income difference between parents is always associated with a 4 percent income difference between their children. The income gap between children raised by rich and poor parents will then depend on the size of the income gap separating rich and poor parents. If inequality between rich and poor parents falls, as it did during the first two-thirds of the twentieth century, and if all else remains equal, the subsequent income gap between their children will also fall. If inequality between rich and poor parents rises, as it did in the last third of the twentieth century, and if all else remains equal, the income gap between their children will also widen. The same logic holds for other parental advantages, like educational attainment and occupational position.

We do not find statistically reliable changes in the effect of parental income, but that is because our estimates are imprecise and our time series only covers the years from 1979 to 1996, not because the point estimates are the same year after year. As we shall see, the effects of a one-year difference in parental education and a one-point difference in occupational SEI do fluctuate between 1960 and 2000. We therefore assume that the effects of parental income also fluctuated, and that the PSID sample is just too small and starts too late to identify such fluctuations. Nonetheless, we assume that the impact of family background also depends on how unequal parents are. All else being equal, the more each parental characteristic varies, the higher the expected correlation between the parental characteristic and children's economic outcomes.

Table 3.1 shows trends in the means and standard deviations of the seven parental characteristics available in OCG and GSS. The last col-

TABLE 3.1

Means and Standard Deviations of Seven Parental Characteristics among
OCG and GSS Respondents Ages 30 to 59, by Decade

Variable	OCG Men		GSS Men and Women			Percent Change in SD[a]
	1962	1973	1970's	1980's	1990's	
Parental occupation						
Mean	−.091	−.038	−.097	.055	.048	
(S.D.)	(.933)	(.983)	(.939)	(1.049)	(1.022)	14.7%
Parental education						
Mean	7.462	7.901	8.612	9.915	11.166	
(S.D.)	(3.87)	(4.08)	(3.86)	(4.00)	(3.79)	3.4%
Number of siblings						
Mean	4.245	3.868	3.989	3.767	3.671	
(S.D.)	(2.76)	(2.73)	(2.87)	(2.76)	(2.61)	−10.2%
Intact family						
Mean	.827	.831	.764	.763	.728	
(S.D.)	(.377)	(.373)	(.425)	(.425)	(.445)	3.7%
Black						
Mean	.093	.091	.113	.112	.137	
(S.D.)	(.291)	(.286)	(.316)	(.315)	(.344)	7.0%
Hispanic						
Mean	.022	.046	.028	.039	.045	
(S.D.)	(.146)	(.210)	(.164)	(.193)	(.207)	26.2%[b]
Southern origins						
Mean	.303	.331	.330	.314	.300	
(S.D.)	(.460)	(.471)	(.470)	(.464)	(.458)	−0.2%
Unweighted N	10,953	21,289	5,143	6,743	8,474	

Notes: [a] (OCG-73/OCG-62)(GSS90s/GSS70s)(100)−100. The shift from Stevens and Featherman's (1981) scale to Stevens and Cho's (1985) scale makes comparisons between pre-1 89 and post-1989 GSS data problematic, but since the standard deviation of fathers' occupation does not change in 1989, we treat the shift as seamless.
[b] Because the OCG-I and OCG-II measures of "Hispanic" are not strictly comparable, this change is based solely on the GSS.

umn of table 3.1 combines the within-survey changes in OCG with the within-survey changes in GSS to estimate the overall trend in the dispersion of each parental characteristic between the early 1960s and the 1990s. Changes in the standard deviation provide a good measure of trends in parental inequality when parental characteristics have linear effects on the log of family income. This requirement is more or less met for all the parental characteristics except number of siblings.

Occupational Inequality. The relationship between the logarithm of respondents' family income and parental SEI scores is approximately linear in the bottom 90 percent of the occupational distribution. But SEI scores have a long tail above the 90th percentile, and differences above the 90th percentile have smaller percentage effects on children's family income than differences below the 90th percentile (results not shown). To assess the impact of this nonlinearity on the estimated trend in occupational inequality among parents, we transformed SEI scores so as to make their effect on logged family income roughly linear. The estimated trend in occupational inequality among parents using this transformed measure of SEI was almost identical to the trend using the original measure.[16] We therefore use the more familiar untransformed measure. Table 3.1 shows that when we use this measure, occupational inequality among parents rose by 14.7 percent between 1962 and the 1990s.

Educational Inequality. Parental education also has essentially linear effects on the log of respondents' family income. In the 1961 OCG, for example, the income gap between respondents whose fathers had sixteen rather than twelve years of schooling was 29 percent, while the income gap between respondents whose fathers had twelve rather than eight years of schooling was 28 percent.[17] Table 3.1 shows that the standard deviation of the number of years of school that a parent had completed rose slightly between the first and second OCG surveys but fell slightly in the GSS between the 1970s and the 1990s. Overall, educational inequality among parents hardly changes.[18]

Inequality in Family Size. Disparities in the size of children's families declined somewhat between the early 1960s and the 1990s. All else being equal, this decline should have reduced the correlation between respondents' family background and their eventual income.

Dichotomous Background Measures. The four remaining measures of parental advantages in table 3.1—intact family, black, Hispanic, and Southern origins—are dichotomous rather than continuous. It is more difficult to think about changes in parental inequality when a measure has only two possible values (coded in this case as zero and one). To see how the distribution of dichotomous parental characteristics affects inequality, suppose that coming from an intact family always doubled a child's expected family income. This would be a sizable advantage, but if almost all children grew up in intact families, family structure could not explain much of the variation in family income, because it would not vary much. This would be equally true if almost everyone grew up in a broken family. Dichotomous characteristics can make their largest contribution to inequality when half the population has an advantage and half does not. The standard deviation of a dichotomous characteristic reflects this fact: it is zero when nobody has the characteristic, rises gradually to 0.50 when half the population has the characteristic, and then falls back gradually to zero when everyone has the characteristic.[19]

The only dichotomous characteristic for which the standard deviation changes appreciably is being Hispanic. For reasons that we have already discussed, the OCG measures provide no information on the actual change in the percentage of the population that was Hispanic. The GSS shows substantial growth in the English-speaking Hispanic population between the 1970s and 1990s. Because Hispanics have relatively low family incomes, the fact that more adults had Hispanic parents implies both an increase in the overall level of inequality among parents and an increase in the fraction of the variance in respondents' incomes explained by their parents' characteristics.

Income Inequality. All else being equal, growing ethnic diversity and growing inequality in the kinds of work that parents did should have led to a small increase in both the income gap between respondents from advantaged and disadvantaged families and the correlation between respondents' family income and their parents' characteristics. But all else was obviously not equal. The most obvious omission in table 1 is parental income. Since we know that the overall distribution of income changed over the course of the twentieth century, it seems likely that income inequality among parents also changed.

There is no reliable data on income inequality among parents prior to 1940. But this was an era when most children lived in families with a male breadwinner, when relatively few women worked for pay while they had children at home, and when government transfer payments to the needy were modest. The dispersion of family income among parents is therefore likely to have tracked the dispersion of mature men's earnings, which depends mainly on the unemployment rate and the dispersion of hourly wages among those with jobs. Men's wages became more equal between 1900 and 1945 (Margo 1999). Thus if we set aside the 1930s, when unemployment was unusually high, it seems likely that parental incomes also became more equal between 1900 and 1945.

We have better information on the distribution of family income after World War II. Figure 3.3 shows that income inequality among families of two or more declined a little between the late 1940s and the late 1960s. After 1969 inequality began to climb. By the late 1970s family incomes were as unequal as they had been in the late 1940s. In the 1980s and 1990s income inequality reached levels not seen since before World War II. Unfortunately, Figure 3.3 covers all families of two or

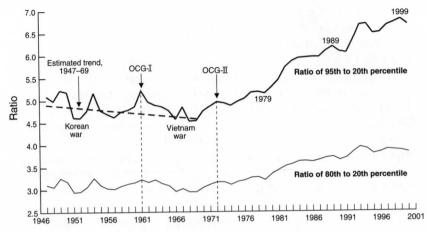

Figure 3.3 Ratio of family incomes at the 95th and 80th percentiles to incomes at the 20th percentile in the United States: 1947 to 2000.

more, regardless of whether they include children. But Jencks, Mayer, and Swingle (forthcoming) have analyzed trends between 1969 and 1999 for households with children, and their trends are quite similar to those in Figure 3.3. In the absence of contrary evidence we therefore assume that trends among parents were similar to trends for all families of two or more throughout the period from 1947 to 2000. If that assumption is correct, income inequality among parents probably declined during the first two-thirds of the twentieth century and rose during the last third of the century.

Neither OCG nor GSS includes a direct measure of parental income, and so the coefficients of parental education and occupation subsume their influence on parental income. When overall wage inequality rose after 1970, inequality between workers with different amounts of education and workers in different occupations rose at roughly the same rate. Such evidence as we have suggests that the opposite pattern prevailed between 1940 and 1970, when wage inequality was falling. Thus if the value of a 1 percent increase in parental income remained constant—a very large "if"—and if all else remained equal, the coefficients of parental education and occupation should have declined between 1940 and 1970 and should then have risen after 1970.

The implications of these income changes for children born in particular years depend on whether the effects of parental income vary for children of different ages. If parental income exerts its strongest effect when children are very young and if all else is equal, the coefficients of parental education and occupation should probably have fallen fairly steadily among respondents born between 1900 and 1970, as ours were. If parental income exerts its largest effect when adolescents are deciding whether to attend college, the coefficients of parental education and occupation should be somewhat larger among children born in the 1960s than among those born in the 1950s or 1940s.[20] If parental income has roughly the same impact on children of all ages, we would expect to see some decline in the impact of parental education and occupation among children born between 1900 and about 1950, followed by some increase among those born after about 1965. Unfortunately, our samples do not include enough individuals born after 1965 to assess this last conjecture.

Changes in Intergenerational Correlations

We turn now to changes in the multiple correlation between mature adults' position in the income distribution and their parents' advantages. We denote this parent-child correlation as R_{pc}.[21] When R_{pc} falls, we can infer that intergenerational changes in rank (what sociologists call "exchange mobility") have become larger or more frequent. When R_{pc} rises, intergenerational changes in rank have become either smaller or less frequent.

Table 3.2 shows multiple correlations between respondents' family income and the seven parental characteristics measured in the OCG and GSS surveys, namely race, ethnicity, Southern origins, intact family, number of siblings, parental education, and parental occupation. For reasons already discussed, differences between the OCG and GSS correlations are likely to be a byproduct of differences between the surveys. For men, one can estimate the overall change between the early 1960s and the 1990s by first comparing the 1961 and 1972 OCG surveys, then comparing GSS men surveyed in the 1970s and 1990s, and then combining these two within-survey changes. But the changes during the 1960s are so different from the changes between the 1970s and 1990s that combining the two changes into a single summary statistic usually conceals more than it reveals.

Among OCG men we see a dramatic decline in R_{pc} between 1961 and 1972. This decline recurs for all age groups. The diagonal arrows track birth cohorts as they get older. Here again we see declines between 1961 and 1972. Men who were between the ages of 30 and 39 in 1961, for example, were almost all between the ages of 40 and 49 in 1972. For these men R_{pc} fell from 0.399 to 0.305. The same pattern holds for men who were between 40 and 49 in 1961. Although it is tempting to assume that these changes reflect a trend that prevailed throughout the 1960s, this need not be the case. Figure 3.3 suggests, for example, that family

TABLE 3.2
Multiple Correlations of Family Income with Seven Parental Advantages
in OCG and GSS, by Age, Sex, and Decade

Respondents' Age	OCG Men		GSS Men			GSS Women		
	1961	1972[a]	1970s	1980s	1990s	1970s	1980s	1990s
30 to 39	.399	.309	.330	.289	.306	.399	.361	.374
40 to 49	.397	.305	.355	.362	.352	.437	.388	.361
50 to 59	.414	.323	.327	.410	.360	.440	.429	.350
Weighted Mean for All 30 to 59 Year Olds	.403	.312	.337	.342	.335	.423	.385	.364[b]
Approximate Sampling Error of Multiple R[c]	(.008)	(.006)	(.014)	(.017)	(.015)	(.012)	(.015)	(.014)
Sample size	12,829	23,824	2,382	3,040	3,817	2,761	3,703	4,657

Notes: The seven measures of family background are race, ethnicity, Southern origins, living with both parents at age sixteen, number of siblings, parental education, and parental occupation (see text for details).
[a] The declines between 1961 and 1972 are significant at the .01 level for all age groups.
[b] The average decline between the 1970s and the 1990s is significant at the .01 level.
[c] Approximated using $[(1-R^2)/(N-8)]^{.5}$.

incomes were unusually unequal in 1961. The changes that drove up measured income inequality could conceivably have produced an analogous short-term jump in R_{pc}.

In any event, the GSS tells a very different story about changes in R_{pc} after 1972. The multiple correlations for men in the same age group show no consistent trend between the 1970s and the 1990s, and none of the changes is statistically significant.[22] When we track the same cohort of men over time, the multiple correlations almost always rise as a cohort ages. This is in sharp contrast to what we saw between 1961 and 1972.

Unlike OCG, GSS provides data on post-1972 trends among women as well as men. Table 3.2 shows that while R_{pc} was essentially stable among GSS men, it declined by about a seventh among GSS women. Whereas R_{pc} was substantially higher among women than men in the 1970s, this gender difference had largely disappeared by the 1990s. This pattern of differences is consistent with the hypothesis that parental advantages influence success in the marriage market somewhat more than they influence success in the labor market, although other explanations are also possible. Regrettably, we cannot test this hypothesis in a rigorous way with either the OCG or GSS data.

The correlations in table 3.2 take no account of parental income. To see how much this omission biases R_{pc} we turn to the PSID. Our PSID data set did not include a measure of either parental occupation or sibship size. Nonetheless, the first equation in table 3.3 shows that even when we omit parental income, the other five parental characteristics measured in the PSID correlate 0.367 with respondents' income at age thirty. Table 3.2, in contrast, suggests that for GSS men and women surveyed in the 1980s and 1990s, the multiple correlation between all seven parental characteristics and family income measured between the ages of 30 and 39 averages 0.333. Adding parental income to the PSID equation in table 3.3 raises R_{pc} by about a tenth (from 0.367 to 0.406), suggesting that omitting parental income does not attenuate the estimated level of intergenerational inheritance as much as some economists assume it does.

TABLE 3.3

Effect of Including Seven Years of Parental Income on Multiple Correlation of Parental Characteristics with PSID Children's Family Income at Age Thirty

	Coefficients (and standard errors)		
Ln of mean parental income when child was 19 to 25		.363 (.043)	.206 (.046)
Income by Year interaction (Ln parental income)(Year)(17)		.038 (.073)	.063 (.073)
Mother's education (in years)	.050 (.006)		.029 (.007)
Intact family	.156 (.039)		.000 (.043)
Black	−.473 (.044)		−.406 (.045)
Hispanic	−.068 (.073)		−.083 (.074)
Southern upbringing	−.074 (.032)		−.047 (.032)
R^2	.135	.117	.165
Multiple R	.367	.342	.406

Notes: Coefficients in bold are significant at $p < .05$. Sample includes all men and women with complete data who turned thirty between 1979 and 1996 (N = 3,509). The standard deviation of logged family income at age thirty is 0.722.

For our purposes, however, the crucial question is not whether adding parental income affects the estimated *level* of R_{pc} but whether it affects the estimated *trend*. The interaction between parental income and survey year in the third column of table 3.3 is positive, suggesting that the independent effect of parental income may have increased over time. But the coefficient of the interaction term is also smaller than its standard error, suggesting that the PSID does not provide enough statistical power to settle this question. Mayer and Lopoo (2001) are also unable to find any consistent trend in R_{pc} using the PSID.

For those who find it hard to decide whether the correlations in table 3.2 are "large" or "small," table 3.4 displays the association between parental advantages and children's family income in a more intuitively accessible form, namely the probability that children with parents in the top or bottom quartile will remain there when they grow up. To construct this matrix we first used the seven measures of parental advantages available in OCG and GSS to rank respondents' parents from least to most advantaged.[23] Then we divided parents into quartiles running from the least to the most advantaged. We also divided respondents into quartiles based on how their family income compared to that of other respondents of the same age and sex who were surveyed in the same year. Finally, we calculated the probability that respondents whose parents were in the top or bottom quartile would have family incomes in each quartile. To keep the discussion simple, we focus on the probability that those born into the top or bottom quartile were in the top or bottom income quartile as mature adults.

Since R_{pc} fell between 1961 and 1972, we also expected the proportions of OCG men who remained in the top and bottom quartiles to decline. Likewise, since R_{pc} did not change much for men after 1972, we did not expect much change in the proportions of GSS men who remained in the top and bottom quartiles. Table 3.4 confirms these expectations.

Among women the story is a little more complicated. Among GSS women, R_{pc} fell between the 1970s and the 1990s, so we expected a parallel decline in the proportions of GSS women who stayed in the top and bottom quartiles. Table 3.4 confirms this prediction for women born into the top quartile: their chances of having slipped into a lower quartile were clearly higher in the 1990s than in the 1970s. But the chances that a woman born into the bottom quartile would remain there did not change much between the 1970s and the 1990s, although women who moved up did move further in the 1990s than in the 1970s.

Table 3.4 also suggests that downward mobility out of the top quartile is more common than upward mobility out of the bottom quartile—an asymmetry that correlation coefficients cannot detect. In the first OCG survey, for example, only 37.6 percent of the mature men

TABLE 3.4

Percent of 30- to 59-Year-Old Sons and Daughters in Each Quartile of Family Income By Quartile of Parental Advantages and Year in OCG and GSS

Parents' Quartile and Survey	Family Income Quartile					Sample Size
	Bottom	Second	Third	Top	Total	
Sons from Bottom Quartile						
OCG: 1961	46.2	27.7	16.7	9.5	100	2,537
OCG: 1972	40.7	29.8	21.2	8.4	100	6,454
GSS: 1970s	40.3	29.6	19.8	10.2	100	595
GSS: 1980s	39.4	30.0	21.2	9.4	100	840
GSS: 1990s	40.6	25.8	21.1	12.6	100	954
Trend: 1961 to 1990s[a]	−5.3	−1.7	5.7	1.4		
Sons from Top Quartile						
OCG: 1961	9.5	20.9	32.1	37.6	100	2,678
OCG: 1972	11.8	24.0	29.2	35.0	100	4,899
GSS: 1970s	11.6	20.5	30.2	37.8	100	596
GSS: 1980s	12.3	19.7	28.8	39.2	100	728
GSS: 1990s	11.6	21.4	29.0	38.0	100	954
Trend: 1961 to 1990s[a]	2.4	3.9	−4.1	−2.3		
Daughters from Bottom Quartile						
GSS: 1970s	44.4	26.2	19.6	9.9	100	690
GSS: 1980s	44.5	25.5	18.8	11.2	100	1,070
GSS: 1990s	43.7	25.9	18.8	11.6	100	1,164
Trend: 1970s to 1990s	−0.6	−0.4	−0.8	1.7		
Daughters from Top Quartile						
GSS: 1970s	10.1	19.1	27.1	42.8	100	691
GSS: 1980s	12.1	19.3	29.7	38.9	100	878
GSS: 1990s	11.7	23.5	27.1	37.7	100	1,164
Trend: 1970s to 1990s	1.5	4.4	0.0	−5.2		

Notes: Parents are assigned to quartiles of parental advantages using the seven measures in table 3.1, with each advantage weighted by its coefficient in the equation predicting log family income. Family incomes are assigned to quartiles after eliminating variation due to age, gender, and survey year.

[a] Sum of within-survey changes: (OCG II–OCG I) + (GSS 1990s–GSS 1970s).

born into the top quartile had family incomes in the top quartile, whereas 46.2 percent of the men who had been born into the bottom quartile were still there. This difference is highly significant ($p < 0.001$). This asymmetry is much less marked among GSS men and is not statistically significant, but it crops up among GSS women. This asymmetry may just reflect the fact that both OCG and GSS asked more questions about characteristics that distinguish people in the bottom quartile of the income distribution from everyone else than about characteristics that distinguish people in the top quartile of the distribution, but the asymmetry could also be real.

Long-Term Income. Tables 3.2 through 3.4 describe the correlation between family background characteristics and family income in a single randomly selected year between the ages of 30 and 59. The PSID data cited earlier suggest that something like half the variance for such an income measure is attributable to some combination of measurement error and real year-to-year fluctuations in income. If half the variance in mature adults' annual income is attributable to measurement error and year-to-year fluctuations, averaging mature respondents' income between the ages of 30 and 59 should roughly double R^2. Doubling R^2 would raise the values of R_{pc} in table 3.2 by about two-fifths, putting them between about 0.4 and 0.6. It would also increase the probability that a respondent born into the top of the bottom quartile of parental advantages had a lifetime income in the same quartile.

Although economists often assume that the study of intergenerational inheritance should focus on lifetime incomes, and that year-to-year fluctuations should be treated as noise, this view only makes sense if families' consumption levels are based on lifetime income rather than income over some shorter interval. Because families often save and borrow so as to neutralize the effects of short-term income changes, R_{pc} in table 3.2 constitutes a lower-bound on the correlation between mature adults' standard of living in a randomly selected year and their parents' advantages. But we also know that short-term income fluctuations have real effects on some forms of consumption, including grocery spending and parents' ability or willingness to help pay their children's college bills. This means that doubling the estimates of R_{pc} in table 3.2 would overstate the correlation between mature adults' standard of living in any given year and the parental advantages measured in OCG and GSS.

CHANGES IN INCOME RATIOS

Up to this point we have focused on the extent to which children's rank in the distribution of income depends on their parents' rank in the distribution of socioeconomic advantages, ignoring the fact that the economic distance between the top and bottom of the income distribution changes over time. But the economic distance between mature adults from advantaged and disadvantaged families depends not just on R_{pc} but on the economic distance between grown children at, say, the 5th and 95th percentiles of the distribution.

One can measure the increase in income associated with growing up in a more advantaged family either as a dollar difference or a percentage difference. Most people find percentage differences more appealing. Doubling your income may not have the same effect on well-being when your income is small as when it is large, but this assumption seems more plausible than the assumption that an extra $10,000 has the same effect on well-being regardless of whether your income is small or large. Increasing the standard deviation of log income by 0.01 implies that the income gap between random families has risen by 1 percent.[24] Thus if a 1 percent increase in income is equally valuable to the rich and the poor, the standard deviation of log income is a good measure of income inequality. The top half of table 3.5 shows trends in inequality among mature adults using this measure. Just as in figure 3.3, inequality fell between 1961 and 1972 and rose steadily between the 1970s and 1990s.[25]

Income Ratios Between the Advantaged and Disadvantaged. One way to measure the income ratio between respondents with advantaged rather than disadvantaged parents is to multiply the intergenerational correlation (R_{pc}) by the standard deviation of mature adults' logged family income. This yields an estimate of the income gap between mature adults whose parents differed by one standard deviation on the index of parental advantages that we used to construct table 3.4. The second panel of table 3.5 shows trends in this measure. Several results deserve attention:

- Because income inequality declined between 1961 and 1972, the income gap between respondents from advantaged and disadvantaged families fell even more than the intergenerational correlation.
- Because women's family incomes are more unequal than men's, the income gap between women from advantaged and disadvantaged families exceeds the gap between men from similar backgrounds even when the values of R_{pc} for men and women are similar.
- Because income inequality grew faster among men than women after 1970, the income gap between advantaged and disadvantaged men rose, while the income gap between advantaged and disadvantaged women remained roughly constant.

TABLE 3.5

Income Gap between Respondents Whose Parents Differed by One Standard Deviation on the Seven-Item Index of Parental Advantages in OCG and GSS, by Age, Gender, and Decade

	OCG Men		GSS Men			GSS Women		
	1961	1972	1970s	1980s	1990s	1970s	1980s	1990s
SD of Log Family Income								
30–39 year olds	.813	.708	.638	.753	.769	.814	.875	.948
40–49 year olds	.860	.764	.697	.763	.901	.813	.932	.929
50–59 year olds	.971	.827	.760	.933	.962	.883	.958	.952
Weighted mean	**.875**	**.765**	**.695**	**.801**	**.860**	**.835**	**.912**	**.942**
Income Gap between Respondents Whose Parents Differ by 1 SD[a]								
30–39 year olds	.325	.219	.211	.218	.236	.325	.316	.354
40–49 year olds	.341	.233	.247	.276	.317	.355	.361	.335
50–59 year olds	.402	.267	.249	.383	.347	.389	.411	.333
Weighted mean	**.353**	**.239**	**.231**	**.277**	**.290**	**.353**	**.352**	**.343**

Notes: [a] SD of log family income in the top panel of this table multiplied by the appropriate multiple correlation in table 3.2.

- Because income inequality rises with age, the income gap between respondents from advantaged and disadvantaged families also rises with age, even though the correlation between family income and parental advantages shows no consistent trend with age.

Table 3.6 presents such income ratios in a more intuitively understandable way by comparing the age-adjusted family incomes of respondents from each quartile of parental advantages.[26] The income gap between respondents raised in the bottom and second quartiles is usually larger than that between respondents raised in the third and top quartiles, regardless of whether we measure the gap as a ratio or as a dollar amount.[27]

Specific Parental Advantages. Column 1 of table 3.7 shows the bivariate relationship of respondents' logged family income in 1961 to each of the seven parental advantages measured in OCG. Column 2 shows the change in this coefficient between 1961 and 1972. Almost all of the coefficients decline significantly between 1961 and 1972. Columns 3 and 4 show the multivariate coefficients from an equation that controls all seven parental advantages simultaneously. Here again, all seven coefficients decline, although only three of the declines are now significant.

The coefficient of parental occupation dropped by about half between 1961 and 1972. This decline is partly attributable to the steady decline in the proportion of respondents whose fathers were farmers. Among respondents not raised on farms, the main reason for decline was that respondents from the top tenth of the occupational distribution enjoyed less of an economic advantage in 1972 than in 1961 (results not shown).

The declining effect of Southern origins probably reflects the narrowing of the income gap between the South and the North. The declining effect of race reflects a decline in the educational gap between blacks and whites, movement of blacks from the South to the North, and some reduction in wage discrimination.

Table 3.8 shows bivariate results from the GSS. Column 1 shows the estimated coefficient of each parental advantage for men in 1971, while the second column shows the estimated change in the bivariate coefficient for men between 1971 and 1999.[28] The bivariate relationships between men's family income and their father's education, number of siblings, and whether they grew up in an intact family become significantly stronger over time. The bivariate effect of father's occupation also grows slightly stronger, but the change is not significant. The bivariate effect of being Hispanic grows weaker over time.

Columns 3 and 5 show that in 1971 almost every parental advantage or disadvantage had more impact on women than on men. But columns

TABLE 3.6
Mean Family Income by Quartile of Parental Advantages for Men and Women Ages 30 to 59 in OCG and GSS, by Decade

	OCG Men		GSS Men			GSS Women		
	1961	1972	1970s	1980s	1990s	1970s	1980s	1990s
Mean of Log Family Income by Quartile of Parental Advantages								
Bottom quartile	9.70	10.30	10.42	10.31	10.27	10.09	9.97	9.98
Second quartile	10.12	10.58	10.75	10.67	10.63	10.54	10.41	10.43
Third quartile	10.31	10.72	10.83	10.82	10.78	10.68	10.65	10.63
Top quartile	10.57	10.91	10.99	10.99	10.96	10.95	10.82	10.84
Interquartile Ratio								
Second-bottom	1.51	1.32	1.39	1.44	1.44	1.56	1.56	1.56
Third-second	1.21	1.14	1.09	1.15	1.17	1.16	1.27	1.23
Top-third	1.30	1.21	1.17	1.19	1.20	1.30	1.18	1.22
Top-bottom	2.38	1.83	1.76	1.98	2.00	2.37	2.34	2.34
Interquartile Gap in 1998 Dollars[a]								
Second-bottom	$8,404	$9,633	$12,961	$13,132	$12,535	$13,573	$11,911	$12,111
Third-second	5,156	5,663	4,109	6,608	6,827	6,041	9,088	7,703
Top-third	9,000	9,475	8,373	9,628	9,466	13,238	7,635	9,285
Top-bottom	$22,560	$24,771	$25,443	$29,368	$28,828	$32,852	$28,634	$29,099
Sample size	10,953	21,289	2,382	3,040	3,817	2,761	3,703	4,657

Notes: [a] Prices are in 1998 CPI-U-X1 dollars, which probably understate actual gains in purchasing power over time.
Dollar gaps are between geometric rather than arithmetic means.

TABLE 3.7

Regression Coefficients of Seven Parental Advantages When Predicting Logged Family Income among Sons Ages 30 to 59 in 1961 and 1972: Bivariate and Multivariate Results from Pooled OCG-I and OCG-II Data

	Bivariate Results		Multivariate Results	
Parental Characteristic	Coefficient in 1961	Change from 1961 to 1972	Coefficient in 1961	Change from 1961 to 1972
Parents' Occupation				
B	**.257**	−.089	**.156**	−.072
(S.E.)	(.007)	(.009)	(.008)	(.011)
Parents' Education				
B	**.053**	−.012	**.016**	.001
(S.E.)	(.002)	(.002)	(.002)	(.003)
Number of Siblings				
B	−.058	−.011	−.024	.003
(S.E.)	(.002)	(.003)	(.003)	(.003)
Intact Family				
B	**.164**	.033	.063	.007
(S.E.)	(.018)	(.024)	(.038)	(.051)
Black				
B	−.824	**.359**	−.559	**.279**
(S.E.)	(.023)	(.031)	(.025)	(.032)
Hispanic				
B	−.405	.082	−.255	.006
(S.E.)	(.047)	(.055)	(.045)	(.053)
Southern Origins				
B	−.424	**.191**	−.203	**.098**
(S.E.)	(.015)	(.019)	(.015)	(.020)
Unweighted sample size:	32,242		32,242	

Notes: Coefficients in boldface are significant at the .05 level.

Missing data on the independent variables were imputed using best-subset estimates. Missing data on family income were imputed by the Census Bureau using its "hot deck" routine. Equations also include dummy variables for missing values on parental occupation, education, siblings, and intact family. Income was age-standardized for each OCG sample by using the regression of log income on a quartic in age.

4 and 6 show that the coefficients for men and women often converged between 1971 and 1999. The effects of parental education, race, and Southern origins all weakened significantly for women and were very close to those for men by the late 1990s. The adverse effect of coming from a large family was significantly larger for women than men in 1971, but this difference had also disappeared by the late 1990s. The

TABLE 3.8

Bivariate Regression Coefficients of Seven Parental Advantages When Predicting Log Family Income at Ages 30 to 59 among GSS Men and Women: 1971–1999 (Coefficients in boldface are significant at the .05 level)

Parental Characteristics	Sons		Daughters		Daughters minus Sons	
	Coefficient in 1971	Change from 1971 to 1999	Coefficient for 1971	Change from 1971 to 1999	Coefficient for 1971	Change from 1971 to 1999
Fathers' Occupation						
B	**.131**	.037	**.207**	-.010	**.076**	-.047
(S.E.)	(.017)	(.026)	(.017)	(.028)	(.024)	(.038)
Parents' Education						
B	**.037**	**.015**	**.057**	-.010	**.020**	**-.025**
(S.E.)	(.004)	(.006)	(.004)	(.007)	(.006)	(.009)
Number of Siblings						
B	**-.043**	**-.029**	**-.067**	.007	**-.024**	**.036**
(S.E.)	(.006)	(.010)	(.006)	(.010)	(.008)	(.014)
Intact Family						
B	**.090**	**.205**	**.262**	.081	**.172**	-.124
(S.E.)	(.039)	(.062)	(.039)	(.062)	(.055)	(.088)
Black						
B	**-.415**	-.065	**-.770**	**.179**	**-.355**	**.244**
(S.E)	(.051)	(.081)	(.051)	(.079)	(.072)	(.113)
Hispanic						
B	**-.573**	**.443**	**-.482**	.168	.091	-.275
(S.E.)	(.095)	(.147)	(.095)	(.144)	(.134)	(.206)
Southern Origins						
B	**-.260**	.093	**-.367**	**.226**	**-.107**	.133
(S.E.)	(.035)	(.057)	(.036)	(.060)	(.050)	(.083)
SD of Log Family Income	0.804		0.907			
Unweighted Sample Size	9,268		11,107			

Notes: Missing data were imputed using best-subset estimates. All equations also include dummies for missing data. Education equations also include an interaction allowing the coefficient to vary when mothers' education is substituted for fathers'.

multivariate GSS results (not shown) are broadly similar to the bivariate results except that the coefficients are smaller.

What is the Optimal Intergenerational Correlation?

Most scholars who study the transmission of economic and social advantages across generations assume that social policy should strive to reduce such linkages. Taken at face value, this view could imply either that the optimal intergenerational correlation is zero or merely that the optimal correlation is lower than the correlation we currently observe. In this section we propose a third possibility. We argue that some of the mechanisms that contribute to intergenerational correlations are normatively acceptable, economically efficient, or both. Others are not. In our view, the numerical magnitude of the observed correlation (which we still denote as R_{pc}) does not tell us anything useful about why it exists. As a result, the value of R_{pc} cannot tell us whether we should invest resources in reducing it. We would need other kinds of evidence to answer that question.

To decide whether the current value of R_{pc} is too high, too low, or just right, one must begin by identifying some criteria for making such judgments. Egalitarians have traditionally advanced three reasons for reducing R_{pc}: increasing economic efficiency, reducing economic inequality, and promoting social justice. Each of these goals probably implies a different optimal value for R_{pc}, but we will not try to justify that conjecture here. Instead, we ask a narrower question, namely whether any of these goals imply that the optimal value of R_{pc} is zero. We start by considering economic efficiency, then turn to economic inequality, and conclude with a discussion of justice.

Economic Efficiency. The earliest arguments for reducing intergenerational inheritance seem to have been based on claims about efficiency. In pre-Revolutionary France, where some public offices passed directly from fathers to sons and others were open only to members of the aristocracy, the regime's critics demanded "careers open to talents." In Britain, too, replacing patronage with selection based on examinations was widely seen as the best way to create an efficient civil service. In both countries the reformers equated the inheritance of privilege with incompetence in high places and wanted to open jobs to able candidates regardless of ancestry. Later, many large private firms adopted the same strategy for raising efficiency, as did many of the professions.

These arguments were almost surely correct in eighteenth-century France and Britain. But if the rationale for reducing intergenerational inheritance is to improve the match between job requirements and job-holders' skills, the benefits that flow from reducing inheritance are almost certainly subject to the law of diminishing returns. If we denote the correlation between a father's occupational rank and his son's rank as r_{fs}, reducing this correlation from 1.00 to 0.80 is almost certain to yield much larger economic gains than reducing it from 0.50 to 0.30. And as long as skills depend partly on either genes or upbringing, the only way to reduce r_{fs} to zero will be to replace occupational selection systems based on expected job performance with systems based on some other criterion. From an efficiency perspective, therefore, the optimal value of r_{fs} is never likely to be zero.

By the late twentieth century observed values of r_{fs} for rich democracies all fell within a fairly narrow range. Using an occupational ranking scheme akin to the SEI scores described earlier in this chapter, Björklund and Jäntti (2000) report father-son correlations for occupational rank in the United States and eight European countries. Their estimates of r_{fs} are all between 0.34 and 0.50. If we set aside the four nations in their sample with fewer than 500 respondents, their lowest estimates are for the United States (0.34) and Britain (0.35), while the highest estimate is for Ireland (0.49). Germany and the Netherlands fell between these extremes with values of 0.42 and 0.40 respectively.[29]

Those who assume that the United States is more economically efficient than Europe may interpret the high rate of occupational mobility in the United States as evidence for the hypothesis that increases in occupational mobility enhance efficiency. But while the material standard of living is higher in the United States than in Europe, the difference is largely explained by the fact that Americans work more than Europeans, not that they produce more per hour. An OECD report that tried to estimate GDP per hour worked in 1996 found little difference between the United States, Germany, and Ireland. The United States ranked ahead of Britain, but it ranked behind the Netherlands (Scarpetta et al. 2000, table A2.6).[30]

Nor are low correlations between fathers' and sons' earnings associated in any obvious way with high levels of economic efficiency. Estimates of r_{fs} for earnings are hard to find, because economists prefer to report the elasticity of a son's earnings with respect to his father's earnings (β_{fs}). Such elasticities are sensitive to both differences in the age at which fathers and sons earnings are measured and intergenerational changes in earnings inequality (Grawe forthcoming).[31] As a result, even intergenerational earnings elasticities derived from the same sample vary dramatically.[32] Solon (1999), for example, identified ten studies that had used the PSID to estimate the elasticity of a son's annual earnings with respect to his father's earnings in the United States. These ten estimates ranged from 0.13 to 0.53, with a median value of 0.39. Although their median is close to Solon's own estimate (0.41), the dispersion of the estimates for the United States shows that cross-national comparisons are worthless unless close attention has been given to achieving comparability.[33]

The most meticulous cross-national comparison seems to be that by Grawe (2001). He concludes that intergenerational earnings mobility in the United States is higher than in Britain but lower than in Canada. Comparisons with Germany are inconclusive. And the best estimates for Finland and Sweden (Solon 2002; Björklund and Chadwick 2002) imply that these nations have more earnings mobility than the United States, although the Finnish and Swedish samples are not entirely comparable to any of the U.S. samples. Still, these data offer no support for the hypothesis that low rates of intergenerational inheritance make an economic system unusually efficient. OECD estimates of output per hour do suggest that the United States is more efficient than Britain, which is consistent with Grawe's conclusion that earnings mobility is higher in the United States than Britain. But the OECD estimates also suggest that the United States is more efficient than Canada, where earnings mobility exceeds the U.S. level. And the OECD estimates hourly output in Finland and Sweden at roughly the U.S. level, even though they appear to have more earnings mobility than the U.S..

None of this evidence contradicts the widespread intuition that very high rates of intergenerational inheritance are likely to reduce economic efficiency. But within the range of values we observe in today's rich democracies, there is no obvious relationship between rates of mobility and economic output per hour worked.

Economic Inequality.   Earnings inequality derives partly from the fact that workers have different skills. Thus, if a nation can improve the skills of its worst paid workers, it can simultaneously raise mean earnings and reduce the dispersion of earnings. Since poorly paid workers are always drawn disproportionately from disadvantaged backgrounds, improving their skills will also reduce the intergenerational inheritance of economic advantages. This logic played an important role in shaping Lyndon Johnson's War on Poverty during the mid-1960s. But while the logic supporting this strategy is compelling, it is hard to see how this strategy can generate a *large* reduction in inequality.

Assume that the correlation between parents' logged earnings and their grown children's logged earnings ($r_{yp,yc}$) is 0.40. Now imagine some policy innovation that raises the mean earnings of adults from all different backgrounds to the same level. Any such policy would by definition reduce the intergenerational correlation of earnings from 0.40 to zero. It would also reduce the variance of children's logged earning by $0.40^2 = 16$ percent. Reducing the variance of earnings by 16 percent would, in turn, reduce the standard deviation of logged earnings (a standard measure of inequality) to $\sqrt{.84} = 91.7$ percent of its previous level.

An 8.3 percent reduction in earnings inequality is not negligible. But this outcome requires a policy that reduces the intergenerational correlation to zero. Such a reduction would not be easy, and it would probably not even be desirable. It requires a world in which genes have no effect on earnings. It also requires a world in which advantaged parents make no special effort to pass along their advantages to their children More realistic assumptions imply a smaller reduction in intergenerational inheritance, which would in turn imply a smaller reduction in inequality.

Reducing intergenerational inheritance of economic advantages may nonetheless be an essential political prerequisite for reducing economic inequality by other means. The most effective strategies for reducing income inequality appear to depend on using the power of the government both to limit the dispersion of earnings and to support households in which earnings fall far short of need. The political will required to implement such policies may well depend partly on persuading the affluent that their children have a reasonable chance of benefiting from these policies.

Justice. Some Americans see *any* correlation between parental advantages and children's economic prospects as evidence that the United States has not lived up to the ideal of equal opportunity. One common version of this argument holds that since children do not get to choose their parents, penalizing children for having the wrong parents is unjust.

There is no American consensus on the definition of equal opportunity, but most discussions seem to assume that it has two basic elements. First, jobs should be distributed on the basis of actual or potential performance, not ancestry. We refer to this ideal as "meritocracy." Second, all children should have the same opportunity to develop the skills required to get a good job. We refer to this ideal as "equal developmental opportunity." (What we call "developmental" opportunity is similar to "educational" opportunity, except that it unambiguously encompasses the activities of parents as well as schools.) Both meritocracy and equal educational opportunity were once strategies for encouraging economic growth. Today, however, these ideals have evolved into claims about justice as well as efficiency, and they are more likely to be invoked by people who care about racism, poverty, and inequality than by people who care about growth.

America does not distribute jobs in a strictly meritocratic way, and American children do not all have the same opportunities to develop their talents. But even if these goals had been achieved, mature adults' family incomes would still be correlated with their parents' characteristics for at least three reasons. First, even if developmental opportunities were equal, both fathers and mothers would still pass on half their genes to their children, and genes would still have some effect on competence. Second, parents would still pass on some of their cultural ideals and personal preferences to their children. As a result, children who had to choose between maximizing their family income and, say, spending time with their children or living near a trout stream would often make the same choice that their parents had made. Third, while most Americans want employers to follow meritocratic principles when distributing jobs, few want to impose such requirements on men and women who are choosing a spouse. Discrimination on the basis of race, ethnicity, and socioeconomic background is still almost universally accepted as a legitimate feature of the marriage market. We discuss these issues in order.

Genes and Justice. There is a latent tension between meritocracy and fairness. A meritocracy, for example, rewards professional athletes for some combination of natural aptitude and effort. It is hard to argue that rewarding athletes for inheriting the right genes is any more fair than rewarding people for inheriting financial assets. Yet a commitment to meritocracy makes this kind of unfairness inevitable in domains where performance varies for genetic reasons. It therefore guarantees that economic status will to some extent be correlated across generations.

Herrnstein (1971) provided a controversial but influential analysis of this issue. His argument went as follows. First, economic success in developed countries depends partly on cognitive skills, which vary partly for genetic reasons. It follows that genetic variation influences an individual's chances of economic success. Second, children get half their genes from each of their parents. This ensures that children of successful parents usually inherit a disproportionate share of whatever genes facilitate success. As a result, children of successful parents tend to be more successful than the average child. Indeed, Herrnstein argued that the relative importance of genetic advantages had increased as social reforms equalized children's opportunities.

Herrnstein probably exaggerated the role of cognitive skills in determining economic success (Jencks et al. 1972). But genetic variation also appears to influence noncognitive traits like empathy, reliability, ambition, impulsiveness, and leadership. John Loehlin's chapter in this volume shows that parents and children are not as similar on measures of such traits as they are on IQ tests. Nonetheless, the parent-child correlations on these personality measures are considerably higher for biological than adopted children, just as they are for cognitive tests. This finding suggests that Herrnstein's argument may also be somewhat applicable to the noncognitive determinants of economic success.

Although the logic of Herrnstein's argument is inescapable, logic alone cannot tell us whether genetic resemblance plays a large or small role in economic resemblance between parents and children. The most obvious way to address this question is to compare economic resemblance between parents and their adopted children to economic resemblance between parents and their biological children. We do not have such data for the United States. In Sweden, as we noted earlier, the father-son earnings elasticity is reduced by two-thirds when sons have never lived with their father.

The implications of genetic inheritance for justice depend partly on whether the genes that contribute to father-son earnings correlations influence men's actual job performance or only their job opportunities. In the United States, for example, both height and beauty influence wages. As far as we know, no one has yet investigated whether either height or beauty affects job performance outside the NBA, Hollywood, and the fashion industry. The implications of genetic inheritance also depend on the economic and social cost of reducing genes' impact on job performance. Medical intervention to minimize the consequences of myopia is relatively cheap and quite effective. Medical intervention to minimize the consequences of mental disorders with a genetic component, such as depression, is currently less effective and more expensive. The list of genetic disorders that yield to treatment is likely to keep growing, however, which should somewhat reduce the economic impact of genetic resemblance between parents and children. In due course it may also become easier to control children's actual genetic endowment. How this controversial possibility would affect genetic resemblance between parents and children is far from clear.

Culture, Preferences, and Justice. Equalizing opportunity presumably means ensuring that everyone faces the same choices, not that everyone actually makes the same choices. Maximizing one's family income usually requires spending less time on other activities, and people differ in their willingness to make this sacrifice. Some women take jobs to earn money for their children's education, while others think it is more important to stay home with their children. Some men spend evenings at the office or on the road so that their family can live in a nicer house or neighborhood, while others regard this as a foolish choice. These choices depend, in part, on both our parents' values and the norms that prevailed in the community in which we grew up. Those who favor equal opportunity seldom argue that society should eliminate these sources of intergenerational resemblance.

Family background seems, for example, to influence people's choices about how many hours they work (Altonji and Dunn 2000). This is not surprising. Neither is it evidence that those who work fewer hours and earn less money have been denied an opportunity to work more, although that is surely true in some cases. Equalizing opportunity appears to imply that everyone should have the same opportunity to work long hours, not that everyone should actually do so.

Wages are also lower in rural than urban areas. To some extent this wage differential reflects the fact that prices are lower in rural areas, but direct measures of material well-being, such as surveys of housing conditions, suggest that living standards are also lower in rural areas. Nonetheless, people raised in rural areas often want to remain there. Many accept a somewhat lower material standard of living to enjoy a life that they judge superior in other respects. The fact that parents and children often have similar preferences in this regard contributes to the intergenerational correlation of earnings. It does not prove that children raised in rural areas have fewer opportunities to develop economically useful skills, although that may also be true.

Marriage and Justice. The intergenerational correlations reported in this chapter reflect the workings of the marriage market as well as the labor market. Indeed, more than half the correlation between married women's family income and their parents' characteristics derives from the tendency of women from advantaged backgrounds to marry men with high incomes. This pattern arises partly because women from advantaged backgrounds are more likely to meet men from similar backgrounds and partly because women from advantaged backgrounds are more likely to have characteristics that make well-paid men want to marry them.

Few advocates of equal opportunity want to make the marriage market follow meritocratic principles. If a young medical resident has been dating several different men and is trying to decide which one to marry, hardly anyone believes that she has a moral obligation to choose the most competent candidate. If she decides to reject the top surgical resident at her hospital in order to marry a n'er-do-well from a privileged background, her colleagues may criticize her choice as foolish, but they are not likely to say it is morally reprehensible, even though it obviously reduces her future husband's chances of ending up as poor as he "deserves" to be. The same logic applies if "she" becomes "he."

That said, it remains true that social policies that reduce the impact of parental advantages on children's characteristics are likely to reduce the chances that people from advantaged backgrounds will marry well. Perhaps the most important way advantaged parents improve their children's marital prospects is by inducing their children to stay in school. Of course, couples also pair off on the basis of shared interests, tastes, habits, and friends. If children from different racial, ethnic, and socio-economic backgrounds were more alike in these respects, family back-ground would exert less influence on people's chances of finding a spouse with a good job. Policies that equalized children's developmental opportunities might therefore increase the likelihood that adults from disadvantaged backgrounds would marry well.

The Politics of Equal Opportunity. We have argued that genetic inher-itance, intergenerational transmission of preferences and values, and as-sortative mating would create a nontrivial correlation between mature adults' family income and their parents' socioeconomic advantages even if the labor market were completely meritocratic and all children had the same opportunity to develop the traits that both labor and marriage markets reward. But we have no way of knowing how large this correla-tion would be. Indeed, we have no way of knowing whether it would be larger or smaller than the values of R_{pc} reported earlier in this chapter. It follows that if what justice requires is a meritocratic labor market and equal developmental opportunities for all children, positive values of R_{pc} are not evidence of injustice, and changes in R_{pc} are not good indicators of whether society is becoming more or less just. If our concern is with justice, we need more direct evidence on the amount of variation in chil-dren's developmental opportunities and the degree to which the labor market follows meritocratic principles.

In theory, employers have an interest in making the labor market more meritocratic. In practice, we have little evidence about the extent to which they hire or promote based on valid predictors of future perfor-mance. We know that job opportunities for women and minorities have improved over the past generation, but those are only indirect indicators that labor markets have grown meritocratic, and we have no direct indi-cators.

Equalizing children's developmental opportunities is an even more formidable task, since it involves changing families as well as schools. It is relatively easy to imagine a society in which all children have equal access to the kinds of goods and services that parents buy for their chil-dren in the market. Indeed, many affluent societies have taken significant steps toward this goal over the past two hundred years. Both the United States and Europe began trying to equalize children's educational oppor-tunities in the nineteenth century by making public education free. Post-secondary students must still pay some of their own bills, especially in the United States, which means that they often have to combine educa-tion and work. In the United States, many post-secondary students are also expected to borrow. But while higher education is more financially accessible in most other rich democracies than in the United States, it is more academically accessible in the United States than elsewhere. American colleges admit more students with poor secondary school records, and they offer a wider menu of nonacademic instruction. Both the European and American systems result in a substantial correlation between family background and young people's educational attainment.

Except for the United States, most affluent nations also make children's medical care almost costless. In addition, some European nations try to provide high-quality childcare for all children with working mothers. In the United States the food stamp program tries to ensure that all children get enough to eat. In Europe children's allowances are sometimes meant to do the same thing. Such efforts have probably lowered the correlation between parental income and children's health, but they have not reduced it to zero in either the United States or Europe.

Political resistance to shifting the costs of childrearing from parents to governments has also been stronger in the United States than in most European nations. All these rich democracies are alike in that families with above-average incomes pay most of the taxes, while families with below-average incomes have most of the children. Shifting the costs of childrearing from families to the government therefore involves a large redistribution of resources from the top to the bottom of the income distribution in every country. This kind of redistribution has been more politically acceptable in Europe than in the United States for both attitudinal and institutional reasons.

Redistributing the cost of childrearing is politically attractive in European countries with low birth rates, because making parenthood less costly seems like a promising way to increase fertility, expand the labor force, and finance future pension payments. Redistribution from the more affluent to the less affluent is also attractive in countries that have strong working-class political parties whose members mostly benefit from redistribution. It is not attractive in countries like the United States, where population decline is not a concern and encouraging the poor to have more children is unpopular. The combination of two-party politics, multiple veto points, and fiscal decentralization also makes it unusually hard to tax the affluent in the United States. Nonetheless, shifting the economic costs of child-rearing from parents to governments remains the most obvious strategy for equalizing children's developmental opportunities.

It is much harder to imagine how a society could equalize the quality of children's home life than to imagine how a society could equalize children's access to the kinds of goods and services that parents buy in the marketplace. Raising poor parents' incomes would presumably lower the amount of conflict and stress in poor children's homes. Ensuring that working mothers have predictable schedules that are compatible with their children's schedule would also improve children's lives, although it is not clear how much impact these changes would have on children's adult characteristics. Some people believe that direct intervention in dysfunctional families can also help parents do a better job raising their children.

But hardly anyone who has raised children believes that equalizing parents' incomes or providing more social services would fully equalize children's developmental opportunities. Nor do many people think that schools can fully compensate children for being shortchanged at home. Such compensation is especially difficult to achieve in the United States, where teachers are hired by local school districts and the best teachers gravitate to affluent districts where the students are easier to teach. Some disparity in children's developmental opportunities is probably an inescapable cost of encouraging parents to care more about their own children than about anyone else's children. How large these disparities need to be remains an open question.

NOTES

We are grateful to Claude Fischer, Michele Landis Dauber, Martina Morris, Arthur Stinchcombe, and participants in seminars at Harvard University's Kennedy School of Government, the Santa Fe Institute, the Stanford University Law School, Statistics Canada, the Sociology Departments at UCLA and Berkeley, and the Institute for Research on Poverty at the University of Wisconsin for helpful comments on earlier drafts. The Russell Sage Foundation provided financial support. In addition, Harding was supported by a National Science Foundation Graduate Research Fellowship and by a National Science Foundation Integrative Graduate Education and Research Traineeship. Lopoo would like to thank the Bendheim-Thoman Center for Research on Child Wellbeing and the Office of Population Research at Princeton University, which is supported by NICHD center grant 5 P30 HD32030, for financial support.

1. Hauser et al. warn that this comparison is not exact, because the Census Bureau introduced a new occupational classification scheme between the 1973 OCG and the 1986 SIPP.

2. Corcoran (2001) estimated the correlation between parents' family incomes and their sons' hourly wages, annual earnings, and total family income between the ages of 25 and 27. All these correlations were smaller among sons who turned twenty in the 1980s than among sons who turned twenty in the 1970s. Fertig (2002) used the PSID to analyze trends in earnings mobility. She too found that the association between fathers' and sons' earnings weakened over time, although this was not true for mothers' earnings. Levine and Ma-

zumder (2002) also found an (insignificant) decline in the intergenerational elasticity of sons' earnings with respect to their parents' family income in the PSID. Mayer and Lopoo (2001) found a downward trend in the effect of parents' family income on both sons' family income and their wages at age 30 among those born after 1952, but the linear trend was no longer significant when they included sons born between 1949 and 1951.

3. With random mating and additive genetic effects, the genetic correlation between fraternal twins is 0.50. Positive assortative mating raises the correlation. Nonadditive genetic effects lower it. If these biases roughly offset one another, the estimated heritability (unadjusted for measurement error) is (0.54–0.30)/(1–0.5) = 0.48.

4. Ashenfelter and Rouse (1998) describe the sampling strategy. Their analysis focuses exclusively on returns to schooling among identical twins, but Cecelia Rouse generously supplied both the MZ and DZ twin correlations for hourly wages, which were 0.63 and 0.37 respectively. Using the simplified model in the previous note, the implied heritability is thus (0.63–0.37)/(1–0.5) = 0.52.

5. If a son had always lived with a nonbiological father, the elasticity of the son's earnings with respect to his nonbiological father's earnings is about 0.15 if his father is at the mean of the distribution for all fathers.

6. These estimates are corrected for underreporting. The data are from U.S. Bureau of the Census (2000, 55 and D-4). Since the self-employed earn less per hour than wage and salary workers with similar characteristics, we assigned their business assets an implicit value of zero. The implicit returns on equity in owner-occupied housing raise family income by another 7 percent for the population as a whole (U.S. Bureau of the Census 2000, 61), but the increase would be smaller for thirty to fifty-nine year olds. In any event, our estimates of family income do not include the implicit return on home equity.

7. Kotlikoff and Summers (1981) reach much the same conclusion. The relative importance of inherited assets for respondents between the ages of 30 and 59 could be either higher or lower than for the general population, depending on whether inheritances or savings accumulate faster as people age.

8. Gifts and bequests also help reduce mortgage debt, which does not show up as money income.

9. Life expectancy increased by six years between 1960 and 2000, so the proportion of thirty to fifty-nine year olds with at least one living parent rose sharply. The proportion who had actually received a bequest probably fell correspondingly, but we have no data on this point.

10. These estimates are from tabulations by Andrew Clarkwest using the Integrated Public Use Microsamples from the decennial census.

11. To standardize income we divided respondents by gender, survey, and year, and regressed the log of family income on Age, Age^2, Age^3, and Age^4. We use the residuals from these regressions as our dependent variable in subsequent analyses. The Census Bureau imputed missing OCG income data using a "hot deck" routine, which assigns respondents the income of the last previous respondent with similar characteristics. The GSS is too small for such imputations, so we drop GSS respondents who did not report their family income.

12. Since we do not know to what degree extended families living in the same

household pool their incomes, it is not clear whether we would be better off including their income, but in the data available to us this is not an option.

13. Once we take logarithms, incomes of $200 and $800 differ as much as incomes of $20,000 and $80,000. As a result, much of the within-category variance is in the bottom income category, which includes families with incomes below $1,000 in 1972 dollars. We do not believe that income differences among such families provide any useful information. There is no obvious way in which even a single individual could have subsisted on less than $1,000 worth of goods and services in 1972. Almost everyone who reported such an income must therefore have had additional resources: unreported money income, noncash income (such as food stamps and housing subsidies), gifts or loans from friends or relatives, or savings that could be drawn down. The 1970 Census shows no relationship between variations in household income below $1,000 and a household's chances of having a telephone, an automobile, or other amenities (data not shown).

14. OCG fathers and sons were classified using the Census Bureau's 1960 categories. Until 1988, GSS fathers and sons were classified using the 1970 Census categories, which are quite similar to those for 1960. Starting in 1988, GSS fathers and sons were classified using the 1980 categories, which differ appreciably from those used earlier.

15. See Duncan (1961) for the original index. We use Stevens and Featherman's (1981) SEI scores to rank 1970 occupations, and Stevens and Cho's (1985) SEI scores to rank 1980 occupations. In both cases we use SEI scores that cover all workers in an occupation rather than just men. These occupational rankings are based on the educational attainment and income of workers at the time of the decennial census in which the Census Bureau introduced a classification scheme, not at the time when the respondent's father was sixteen. OCG men whose fathers owned farms, for example, are assigned an SEI score based on the education and income of farmers in 1960, even if the respondent was sixteen in 1920. This could be a problem if, as seems likely, the education and income gaps between farmers and the rest of the population were wider in 1920 than in 1960. The relative ranking of most other occupations has, however, been surprisingly stable since 1940.

16. Occupational inequality increased by 16.8 percent using transformed SEI scores compared to 15.5 percent using untransformed SEI scores.

17. Children whose parents attended graduate school do not earn significantly more than children whose parents merely earned a BA, but so few fathers had any graduate education that we cannot draw any firm conclusions from this finding.

18. For a contrasting approach that treats the ratio of the standard deviation to the mean as a measure of educational inequality, see Hauser and Featherman (1976). Using this measure, educational inequality falls sharply over the course of the twentieth century. But Hauser and Featherman's data also show that the standard deviation of years of schooling falls for successive cohorts of men born during the first half of the twentieth century even when it is not divided by the mean. This decline appears to have slowed in the second half of the century. The absence of such a trend in our data on fathers may be a byproduct of changes in differential fertility.

19. The standard deviation of a dichotomous characteristic is equal to $[(p)(1-p)]^{.5}$ where p is the proportion of individuals who have the characteristic.

20. This prediction assumes that the post-1969 trend in income inequality among parents of college-age children matched that for parents of children under eighteen.

21. The square of the multiple correlation is the percentage of the income variance explained by parental characteristics.

22. The estimated within-cohort trends are much noisier in GSS than in OCG, partly because the samples are much smaller and partly because the match between cohorts is less exact. Those who were between the ages of 30 and 39 in the 1980s, for example, were born between 1940 and 1949 if they were surveyed in 1980 but were born between 1949 and 1959 if they were surveyed in 1989. When we compare those aged 30 to 39 in the 1980s to those aged 40 to 49 in the 1990s, the degree of overlap between birth cohorts varies with the precise survey year.

23. These rankings weight each parental advantage by its coefficient in an equation that predicts age-adjusted family income for respondents of a given age and gender in a given period.

24. These effects compound, so a standard deviation of 0.70 implies that when families differ by one standard deviation their incomes differ by a factor of $e^{.70} = 2.01$.

25. The standard deviation of logged income is quite sensitive to small errors near the bottom of the distribution, which means that it is also sensitive to certain methodological changes. Figure 3.3 suggests that income inequality spiked in 1961. This could have been linked to the unusually high rate of unemployment, but the Census Bureau also introduced its "hot deck" routine for imputing missing income values in 1961. Introducing hot deck imputations could perhaps account for the sharp jump in inequality between 1960 and 1961, but it could not account for the equally sharp decline between 1961 and 1962 unless the new imputation procedures had problems that were corrected in 1962. The standard deviation of logged family income in the GSS increases when the number of income intervals changes. But the GSS only adds new intervals at the top, not the bottom, and we did not find sharp discontinuities in the standard deviation for years when the GSS added new intervals.

26. When we convert a normal distribution into quartiles, the distance between the second and third quartiles is always smaller than that between the first and second quartiles or that between the third and fourth. We therefore expect more mobility in the middle two quartiles than in the extreme quartiles, and that is what we observe. To avoid clutter we show only the results for the top and bottom quartiles.

27. The dollar gaps in table 3.6 were calculated from the geometric means for each quartile. The pattern might change if we calculated the gaps using arithmetic means.

28. The estimated change is extrapolated from the linear interaction between the measure of parental occupation and survey year. We did not have enough statistical power to estimate more complex interactions.

29. The sampling errors for these estimates are roughly 0.007 for the United

States, 0.011 for Britain, 0.017 for Germany, 0.019 for the Netherlands, and 0.021 for Ireland.

30. The correlation between GDP per hour (measured at purchasing power parity) and r_{fs}, should be negative if mobility enhances efficiency. For the five nations with large samples, the correlation between r_{fs} and Scarpetta et al.'s estimates of output per hour is actually positive (0.189), albeit insignificant. If we add the other four nations for which Björklund and Jäntti estimate r_{fs} (Austria, Finland, Italy, and Switzerland), the correlation between r_{fs} and GDP per hour worked falls to 0.006.

31. $\beta_{fs} = (r_{fs})(\sigma_{lnYS}/\sigma_{lnYF})$, where σ_{lnYS} and σ_{lnYF} are the standard deviations of logged earnings for sons and fathers. Most studies compare fathers and sons earnings when the fathers are older than their sons. Because earnings inequality rises with age (at least after about thirty), this practice often makes β_{fs} less than r_{fs}. In some cases, however, studies try to compare the earnings of fathers and sons who were roughly the same age. This strategy means that sons earnings are measured a generation later than fathers earnings. The ratio of σ_{lnYS} to σ_{lnYF} then depends on the trend in earnings inequality. In countries like the United States and Britain, where earnings have grown substantially more unequal, this approach will yield values of β_{fs} that exceed r_{fs}.

32. Different approaches to measurement error also contribute to this problem.

33. Cross-national comparisons of occupational mobility are, of course, also sensitive to national differences in occupational classification schemes, and some Europeans believe that the high rate of measured mobility in the United States is attributable to deficiencies in the Census Bureau's categories. Björklund and Jäntti's use of a consistent ranking scheme cannot solve this problem.

Chapter Four

INFLUENCES OF NATURE AND NURTURE ON
EARNINGS VARIATION

A Report on a Study of Various Sibling Types in Sweden

ANDERS BJÖRKLUND, MARKUS JÄNTTI, AND GARY SOLON

UNDERSTANDING the sources of earnings inequality is a central topic in labor economics. Indeed, accounting for the rise in earnings inequality that has occurred in most developed countries over the last quarter-century probably has been the field's most active research area in recent years (Katz and Autor 1999). Another active area of inequality research has focused on the role of family and community origins. One line of this research has used sibling correlations to measure the proportion of earnings variation that can be attributed to the family and community background factors that siblings have in common. The basic idea is that, if family and community origins account for a large portion of earnings inequality, siblings will show a strong resemblance in earnings; if family and community background matters hardly at all, siblings will show little more resemblance than would randomly selected unrelated individuals.

Most of the empirical evidence on sibling correlations in earnings (reviewed in Solon 1999) pertains to brothers in the United States. A reasonable summary of that evidence is that the correlation among U.S. brothers in the permanent component of their logarithmic earnings may be around 0.4. Bjorklund et al. (2002) present evidence that brother correlations in long-run earnings are lower in Sweden, Denmark, Finland, and Norway. Another strand of research has focused on twins. Most of the studies of monozygotic twins, both in the United States and elsewhere, have estimated earnings correlations of around 0.6. Estimates for dizygotic twins have tended to be lower than those for monozygotic twins, but higher than those for non-twin brothers.

While these brother correlations are far less than 1, they are large enough to suggest a substantial role for family and community origins in accounting for earnings inequality. Once that is recognized, it is natural to ask which specific background factors make a difference. One aspect of that question is whether the brother resemblance in earnings

stems from similarities between brothers in their genetic endowments
or from similarities in their family and community environments. That
question has been hotly debated—most recently in response to Herrnstein and Murray's *The Bell Curve* (1994)—with respect to scores on
intelligence tests. Much less attention has been devoted to nature vs.
nurture as sources of earnings inequality. The main exception is the
work during the 1970's by Paul Taubman and colleagues (Taubman
1976; Behrman et al. 1977). Using the National Research Council sample of monozygotic and dizygotic twins, Taubman et al. attempted to
disentangle the roles of nature and nurture on the assumption that the
greater correlation typically observed for monozygotic twins occurs
mainly because monozygotic twins (so-called identical twins, who come
from one fertilized egg that splits in two) have identical genes, whereas
the genes of dizygotic twins (fraternal twins, who come from two different eggs fertilized by different sperm) are correlated only in the same
way as the genes of non-twin siblings.

In this chapter, we use an extraordinary Swedish data set on various
types of sibling pairs to reconsider the extent to which sibling correlations in earnings stem from genetic and environmental sources. Following the suggestion of Feldman et al. (2000), we make use of a wide
variety of sibling types, differing in both their genetic connectedness and
the extent to which they were reared together. Contrasting sibling correlations across a wider variety of sibling types provides additional lever-
age for disentangling nature and nurture effects, and for examining the
sensitivity of results to alternative modeling assumptions.

Although we believe it is worthwhile to use sibling comparisons to
generate new clues about the sources of earnings inequality, we stress
that the policy implications are far less clear than is sometimes supposed.
The notion that environmentally induced inequality is easily susceptible
to policy remediation, and that genetically based inequality is not, is a
non sequitur. To borrow an example from Goldberger (1979), a finding
of a large genetic role in poor eyesight would in no way indicate that
remediation with eyeglasses is ineffectual. Whether earnings status is determined largely by nature or nurture, any proposed policy ought to be
evaluated on the basis of the particular policy's benefits and costs.

In the next section, we outline some simple models of the dependence
of sibling correlations on variation in genetic and environmental factors.
In the process, we highlight how results from the previous literature and
from our own analysis might be sensitive to arbitrary modeling assumptions. After describing our data on Swedish siblings, we then use those
data to estimate alternative models, and we discuss what the results do
(and do not) reveal about nature and nurture as sources of earnings
variation. We offer a summary and conclusion in the final section.

MODELS

A simple model of genetic and environmental influences on an earnings measure Y is

$$Y = gG + sS + uU, \qquad (1)$$

where G represents the genetic factor; S is an environmental factor that may be at least somewhat shared between siblings; U is an environmental factor totally idiosyncratic to the individual (i.e., not shared at all between siblings); Y, G, S, and U are all standardized to have mean 0 and variance 1; and g, s, and u are parameters that will be related to the relative importance of genes, shared environment, and non-shared environment in accounting for variation in Y. The variables G, S, and U are all "latent," that is, they are not directly observed.

With U defined as perfectly idiosyncratic to the individual, it is natural to assume that U is uncorrelated with both G and S. With one exception, the models that follow also will make the simplifying assumption that G and S are uncorrelated. In that case, g^2 is the fraction of the variance in Y that is due to genetic variation, and $1 - g^2 = s^2 + u^2$ is the fraction due to the combination of shared and non-shared environments.

When this model is combined with sufficiently strong assumptions about the extent to which G and S are correlated between different sibling types, it becomes possible to use data on sibling correlations in Y to infer how much of earnings inequality can be ascribed to each source. We will illustrate with a simplified caricature of the Taubman et al. analysis of monozygotic and dizygotic twins. Let Y and Y' denote the earnings measures for the two members of a twin pair. In addition to the assumption that G, S, and U are mutually uncorrelated *within* individuals, assume that they are uncorrelated *between* twins—for example, one twin's G is uncorrelated with the other twin's S'. Let $Corr(G,G') = 1$ for monozygotic twins, who have identical genes, and assume that $Corr(G,G')$ is 0.5 for dizygotic twins, whose genetic resemblance is the same as for non-twin full siblings. (See Otto, Christiansen, and Feldman 1995 for a thorough discussion of genetic resemblance among various family members.) Finally, assume that $Corr(S,S') = 1$ for both monozygotic and dizygotic twins. This last assumption implies that the twin correlation in environmental influences on earnings is $s^2/(s^2 + u^2)$ for both twin types, and so the assumption is that monozygotic twins experience no more (and no less) similarity in environment than dizygotic twins do.

It follows from these strong assumptions that $Corr(Y,Y')$ is $g^2 + s^2$ for monozygotic twins and $0.5\, g^2 + s^2$ for dizygotic twins. Therefore, g^2 can

be estimated by doubling the difference between the earnings correlations observed for monozygotic and dizygotic twins, and s^2 can be
estimated by subtracting the estimated g^2 from the earnings correlation
observed for monozygotic twins. For example, in the Taubman et al.
sample, the earnings correlation was 0.54 for monozygotic twins and
0.30 for dizygotic twins. Processing these correlation estimates through
the assumed model leads to an estimated g^2 of 0.48 and an estimated s^2
of 0.06. These estimates imply that 48 percent of earnings inequality
stems from genetic variation, that 0.48 of the 0.54 earnings correlation
for monozygotic twins is due to their identical genes, and that 0.24 of
the 0.30 earnings correlation for dizygotic twins is due to their similar
genes.

   While this example illustrates the possibility of disentangling nature
and nurture effects by contrasting the earnings correlations of different
sibling types, it also can be used to illustrate the possibility that inferences may be very sensitive to the modeling assumptions. Following
Goldberger (1979), replace the assumptions above with the assumptions
that $g = 0$ (i.e., genetic variation is of absolutely no consequence in determining earnings) and that $Corr(S,S')$ for dizygotic twins is a fraction ρ
of the corresponding correlation for monozygotic twins (i.e., dizygotic
twins may be treated less similarly than monozygotic twins). Processing
the same observed earnings correlations through this alternative model
leads to an estimated g^2 of 0 (by assumption), an estimated s^2 of 0.54,
and an estimated ρ of 0.30/0.54 = 0.56. These estimates imply that 0
percent of earnings inequality stems from genetic variation and that the
entirety of the 0.54 and 0.30 earnings correlations for monozygotic and
dizygotic twins is due to similarity in environment. Like the preceding
model, this one delivers an exact fit to the observed correlations, and so
the two models (and their dramatically different implications) cannot be
distinguished empirically on the basis of comparing correlations for only
these two types of sibling pairs.

   The empirical strategy in our study is to use a wider variety of sibling
types to enable estimation of more general (i.e., less restrictive) models
and to examine the sensitivity of our results to variation in modeling
assumptions. As described in more detail in the next section, we use
observed sibling correlations in earnings for nine types of sibling pairs:
monozygotic twins reared together, monozygotic twins reared apart, dizygotic twins reared together, dizygotic twins reared apart, non-twin full
siblings reared together, non-twin full siblings reared apart, half-siblings
reared together, half-siblings reared apart, and adoptive siblings. As with
the simple models described earlier, we can process the observed correlations through a set of assumptions about the relative genetic and

environmental connectedness of the various sibling types to obtain estimates of parameters related to the importance of genes and environment in accounting for earnings variation. The advantage of working with a wider variety of sibling types is that we will be able to use models that invoke somewhat less restrictive assumptions, and we will have greater latitude for checking the robustness of our results to alternative assumptions.

In our work so far, we have estimated four models. Model 1 extends the previously described first model to the setting with nine different types of sibling pairs. In this model, $Corr(G,G') = 1$ for monozygotic twins (reared together or apart), and we continue to assume that $Corr(G,G') = 0.5$ for dizygotic twins (reared together or apart) as well as for non-twin full siblings (reared together or apart). We also assume that $Corr(G,G') = 0.25$ for half-siblings (reared together or apart) and $Corr(G,G') = 0$ for adoptive siblings. We continue to assume that $Corr(S,S') = 1$ for all types of sibling pairs reared together, and we assume that $Corr(S,S') = 0$ for sibling pairs reared apart. In effect, the model assumes that all types of sibling pairs reared together experience the same degree of environmental similarity and that the environments of siblings reared apart are absolutely unrelated. Although this model is similar to models frequently used in twins-based research on intelligence and personality traits, we recognize that the assumptions are terribly restrictive, and we do not mean them to be taken very seriously. Rather, we will use this model as a point of departure for considering several less restrictive models.

Model 2 dispenses with the simplifying assumption that G and S are uncorrelated. Instead, recognizing the possibility that those with genes conducive to high earnings also tend to have advantaged environments, this model treats $Corr(G,S')$ as a quantity to be estimated. In particular, model 2 adds two new parameters that allow for three distinct nonzero correlations between G and S': one for biological siblings reared together, one for siblings reared apart, and one for adoptive siblings.

Model 1's assumptions that the genetic correlation is 0.5 for dizygotic twins and non-twin full siblings, 0.25 for half-siblings, and 0 for adoptive siblings are frequently used in siblings research, but they are highly questionable. The assumptions of 0.5 and 0.25 correlations fail in the presence of assortative mating, genetic dominance, or non-additivities in the effects of different genes. The assumption of a zero correlation for adoptive siblings fails in the presence of nonrandomness in adoption placements. Therefore, in model 3, we replace these three assumed values of 0.5, 0.25, and 0 with three parameters to be estimated.

Finally, we need to loosen up the restrictions that $Corr(S,S') = 1$ for all sibling pairs reared together and $Corr(S,S') = 0$ for all those reared apart. As emphasized by Goldberger (1979), the implication that the sibling correlation in environmental influences on earnings is the same $s^2/(s^2 + u^2)$ for all types reared together is hard to believe. This assumption is false, for example, if monozygotic twins are treated more similarly than dizygotic twins, or if twins are treated more similarly than non-twins. Kamin and Goldberger (2002) caution that the assumption of zero environmental correlation for siblings reared apart also is questionable. Twins classified as reared apart, for example, shared the same womb; after birth, they may have been reared together for some time before they were separated; and, even after they were separated, they may have experienced correlated environments, an obvious example being if they were reared by relatives. Therefore, in model 4, instead of imposing correlations of 1 for all pairs reared together and 0 for all those reared apart, we normalize $Corr(S,S')$ to 1 for monozygotic twins reared together, and we introduce three new parameters to represent this correlation for other sibling types: one for dizygotic twins reared together, one for non-twins reared together, and one for siblings reared apart.

Of course, each of these embellished models is still a very stylized model of how nature and nurture affect earnings. In principle, we would like to estimate more general and realistic models, for example, by combining the features of models 2, 3, and 4. Unfortunately, simultaneously incorporating the features of even any two of these extended models results in under-identification; that is, the combined model does not lead to well-defined parameter estimates because very different sets of parameter values produce the exact same fit to the data. Nevertheless, as we will see in the section "Results from Model Estimation," the estimates from models 1–4 do shed some light on the range of conclusions about nature vs. nurture that can be supported under various assumptions. First, however, we will describe the extraordinary data set on which our estimates are based.

DATA

Our samples of twins and non-twins come from different sources. Our twins sample comes from the middle cohort of the Swedish Twin Registry, developed and administered at the Karolinska Institutet in Stockholm. The starting point for this sample is the population of all twins born in Sweden between 1926 and 1967, in all 54,890 pairs. Out of these, all 17,992 same-sex twin pairs born between 1926 and 1958 who were alive and living in Sweden in 1970 were sent a questionnaire in

1972 (Medlund et al. 1977). Responses were received from both members of 13,664 pairs.

One of the variables elicited in the questionnaire was the twins' own report of their zygosity. More objective information on zygosity is available for a small subsample included in SATSA (the Swedish Adoption/ Twin Study of Aging). In that project, 351 twin pairs reared apart and a control sample of 407 twin pairs reared together have been subjected to intensive study, including a medical determination of zygosity based on blood samples. Whenever possible, we classify twins as monozygotic or dizygotic on the basis of the SATSA information, but for the majority of our twins sample that is not in the SATSA subsample, we must rely on self-reports of zygosity. Fortunately, cross-tabulations of the two zygosity measures for the SATSA subsample have shown that the self-reports conform remarkably well with the determinations from the blood tests (Pedersen et al. 1991).

The 1972 questionnaire also asked, "How long did you live with your twin partner?" We follow previous studies of the Swedish twins in categorizing the pairs as reared together or apart on the basis of whether they were separated before age ten. That some of the twins "reared apart" did live together for a substantial period before age ten is part of the motivation for our model 4, which estimates the correlation in shared environment for siblings "reared apart" instead of assuming that the correlation is zero.

Our data on non-twin siblings stem from two simple random samples of the Swedish population drawn by Statistics Sweden. The first was a sample of 100,000 persons born in Sweden between 1951 and 1964. A further requirement was that the persons had not been adopted by either parent. The second sample consists of 3,000 persons born in Sweden between 1951 and 1964 who were adopted by both parents. A further requirement in both samples was that the persons must have lived in Sweden in 1993. Because these data were collected from population registers, there is no nonresponse.

For the members of these two samples, Statistics Sweden identified their siblings according to several definitions. First, full siblings were identified as siblings with the same two biological parents. From the resulting sample of full-sibling pairs, we drew our sample of non-twin full siblings as those who were not born in the same year and the same month (or adjacent months). Second, half-siblings were identified, and a distinction was made between half-siblings on the mother's side and on the father's side. Because our preliminary analyses showed similar results for both types of half-siblings, we pool them together in the current analysis. Third, siblings related by adoption were identified by means of an adoption code recorded in a special population register held by Statistics Sweden. In our present analysis, we use only pairs containing a biological child and an adopted child. We suspect that the higher correlations observed for pairs of adopted children might reflect biological relationships between the two adopted children. Finally, Statistics Sweden also recorded whether the siblings lived together in the censuses of 1960, 1965, 1970, 1975, and 1980. We classify non-twin siblings as reared apart if they never lived in the same household in any of the censuses.

We confine our present analysis to brother-brother pairs and sister-sister pairs. When more than two same-sex siblings from the same family meet our sample restrictions, we use all available pairs. For example, a family with three brothers contributes three brother pairs to our sample. Our standard error estimates do not account for the nonindependence of the overlapping sibling pairs from the same family.

What distinguishes our study from the many previous studies of Swedish twins is our focus on earnings as the variable of interest. We obtained special permission from Statistics Sweden to access longitudinal data on annual labor earnings for the members of our siblings samples. The earnings data are for 1987, 1990, and 1993. They come from compulsory reports by employers to tax authorities and should be very reliable. Earnings of the self-employed are included.

With earnings as our variable of interest, we wish to observe our sample members when they were of working age. The participants in the twins survey were born between 1926 and 1958, and so they were between the ages of 29 and 61 in 1987. We restrict our sample of non-twin siblings to those born between 1943 and 1965, and so they were between 22 and 44 in 1987. (Note that although our non-twins sample began with individuals born between 1951 and 1964, their siblings could have been born outside that range.) We include individuals only if they had positive earnings in at least one of the years 1987, 1990, and 1993.

Ideally, we would like to use a long-run measure of earnings that is not greatly influenced by transitory fluctuations in a single year's earnings and that is adjusted for stage of life cycle. For smoothing out transitory fluctuations, we are fortunate to have access to up to three years of earnings data over a span of seven years. We also have performed a first-stage regression adjustment to account for stage of life cycle. In particular, for a more inclusive preliminary sample (e.g., including individuals in sister-brother pairs), we pooled all observations of positive earnings in 1987, 1990, and 1993. Then, separately for women and men, we applied least squares to the regression of the natural logarithm of annual earnings on year dummy variables and a cubic in age. Then, taking the residual from that regression as an age-adjusted measure of log annual earnings, we smoothed out transitory earnings variation by averaging each individual's residualized log earnings variable over all of his or her available observations from the three years. The resulting multiyear average of age-adjusted log earnings is the earnings measure Y for which we measure sibling correlations, which in turn are used to decompose earnings inequality into genetic and environmental components.

The first column of table 4.1 restates the nine types of sibling pairs used in our analysis, and the second column shows our sample's number of pairs of each type. Our sample sizes for monozygotic and dizygotic twins reared apart are very small, so our estimates of the sibling correlations for those sibling types will be very unreliable. Accordingly, the model-fitting method that we will present in the next section will be designed to give relatively little weight to imprecise correlation estimates based on small samples. The sample sizes for our other seven types of sibling pairs, however, are quite substantial, especially relative to the tiny sample sizes often used in siblings research.

The third column of table 4.1 shows the sample estimates of the sibling correlation $Corr(Y,Y')$ for each type of sibling pair. Letting N denote the sample's number of pairs of a particular type, we calculate our estimate of $Corr(Y,Y')$ as the ratio of the siblings' sample covariance in Y to the sample variance:

$$\hat{C} = \frac{\left(\sum_{i=1}^{N} Y_i Y_i'/N\right) - \bar{Y}^2}{\left[\sum_{i=1}^{N} (Y_i^2 + Y_i'^2)/(2N)\right] - \bar{Y}^2} \tag{2}$$

where

$$\bar{Y} = \sum_{i=1}^{N} (Y_i + Y_i')/(2N). \tag{3}$$

In parentheses below each estimated sibling correlation is the associated standard error estimate, computed as

$$\hat{\sigma} = \sqrt{(1 - \hat{C}^2)/N}. \tag{4}$$

For our very large samples (over 40,000 each) of non-twin full siblings reared together, we estimate the sibling correlation in our earnings measure Y to be 0.17 for brothers and 0.13 for sisters. While significantly

TABLE 4.1
Results from Model 1

Type of Sibling Pair	Number of Pairs	Sibling Correlation	Fitted Value from Model	Genetic Component	Env. Component
Brothers					
MZ twins reared together	2,052	0.363 (0.021)	0.319	0.281 (0.080)	0.038 (0.037)
MZ twins reared apart	45	0.072 (0.149)	0.281	0.281	0
DZ twins reared together	3,269	0.166 (0.017)	0.179	0.141	0.038
DZ twins reared apart	41	0.165 (0.154)	0.141	0.141	0
Full siblings reared together	48,389	0.174 (0.004)	0.179	0.141	0.038
Full siblings reared apart	3,297	0.159 (0.017)	0.141	0.141	0
Half-siblings reared together	2,862	0.138 (0.018)	0.108	0.070	0.038
Half-siblings reared apart	4,782	0.068 (0.014)	0.070	0.070	0
Adoptive siblings	1,954	0.082 (0.023)	0.038	0	0.038
Sisters					
MZ twins reared together	2,395	0.309 (0.019)	0.254	0.245 (0.080)	0.009 (0.037)
MZ twins reared apart	41	−0.048 (0.156)	0.245	0.245	0
DZ twins reared together	3,474	0.116 (0.017)	0.131	0.123	0.009
DZ twins reared apart	64	0.177 (0.123)	0.123	0.123	0
Full siblings reared together	42,510	0.127 (0.005)	0.131	0.123	0.009
Full siblings reared apart	3,310	0.102 (0.017)	0.123	0.123	0
Half-siblings reared together	2,747	0.069 (0.019)	0.070	0.061	0.009
Half-siblings reared apart	4,321	0.086 (0.015)	0.061	0.061	0
Adoptive siblings	1,705	0.066 (0.024)	0.009	0	0.009

Notes: Numbers in parentheses are estimated standard errors. For men, the chi-square goodness-of-fit statistic is 15.6 with 7 degrees of freedom (p-value 0.030). For women, it is 22.9 (p-value 0.002).

positive, these estimates accord with the finding of Bjorklund et al. (2002) that sibling correlations in earnings are lower in Sweden than in the United States. Our measured sibling correlations for monozygotic twins reared together are 0.36 for brothers and 0.31 for sisters. As expected, these estimates are larger than for the other types of sibling pairs, but again they are distinctly lower than most of the corresponding estimates for the United States. The correlation estimates for dizygotic twins reared together are similar to those for non-twin full siblings, while those for half-siblings and adoptive siblings are somewhat lower. At first glance, the estimates for monozygotic twins reared apart seem surprisingly low, but, as they are based on samples of only slightly more than forty pairs, they are extremely unreliable.

Just from eyeballing these numbers, one might notice some patterns consistent with a genetic role in earnings inequality. For example, the measured earnings correlations for monozygotic twins reared together are greater than those for dizygotic twins and non-twin full siblings, which in turn exceed the correlations for half-siblings and adoptive siblings. Possible signs of a contribution of shared environment to the sibling correlations are that the correlation estimates for adoptive siblings are significantly positive (though not very large) and that the measured correlations for particular genetic types of sibling pairs are often (though not always) greater for those reared together than for those reared apart. That none of the observed earnings correlations exceeds 0.36 suggests a predominant role for non-shared environment. In the next section, we proceed to a more formal analysis of these patterns.

Results from Model Estimation

We begin by estimating model 1 as described earlier. Recall that this simple model makes very strong assumptions: that all types of sibling pairs reared together experience the same degree of environmental similarity; that those reared apart experience *no* similarity in environment; that the genetic and environmental factors are uncorrelated with each other; and that the genetic similarity of dizygotic twins and non-twin full siblings is half that of monozygotic twins, the genetic similarity for half-siblings is a quarter of that for monozygotic twins, and adoptive siblings have no genetic resemblance at all. In terms of equation (1), these assumptions imply that the earnings correlation is $g^2 + s^2$ for monozygotic twins reared together, $0.5g^2 + s^2$ for dizygotic twins and non-twin full siblings reared together, $0.25g^2 + s^2$ for half-siblings reared together, s^2 for adoptive siblings, g^2 for monozygotic twins reared apart,

$0.5g^2$ for dizygotic twins and non-twin full siblings reared apart, and $0.25g^2$ for half-siblings reared apart.

Taken literally, the model delivers all too many ways of estimating the parameters. Consider the estimation of g^2, which is the fraction of earnings inequality attributable to genetic variation. As noted in the section "Models," one way of estimating g^2 from this model is to double the difference between the measured correlations for monozygotic twins and dizygotic twins reared together. With our correlation estimates for brothers, that delivers an estimated g^2 of 0.39, which is *too* large for explaining even our very highest correlation estimate, even if environmental variation is of no consequence at all. Another way to estimate g^2 is by doubling the difference between the measured correlations for monozygotic and dizygotic twins reared apart. With our correlation estimates for either brothers or sisters, that delivers a ridiculous negative estimate of g^2, but of course the estimate is very unreliable because of the small sample sizes for twins reared apart. Clearly, the statistical challenge is how best to combine the available evidence from the nine different types of sibling pairs.

We use the approach of "minimum distance estimation," which chooses parameter estimates so as to match the implied population values of the sibling correlations as closely as possible to the values observed in our sample. In other words, we estimate g^2 and s^2 by taking the nine sample sibling correlations as nine observations of our dependent variable and then applying least squares to the regression of those observed correlations on the functions of g^2 and s^2 listed in the first paragraph of this section. To improve the precision of our parameter estimation, we use weighted least squares, with the nine observations' contributions to the sum of squares weighted by the sample sizes on which they are based.[1] For example, in our model estimation for brothers, the observed correlation for non-twin full siblings reared together, which is based on almost 50,000 brother pairs, gets more than 1,000 times as much weight as the correlation estimate for monozygotic twins reared apart, which is based on only 45 pairs. This is appropriate because the latter correlation estimate is subject to vastly greater sampling error and therefore is vastly less informative. Thus, our estimation procedure will labor mightily to get a close fit to the sample correlation for full siblings reared together and will hardly bother at all with fitting the sample correlations for monozygotic and dizygotic twins reared apart. Our estimates of g^2 and s^2 will be based mainly on contrasts among the seven types of sibling pairs for which we do have sizeable samples and will depend very little on the other two.

Estimating model 1 with our samples of brothers produces an estimated g^2 of 0.281 (with estimated standard error 0.080) and an estimated s^2 of 0.038 (0.037). The estimated value of $u^2 = 1 - g^2 - s^2$ therefore is 0.681, suggesting that non-shared environment is responsible for most earnings variation. The implied values of the population sibling correlations for the nine types of sibling pairs are listed in the fourth column of table 4.1, and the fifth and sixth columns decompose the implied correlations into their genetic and environmental components. The results imply that genetic variation accounts for 28 percent of earnings inequality, 0.28 of the 0.32 earnings correlation fitted for monozygotic twins reared together, and 0.14 of the 0.18 correlation fitted for dizygotic twins and non-twin full brothers reared together. The results for sisters, shown in the lower panel of table 4.1, are qualitatively similar to those for brothers.

Our weighted estimation scheme assures a good fit to the observed correlations for the huge samples of non-twin full siblings reared together, with the fitted value of 0.179 for brothers coming very close to the observed value of 0.174. Similarly, the fitted value of 0.131 for sisters only slightly overpredicts the observed value of 0.127. The model comes nowhere near fitting the observed values for monozygotic twins reared apart, but that is just as well because those strangely small sample correlations are based on tiny samples and are probably far from the true population values. For the other sibling types with sizeable samples, the fitted values from the model are fairly close to the observed values, though not close enough to satisfy a chi-square goodness-of-fit test, which rejects the model at the 0.05 level for both brothers and sisters. For brothers, the most noticeable failures of the model are that it underpredicts the correlations for monozygotic twins reared together and adoptive siblings by 0.04, for half-siblings reared together by 0.03, and for full siblings reared apart by 0.02. Some similar discrepancies appear for the sisters sample.

If anything, it is surprising that the model fits as well as it does. As emphasized in the second section, many of the model's assumptions are highly implausible, so we ought to consider several less restrictive models. Bearing in mind the expectation that individuals with genes conducive to high earnings also tend to enjoy advantagous environments, model 2 loosens up the assumption of zero correlation between the genetic factor G and the shared-environment factor S. In particular, the new model allows three distinct nonzero values of $Corr(G,S')$, one each for biological siblings reared together, siblings reared apart, and adoptive siblings. To our surprise, for both brothers and sisters, these estimated cross-correlations turn out to be insignificantly *negative*.

As shown in table 4.2, except for the exact fit enabled by a free parameter for adoptive siblings, the addition of parameters does not dramatically improve the fit to the data; indeed, for brothers, the chi-square

TABLE 4.2
Results from Model 2

Type of Sibling Pair	Number of Pairs	Sibling Correlation	Fitted Value from Model	Genetic Component	Env. Component
Brothers					
MZ twins reared together	2,052	0.363 (0.021)	0.334	0.250–0.314	0.020–0.084
MZ twins reared apart	45	0.072 (0.149)	0.307	0.307–0.314	−0.007–0
DZ twins reared together	3,269	0.166 (0.017)	0.177	0.093–0.157	0.020–0.084
DZ twins reared apart	41	0.165 (0.154)	0.150	0.150–0.157	−0.007–0
Full siblings reared together	48,389	0.174 (0.004)	0.177	0.093–0.157	0.020–0.084
Full siblings reared apart	3,297	0.159 (0.017)	0.150	0.150–0.157	−0.007–0
Half-siblings reared together	2,862	0.138 (0.018)	0.098	0.015–0.079	0.020–0.084
Half-siblings reared apart	4,782	0.068 (0.014)	0.072	0.072–0.079	−0.007–0
Adoptive siblings	1,954	0.082 (0.023)	0.082	−0.002–0	0.082–0.084
Sisters					
MZ twins reared together	2,395	0.309 (0.019)	0.274	0.201–0.289	−0.015–0.073
MZ twins reared apart	41	−0.048 (0.156)	0.277	0.277–0.289	−0.012–0
DZ twins reared together	3,474	0.116 (0.017)	0.129	0.057–0.145	−0.015–0.073
DZ twins reared apart	64	0.177 (0.123)	0.132	0.132–0.145	−0.012–0
Full siblings reared together	42,510	0.127 (0.005)	0.129	0.057–0.145	−0.015–0.073
Full siblings reared apart	3,310	0.102 (0.017)	0.132	0.132–0.145	−0.012–0
Half-siblings reared together	2,747	0.069 (0.019)	0.057	−0.016–0.072	−0.015–0.073
Half-siblings reared apart	4,321	0.086 (0.015)	0.060	0.060–0.072	−0.012–0
Adoptive siblings	1,705	0.066 (0.024)	0.066	−0.007–0	0.066–0.073

Notes: Numbers in parentheses are estimated standard errors. For men, the chi-square goodness-of-fit statistic is 10.3 with 5 degrees of freedom (p-value 0.07). For women, it is 14.9 (p-value 0.01).

statistic for improvement of fit is insignificant at the 0.05 level. Summarizing the implications for nature vs. nurture is complicated by the fundamental ambiguity about which should be credited for the correlation between the two. The decompositions in table 4.2 provide a range between the two polar extremes of attributing all of the cross-term to either nature or nurture. For the most part, the qualitative implications are similar to those from model 1. For both brothers and sisters, the larger part of most of the fitted correlations is attributed to the siblings' genetic resemblance. Although the results of this exercise should not be read as proving the absence of a positive correlation between nature and nurture, it appears that the arbitrary practice of assuming zero correlation among the factors in the variance decomposition (which is quite common in many applications, not just in siblings research) does not cost much in the present context.

Another of the questionable assumptions in model 1 is that the genetic correlation is 0.5 for dizygotic twins and non-twin full siblings, 0.25 for half-siblings, and 0 for adoptive siblings. This set of restrictions, quite commonly imposed in siblings research, assumes away the effects of assortative mating, genetic dominance, nonadditivities in influences of different genes, and nonrandomness in adoption placements. Model 3 therefore replaces the previously assumed values of 0.5, 0.25, and 0 with three new parameters to be estimated. For brothers, the respective estimates turn out to be 0.43 (with estimated standard error 0.01), 0.25 (0.04), and 0.14 (0.09); for sisters, they are 0.39 (0.02), 0.26 (0.04), and 0.18 (0.10). Although the joint hypothesis that the 0.5, 0.25, and 0 values were correct is rejected at the 0.05 significance level for both brothers and sisters, the newly estimated values are not hugely different from the values previously assumed. Consequently, the qualitative implications from model 1 are preserved again. The results for brothers imply that genetic variation accounts for 32 percent of earnings inequality, 0.32 of the 0.36 earnings correlation fitted for monozygotic twins reared together, and 0.14 of the 0.18 correlation fitted for dizygotic twins and non-twin full siblings. The implications for sisters are similar (table 4.3).

Finally—and, we think, most importantly—we turn to the assumption that all siblings reared together experience the same degree of environmental similarity and that all siblings reared apart experience no environmental similarity at all. This assumption of model 1 ignores the likelihood that monozygotic twins are treated more similarly than other sibling pairs are, and it overlooks the many reasons why siblings classified as "reared apart" might have correlated environments (e.g., some of them did live together for a substantial time before being separated, or they were raised by relatives). As explained in the section "Models," it is easy to see how misspecification of environmental effects could dis-

TABLE 4.3
Results from Model 3

Type of Sibling Pair	Number of Pairs	Sibling Correlation	Fitted Value from Model	Genetic Component	Env. Component
Brothers					
MZ twins reared together	2,052	0.363 (0.021)	0.357	0.320 (0.059)	0.037 (0.026)
MZ twins reared apart	45	0.072 (0.149)	0.320	0.320	0
DZ twins reared together	3,269	0.166 (0.017)	0.175	0.138	0.037
DZ twins reared apart	41	0.165 (0.154)	0.138	0.138	0
Full siblings reared together	48,389	0.174 (0.004)	0.175	0.138	0.037
Full siblings reared apart	3,297	0.159 (0.017)	0.138	0.138	0
Half-siblings reared together	2,862	0.138 (0.018)	0.118	0.080	0.037
Half-siblings reared apart	4,782	0.068 (0.014)	0.080	0.080	0
Adoptive siblings	1,954	0.082 (0.023)	0.082	0.044	0.037
Sisters					
MZ twins reared together	2,395	0.309 (0.019)	0.303	0.291 (0.064)	0.012 (0.027)
MZ twins reared apart	41	−0.048 (0.156)	0.291	0.291	0
DZ twins reared together	3,474	0.116 (0.017)	0.126	0.114	0.012
DZ twins reared apart	64	0.177 (0.123)	0.114	0.114	0
Full siblings reared together	42,510	0.127 (0.005)	0.126	0.114	0.012
Full siblings reared apart	3,310	0.102 (0.017)	0.114	0.114	0
Half-siblings reared together	2,747	0.069 (0.019)	0.086	0.074	0.012
Half-siblings reared apart	4,321	0.086 (0.015)	0.074	0.074	0
Adoptive siblings	1,705	0.066 (0.024)	0.066	0.054	0.012

Notes: Numbers in parentheses are estimated standard errors. For men, the chi-square goodness-of-fit statistic is 6.7 with 4 degrees of freedom (p-value 0.17). For women, it is 7.4 (p-value 0.12).

tort decompositions of genetic and environmental influences. For example, the assumption that monozygotic and dizygotic twins differ only in their genetic resemblance, and not at all in their environmental similarity, forces the greater earnings correlation observed for monozygotic twins to be attributed to an important role for genetics.

Therefore, in model 4, we explore the implications of a more flexible specification of environmental effects. Normalizing $Corr(S,S')$ to 1 for monozygotic twins reared together, we estimate three new parameters to represent this correlation for dizygotic twins reared together, non-twins reared together, and siblings reared apart. For brothers, the respective estimates are 0.406 (with estimated standard error 0.147), 0.461 (0.216), and 0.209 (0.311); for sisters, they are 0.282 (0.131), 0.340 (0.074), and 0.254 (0.180). As suspected, the estimates for reared-together siblings other than monozygotic twins are significantly less than 1 (in both the statistical and substantive senses), and the estimates for siblings reared apart are also more than 0, although not significantly so in the statistical sense. For both brothers and sisters, chi-square tests of model 1 vs. model 4 show that model 4's improvement of fit is statistically significant. Furthermore, model 4 fits the data better than models 2 and 3. For both brothers and sisters, goodness-of-fit tests of model 4 fail to reject it at even the 0.20 significance level.

Table 4.4 displays model 4's implications for decomposing earnings variation between nature and nurture. This time the qualitative findings are somewhat altered. The fraction of men's earnings inequality attributable to genetic variation, which had been estimated at about 0.3 in previous models, is now estimated at 0.2. With previous models, about 80 percent or more of the earnings correlations for twin brothers and non-twin full brothers usually had been attributed to their genetic resemblance. Now the proportion from genetic resemblance is more like 60 percent, with shared environmental influences now playing a larger role than before. For sisters, the estimated fraction of earnings inequality attributable to genetic variation, previously between 0.2 and 0.3, now falls to 0.13. The estimated genetic share of the earnings correlations for twin sisters and non-twin full sisters, which typically had been estimated at about 90 percent before, now has about a 50/50 split with shared environment.

The intuition for the change in results is straightforward. In model 1, which assumed that all siblings reared together experience the same environmental similarity, the only way to account for the large gap between the earnings correlation for monozygotic twins reared together and the much lower correlations for dizygotic twins and full siblings reared together was to estimate a large value for g^2, the genetic component of earnings variation. For brothers, for example, explaining the gap

TABLE 4.4
Results from Model 4

Type of Sibling Pair	Number of Pairs	Sibling Correlation	Fitted Value from Model	Genetic Component	Env. Component
Brothers					
MZ twins reared together	2,052	0.363 (0.021)	0.363	0.199 (0.157)	0.164 (0.158)
MZ twins reared apart	45	0.072 (0.149)	0.233	0.199	0.034
DZ twins reared together	3,269	0.166 (0.017)	0.166	0.100	0.067
DZ twins reared apart	41	0.165 (0.154)	0.134	0.100	0.034
Full siblings reared together	48,389	0.174 (0.004)	0.175	0.100	0.076
Full siblings reared apart	3,297	0.159 (0.017)	0.134	0.100	0.034
Half-siblings reared together	2,862	0.138 (0.018)	0.125	0.050	0.076
Half-siblings reared apart	4,782	0.068 (0.014)	0.084	0.050	0.034
Adoptive siblings	1,954	0.082 (0.023)	0.076	0	0.076
Sisters					
MZ twins reared together	2,395	0.309 (0.019)	0.309	0.130 (0.085)	0.179 (0.044)
MZ twins reared apart	41	−0.048 (0.156)	0.176	0.130	0.045
DZ twins reared together	3,474	0.116 (0.017)	0.116	0.065	0.050
DZ twins reared apart	64	0.177 (0.123)	0.111	0.065	0.045
Full siblings reared together	42,510	0.127 (0.005)	0.126	0.065	0.061
Full siblings reared apart	3,310	0.102 (0.017)	0.111	0.065	0.045
Half-siblings reared together	2,747	0.069 (0.019)	0.093	0.033	0.061
Half-siblings reared apart	4,321	0.086 (0.015)	0.078	0.033	0.045
Adoptive siblings	1,705	0.066 (0.024)	0.061	0	0.061

Notes: Numbers in parentheses are estimated standard errors. For men, the chi-square goodness-of-fit statistic is 5.21 with 4 degrees of freedom (p-value 0.27). For women, it is 4.65 (p-value 0.34).

between the 0.36 correlation measured for monozygotic twins reared together and the 0.17 correlations measured for both dizygotic twins and full siblings reared together would require a g^2 of almost 0.40. Even with no role whatsoever for shared environment, a g^2 of almost 0.40 would lead to overprediction of the earnings correlations for every type of biological sibling. Furthermore, avoiding overprediction of those correlations requires a small value of s^2, the shared environment component, which leads to underprediction of the correlation for adoptive siblings. The reason that model 4 fits the data better is that it interprets the much higher correlation observed for monozygotic twins reared together as reflecting greater similarity in environment in addition to greater genetic resemblance. Model 4 therefore can fit the relatively high correlation for monozygotic twins reared together without having to overpredict the correlations for other biological siblings. At the same time, by assigning a substantial role to shared environment, model 4 can explain the significantly positive correlation observed for adoptive siblings, and, by allowing for some environmental similarity among siblings reared apart, it can fit the reared-apart correlations without requiring quite so large a genetic component.

Conclusions

In this chapter, we have used new evidence from Sweden on earnings correlations among a variety of sibling types in an attempt to shed new light on nature vs. nurture as sources of earnings inequality. The richness of our data set has enabled us to explore the robustness of our results to variations in model specification. We have found that the results are indeed sensitive to flexibility in modeling the variation across types of sibling pairs in the similarity of their environments. Models that assume monozygotic twins experience the same environmental similarity as other sibling pairs and that assume no environmental resemblance among siblings reared apart tend to exaggerate the importance of nature relative to nurture. Even our smallest estimates of the genetic component of earnings variation, however, suggest that it accounts for about 20 percent of earnings inequality among men and more than 10 percent among women.

Although our results point to a significant role for genetic variation, perhaps the most striking finding is the most obvious one—about the importance of *non*-shared environment. The largest sibling correlation in earnings that we estimate is a 0.36 correlation for monozygotic twin brothers. Even though these brothers have identical genes and, according to our preferred model, experience even more similar environments than other sibling pairs do, an estimated 64 percent of their earnings variation is explained by neither genetic nor environmental resemblance. In other words, much and perhaps most of earnings variation in Sweden stems from environmental factors that are not shared even by monozygotic twins.

NOTES

We are grateful to Nancy Pedersen at the Swedish Twin Registry for making the twins data available for this study. Ake Nilsson at Statistics Sweden provided indispensable guidance in constructing the siblings data set. Financial support from the Joint Committee of the Nordic Social Science Research Councils, the Swedish Council for Research in the Humanities and Social Sciences, and the Swedish Council for Social Research is gratefully acknowledged. We have received useful comments from John Bound, Arthur Goldberger, an anonymous reviewer, participants at the Russell Sage Foundation conference held at the Santa Fe Institute in October 2001, and seminar participants at Southampton University, Nuffield College, the Stockholm School of Economics, and SOFI at Stockholm University.

1. In principle, we could improve the asymptotic efficiency of our estimation still further by using weights that incorporate the influence of the sibling correlations, as well as the sample sizes, on the error variance in our regression equation. We do not do so because, as explained by Altonji and Segal (1996) and Clark (1996), basing the weights on the estimated correlations themselves might induce a large finite-sample bias in our parameter estimation. We do, however, take account of how the error variance depends on the sibling correlations when we perform our standard error estimation, which relies on standard results on the asymptotic covariance matrix for nonlinear least squares estimation.

Chapter Five

RAGS, RICHES, AND RACE

The Intergenerational Economic Mobility of Black and

White Families in the United States

TOM HERTZ

THIS chapter demonstrates that the observed degree of intergenerational economic mobility in the United States depends critically on the race of the parents. Using a representative sample of 6,273 African American and white families observed over thirty-two years and in two generations, I first confirm that the intergenerational correlation in long-run average income in the United States is on the order of 0.4 or higher, consistent with the findings surveyed in Solon (1999) and Bowles and Gintis (2002), and extended by Mazumder (this volume). I then show that this correlation is driven to a large extent by black families' especially low rate of upward mobility from the bottom of the income distribution. While only 17 percent of whites born to the bottom decile of family income remained there as adults, for blacks the figure was 42 percent. Similarly, "rags-to-riches" transitions from the bottom to the top quartile were less than half as likely for black as for white families.

This black-white mobility gap is also evident in regression analyses in which own income is modeled as a function of parental income and an indicator variable for African American parents. These reveal a 40 percent gap between the adult incomes of blacks and whites who grew up in families with identical long-run average incomes. This gap narrows to 25–30 percent when family income is measured on a per-adult-equivalent basis, in a manner described later, to take account of differences in family size between races and across generations. It is also observed that these black-white gaps in both the probability of upward mobility and in the conditional expectation of income are virtually unchanged by the inclusion of parents' level of education on the right-hand side of the regression, implying that group differences in parental human capital (at least insofar as this is captured by years of schooling) cannot explain the disparity in mobility outcomes by race.

Measures of Mobility

Intergenerational mobility involves two components: the conditional expectation of income given parents' income, and the degree and structure of variation around this expectation. Both of these may differ by demographic group. The standard intergenerational regression equation captures the first of these two components but says nothing about the probability of observing outcomes other than the expected one. Transition matrices, on the other hand, allow us to estimate the observed probability of moving from one point in the income distribution to another, which is a function of both the expected and unexpected components of mobility. Neither approach is adequate by itself: whereas linear regression equations collapse a complex relation between two distributions down to a single parameter, obscuring valuable information, the transition matrix invites us to lose ourselves in a forest of detail, and may leave us with little understanding of "overall" mobility. I try to make judicious use of both approaches: I look at the overall regression estimates along with measures of persistence at the top and bottom of the distribution, and rates of transition between these extremes.

To start, consider the standard linear intergenerational equation, where y_i denotes the long-run average income (in logs) of the ith family in the current generation and x_i is the corresponding value from the previous generation; where both are age-adjusted by rules that will be described in the next section; and ε_i is a stochastic disturbance term of mean zero:

$$y_i = \alpha + \beta x_i + \varepsilon_i$$

I will refer to the simple difference between the child's and the parents' incomes $(y_i - x_i)$ as the child's *experienced mobility*. It is the sum of two components: *expected mobility* is the difference between the conditional expectation of the child's income and the income of their parents. This will depend on the value of x_i, as below:

$$\hat{y}_i - x_i = \hat{\alpha} - (1 - \hat{\beta})x_i$$

The second, *residual mobility,* is just the difference between actual and predicted income, or the residual, whose value does not depend on x_i, by construction, although its variance and higher moments might (i.e., if the residuals are heteroskedastic):

$$\hat{\varepsilon}_i = y_i - \hat{y}_i$$

Graphically, expected mobility is the signed vertical distance from the line $y = x$ to the regression line, indicated by the arrow in figure 5.1a,

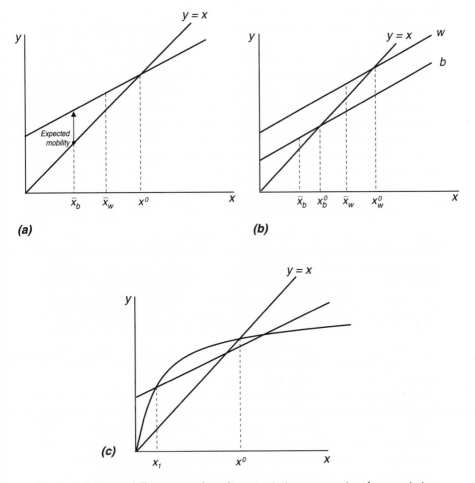

Figure 5.1 Group differences and nonlinearity in intergenerational transmission.

and residual mobility is the vertical distance from the regression line to any point (x_i, y_i). Expected mobility may also be estimated about the conditional median instead of the mean by using least absolute deviations (LAD) instead of least squares to fit the regression line; this places less weight on extreme values.

The elasticity $\hat{\beta}$ is a common summary measure of intergenerational persistence; it is the derivative of predicted income with respect to parental income $(d\hat{y}_i/dx_i)$; the term $(1 - \hat{\beta})$ is then a measure of mobility. The assumption of linearity assures that $\hat{\beta}$ is both locally and globally informative: it measures the change in expected income due to small changes in parents' income, and also allows us to calculate the difference in predicted incomes between the children of the rich and of the poor. Note, however, that $\hat{\beta}$ does not in itself tell us anything about the probability of unexpected outcomes: to determine the probability of moving from rags to riches in one generation, for instance, we need to estimate (or assume) a joint distribution function for child and parent incomes,[1] or to examine transition probabilities directly in a quantile-to-quantile transition matrix. Furthermore, once we allow for a nonlinear relation between parent and child incomes, then *local* slope estimates no longer suffice to summarize *global* differences in expected incomes, as between the offspring of the rich and of the poor.

Expected Mobility by Group and Level of Income

Now let there be two groups in the population, indexed by b and w, one of which is poorer than the other, on average, in both generations, so that $\bar{x}_b < \bar{x}_w$ and $\bar{y}_b < \bar{y}_w$. The question is how to compare intergenerational mobility in the two subpopulations. Suppose that upon running separate regressions we discovered that the groups had identical slopes and intercepts, yielding figure 5.1a. Assume that the variances of incomes were the same for both groups and in both generations (i.e., leave aside differences in residual mobility) and that the only thing that distinguished the groups was their mean parental income. Group b would, on average, have *higher* expected mobility (more upward mobility) than group w, but lower predicted incomes. This would not be because of heterogeneity in the transmission process, but simply because their parents are poorer: in a homogenous mean-reverting system, the average child in group b could expect larger intergenerational income gains than the average child in group w.[2] Expected mobility would be the same for a w and a b whose parents earned the same amount; and in principle all family dynasties would eventually end up at x^0.

In figure 5.1b the two groups have identical slopes but different intercepts. As a result, group b has lower expected mobility (meaning either less upward or more downward mobility), and hence lower predicted income, than group w at any given parental income level; it may or may not be lower at the respective means. Which statistics should we now compare: slopes or intercepts? The identical slopes tell us that the two groups display identical rates of regression toward an intergenerational equilibrium; but they are regressing toward *different* equilibria. Within-group mobility, as summarized by the intergenerational elasticity, is the same for both, but it is not the case that members of each group are equally mobile throughout the pooled income distribution. Children of group b have uniformly lower expected incomes than children of group

w who are born to similarly well-off parents. Parental income does not appear to buy the same level of long-run economic status for the children of one group as it does for the other. This is an example of group-related heterogeneity in the transmission process; it is captured by the systematic difference in what I call expected mobility (conditional on x), but not captured by differences in slope. The difference in expected income between groups at a given level of x may be called the *mobility gap*.

A simple test for group-based heterogeneity is thus to include a race indicator in the standard intergenerational equation and test the hypothesis that this coefficient is zero.[3] Assuming the regression line for the group with poorer parents lies below the line for the richer group, and that the two lines have similar slopes, a consequence of heterogeneity is that the pooled estimate will be steeper than either of the within-group estimates. This is a straightforward example of omitted variables bias: if we are not aware of the group difference we will arrive at an estimate of the elasticity that applies to neither group. Whether this bias matters depends on the question we are asking. If our aim is to estimate the effect of marginal increases in parental income on the child's future economic prospects (for example, to evaluate the long-run impact of an income transfer program) then the bias is problematic, as neither group's children will benefit to the degree implied by the pooled estimate. If our aim, however, is to characterize the overall level of intergenerational transmission in the society, then the pooled estimate of β remains an important summary statistic. The elasticity between parent and child incomes in a heterogenous society is a well-defined concept whether or not it obscures differences in the underlying elasticities by group or income level.

Figure 5.1c allows the relation between incomes in the two generations to be nonlinear, but pools the two groups for clarity. The linear approximation is also plotted, and this need not pass through the same equilibrium. Any number of techniques, from polynomials in parents' income to nonparametric methods such as locally weighted regression, may be used to generate the nonlinear prediction. The local slopes still tell us the local relation between predicted income and parents' income, and this can answer some interesting questions: for example, do small differences among the incomes of the poor make larger or smaller differences in the expected incomes of their kids than similar marginal changes do for the rich? (In the case illustrated, however, the answer is "larger.") The comparison of local slopes, however, does not provide information about the difference in the expected incomes of rich and poor children, nor do local slopes tell us anything about the chances of experiencing something other than the expected outcome.[4] Furthermore, what I have called expected mobility may be higher at a point with steeper slope (as at x_1, where it is positive, versus x^0, where it is zero). Finally, note that the mobility gap as defined above may likewise be calculated according to the linear and nonlinear specifications, to see how group heterogeneity and nonlinearity interact.

Experienced Mobility

The intergenerational correlation coefficient contains information about both expected and residual mobility, and thus serves as summary measure of total experienced mobility. Letting r_{xy} denote this correlation we have

$$r_{xy} = \hat{\beta}\,\frac{\sigma_x}{\sigma_y} = \frac{Cov(x,y)}{\sigma_x\sigma_y}.$$

A typical U.S. result of $r_{xy} = 0.4$ corresponds to an R^2 of 0.16, reminding us that 84 percent of the variance of own (log long-run average) income is *not* explained by variations in parental income. Knowing only the elasticity we cannot specify the R^2: a society with an intergenerational elasticity of 0.6 could be one in which parental income explained virtually all of the variance in own income, or virtually none.[5] By most accounts, the variance of log income has risen over time in the United States, so that $\sigma_y > \sigma_x$, and the correlations are uniformly lower than the corresponding elasticities. Note that neither measure would appear to be a fundamental economic parameter; they are descriptive statistics.

Within-group correlation coefficients from a stratified analysis may differ even if the respective elasticities are the same, provided the ratio of parent and child variances differs by group. However, the within-group correlations do not describe the ease of mobility of a member of a given group with respect to the full population's income distribution since any systematic between-group effects are ignored.

Quantile-to-quantile transition matrices reveal the probabilities of movements from and to any point in the income distribution, thus providing information about total experienced mobility, usually in terms of income rankings.[6] The problem, however, is that there is no best way to summarize their contents. For example, suppose the probability of moving from decile 1 to 2 is higher than that of moving from decile 10 to 9, but the probability of moving from 1 to 5 is *lower* than that of moving from 10 to 6. If so, is mobility higher for the rich or the poor? This problem is inherent in the comparison of two income distributions. It is the reason that we frequently resort to comparisons of expected outcomes, rather than an exhaustive accounting of the probabilities of all possible outcomes.

I present two rich / poor black / white comparisons that measure experienced mobility on two different scales. The first reports the rate of within-quantile persistence, implying that any change in income quantile constitutes mobility; I look at both deciles and quartiles. I will ask, for example, whether black children in the bottom decile are more or less likely to remain in that decile than are whites; and whether movements out of the top quartiles are more likely than movements out of the bottom. The second focuses on extreme mobility, the so-called rags-to-riches transitions from one end of the income distribution to the other.

CONSTRUCTION OF THE THIRTY-TWO-YEAR FAMILY INCOME PANEL

I use data from the Panel Study of Income Dynamics, which began in 1968 with a sample of 4,800 U.S. families in which low-income households are overrepresented,[7] allowing for black-white comparisons of considerable statistical precision despite the fact that blacks are a relatively small minority of the population.[8] Weights are provided that make the sample representative of the U.S. population at that time, and these have been updated every year to account for sample attrition.[9] As recommended by Hill (1992) for panels of varying length, I use the individual-level weights associated with the last year each person appeared in the data set. The PSID attempted to follow all members of these original families, as well as all those who have joined them as they set up new households, until 1997 when the costs of following an ever-growing number of people forced a significant reduction in the rate of follow-up coverage and a biannual interview cycle. Annual family income data have been released through 1996 (in the 1997 survey) as well as for 1998 (in the 1999 survey).

My sample consists of the set of all children of black and white participants who were born between 1942 and 1972, inclusive, who were observed both as children or young adults (25 or less) in a household of which they were not the head, and later as adult heads (26 or older) of household, or adult spouses or partners thereof, for a total of 6,273 individuals.[10]

Income in the second generation is defined as the age-adjusted average annual money income (total family income), in logs, of the adult sample member's household for all years for which it was observed, in constant dollars using the national Consumer Price Index as the deflator.[11] The age-adjustment was based on a time-series regression of log family income against the average age of the head and spouse (if any) and its square, with family-specific fixed effects. The predicted value at age forty, including the fixed effect, was retained as the outcome variable for analysis. Separate regressions were run for blacks and whites in each generation.

This method of estimating age-adjusted long-run average income differs in two important ways from a more common method, namely, forming the average of income across however many years it is observed, taking the log of this average, and then including controls for parents' and children's ages in the intergenerational regression equation. First, because the annual incomes that enter into my time-series regressions are already in logarithms, the resulting long-run income measures are effectively means of logs, not logs of means. This turns out to make very little difference for the pooled intergenerational elasticity estimates, but it does have a significant impact on the estimated black-white mobility gap. The difference between black and white long-run average family income is about five percentage points larger when measured by the mean of log annual income than when measured by the log of mean annual income, reflecting a greater prevalence of unusually low-income years among black families.[12]

Second, my method allows for different age-income profiles for black and white families. Both black and white incomes are increased by the age adjustment, which projects their earnings from an observed mean age of about 33 to a standardized age of 40. But since the white age-earnings gradient is steeper, the age adjustment increases white incomes by about ten percentage points more than it raises black incomes. This is an important correction, bringing us closer to the ideal of observing all incomes at the same age.[13]

Note also that the adjusted income measures are not of mean zero, allowing us to ask questions about changes in actual income as well as in rank. The mean number of years of data on which the second generation's predicted income values were based was 11.3; the minimum was 1 and the maximum was 30 (see table 5.1). The proportion of the second generation with fewer than three years of income data was 11.8 percent. The adult age requirement is imposed to omit the earliest years of working life, when earnings are quite variable and so constitute poor measures of the lifetime average (Solon 1992). I chose a rather low age-threshold (26) to maximize the size of the sample. In principle this comes at the price of observing a high transitory variance of incomes, biasing the correlation coefficient downward.

Total family income is preferred to individual earnings because it is available in a reasonably consistent form for all survey years;[14] because it includes income from transfers (which are important at the lower end

TABLE 5.1
Summary Statistics by Race

Ages and Years Observed	Mean	SD	Min	Max
Whites (n = 3471)				
Average Age	32.5	4.3	22	53
Parents' Average Age	42.9	7.4	18	75
Number of Years of Income Data	11.5	7.3	1	29
Parents' Number of Years of Income Data	11.9	7.0	1	27
Blacks (n = 2802)				
Average Age	32.5	4.4	22	55
Parents' Average Age	44.4	9.7	19	81
Number of Years of Income Data	10.3	6.7	1	30
Parents' Number of Years of Income Data	12.0	6.7	1	28
Total (n = 6273)				
Average Age	32.5	4.3	22	55
Parents' Average Age	43.1	7.9	18	81
Number of Years of Income Data	11.3	7.2	1	30
Parents' Number of Years of Income Data	11.9	7.0	1	28

| | | | | | | Changes in: | |
Family Income (Logs)	Median	Mean	SD	Min	Max	Median	Mean
Whites							
Age-Adjusted Log Family Income	10.91	10.83	0.65	6.06	12.91	0.052	0.035
Parents	10.85	10.79	0.53	7.18	12.81		
Age and Size-Adjusted Log Family Income	10.09	10.04	0.65	5.57	12.53	0.422	0.424
Parents	9.67	9.62	0.56	5.98	11.83		
Blacks							
Age-Adjusted Log Family Income	10.17	10.00	0.92	3.93	11.99	0.086	−0.092
Parents	10.08	10.09	0.62	7.63	11.43		
Age and Size-Adjusted Log Family Income	9.49	9.32	0.87	3.40	11.42	0.743	0.541
Parents	8.75	8.78	0.66	6.14	10.63		
Total							
Age-Adjusted Log Family Income	10.81	10.68	0.78	3.93	12.91	0.043	0.012
Parents	10.77	10.66	0.61	7.18	12.81		
Age and Size-Adjusted Log Family Income	10.01	9.91	0.75	3.40	12.53	0.451	0.445
Parents	9.56	9.47	0.67	5.98	11.83		

Notes: Household size calculated as described in text. Nationally representative sample of black and white families from the Panel Study of Income Dynamics, as described in text. When sampling weights are applied, whites make up 82 percent of the sample. Incomes are adjusted to 1997 dollars using the national Consumer Price Index (CPI-U / CPI-RS). The final columns in the lower panel report the changes from one generation to the next in median and mean log income.

of the income distribution) and from assets (which are important at the upper end of the income distribution, but hard to attribute to husband versus wife); because family incomes are less likely to be zero than are personal earnings; and because family income is arguably a better measure of adult economic status than personal income, especially for women, who are often simply dropped from analyses of intergenerational mobility that are based on labor earnings alone.[15] It should be noted that unlike personal earnings, family or household income will depend on assortative marriage patterns, including the relative infrequency of interracial marriages.

A drawback of total family income is that it does not capture the higher consumption needs of larger families and so may be a poor measure of well-being, or of childhood advantage. To address this I created a measure of income per adult equivalent along the lines suggested by Deaton (1997): I divided total family income for each year by an adjusted household size equal to the number of adults (over 18) plus half the number of children, all raised to the power of 0.9 to capture the probable economies of scale in larger households. Because family size varies over the life cycle in ways that are not identical to the rise and fall of earnings, these income-per-person estimates were age-adjusted in a separate set of generation- and race-specific equations.

Various definitions of parental income are possible, some yielding more usable data than others. The biological father's income, for example, will not be observed for children whose biological father was not a PSID participant. Since marriage rates and the prevalence of female-headed households vary significantly by race, defining parental income in this way might distort the analysis, in addition to reducing the working sample size. I therefore adopt a broad definition of "parental" income, consisting of the age-adjusted log of real family income for the child's household of residence from ages 0 to 25, or any fraction thereof for which this household was observed, without regard to whether the child was living with either of her natural parents, and without worrying about any changes over time in the marital status of the household head(s) or in the family's composition. An additional restriction was imposed to ensure that these "parents" were not in fact members of the second generation who had already started their own households. It is likely, however, that some young adult earnings are counted in total family income, alongside that of their parents. The average number of years of observation of parents' income was 11.9 with a minimum of one and a maximum of twenty-eight (see table 5.1). Some 8.7 percent of parents were observed for fewer than three years.

Parental race was defined by the race of the head of the household(s) the child lived in prior to age 26; in the few cases where this value changed over time, the modal value was chosen. Parental education was defined as the average of the highest year of schooling completed by the head of household and by the spouse (if present); these values were then averaged over the period during which the child lived in that household.

Findings

Table 5.1 describes the dataset. The mean age at which the second generation was observed was 33 (range 22–55) and these figures were comparable for whites and blacks.[16] The average for parents was 43 (range 18–81). Black families made up 18 percent of the weighted sample; in unweighted terms they represent 45 percent. Mean log family incomes (in log 1997 dollars and standardized to age 40) grew from 10.79 ($48,530) for white parents to 10.83 ($50,510) for white children, an increase of roughly 3.5 percent; growth in the median was somewhat faster, at 5.2 percent.[17] For blacks, median incomes rose by 8.6 percent, but mean incomes fell by 9.2 percent. This reflects the influence of a significant number of low outliers in the second generation, which pull the mean of logs down but leave the median unscathed.[18] The influence of low outliers for the children is also apparent in the sharp decrease in the minimum observed income values from one generation to the next, and in the rise in standard deviations.

When incomes are adjusted for family size, however, a different picture emerges. The average number people in a household (of all ages) fell from 4.8 to 2.9 for whites, and from 6.1 to 2.9 for blacks (numbers not shown in table). As a result, incomes per adult equivalent rose by about 42 log points (53 percent) for whites from one generation to the next, and by 54 to 74 log points for blacks (72 to 110 percent), reflecting their more significant reduction in family size. As we shall see, by most measures the black-white mobility gap is smaller when changing household sizes are taken into account.

Figure 5.2 graphs the raw data (with no adjustment for household size) along with both the pooled and the group-specific OLS regression lines. The increase in variance from one generation to the next is immediately apparent as is the gap between the black and white regression lines and the upward bias that this imparts to the pooled estimate. The underlying regression results appear in table 5.2. OLS and LAD estimates (least absolute deviations, or quantile regression at the median) are compared, using log age-adjusted family income, with and without the adjustment for family size. In the pooled sample, the OLS parent-child elasticity is 0.53 with or without the family-size correction; under LAD the elasticity is somewhat lower, at 0.47 to 0.48. For whites, elasticities range between 0.35 and 0.44, depending on the method and the income measure; for blacks the range is 0.32 to 0.42. This confirms that the within-group elasticities are lower than the pooled results. Note also that the OLS elasticities are lower for blacks than whites, while under LAD they are comparable.

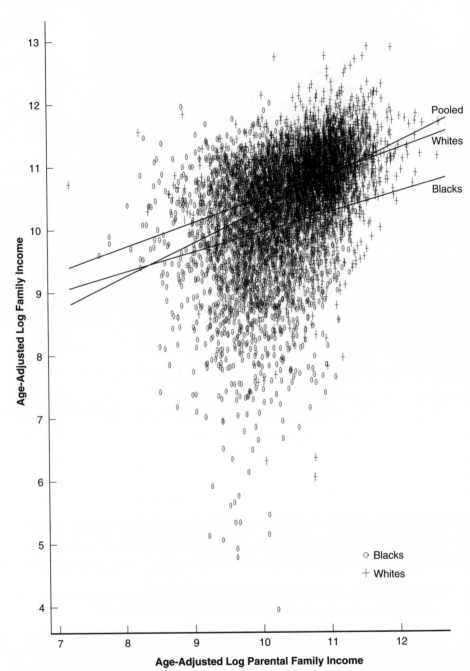

Figure 5.2 OLS regression estimates, by race (no adjustment from family size).

TABLE 5.2
OLS and LAD Regression Estimates of Intergenerational Elasticities
and Correlations Pooled and Stratified by Race

OLS		Elasticity	Robust Standard Error	Pearson's Correlation
Log Age-Adjusted Family Income	Pooled	0.534	0.023	0.421
	White	0.393	0.027	0.322
	Black	0.317	0.050	0.211
Log Age-Adjusted Family Income	Pooled	0.531	0.019	0.474
Per Adult Equivalent	White	0.443	0.024	0.386
	Black	0.392	0.045	0.300
LAD Estimates		Elasticity	Standard Error	Spearman's Correlation
Log Age-Adjusted Family Income	Pooled	0.478	0.019	0.487
	White	0.354	0.020	0.344
	Black	0.343	0.043	0.197
Log Age-Adjusted Family Income	Pooled	0.474	0.016	0.530
Per Adult Equivalent	White	0.407	0.020	0.387
	Black	0.418	0.054	0.280

Notes: LAD stands for least absolute deviations, or quantile regression at the median; sample weights are applied to these regressions as well as the OLS results. Robust standard errors in the top panel allow for clustering at the household level. Spearman's correlation is based on rank order and is calculated without sampling weights (see note 19 in text).

Pearson correlation coefficients in the pooled sample are lower than the OLS elasticities, reflecting the rise in variance from one generation to the next; they are 0.42 in the unadjusted data and 0.47 in the family-size adjusted data. Spearman's rank order correlations, reported in conjunction with the LAD estimates, are noticeable higher at 0.49 and 0.53 in the pooled sample.[19] In all cases the within-group correlation coefficients are lower than the pooled estimates, and lower for blacks than for whites; but as I have argued earlier and will soon document, this does not imply that blacks are more mobile across the full range of the pooled income distribution.

Table 5.3 repeats the pooled regression estimates just discussed and juxtaposes them to extended specifications that control first for race, then for parents' education, then for both. Under OLS, the black-white difference in expected incomes, conditional on parents' income, is 57 log points (50 under LAD); after correcting for family size it is smaller (36 log points under OLS and 29 under LAD).[20] The relative explanatory

TABLE 5.3
OLS and LAD Regression Estimates of Intergenerational Elasticities
with Controls for Race and Parents' Education

	(1)	(2)	(3)	(4)
OLS: Log Age-Adjusted Family Income				
Parental income	0.534	0.376	0.426	0.297
	(0.023)	(0.024)	(0.028)	(0.026)
Parents black		−0.566		−0.545
		(0.039)		(0.038)
Parents' years of schooling			0.041	0.032
			(0.006)	(0.006)
R-squared	0.177	0.240	0.191	0.249
OLS: Log Age-Adjusted Family Income per Adult Equivalent				
Parental income	0.531	0.431	0.414	0.321
	(0.019)	(0.022)	(0.024)	(0.024)
Parents black		−0.358		−0.350
		(0.038)		(0.036)
Parents' years of schooling			0.044	0.042
			(0.006)	(0.006)
R-Squared	0.225	0.251	0.240	0.265
LAD: Log Age-Adjusted Family Income				
Parental income	0.478	0.353	0.383	0.272
	(0.019)	(0.018)	(0.023)	(0.023)
Parents black		−0.495		−0.485
		(0.025)		(0.028)
Parents' years of schooling			0.038	0.033
			(0.005)	(0.005)
Pseudo R-squared	0.090	0.123	0.098	0.129
LAD: Log Age-Adjusted Family Income per Adult Equivalent				
Parental income	0.474	0.408	0.330	0.292
	(0.016)	(0.019)	(0.020)	(0.020)
Parents black		−0.294		−0.283
		(0.030)		(0.026)
Parents' years of schooling			0.052	0.047
			(0.005)	(0.005)
Pseudo R-squared	0.115	0.126	0.129	0.139

Notes: LAD stands for least absolute deviations, or quantile regression at the median; sample weights are applied. Robust standard errors in the top two panels allow for clustering at the household level. All equations also include an intercept term, which is not reported. For the LAD equations, the pseudo-R-squared is calculated as 1 minus the ratio of the sum of the absolute values of the regression residuals to the sum of the absolute values of the deviations of own log income (the dependent variable) about its median.

power of race versus parental education, considered separately, may be assessed by comparing the R-squareds in columns 2 and 3. (Under LAD a pseudo-R-squared, based on sums of absolute deviations about the median, is reported.) When parental education is added to the equation with the race indicator (column 4), that coefficient falls by just one or two log points: differences in years of parental schooling do not explain much of the race-based mobility gap, although they noticeably reduce the residual effect of parental income.[21]

Table 5.4 reports the proportions of those born in the top and bottom

TABLE 5.4

Rate of Intergenerational Persistence in Lower and Upper Deciles, by Race
(age-adjusted log family income)

	Bottom Decile	Top Decile[§]	Difference: Bottom-Top	t-score
All	0.315	0.296	0.019	0.52
	(0.023)	(0.029)	(0.036)	
White	0.169	0.297	−0.128	−2.65***
	(0.039)	(0.029)	(0.048)	
Black[§]	0.415	0.040[§]	0.375[§]	6.67***
	(0.025)	(0.050)	(0.056)	
Difference: black-white	0.246	−0.257[§]		
	(0.046)	(0.058)		
t-score	5.31***	−4.44***		
z-score: probit equation	4.44***	−2.07**		
Difference: black-white, controlling	0.248	−0.242[§]		
for parents' income	(0.046)	(0.069)		
z-score	4.48***	−1.81*		
Difference: black-white, controlling	0.243	−0.263[§]		
for parents' income and education	(0.046)	(0.045)		
z-score	4.45***	−2.13**		
Unweighted Sample Size	1165	379		

Notes: The first three rows report the proportion of those born to the bottom decile (first column) or top decile (second column) of the pooled income distribution of age-adjusted family income for that generation who remained in that decile as adults; robust standard errors allowing for clustering at the household level are reported in parentheses. Sample weights are applied. The third column reports the difference between the bottom- and top-decile persistence rates by race, and the fourth column tests the hypothesis that this difference is zero. The difference between the decile persistence rates for whites and blacks is calculated in the fourth row; the significance of this difference is tested first by a simple two-tailed t-test, and then by means of a probit equation. This probit equation is then extended to include parents' income and education.

[§] Only six blacks in the sample were born in the top decile.

* Significant at 10%. ** Significant at 5%. *** Significant at 1%.

deciles (of the pooled distribution of age-adjusted family income) who remained in those deciles as adults. When white and black families are considered together (first row) this measure of intergenerational persistence was similar at the two ends of the income distribution, at about 30 percent. The final column indicates that the hypothesis of equal rates of persistence for rich and poor cannot be rejected.[22] This symmetry vanishes, however, when we stratify by race: for whites, the rate of persistence at the bottom was about half that at the top (17 versus 30 percent), while for blacks persistence at the bottom was ten times higher than at the top (42 versus 4 percent). Both of these bottom-minus-top differences were statistically significant at the 1 percent level, as were the black-minus-white differences calculated vertically in each column. That the top parental decile contained only six black families limits the precision of our estimates, but there is no such data constraint at the bottom: we may safely conclude that black families had a much lower rate of upward mobility from the bottom decile than did whites, and thus that the pooled estimates of the degree of persistence at the bottom are potentially misleading.

The next row repeats the significance test of the black/white comparison using the z-scores from a probit equation in which a race indicator alone predicts for the subset of those born to a given decile whether one remains in that decile; significance levels are reduced, but the hypothesis of equality between the black and white persistence rates is still rejected at the 5 percent level or better. This probit equation is then extended to include parents' log income, to control for the fact that white families had higher average incomes than blacks in the same decile; no major change in the estimated difference in rates of persistence is observed. Finally, parents' education is added to the regression to see whether group differences in the quantity (if not the quality) of parental education might explain their different rates of mobility. This does not appear to be the case, as the black-white mobility gaps are not appreciably altered by controlling for parents' years of schooling.[23]

Table 5.5 presents the identical estimates based on family income per adult equivalent. Now in the pooled sample the rate of persistence in the bottom decile is significantly higher than at the top (37 versus 27 percent). Again the proportions differ by race: white families' top and bottom rates are now indistinguishable (27–28 percent), but for black families the rate of persistence at the bottom was 41 percent, compared to zero (in a very small sample) at the top. The vertical comparisons again demonstrate that blacks had higher persistence than whites at the bottom, but lower at the top; and that the difference by race in persistence at the bottom cannot be explained by differences in income within the decile or in parental education. (Because no black families remained

TABLE 5.5
Rate of Intergenerational Persistence in Lower and Upper Deciles, by Race
(age-adjusted log family income per adult equivalent)

	Bottom Decile	Top Decile[§]	Difference: Bottom-Top	t-score
All	0.366	0.267	0.100	2.64***
	(0.026)	(0.028)	(0.038)	
White	0.279	0.272	0.007	0.13
	(0.047)	(0.028)	(0.055)	
Black[§]	0.407	0.000[§]	0.407	12.85***
	(0.032)	(0.000)	(0.032)	
Difference: black-white	0.127	−0.272[§]		
	(0.057)	(0.028)		
t-score	2.24**	−9.67***		
z-score: probit equation	2.15**	na		
Difference: black-white, controlling	0.125	na		
for parents' income	(0.057)			
z-score	2.12**			
Difference: black-white, controlling	0.133	na		
for parents' income and education	(0.052)			
z-score	2.41**			
Unweighted Sample Size	1131	380		

Notes: See notes to table 5.4.
[§] Seven blacks in the sample were born to the top parental decile of income per adult equivalent, and none remained there as adults, making it impossible to run the probit equation.
* Significant at 10%. ** Significant at 5%. *** Significant at 1%.

in the upper decile in the second generation, no probit estimates of their adjusted rates of persistence are possible.) Note, however, that the black-white gap in bottom-decile persistence rates is much smaller when measured on a per-adult-equivalent basis (about 13 percentage points compared to 25 points in table 5.4).

Tables 5.6 and 5.7 repeat the calculations for the top and bottom income quartiles, instead of deciles. In the first row of table 5.6 we observe that persistence was not much higher in the bottom quartile than the top for the pooled sample. For whites, however, persistence was significantly higher at the top, and for blacks it was significantly higher at the bottom. The corresponding black-white differences are both large (30 percentage points) and significant at the 1 percent level. They are reduced by 2 to 5 percentage points with the inclusion of parental income (to control for position within the quartile) and education. Table 5.7 looks at quartiles of family income on a per-adult equivalent basis;

TABLE 5.6
Rate of Intergenerational Persistence in Lower and Upper Quartiles, by Race
(age-adjusted log family income)

	Bottom Quartile	Top Quartile	Difference: Bottom-Top	t-score
All	0.466	0.436	0.030	1.16
	(0.017)	(0.019)	(0.026)	
White	0.323	0.448	−0.125	−4.06***
	(0.024)	(0.019)	(0.031)	
Black	0.629	0.148	0.481	6.04***
	(0.020)	(0.077)	(0.080)	
Difference: black-white	0.306	−0.300		
	(0.031)	(0.079)		
t-score	9.74***	−3.79***		
z-score: probit equation	9.20***	−2.72***		
Difference: black-white, controlling	0.289	−0.271		
for parents' income	(0.032)	(0.088)		
z-score	8.63***	−2.36**		
Difference: black-white, controlling	0.282	−0.254		
for parents' income and education	(0.031)	(0.090)		
z-score	8.57***	−2.26**		
Unweighted Sample Size	2604	982		

Notes: See notes to table 5.4.
* Significant at 10%. ** Significant at 5%. *** Significant at 1%.

as in table 5.5, persistence at the bottom of the pooled income distribution is now significantly higher than at the top (51 versus 45 percent).
This again reflects the sum of opposite effects for white and black families. The black-white gap in top-quartile persistence rates shrinks, however, to 9 percentage points (46 for whites versus 37 percent for blacks)
and loses its statistical significance. At the bottom, the racial gap in persistence rates remains large (20 percentage points) and significant; it falls
to about 14 percentage points, but remains clearly significant, after controlling for parents' income within the quartile and for their schooling.

Tables 5.8 and 5.9 examine the rate of mobility between the bottom
and top quartiles, the proverbial rags-to-riches transition (and vice
versa).[24] In table 5.8, using family income with no adjustment for household size, we observe a rough symmetry in the overall likelihood of upward and downward transitions: about 9 percent of families move from
the bottom quartile to the top in a generation compared to 10 percent
who move the other way. For white families, however, extreme upward

TABLE 5.7
Rate of Intergenerational Persistence in Lower and Upper Quartiles, by Race
(age-adjusted log family income per adult equivalent)

	Bottom Quartile	Top Quartile	Difference: Bottom-Top	t-score
All	0.509	0.453	0.056	2.13**
	(0.018)	(0.019)	(0.026)	
White	0.414	0.455	−0.042	−1.23
	(0.028)	(0.020)	(0.034)	
Black	0.610	0.368	0.242	1.67*
	(0.021)	(0.143)	(0.145)	
Difference: black-white	0.196	−0.088		
	(0.035)	(0.145)		
t-score	5.63***	−0.61		
z-score: probit equation	5.53***	−0.59		
Difference: black-white, controlling	0.134	−0.069		
for parents' income	(0.036)	(0.142)		
z-score	3.70***	−0.47		
Difference: black-white, controlling	0.135	−0.056		
for parents' income and education	(0.035)	(0.146)		
z-score	3.81***	−0.37		
Unweighted Sample Size	2662	983		

Notes: See notes to table 5.4.
* Significant at 10%. ** Significant at 5%. *** Significant at 1%.

mobility was significantly more likely than extreme downward mobility (14 versus 9 percent); and for blacks the reverse is true (4 versus 35 percent). The black-white mobility gaps are again robust to the inclusion of controls for parental income within the quartile and education.

In table 5.9 the correction for household size again weakens our conclusions somewhat. None of the up-versus-down comparisons achieve statistical significance at the 10 percent level. Similarly, the black-white gap in the rate of riches-to-rags mobility is smaller and no longer significant. However, the racial gap in rags-to-riches mobility rates (10 for whites and 4 percent for blacks), while smaller in magnitude than in the previous table, remains significant at the 1 percent level and is robust to the inclusion of controls for initial position within the quartile and education.

Table 5.10 presents the decile transition matrix for the pooled income distribution. The figures can be read either as row or column percentages since the weighted number of observations in each column and row is

TABLE 5.8
Mobility between Top and Bottom Quartiles, by Race
(age-adjusted log family income)

	Bottom Quartile to Top	Top Quartile to Bottom	Difference: Up-Down	t-score
All	0.093	0.102	−0.009	−0.60
	(0.009)	(0.012)	(0.015)	
White	0.142	0.092	0.051	2.56**
	(0.017)	(0.011)	(0.020)	
Black	0.036	0.353	−0.316	−3.26***
	(0.006)	(0.097)	(0.097)	
Difference: black-white	−0.106	0.261		
	(0.018)	(0.098)		
t-score	−5.99***	2.68***		
z-score: probit equation	−6.73***	3.54***		
Difference: black-white, controlling	−0.103	0.209		
for parents' income	(0.018)	(0.094)		
z-score	−6.57***	3.00***		
Difference: black-white, controlling	−0.094	0.226		
for parents' income and education	(0.017)	(0.100)		
z-score	−6.32***	3.06***		
Unweighted Sample Size	2602	982		

Notes: The first three rows report the proportion of those born to the bottom quartile who achieve the top quartile as adults (first column); or vice versa (second column). Robust standard errors with clustering at the household level appear in parentheses; sample weights are applied. Probit equations are as in previous tables.
* Significant at 10%. ** Significant at 5%. *** Significant at 1%.

the same. Using the household-size-adjusted data (lower panel), for instance, we see that a child born in the bottom decile has a 0.5 percent chance of reaching the top decile; by contrast, a child born to the top decile has a 26.7 percent chance of remaining there. Dividing these two figures yields a ratio of 53, meaning that the rich child is 53 times more likely to be rich as an adult.

In the upper panel this ratio is somewhat less extreme, at about 23, and similar ratios characterize the relative probability of ending up in the bottom decile for those starting at the bottom versus the top. As we have seen, however, the pooled transition probabilities *overstate* mobility for black children and *understate* it for whites. As noted in table 5.5, the 36.6 percent rate of persistence in the bottom decile is a weighted average of 27.9 percent for whites and 40.7 percent for blacks.

TABLE 5.9
Mobility Between Top and Bottom Quartiles, by Race
(age-adjusted log family income per adult equivalent)

	Bottom Quartile to Top	Top Quartile to Bottom	Difference: Up-Down	t-score
All	0.073	0.092	−0.019	−1.44
	(0.008)	(0.011)	(0.013)	
White	0.102	0.090	0.012	0.70
	(0.014)	(0.011)	(0.018)	
Black	0.042	0.185	−0.143	−1.50
	(0.006)	(0.095)	(0.096)	
Difference: black-white	−0.060	0.095		
	(0.016)	(0.096)		
t-score	−3.85***	0.99		
z-score: probit equation	−4.36***	1.23		
Difference: black-white, controlling	−0.038	0.073		
for parents' income	(0.014)	(0.080)		
z-score	−3.01***	1.10		
Difference: black-white, controlling	−0.037	0.069		
for parents' income and education	(0.013)	(0.079)		
z-score	−3.00***	1.06		
Unweighted Sample Size	2662	983		

Notes: See notes for table 5.8.
* Significant at 10%. ** Significant at 5%. *** Significant at 1%.

The final two figures use a nonparametric running line smooth to look for nonlinearities in the intergenerational relationship. Figure 5.3, which is not adjusted for household size, reveals that the slope of this relation is relatively flat for blacks in the bottom decile: for the poorest black families, small increases in parental income appear to have no consistent effect on one's expected income as an adult, and as a result the black-white mobility gap rises with income. Between the 10th and 25th percentiles of the pooled distribution, however, the mobility gap narrows somewhat, remaining constant at about 50 log points thereafter. In figure 5.4, after adjusting for household size, the flatness of the regression line for blacks in the bottom 5 percent is still more striking. From here to about the 75th percentile we see a black-white income gap on the order of 30 log points (consistent with the regression results in table 5.3); this gap then gets narrower in the upper quartile (consistent with the results from table 5.7).

TABLE 5.10
Decile Transition Matrix for the Pooled Income Distribution (Percentages)

Income Measure: Age-Adjusted Log Family Income

						Children					
		Bottom	*2*	*3*	*4*	*5*	*6*	*7*	*8*	*9*	*Top*
	Bottom	31.5	19.8	11.1	8.8	10.0	5.8	3.7	5.0	3.0	1.3
	2	18.2	15.0	16.9	11.4	11.1	6.0	7.5	5.5	4.8	3.6
	3	13.1	15.6	13.3	10.5	11.7	8.9	7.9	7.1	8.4	3.7
Parents	4	10.4	10.0	15.5	13.2	10.0	10.5	10.7	8.1	6.3	5.3
	5	7.3	11.8	10.0	10.4	11.3	12.6	13.7	8.4	7.3	7.3
	6	5.6	6.0	8.9	9.0	10.9	15.2	12.7	11.8	13.0	7.0
	7	4.8	7.5	8.3	11.1	11.6	10.5	9.4	11.0	14.3	11.5
	8	4.9	4.2	7.4	12.2	9.4	7.8	12.6	12.8	14.9	13.8
	9	3.0	8.1	5.4	6.6	8.3	11.1	11.8	14.5	14.3	17.1
	Top	1.5	2.0	3.1	6.9	5.9	11.6	9.9	15.8	13.7	29.6

Income Measure: Age-Adjusted Log Family Income per Adult Equivalent

						Children					
		Bottom	*2*	*3*	*4*	*5*	*6*	*7*	*8*	*9*	*Top*
	Bottom	36.6	20.5	13.4	9.6	6.6	4.7	4.3	2.1	1.8	0.5
	2	20.7	18.1	11.0	13.0	8.9	11.1	6.6	5.3	3.0	2.2
	3	13.7	13.1	14.4	13.1	11.0	8.5	8.4	8.9	5.1	3.9
Parents	4	8.3	11.7	11.7	10.8	12.0	10.0	9.6	10.1	7.4	8.4
	5	5.6	8.2	12.3	11.4	13.8	13.0	13.1	8.1	7.0	7.6
	6	4.5	9.1	9.4	5.9	14.4	12.7	10.4	11.5	13.7	8.3
	7	3.1	6.1	11.2	14.4	11.0	9.1	9.4	14.9	11.9	8.9
	8	3.7	6.0	7.2	9.3	8.5	10.8	10.7	12.5	16.8	14.7
	9	2.6	3.8	5.2	7.3	5.7	8.1	15.6	16.1	16.8	18.8
	Top	1.4	3.6	4.2	5.0	8.1	12.4	11.5	10.6	16.5	26.7

Notes: These are the observed transition probabilities from the parental decile to child's decile as an adult, using the pooled income distribution for both blacks and whites, and based on the long-run average income measures described in the text. Decile boundaries are specific to each generation. All rows and columns sum to 100, up to rounding error. In the upper panel, for example, we may observe that 31.5 percent of those born to the bottom parental decile remained in that decile as adults, while 19.8 percent moved up to the second decile. The numbers may also be read in the other direction: 19.8 percent of those found in the second decile as adults originated in the bottom decile.

CONCLUSIONS

In 1968, not entirely coincidentally the first year of the PSID survey, the sociologist Otis Dudley Duncan took exception to the growing belief in the research community that poverty per se was largely inherited, arguing that the discussion had failed to confront the question of race:

Negroes (that is, disproportionate numbers of them) are poor mainly because they are "Negroes" and are defined and treated as such by our society. . . . [T]heir poverty stems largely not from the legacy of poverty but
from the legacy of race.

These words were written thirty-five years ago, but intergenerational
mobility analyses are inherently long-run in scope; recall that the children in my sample were born between 1942 and 1972 with the median
year of birth being 1957.[25] For this group, at least, race has been a key
determinant of mobility. As a result, much of the currently measurable
intergenerational persistence of poverty in the United States is due to the
significantly higher rate of persistence among poor African-American as
opposed to poor white households. Similarly, any evidence of a higher
rate of persistence at the bottom of the income distribution than the top
is driven by the experience of black families. The independent effect of
race is also manifest in the fact that intergenerational elasticities and
correlations are larger when black and white families are pooled than
when they are considered separately. In other words, part of the reason
that the pooled intergenerational correlations are so high is that race is
inherited, and race has important economic correlates.[26]

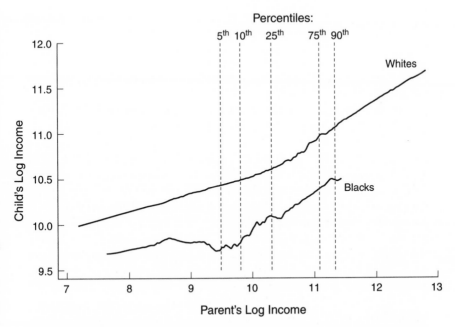

Figure 5.3 Nonparametric depiction of the intergenerational income elasticity
(age adjusted log family income).

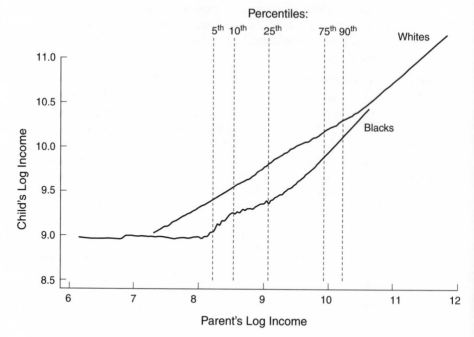

Figure 5.4 Nonparametric depiction of the intergenerational income elasticity (age-adjusted log family income, adjusted for household size).

Also striking is the relative insensitivity of own income to parental income for blacks at the very bottom of the income distribution, which has discouraging implications for the effect, at the margin, of income-transfer programs on poverty in the next generation. These findings are robust to the correction for family size. Moreover, this correction does not reduce the overall importance of parental income, but rather raises it. The pooled correlations in table 5.2 for the size adjusted data are 0.47 using the standard correlation coefficient and 0.53 using Spearman's rank order statistic. Although elasticity estimates have been reported that exceed these figures (e.g., by Mazumder, this volume), I am not aware of any larger previous estimates of correlations. Part of the reason my estimates of the parent-child correlation exceed those of others is that I have averaged *both* parent and child incomes over the longest time frame possible using the currently available PSID data.

Finally, it must be stressed that these findings are purely descriptive, and do not constitute proof of differential economic treatment, or discrimination, by race. I explore only one of the many channels through which the difference in adult economic outcomes between black and white children born to comparably well-off parents might have been generated, namely, the possibility that their parents differ in terms of the number of years of schooling they have attained. This factor, however, does not appear to be important in explaining the black-white mobility gap.

Notes

Thanks to Josh Angrist, Jared Bernstein, Sam Bowles, Angela Fertig, Herb Gintis, Christopher Jencks, Len Lopoo, Darren Lubotsky, Derek Neal, Melissa Osborne Groves, and Gary Solon for comments and advice; to the ever-helpful staff of the PSID for their assistance; and to the Center for Health and Well-being, Princeton University, for financial support.

1. Solon (1992) notes that the common assumption of bivariate log-normality precludes a nonlinear relation between incomes in the two generations, and is not always supported by the data. In the dataset to be analyzed here, log normality is rejected (using D'Agostino's 1990 test as modified by Royston 1991) due to negative skewness (long left-hand tails) and excess kurtosis (too much mass in tails); these are most evident in the second generation.

2. In logged data these gains will be larger in proportionate terms, but may not be so in absolute terms.

3. Another approach is to allow both slopes and intercepts to differ by group and then test the hypothesis that the predicted values for each group at each level of x are the same.

4. I thus disagree with Corak and Heisz (1999), who take the finding that local slopes are steepest at the top of the Canadian income distribution to imply that intergenerational mobility is lowest there.

5. The latter would require a large secular increase in the variance of incomes, but such increases are by no means unheard of, even if they are not typically of the scale just implied. The United States in the 1990s is one apparent example; the postsocialist economies are another; China is a third.

6. Quantile transition matrices have the advantage of being insensitive to the choice of whether to work in levels or logarithms, as is Spearman's rank order correlation. Alternatively, these transitions can be studied in absolute terms by applying the first generation's quantile boundaries to the second generation's income distribution.

7. I use data from both the self-weighting Survey Research Center component of the PSID and the nonrandomly sampled Survey of Economic Opportunity portion. Solon (1992) notes that the latter were selected on the basis of their low incomes in 1966; if their low-income status was partly a reflection of transitory rather than permanent earnings, and if their transitory earnings are serially correlated, then their inclusion would mean that the parental sample is nonrandom in ways that are not captured by the sampling weights. I chose to ignore

this problem on the grounds that I observed the average parent for twelve years, compared to Solon's five.

8. The number of Latino and other households who have been tracked over the thirty-year period is too small to produce reliable results. (The PSID's sample of Latinos was augmented in 1990.)

9. Although the weights can adjust the sample's demographic proportions to mitigate the effects of attrition over time, they by no means eliminate the problem of possible attrition-induced biases. Fitzgerald, Gottschalk, and Moffitt (1998) find some evidence that sample attrition has biased the father-son income elasticity upward, but they note that these effects are not statistically significant.

10. Many of these children grew up in the same households, in which case their parents' incomes appear more than once on the right side of the equation. Robust standard errors are used to allow for the possibility of correlated disturbances due to this clustering.

11. I use the CPI-U until 1977 and thereafter the CPI-RS (a "research series" that retroactively applies recent improvements in the design of the index).

12. Both methods yield meaningful measures of the central tendency of income over time. The mean of logs could be seen as a measure of long-run average utility if we assume that utility is a logarithmic function of consumption, and that families have no ability to smooth consumption over time in the face of fluctuating annual income. If families can smooth consumption perfectly, then the log of mean income is the more appropriate long-run measure of utility.

13. Haider and Solon (2003) observe that individual heterogeneity in the rate of growth of earnings with age is an important source of downward bias when estimating the intergenerational elasticity, if the age at which the second generation is observed is well below 40. Because earnings rise more slowly with age for blacks than for whites, race-specific age adjustments remove one component of this heterogeneity, which reduces the downward bias.

14. The history of the PSID's income measurements and the difficulty of creating a consistent time series are discussed in Kim et al. (2000).

15. Harding et al. (this volume) make some of the same arguments in favor of family income, and note that its adoption is a departure from convention.

16. Average ages below 26 occur when an eligible adult (26 or older) lives with a spouse who is younger than 26.

17. Changes in logs are approximations of the percentage change in levels divided by 100. This approximation is less accurate for larger changes; additional discrepancies arise due to rounding error.

18. These conclusions regarding the rise or fall of income from one generation to the next are sensitive to the method used to standardize on age, and should be interpreted with some caution. The estimated intergenerational correlations and elasticities, however, were robust to changes in the age adjustment.

19. Spearman's rank order correlations are calculated with no sampling weights, and this explains part but not all of the difference between these figures and the conventional Pearson's correlations, which are weighted. For comparison, the *unweighted* Pearson correlations are 0.44 and 0.49, about two points higher than when weighted, but still four or five points below the rank order results.

20. A gap of 0.566 log points implies that blacks earned 43 percent less than whites, or that whites earned 76 percent more than blacks. For effects of this size, the log point estimate is thus a poor approximation of either statement of the percentage difference. Its virtue, however, is that by "splitting the differences" it eliminates the need to specify the denominator of the calculation. Interested readers may convert the log point estimates to percentages according to $100[\exp(\pm\hat{\beta}) - 1]$.

21. These estimates of the effect of parents' race are subject to bias from two sources. On the one hand, the fact that these calculations are based on an average of twelve years of parental income data (as opposed to a true lifetime average) leads us to overstate the magnitude of the race coefficient. The inclusion of parental education should mitigate this bias somewhat, and does appear to reduce the coefficients slightly (in absolute value). On the other hand, the arguments of Haider and Solon (2003) can be extended to demonstrate that by observing the second generation at an average age of 33 we will tend to *understate* the race effect. I have estimated the sizes of these two biases and they appear to roughly offset one another in this dataset.

22. Significance tests are based on robust standard errors (in parentheses) that allow for clustering at the household level, which may result in correlations among the unobserved determinants of adult incomes of children who grew up in the same household.

23. The parameter estimates for parental education are not shown in the table, but they are significant and of the expected signs. An extra year of parental schooling reduces the probability of remaining in the bottom decile (for both blacks and whites) by 1.7 percentage points (significant at the 5 percent level) and increases the probability of remaining in the top decile by 5.1 percentage points (significant at the 1 percent level). Comparable effects were observed in the regressions for tables 5.5, 5.6 and 5.7.

24. The small number of upper-decile black families, combined with the relative scarcity of transitions between top and bottom deciles, make it difficult to generate robust estimates of the black-white difference at the decile level.

25. Harding et al. (this volume) find some evidence that overall intergenerational mobility is higher for later birth cohorts, but this question is still being debated.

26. More precisely, what is biologically inherited is not race per se, but rather the physical characteristics such as skin color from which racial categories are constructed.

Chapter Six

RESEMBLANCE IN PERSONALITY AND ATTITUDES

BETWEEN PARENTS AND THEIR CHILDREN

Genetic and Environmental Contributions

JOHN C. LOEHLIN

PSYCHOLOGISTS, sociologists, and others have been interested in parent-offspring resemblance for a long time, and have calculated many parent-offspring correlations for personality and attitude measures since the 1930s—maybe longer, but I will not be going back farther than that.

The reasons for this interest have varied. Sociologists and anthropologists have been concerned with the transmission of attitudes and values from one generation to the next. Economists (as evidenced in this volume) have explored cross-generational transmission of status. Developmental psychologists have been interested in the mechanisms whereby children come to resemble their parents in attitudes and personality. Most such psychologists have emphasized the role of mechanisms centered on learning, such as imitation and identification, in accounting for parent-child resemblance. Behavior geneticists have pointed out, however, that insofar as the genes influence the development of personality traits and attitudes in each generation, the fact that parents and children share genes could contribute to their resemblance.

For all these groups, the extent to which children actually do resemble their parents is an important datum. To give a sense of the extent and nature of such resemblance, I have compiled a table of 1279 correlations between a parent and a child on some measured personality trait or attitude, based on fifty-nine samples from the published literature. I think the collection is fairly complete in some of the more exotic categories that I will be discussing. It is almost certainly incomplete in the more prosaic categories, such as the resemblance between parents and offspring in ordinary families. Although I may not have all the parent-child correlations ever published, I have at least captured a good many of them.

The tabulation was restricted in several ways. I included only correlations based on at least fifty pairings, to minimize sampling fluctuation.

(If a particular study had categories that fell short of that number, such as separate father-child and mother-child correlations each based on forty pairings, I averaged them and entered the result as a parent-child correlation based on eighty pairings. This isn't exactly equivalent, but when the correlations are fairly low—which these tend to be—it should be close enough. If the author provided a pooled correlation, I used that.) I also restricted the compilation to studies based on Western populations. This ruled out only a very small number of studies—too few to consider separately in any case. In fact, the great majority of the correlations are from studies in the United States, with some representation from Britain, Canada, Australia, and Scandinavia. If a given study provided the data in several ways—with the sexes separate and combined, for example, or for subscales and a total score, I used the most detailed breakdown that met the criteria.

The samples in these studies are often far from ideal. They vary considerably in scope, as well as in the completeness with which they are reported. The majority are samples of convenience, in many cases starting with high school or college students and recruiting their parents. Minority groups and families of lower socioeconomic status are doubtless underrepresented (though not *un*represented) in these data. The attitudes and personality traits included in the studies are very diverse, and the measuring instruments (for the adults, usually pencil-and-paper questionnaires) are of varying quality. Nevertheless, it seemed worthwhile to take a broad first look at what is out there in the published literature.[1]

Based on this tabulation, the questions to be addressed in this chapter include the following:

1. How large are typical parent-child correlations for personality traits?
2. How do these compare with parent-child correlations for attitudes?
3. What can we say regarding the genetic and environmental sources of these correlations?
4. How do parent-child correlations compare across different aspects of personality?
5. How do parent-child correlations compare for different parent-child combinations?
6. Are there important trends with age? Over time?

And then:

1. What do these facts tell us about the contribution of personality to the intergenerational transmission of status?
2. What do they tell us about the behavior genetics of personality?

Table 6.1 gives an overview of how the 1279 correlations are distributed. The rows of table 6.1 represent four categories of parent-child correlations. The first, and by far the most common, is parent-offspring correlations in ordinary intact families. The second category is correlations between parents and children whom they have reared, but who are genetically unrelated to them—that is, parent-offspring correlations in adoptive families. A fair number of such correlations have been reported in the literature, although, of course, the number is far less than parent-offspring correlations in ordinary families. (It should be noted that the ordinary families category probably includes a few adoptive pairs, since studies of such families did not always screen for adoptive status. Presumably, not enough such cases will have crept in to have much effect on overall average correlations.) The third and fourth categories represent rarer but theoretically interesting correlations. In the third we have correlations between birth parents and their adopted-away offspring—most are mother-offspring correlations. In the fourth, we have another correlation that to some extent separates genes and environments: the correlation between a monozygotic (MZ) twin and his or her twin's child. Because MZ twins are genetically identical, a parent is as closely related genetically to his twin's children as to his own children, but the twin's children grow up in a different family.

In each row of the table we find two entries—the first is the number of correlations on scales purporting to measure personality traits, the second, correlations on scales of attitudes, values, and interests. For brevity I will usually refer to these latter simply as attitudes. In a broad theoretical sense one could claim that values and interests are subcategories of attitude, and in a practical sense, far more of these correlations are from scales labeled "attitude" than from scales labeled "interests" or "values."

TABLE 6.1
Number of Parent-Child Correlations of Different Types

	Number of Correlations	
Parent-Child Type	Personality	Attitudes
Ordinary Parent and Child	592	361
Parent and Adopted Child	200	36
Birth Parent and Adopted-Away Child	23	2
Parent and Child of MZ Twin	44	21
Total	859	420

Notes: Personality correlations from twenty-nine samples, attitude correlations from forty samples (ten include both).

Overall, in the compilation on which table 6.1 is based, correlations on personality scales outnumber correlations on attitude scales by about two to one. This mostly reflects the common use of multiscale inventories in personality studies. In conjunction with multiple subgroups, they generate correlations rapidly. In fact, there were more individual studies reporting parent-offspring correlations for attitudes than for personality, but the personality researchers tended to report many more correlations per study. In any case, the 420 parent-offspring correlations available for attitudes will be sufficient to give some sense of the similarities and differences between parent-offspring resemblance in attitudes and in personality.

Table 6.2 presents an overview of average correlations. The rows represent three categories of correlation. The first row represents personality scale correlations between parents and children of theirs who were old enough to take the same questionnaire as the parents—typically, high school or college-age children. The second row involves younger children, either measured with a children's version of the parent personality scale or by ratings. The third row includes the attitude measures. Because there were only two attitude correlations that involved young

TABLE 6.2

Mean Unweighted and Weighted Parent-Offspring Correlations for Personality and Attitude Measures, for Three Parent-Child Types

| | Parent-Child Type | | | | | | | | |
| | Biological and Social | | | Social, not Biological | | | Biological, not Social | | |
Category	wt0	wt1	wt2	wt0	wt1	wt2	wt0	wt1	wt2
Personality: parent-child	.13	.13	.14	.04	.04	.04	.13	.13	.12
	(532, .005)			(176, .006)			(63, .012)		
Personality: parent–young child	.11	.11	.12	.09	.09	.08	.03	.03	.03
	(60, .011)			(24, .013)			(4, .030)		
Attitudes: parent-child	.26	.27	.26	.07	.07	.07	.20	.21	.20
	(359, .015)			(36, .020)			(23, .023)		

Notes: wt0 = unweighted mean of *r*s. wt1 = mean of *r*s weighted by the square root of number of pairings. wt2 = mean of *r*s adjusted for redundancy within study. In parentheses are the number of correlations and standard error of the mean for unweighted correlations.

children (both in ordinary families), these have simply been dropped from the table. The columns of the table represent the same family categories as the rows of table 6.1, except that the third and fourth have been merged together as reflecting cases in which genes are shared but not family environments.

In each case an ordinary unweighted mean of the correlations in the category is given, plus two different weighted means. The first of these, wt1 in the table, weights each correlation by the square root of the number of pairings on which it is based (the range was from 50 to upward of 4500 pairings). This weights correlations inversely to their standard errors, giving statistically stable correlations more weight. The second, wt2, down-weights for redundancy. If there are, say, three extraversion scales for a given sample, each is weighted one-third. As is evident from the table, the alternative weightings give figures essentially the same as the unweighted means. For simplicity, I will confine myself to unweighted means from here on.

Below each mean correlation are two numbers in parentheses. The first is the number of correlations on which it is based. The second is an estimate of its standard error, which was obtained by dividing the standard deviation of the unweighted correlations by the square root of N, the number of correlations. As a check on the possible effects of oddities of distribution, standard errors were also obtained for the unweighted correlations by a bootstrap procedure (Efron 1982), in which 1000 samples of size N were drawn with replacement from the relevant data set, the mean calculated in each, and the empirical standard deviation of these means obtained. The bootstrap estimates are not separately shown, because with one exception they all agreed to three decimal places with the directly calculated values given in the table. The exception involved the very small sample of four cases in the third column for the young children, for which the bootstrap estimate was .027 instead of .030. Given this level of agreement, in subsequent tables only directly calculated standard errors are used.

In any case, these standard errors must be regarded as approximate. Often, strict independence will not obtain among the correlations from a single study. For example, the same fathers' scores may enter into father-son and father-daughter correlations. Nevertheless, the standard errors should provide at least rough guidance in assessing differences among the means.

Table 6.2 tells us several interesting things. Consider the first two rows of the table, the personality measures. The first thing to notice about these correlations is that they are all small. A child and a parent measured on a given personality scale do not resemble each other very much. As the first entry in the table, we find this correlation for ordinary families with older or adult children: the average r is .13. In the second row of the first column, we learn that the correlation is about the same with young children as with older children—an average r of .11. Finally, in the third row, we see that parent-child correlations for attitudes and interests, while not huge, are definitely higher than for personality traits, averaging about .26. With standard errors of these means in the neighborhood of .01, this is a large and dependable difference.

The second and third columns of the table give us some clues as to the genetic and environmental origins of these modest parent-child correlations. What they tell us is that (at least for older children and adults) they are mostly due to shared genes, rather than to instruction, imitation, or shared environments. In the second column of the first row, the adoptive families, in which genes are not shared but environments are, the correlations are much lower. In the third column, where genes are shared but not families, the average personality correlation is as high as in intact families. For younger children's personalities (second row), however, social factors appear to loom larger than biological ones. For attitudes (third row), the correlation mediated by the genes alone is a little lower than that for genes plus family, but it is markedly higher than that produced by family alone.

On the face of it, then, these data make a case for greater influence of families on personality among younger children. One way of looking at it is that the younger children have yet to "grow into" their adult personalities, which they will do under the persisting influence of their genes. In the meantime, transitory environmental influences will be important.

Is this also plausible for attitudes? Specific attitudes are acquired, necessarily, from parents, peers, or the wider culture, but genetically based dispositions can influence which attitudes are chosen from among the many available. Thus children may "grow into" their adult attitudes and interests as well as into their adult personalities.

Before we come back to puzzle further about these results, let us look at the data broken down in a couple of ways. Table 6.3 gives personality correlations (based only on the older children) for scales classified according to the currently popular five-factor scheme familiarly known as the "Big Five." The five dimensions are: extraversion, which includes such subtraits as dominance, outgoingness, and impulsivity; agreeableness, which includes friendliness and likeability—with hostility at the negative pole; conscientiousness, which includes orderliness, responsibility, and thoroughness; neuroticism, which includes fears, worries, and emotional instability; and openness, which includes openness to experience and wide-ranging interests. These five dimensions were originally derived by the factor-analysis of trait terms from the English language

TABLE 6.3

Mean Parent-Offspring Correlation on Personality Traits by Big-Five
Personality Dimensions, for Three Parent-Child Types

	Parent-Child Type					
Dimension	Biological and Social		Social, not Biological		Biological, not Social	
Extraversion	.14	(117, .010)	.03	(40, .011)	.16	(15, .019)
Agreeableness	.11	(65, .013)	.01	(16, .021)	.14	(3, .067)
Conscientiousness	.09	(64, .013)	.02	(26, .012)	.11	(2, .110)
Neuroticism	.13	(131, .010)	.05	(40, .011)	.11	(21, .022)
Opennness	.17	(24, .028)	.07	(12, .031)	.14	(1, —)

Notes: Young children excluded. Number of correlations and standard error are given
in parentheses.

(e.g., Fiske 1949; Norman 1963). Similar structures have subsequently
been found in other languages and in existing personality tests and other
descriptive procedures (for reviews, see Digman 1990; John 1990; and
McCrae 1989). There is no special magic about the number five—
individual personality theorists have frequently chosen to work with a
larger or smaller number of major traits, and many eschew trait concepts
altogether. However, the Big Five provide a convenient level at which to
summarize personality (e.g., Loehlin 1992). The classifications of the
various personality scales into these categories were admittedly subjec-
tive—a sixth category (not shown) for "none of the above" was also
used. Nevertheless, the results may serve to give us at least an initial
look at various subdomains of personality.

That initial look suggests that each of these personality domains is
pretty much like the whole. The parent-child correlations in ordinary
families mostly lie between .10 and .15. The adoptive family correlations
are clearly lower, mostly in the .00 to .05 range. The data for the genetic
relationships in column 3 are spotty, but appear similar to those for
ordinary families. It is interesting to note that if any of the Big Five
shows lower parent-child correlations than the rest it is "conscientiousness," an area in which one might have supposed a priori that family
socialization practices would be particularly important. Among the five
dimensions, "openness" may show a slightly higher level of correlation,
although the data for this dimension are limited. If the difference is real,
it may reflect a slight shift into the realm of attitudes and interests with
this dimension.

What about different parent-child pairings? Do mothers or fathers
affect their children more? Are girls or boys more influenced by their

TABLE 6.4

Mean Parent-Offspring Correlation on Personality Traits by Different
Gender Combinations, for Three Parent-Child Types

| | Parent-Child Type | | | | | |
Pairing	Biological and Social		Social, not Biological		Biological, not Social	
Father-Son	.11	(90, .011)	.09	(24, .019)	.01	(5, .022)
Father-Daughter	.13	(90, .011)	.05	(28, .016)	.08	(5, .037)
Mother-Son	.15	(88, .013)	.03	(24, .018)	.12	(9, .035)
Mother-Daughter	.15	(96, .013)	.02	(28, .013)	.14	(9, .031)

Notes: Young children excluded. Number of correlations and standard error are given
in parentheses.

families? Are the cross-sex pairings especially important, as Freud supposed? Or are all four kinds of pairings about equal, as a simple genetic hypothesis might predict? The answer for personality is given in table 6.4, and for attitudes in table 6.5.

The differences in the personality data are not overwhelming, but they are provocative. If there is any real difference among the four kinds of pairing, it is the father-son relationship that is the most social and the mother-daughter relationship that is the most biological. I don't know what this means. Some hormonal effect expressed only in women could make mothers and daughters similar, but would not account for a difference between fathers and sons and the cross-sex pairs.

Do attitudes show the same phenomenon? The answer is in table 6.5, and on the whole it is no. To my eye, the four kinds of pairing look

TABLE 6.5

Mean Parent-Offspring Correlation on Attitudes and Interests by Different
Gender Combinations, for Three Parent-Child Types

| | Parent-Child Type | | | | | |
Pairing	Biological and Social		Social, not Biological		Biological, not Social	
Father-Son	.29	(53, .026)	.10	(8, .028)	.25	(5, .054)
Father-Daughter	.33	(42, .030)	.04	(8, .056)	.19	(5, .050)
Mother-Son	.33	(42, .029)	.10	(8, .050)	.19	(5, .045)
Mother-Daughter	.36	(66, .021)	.02	(8, .032)	.23	(5, .033)

Notes: Young children excluded. Number of correlations and standard error are given
in parentheses.

pretty much alike (and the resemblances look pretty much like those that genes would predict, with a modest contribution from family environment). However, the relevant data in the right-hand columns of the table are quite limited—only eight adoptive and five biological correlations are available for each kind of pairing.

Finally, what about temporal trends? With respect to individuals, table 6.2 suggested that the personalities of young children were less strongly influenced by their genes and more strongly influenced by their family environments than those of older children and adults. Were there also temporal trends for the compilation as a whole? To see, I correlated the size of parent-child correlations with the year in which they were obtained. (If this was not specified in the study, and frequently it was not, I took it to be three years prior to the study's publication date.) The correlations for personality and attitude (in ordinary families for older children) were negative, suggesting a decline in parent-offspring resemblance over time. The correlations were −.08 for personality traits and −.32 for attitudes (Ns of 532 and 359, respectively). The correlation for personality is of marginal statistical significance ($.10 > p > .05$), and is in any case too small to account for much variance. Presumably there have been no great genetic changes in these populations between the 1930s and the present, and so any decline most likely reflects a declining influence of families on the personalities and attitudes of their members. One methodological possibility—declining reliabilities of the tests, perhaps in connection with the use of shorter tests in larger-scale studies— seems not to be an important factor. The correlation of scale reliability with year of testing, in those cases where reliability is reported, is essentially zero (.006).

DISCUSSION

I want to comment briefly on two points. The first concerns the implication of results like these for the main topic of this book: the intergenerational transmission of status. The second concerns their implication for broader questions about the inheritance of personality.

On the face of it, parent-child correlations on the order of .13 don't suggest much predictability of a child's personality from a parent's personality. If we assume that the association between a personality trait and a measure of economic status in either generation is also quite modest, we wind up with an extremely small contribution of personality to the correlation of status across generations (figure 6.1).

The correlation of .13 between a personality trait and occupational status is the median value from Jencks et al. (1979), who reported corre-

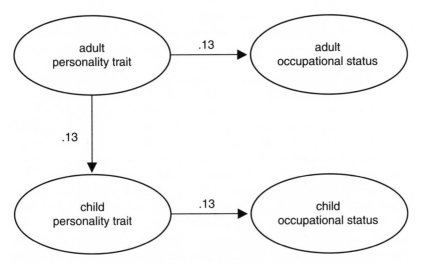

Figure 6.1 Parent-child correlation in occupational status mediated by a personality trait.

lations ranging from .02 to .18 between self-assessed personality traits in high school boys and their occupational status twelve years later. The paths in the figure imply a contribution of $.13 \times .13 \times .13 = .002$ to the correlation between parent's and child's occupational status.

The correlation of .13 between parent and child for personality traits might be, however, a bit on the low side, for several reasons.

First, the personality scales used in these studies are less than perfectly reliable. Better measures would help some. For a little over half the correlations in these studies, an estimate of the reliability of the scale is reported. The mean of these reliability coefficients is .72. Improving scale reliability from .72 to, say, .90, which is about as high as the reliabilities of personality scales go, would boost the .13 to about .16.

Another possibility would be to measure personality from multiple viewpoints, by the use of peer, spouse, or observer ratings in addition to self-report questionnaires. It is unclear whether this would improve parent-offspring correlations more than would be achieved by simply increasing the reliability of questionnaire scales, but such procedures have increased heritability estimates substantially with twin and sibling data (Riemann, Angleitner, and Strelau 1997; Reiss et al. 2000). This is a point to which I return later.

The discussion so far has dealt with correlations between one parent and a child. Using both parents might improve matters. If we assume spouses to be uncorrelated for the trait in question, the use of two parents would turn a .16 parent-offspring correlation into about a .23 [i.e., $(.16^2 + .16^2)^{1/2} = .23$]. This random mating assumption is reasonable as a first approximation in the case of personality traits, where marital correlations tend to be low (e.g., Price and Vandenberg 1980), although it would not do for attitudes, where spouse correlations are substantial (Eaves et al. 1999). One limitation of this approach is that both parents' personalities may not be equally correlated with the status variable—if only one is, we gain no advantage.

What about restriction of range, which can reduce correlations? A fair number of the studies involved college students and their families, which could involve restriction on personality traits related to socioeconomic status and academic achievement. Families who adopt children are also known to be restricted on ability and socioeconomic variables (Stoolmiller 2000). But how much would this affect personality generally? I do have some evidence relevant to restriction of range on personality variables in adoptive families. Results from one of our adoption studies are summarized in table 6.6.

This was a sample based on adoptions from a Texas home for unwed mothers; the adoptive families were tested by mailed questionnaires. The entries in the table are ratios of the standard deviations in the sample to those in the normative population of the test, and they apply to twelve of the eighteen scales of the California Psychological Inventory that I had been able to classify according to the "Big Five." Ratios less than 1.00 mean that the sample was restricted in range relative to the normative population; ratios over 1.00 mean that the sample varied more widely.

The quick answer from table 6.6 is that there is no *general* restriction of range of personality in this tested-by-mail adoption sample. On the contrary, more entries in the table are above 1.00 than below it; but it makes a difference which trait one is looking at. There seems to be above-average variability in traits related to "extraversion": seventeen of the eighteen entries in the table are higher than 1.00. "Agreeableness" is not well represented in this inventory, but insofar as the "femininity" scale can stand for this domain, there may be mild restriction here (coefficients in the range .80 to .97). On the whole, "neuroticism" and "openness" don't show a systematic tendency one way or the other. "Conscientiousness" is more complicated. The parents show restriction in range; the children, especially the adopted children, do not. One might expect conscientiousness to be related to responding to a mail survey. The means (not shown) for the adoptive fathers and mothers on these traits are mostly elevated relative to the norms—by about .25 and .30 standard deviations, respectively. It is likely that the parents played a primary role in determining whether the family participated in the

TABLE 6.6
Little, If Any, Restriction of Range on Twelve Personality Variables in a Sample of Texas Adoptive Families

Personality Scale	Adoptive Fathers	Adoptive Mothers	Adopted Sons	Adopted Daughters	Biological Sons	Biological Daughters
Extraversion						
Dominance	1.17	1.16	1.24	1.20	1.47	1.21
Sociability	1.04	1.11	1.04	1.32	1.02	1.11
Social Presence	1.17	1.11	1.13	1.09	1.19	.93
Agreeableness						
Femininity	.85	.80	.97	.97	.87	.86
Conscientiousness						
Responsibility	.94	.77	1.16	1.23	1.14	1.26
Socialization	.82	.79	1.25	1.30	.86	.98
Self-control	.91	.86	1.18	1.17	1.17	1.17
Neuroticism (reversed)						
Self-acceptance	1.00	1.03	.95	1.11	.97	1.08
Sense of well-being	.95	.95	1.45	1.43	1.02	1.23
Good impression	.93	.92	.95	.93	.77	.89
Openness						
Achievement via independence	1.02	.85	1.07	1.05	1.05	.88
Flexibility	1.14	1.00	1.09	.97	.91	.83

Notes: Data from Loehlin, Willerman, and Horn (1985). California Psychological Inventory scales classified according to the Big Five. Entries are ratios of the standard deviations in the sample to those of males or females in the normative population of the test.

study—the invitation was addressed to them—but we have no direct evidence on this point. The children's means are below the norms, the adopted children lowest. We may guess that the genetic parents of the adopted children were below average in conscientiousness, and so genes may be involved. The median ages for the child generation were 17.5 for the adopted and 19.4 for the biological children, and so age might also enter in. But at any rate, it does not appear that generally adjusting parent-child correlations for restriction of range would materially affect the overall picture with respect to personality.

Finally, what about using multiple traits? We have at least five more-or-less independent dimensions to work with. (The Big Five in theory are orthogonal, although measures of them often show some correlation in practice.) If each of these dimensions provides a small independent path between generations, will these sum together into something respectable? The key question, to which I do not know the answer, is, Will each of these personality domains have an independent association with occupational status? If they do, and the association between the personality trait and status is .13 in each case, and we boost the parent-child correlation to .23 by the use of two parents and highly reliable tests, where are we? Well, we now have $5 \times .004$ or .02 as the correlation between generations in occupational status that is mediated by personality. Still pretty small. The inheritance of traits could account for a little of what is left after the inheritance of ability and of wealth, but not very much of it.

Moreover, it seems doubtful that all five dimensions would contribute equally to occupational status. "Extraversion" and "conscientiousness" have some promise, and as does low "neuroticism." "Agreeableness" might help in some circumstances, but it also seems likely to go along with persistence in a low-status job. The creativity associated with "openness" to experience might sometimes lead to high-level performance, but openness as a personality trait shows some association with intelligence (Loehlin et al. 1998); whether it would contribute much independently of this to the prediction of status is moot.

In short, the low correlations between parents and children on personality traits, assuming modest associations of such traits with status in both generations, make it unlikely that they will contribute much to the transmission of economic status across generations, although improvements in measurement, the use of both parents in studies, and the inquiry into multiple traits could improve things a little.

Well, if not personality, how about attitudes? Average parent-child correlations were higher for attitudes, by a factor of 2, averaging .26 instead of .13. Using both parents is less helpful here, because spouse correlations tend to be decidedly higher for attitudes than for personality

(Eaves et al. 1999). Presumably, improvements in measurement and the use of multiple attitudes will still be beneficial. The critical unknown remains the strength of the association between attitude and economic status (and perhaps, in this case, its causal direction—if status to some degree affects attitude, as seems likely, then figure 6.1 analysis gets more complicated and the explanatory power of attitude shrinks). On the plus side, existing evidence suggests that at least some attitudinal and motivational characteristics may have larger correlations with economic status than do typical personality traits (e.g., Duncan and Dunifon 1998). I leave this issue with the standard dictum that "more research is needed."

The second of my major points of discussion concerns how these low parent-child personality correlations fit into the broader picture of the heritability of personality traits. On the whole, these data suggest that whatever parent-child resemblance there is in personality is mostly, although not entirely, due to shared genes. Suppose the most extreme case: that parent-child resemblance is wholly due to genes, and that spouse correlations are nil. Our best estimate of the heritability of the trait would then be twice the correlation of a parent and a child: that is, on average, .26. This is *considerably* lower than estimates of the heritability of personality traits based on twin studies.

Table 6.7 illustrates this. It gives heritability estimates for the Big Five traits, obtained by doubling the average parent-child correlations in table 6.3, as compared with estimates from three recent twin studies. The latter estimates are almost twice as large. Why this difference? One explanation sometimes proposed is that identical twins may be treated more alike than fraternal twins, and hence that heritability estimates based on twins may be biased upward. There is no doubt that identical

TABLE 6.7

Heritabilities for the Big Five Estimated from Table 6.3 Parent-Offspring Correlations, and Estimates from Three Recent Twin Studies

Dimension	From Parent-Offspring Correlations	Twin Study, United States	Twin Study, Canada	Twin Study, Germany
Extraversion	.28	.49	.53	.56
Agreeableness	.22	.33	.41	.42
Conscientiousness	.18	.48	.44	.53
Neuroticism	.26	.42	.41	.52
Openness	.34	.58	.61	.53
Mean	.26	.46	.48	.51

Notes: Twin data: United States, Waller (1999); Canada, Jang et al. (1996); Germany, Riemann et al. (1997).

twins are treated more alike in some respects than fraternal twins (e.g., Loehlin and Nichols 1976), but the bulk of the evidence suggests that this is a consequence rather than a cause of their greater similarity in personality. A number of direct investigations of the so-called equal environments assumption have failed to support the notion that failures of it constitute a major bias in twin studies of personality (see Loehlin 1992). Moreover, if shared environments seem to play so limited a role in creating personality resemblance, it is hard to see why minor differences in these should be crucial.

In my view, the most likely explanation for the observed difference is that the genetic contribution to personality depends only partly on the effects of genes individually, and to a considerable extent on the so-called nonadditive effects of genes—that is, on the effects of gene configurations rather than individual genes (Finkel and McGue 1997; Plomin et al. 1998). These genetic patterns may include the way in which genes are paired at a particular locus ("dominance" in the geneticist's terminology) or effects involving the genes at more than one locus ("epistasis"). Configurations get broken up in the random selection of the half of the genes that a parent passes on to his or her child, and this decreases the resemblances of ordinary siblings (including fraternal twins) as well as of parents to their offspring, as compared with the resemblances of identical twins, who share all of their genes and hence all of their gene configurations as well. The likely presence of considerable nonadditive genetic variation in the personality domain means that the gene-based resemblance between generations will be considerably less than the contribution of genes to individual differences within a generation.

Within-generation heritabilities of near .50, such as those in table 6.7, are not all that recent behavior genetic studies of personality have to tell us. The measurement of traits from multiple perspectives yields heritability estimates for personality that are even higher than this. In the German study included in table 6.7, the self-report questionnaires were supplemented by ratings from two peers (Riemann et al. 1997). This raised the heritability estimates appreciably. Instead of the heritabilities of .42 to .56 shown in table 6.7 for a self-report questionnaire, heritabilities of .66 to .79 were estimated for the composite of questionnaire and ratings.

A recent study based on U.S. adolescents included six kinds of sibling pairings: identical and fraternal twins, ordinary siblings, and full, half, and unrelated siblings in families resulting from remarriages (Reiss et al. 2000). Six dimensions of adjustment were measured by multiple means: self-report questionnaires, ratings by each parent, and in some cases ratings by observers based on videotaped interactions. The heritabilities ranged from .40 (for autonomy) to .90 (for social responsibility), with a median of .72 (Bouchard and Loehlin 2001). Again, what is common to various perspectives on an individual is more reflective of the genes than that which depends on the specificities of one particular viewpoint. Note that identical twins were included in this study, so nonadditive genetic variance remains in the picture.

CONCLUSIONS

It appears that much of the quite substantial genetic contribution to individual differences in personality does not translate into heritability in the sense of transmission of traits across generations. This makes it unlikely that there will be a large genetic contribution to the intergenerational transmission of status via personality. The data from special family types reviewed in tables 6.1 through 6.5 makes even less likely a large *environmental* contribution to intergenerational transmission by this route. A small joint contribution by personality and attitudes cannot, however, be excluded, and may justify further investigation with more focused methods.

NOTES

I am grateful to Bruce Sacerdote for his helpful comments on an earlier version of this chapter.

1. The tabulation and associated reference list are too bulky for publication here, but are available on request from the author.

Chapter Seven

PERSONALITY AND THE INTERGENERATIONAL
TRANSMISSION OF ECONOMIC STATUS

Melissa Osborne Groves

EDUCATIONAL attainment, cognitive performance, and the receipt of wealth transfers have been shown to be strong indicators of economic success across occupations and explanatory variables in the intergenerational transmission of socioeconomic status. Research also suggests, however, that these three mechanisms are not able to explain the bulk of the large intergenerational persistence of earnings. Few researchers have explored the economic implications of the transmission of personality that occurs in the household. While personality has been shown to be highly heritable through a combination of environmental and genetic mechanisms and rewarded in the labor market, its influence on the transmission of earnings remains unclear.

This chapter will estimate the influence of personality on the intergenerational transmission of earnings using matched father-son pairs from the mature and young male cohorts of the National Longitudinal Surveys (NLS). This is an extension to traditional explanations focusing on the transmission of IQ and education in explaining the high degree of familial similarity in the United States. Current estimates of the correlation between fathers' and sons' earnings in the United States are around 0.40 (Mulligan 1997; Solon 1999), and while education and the transmission of IQ have received considerable attention through such books as *The Bell Curve*, with their controversial statements and policy implications related to the heritability of IQ, a significant portion (almost half) of the relationship between parents' and children's earnings operates independently of these variables. Because personality is highly heritable (Plomin 1986; Loehlin 1992b; Ahern et al. 1982) and a significant determinant of earnings in both generations, it is reasonable to believe that personality accounts for a significant portion of the unexplained relationship between parents' and children's earnings.

Therefore, we will investigate a behavioral explanation for the intergenerational transmission of economic status. To do this, father-son pairs from the NLS are used to estimate (1) if the inclusion of personality variables, controlling for standard human capital variables, reduces the unexplained persistence of earnings and (2) the magnitude by which similarities in personality explain the transmission of earnings from father to son. This research contributes to previous literature by using a representative and longitudinal data set that includes personality measures for parents and children, and a reasonable model of how personality is related to earnings and the intergenerational transmission of earnings. The longitudinal nature of the data set facilitates the correction of classical measurement error and allows for more accurate measures of fathers and sons permanent income.[1] Because the NLS provides self- and family reports of many variables of interest, the degree of measurement error can be estimated from correlations among multiple reports of identical information. These reliabilities are used to correct the correlation matrices and regression results, preventing noisy measures from attenuating the estimates. The NLS also provides multiple-year measures of income over short time intervals, allowing for reasonable estimations of permanent income for both fathers and sons. Reducing the year-to-year noise in earnings measures is found to be more accurate in evaluating the degree of intergenerational transmission in earnings (Solon 1999).

The findings indicate that the inclusion of personality, independent of standard human capital variables, improves our understanding of the transmission of earnings. The unexplained portion of the intergenerational transmission of earnings is reduced by a nontrivial amount when the model is extended to incorporate personality traits. In addition, almost 11 percent of the intergenerational correlation in earnings is attributable to the familial similarity in personality. These estimates are found to be similar in magnitude to the contribution made by the inheritance of IQ, and larger than those found by Loehlin in this volume.[2] It is hoped that this research will improve our understanding of the intergenerational transmission of earnings.

THE INFLUENCE OF PERSONALITY ON EARNINGS

Psychology and sociology are at the forefront of research on the role of personality traits in the determination of personal and economic success. Traits such as the Big Five personality inventory as well as locus of control, impulsivity, machiavellianism, self-esteem, and emotional intelligence have been recognized for their ability to explain differences in educational attainment and occupational success.[3] For example, Jencks et al. (1979) and Filer (1981) have found that traits such as social sensitivity, sociability, emotional stability, self-control, culture, and leadership have statistically significant effects on earnings and occupational success, independent of schooling and cognitive performance. Also, Dunifon and Duncan (1998) and Andrisani and Nestel (1976) estimate that an individual's perception of control over outcomes has a statistically significant influence on various measures of occupational success, independent of the standard explanatory variables.

Economic research has also considered a more inclusive definition of skills, alluding to the importance of noncognitive, or psychological traits in the determination of earnings. For example, Bowles, Gintis, and Osborne (2001b) as well as Juhn, Murphy, and Pierce (1993) suggest that there are "skills" other than education, experience, and IQ, that are able to explain variance in earnings. They find that a large portion of the variance in earnings cannot be explained by standard human capital models of wage determination and, "seemingly irrelevant personal characteristics, including beauty, height, obesity, and even whether one keeps a clean house, are often robust predictors of earnings" (Bowles, Gintis, Osborne 2001b). Using specific personality traits, Osborne (2000), Heckman et al. (2000), Heckman and Rubinstein (2001), Edwards (1977) and Goldsmith et. al. (1997) all find that measured personality variables have significant influences on economic success. For example, using data from the United States and the United Kingdom, personality traits such as externality, aggression, and withdrawal have statistically significant influences on wages. In the United States, a one-standard deviation increase in externality—the belief that outcomes are the result of fate or luck rather than hard work—decreases wages by almost 7 percent while in the United Kingdom, a one-standard deviation increase in aggression or withdrawal is found to decrease wages by 7.6 and 3.3 percent, respectively (Osborne 2000). Additional support for the role of personality in earnings determination is found in Edwards (1977) and Goldsmith et al. (1997). Richard Edwards (1977) finds that a worker's loyalty and self-direction are statistically significant in regressions on wages and supervisor ratings independent of background and human capital variables. Also, Goldsmith et al. (1997) find that predicted values of self-esteem are statistically significant in wage determination equations and that a 10 percent increase in self-esteem improves real wages by almost 5 percent in 1980 and by 13 percent in 1987 (1997, 824). Heckman et al. (2000) and Heckman and Rubinstein (2001) also suggest a mechanism for how personality traits such as externality, aggression, self-esteem or self-direction influence labor market outcomes. They find that General Education Development (GED) recipients are not able to capture labor market rewards predicted by their cognitive performance and educational attainment because they are deficient in personality traits that are important for economic success. According to the authors, the GED sends a mixed signal to employers that recipients may lack specific desirable personality traits such as perseverance and self-discipline.

TRANSMISSION OF EARNINGS — STANDARD EXPLANATIONS

"Like father, like son."

Children resemble their parents in many ways, and economists have a long history of interest in the degree to which the economic outcomes of parents are mirrored in their children. A selection of recent estimates of the father-son intergenerational transmission of earnings in the United States are presented in table 7.1 and are found to range around 0.40 depending upon age, income measure, and measurement-error correction method.[4] While most researchers would agree that 0.40 indicates a high degree of persistence, or a low level of social mobility, there is little agreement about what explains the similarities or what should be done about parent-child similarities.

The human capital model focuses on the mediating roles of schooling and cognitive performance in explaining intergenerational similarities in earnings. In particular, much of the debate has focused on the mechanism by which each influences the transmission of earnings. While the returns to schooling are well accepted to range between 7 and 16 percent, it is not clear what accounts for these rewards and the mechanism by which schools explain the transmission of earnings.[5] Some researchers argue that schools mediate the intergenerational transmission of earnings because they are an indicator of cognitive performance. Arguably the most politically laced research on inequality and social mobility is that which focuses on the importance of cognitive performance in the intergenerational transmission of earnings, because such issues have been infused with controversy over the genetic heritability of cognitive measures. For example, Herrnstein (1973) and Herrnstein and Murray (1994) contend that a significant portion of intergenerational persistence is accounted for by the genetic transmission of IQ (1973, 206) and therefore, "School is not a promising place to try to raise intelligence or to reduce intellectual differences" (1994, 414).

Both education and cognitive performance are significant determinants of earnings, and help to explain the intergenerational transmission of earnings. A surprising amount of the variance in earnings and transmission of economic status, however, remains unexplained with the inclusion of these human capital variables.[6] While there is little agreement over the magnitude of influence each has on the transmission of earn-

TABLE 7.1
The Intergenerational Transmission of Earnings Between Fathers and Sons

Study:	Intergenerational Transmission	Measure of Earnings
Altonji and Dunn (1991)	0.18	Multiyear average lnY
	0.26	Multiyear average lnW
	0.27	Multiyear average ln family Y
Björklund and Jäntti (1997)	0.39	Son lnY and father five-year average lnY
Couch and Lillard (1994)	0.37	Son lnY and father four-year average lnY
	0.53	Son lnY and father five-year average lnY
Mulligan (1997)	0.32	Five-year average lnY
	0.33	Five-year average lnW
	0.48	Five-year average family Y
Peters (1992)	0.14	Multiyear average lnY
	0.24	Multiyear average family Y
Solon (1992)	0.41	Son lnY and father five-year average lnY
	0.29	lnW
	0.48	ln family Y
	0.48	Ratio of family Y to poverty line
Zimmerman (1992)	0.54	Son lnY and father four-year average lnY
	0.39	Son lnW and father four-year average lnW

Notes: Information for this table is taken directly from Solon (1999) and represents only studies using data from the United States. The intergenerational transmission is the elasticity of son's earnings with respect to parental income.

ings, it is well accepted that over 50 percent of the transmission of earnings is unaccounted for by cognitive skills and educational attainment.

PERSONALITY AND THE TRANSMISSION OF EARNINGS

While researchers may have long suspected that factors inside the household contribute to the transmission of earnings, it remains a difficult task to evaluate. To what degree do children resemble their parents, and what is it about families and what they teach their children that influences their children's earnings independent of educational attainment and measured cognitive performance? Personality offers a likely answer because of the high degree of heritability of personality traits (both genetic and environmental) and personality is relatively stable over time.

Current research estimates that the intergenerational correlation of personality traits is between 0.14 and 0.29 for various personality traits. Estimates from a selection of studies are presented in table 7.2.[7] While these intergenerational similarities are the result of both genetic and behavioral inheritance, there is little agreement in the literature as to the relative importance of these two factors. In this volume, Loehlin finds that across many different studies from the literature, average parent-child correlations for the Big Five personality traits range from 0.09 to 0.17, resulting in a mean heritability coefficient of 0.26.

Personality traits are also found to be stable over time, with test-retest correlations as high as 0.85, depending on the initial age of respondents and measure of personality. Using single personality traits, estimates of nine- to nineteen-year stabilities are estimated to be around 0.5 to 0.80,

TABLE 7.2
Intergenerational Correlation of Personality

Study:	Parent-Child Correlation	Personality Trait
Loehlin (this volume)	0.14	Extraversion
	0.13	Neuroticism
	0.11	Agreeableness
	0.09	Conscientiousness
	0.17	Openness
Carmichael and McGue (1994)	0.03	Extraversion
	0.27	Neuroticism
	0.25	Lie (social desirability)
Crook (1937)	0.29	Neuroticism
	0.22	Dominance
	0.15	Self-sufficiency
Insel (1974)	0.24	Extraversion
	0.21	Neuroticism
Loehlin (1992)	0.15	Big Five Inventory[a]
	0.18	Extraversion
	0.14	Emotional stability
Rowe (1993)	0.16	Extraversion

Notes: This table is a sample of the literature, and is presenting correlations between one parent and biological child.

[a] The Big Five Inventory includes neuroticism, extraversion, openness to experience, agreeableness, and conscientiousness.

with values slightly lower for respondents less than 20 years of age.[8]
Costa and McCrae (1997) also provide stability coefficients ranging
from 0.35 to 0.75 for recent longitudinal studies of personality inventories such as the NEO-PI, 16PF, GZTS, MMPI, and CPI, with test-retest
intervals between six and thirty years.[9] It has also been suggested that
these correlations underestimate the true stability because of measurement error that, when corrected, increases the stability of personality
inventories to more than 0.90 (Costa and McCrae 1997).

From the literature we know that the transmission of economic status
is a real phenomenon, one that is not fully explained by the transmission
of educational attainment, cognitive performance, or previously estimated factors of family background. We also know that there exist personality traits that parents pass on to their children that are likely to
influence children's choices and economic success. But, what remains
unknown is the magnitude of influence this similarity in personality has
on the intergenerational transmission of earnings. This chapter asks
what else is unique to a family that might be contributing to the high
degree of similarity between parents and children, and what is the magnitude of this behavioral influence on the intergenerational transmission
of earnings.

METHODS

This chapter uses data from the National Longitudinal Surveys (NLS)
sponsored by the Bureau of Labor Statistics of the U.S. Department of
Labor. These surveys are chosen because they contain large and nationally representative samples, information on personality traits, and allow
parents from the mature men cohort to be paired with their sons in the
young men cohort. Additional information on the data set is presented
in the appendix.

Using matched father-son pairs from the NLS, this chapter decomposes the intergenerational transmission of permanent earnings to investigate the influence personality has on this relationship. Starting from
an estimation of the relationship between fathers' and sons' permanent
earnings from the NLS data, we will consider three models of the mechanisms by which fathers' earnings influence the earnings of their sons.
The first two models investigate the influence that human capital variables have on the intergenerational correlation in earnings with and
without measures of cognitive performance. The final model is a behavioral model allowing us to evaluate the magnitude by which similarities
in personality account for the transmission of earnings.

Using matched father-son pairs from the NLS, the intergenerational transmission of permanent earnings ($b_{y'y}$) can be estimated from the earnings equation

$$\ln Y = \alpha_{0y} + b_{y'y}\ln Y' + \mu, \qquad (1)$$

where Y and Y' represent sons' and fathers' permanent earnings respectively, and where μ is the error term. For the United States (table 7.1), the elasticity of sons' earnings with respect to fathers' earnings (equal to $b_{y'y}$ because earnings are presented in natural log) is estimated around 0.40, with values depending on measurement error correction, form of earnings, and the age at which earnings are measured. To reduce the likelihood that the transmission of earnings is attenuated by these problems, variables are corrected for classical measurement error and the earnings of fathers' and sons' are multiyear averages to approximate more closely lifetime permanent earnings. Variables are assumed to be noisy measures and are corrected using reliability estimates from reports of identical information made by family members.[10] What makes children so similar to their parents? Current explanations focus on human capital variables such as cognitive performance and educational attainment to explain the familial similarities.

It has been argued that human capital variables such as school and job tenure (or similar measures such as age or experience) play strong mediating roles in the intergenerational transmission of earnings. In this human capital model, the relationship between fathers' and their sons' earnings can be represented as in figure 7.1, where the son's earnings equation is

$$\ln Y = \alpha_{0y} + b_{y'y}^{1}\ln Y' + b_{ty}T + b_{sy}S + \mu_{y}. \qquad (2)$$

The magnitude by which the human capital variables (tenure and schooling) mediate the intergenerational transmission of earnings can be measured as the degree of change in the standardized coefficient repre-

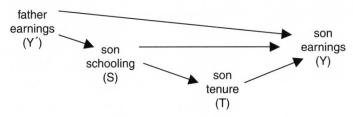

Figure 7.1 Human capital model.

senting the effect of fathers' earnings on sons' earnings $(b^1_{y'y})$ when controls are added for schooling and tenure. The portion of the elasticity of persistence that remains unaccounted for after including the indirect effects of schooling and tenure can be measured by theta, $\theta_1 = b^1_{y'y}/b_{y'y}$.

In addition to schooling and tenure, cognitive performance is believed to explain a portion of the transmission of earning, especially via education. Including IQ as a determinant of educational attainment, tenure, and earnings extends the model of transmission as shown in figure 7.2.[11] With this inclusion, the sons' earnings equation is,

$$lnY = \alpha_{0y} + b^2_{y'y}Y' + b_{ty}T + b_{sy}S + b_{iqy}IQ + \mu_y. \tag{3}$$

If cognitive performance explains a portion of earnings transmission independent of schooling and tenure, the coefficient on parents' earnings $(b^2_{y'y})$ will fall, and our estimate of the portion of the intergenerational correlation not accounted for by this extended human capital model $(\theta = b^2_{y'y}/b_{y'y})$ will decrease.

In addition to the human capital variables considered in figure 7.2, personality traits have been shown to be important determinants of occupational success and transmitted from parents to children. Therefore, personality is likely to serve as a mechanism by which earnings are transmitted across generations. Including personality in our model allows for a behavioral explanation of the intergenerational transmission of earnings, shown in figure 7.3.[12] This behavioral model also extends the sons' earnings equation to

$$lnY = \alpha_{0Y} + b^3_{y'y}Y' + b_{ty}T + b_{sy}S + b_{iqy}IQ + b_{py}P + \mu_y. \tag{4}$$

As done in the previous models, the portion of the intergenerational transmission of earnings that remains unaccounted for by the behavioral model $(\theta_3 + b^3_{y'y}/b_{y'y})$ can be estimated. It is believed that the contribution of personality, independent of the extended human capital model, will

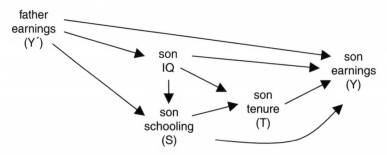

Figure 7.2 Extended human capital model.

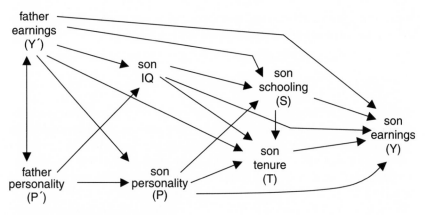

Figure 7.3 Behavioral model.

result in a lower remaining direct influence of fathers' earnings on sons' earnings ($b^3_{y'y}$) and a lower estimate of theta (θ_3).

The second objective of this chapter is to estimate the extent to which similarities in personality account for the transmission of earnings, which we will call omega ($\Omega_{p'p}$). This is estimated by decomposing the correlation between fathers' and sons' earnings so that the portion of the total correlation explained by the transmission of personality can be evaluated. The total correlation between fathers' and sons' earnings is, for the general case, $r_{yy'} = \sum_q \beta_{qy} r_{qy'}$ where β_{qy} is a normalized regression coefficient and $r_{qy'}$ is a simple correlation.[13] For the behavioral model, the total correlation is the sum of all standardized coefficients on variables predicting sons' earnings times their respective correlations with fathers earnings:

$$r_{y'y} = \beta_{y'y} + r_{y'iq}\beta_{iqy} + r_{y's}\beta_{sy} + r_{y't}\beta_{ty} + r_{y'p}\beta_{py}. \tag{5}$$

From the full decomposition (equation 7.A5 in the appendix) the portion of the total correlation that is explained by the father-son transmission of personality is

$$\Omega_{p'p} = r_{y'p}\beta_{p'p}(\beta_{ps}\beta_{sy} + \beta_{pt}\beta_{ty} + \beta_{py} + \beta_{ps}\beta_{st}\beta_{ty})/r_{y'y} \tag{6}$$

The role of similarities in personality in the transmission of earnings ($\Omega_{p'p}$) is therefore the ratio of all paths in our behavioral model that travel through both a father's and son's personality, to the total correlation in earnings (equation 5). To estimate the magnitude of $\Omega_{p'p}$, normalized regression coefficients are estimated from regressions on son's earnings, job tenure, schooling, and personality—models and regression results are presented in the appendix.[14]

RESULTS

This chapter utilizes perhaps the most widely used personality variable in sociological and economic research: the Rotter locus of control scale. Higher scores on the Rotter scale indicate that an individual is more external or fatalistic, believing that hard work and effort are not rewarded and rather it is luck, fate, or good fortune that determines success and achievement. Two econometric problems arose with the use of the Rotter score measured in 1968; the possibility that Rotter is endogenous to earnings, and that a portion of the variation in Rotter scores is age related. The question of endogeneity is addressed by reducing the sample to include only sons still in school in 1968 when the score was evaluated, assuring that Rotter scores were free from labor market influence. This sampling resulted in seventy-one observations with full information for which Rotter was truly exogenous to earnings. The estimates from this restricted sample were not found to be qualitatively different from the full sample of 195, therefore analyses use the larger sample. Descriptive statistics, correlations, and selected regression results appear in the appendix for comparison of the two groups. The possibility of age effects arises because personality measures are shown to be more stable after adolescence, and therefore a portion of the variance in Rotter can be explained by the age at which respondents are evaluated. To remove the influence of age, the Rotter score is regressed on age and the predicted residuals are used as an instrument for Rotter score, called Residual Rotter.[15]

Regression results using the 195 father-son pairs from the NLS and the Rotter Residual indicate that personality contributes to our understanding of the intergenerational transmission of earnings, and that parent-child similarities in personality explain a significant portion of the earnings transmission. Estimates of the contribution made from expansion of the transmission model are in table 7.3 along with estimates of theta for the human capital model, the extended human capital model, and the behavioral model.

The estimates in columns A and B of table 7.3 are consistent with the literature and indicate that almost 70 percent ($\theta_1 = 0.6988$) of the intergenerational transmission of permanent earnings is unaccounted for by tenure and schooling.[16] Comparing this with the final row in column C of table 7.3, we see that the unexplained portion of the transmission of earnings is reduced by less than 2 percentage points with the inclusion

TABLE 7.3
Reduced-Form and Full Models Predicting Sons' Earnings from
Fathers' Earnings to Estimate Theta (θ_i)

Variables:	Simple Transmission A b (t-stat)	Human Capital Model B b (t-stat)	Extended Human Capital Model C b (t-stat)	Behavioral Model D b (t-stat)
Fathers perm. lnY	0.249 (3.927)	0.174 (2.560)	0.170 (2.411)	0.160 (2.309)
Tenure		0.018 (1.907)	0.018 (1.882)	0.016 (1.863)
Education		0.072 (3.362)	0.068 (2.566)	0.067 (2.638)
IQ			0.0076 (0.178)	−0.0081 (−0.197)
Residual Rotter				−0.056 (−2.941)
Adjusted R^2	0.069	0.140	0.135	0.170
Theta ($\theta_i = b^i_{y'y}/b_{y'y}$)		0.6988	0.6827	0.6426

Notes: The dependent variable in all regressions is the natural log of sons' mean self-disclosed earnings between 1980 and 1981. Only unstandardized regression coefficients are presented here, but full results appear in the appendix. The residual Rotter is the Rotter measured in 1968 with age effects removed.

of cognitive performance. While a powerful predictor of educational attainment, cognitive performance explains very little of the transmission of earnings after controlling for the other human capital variables.

Estimates of the earnings equation from the behavioral model are presented in column D of table 7.3. The coefficient on the residual Rotter indicates that a one standard deviation increase in a son's measure reduces wages by over 13 percent ($b' = b_p\sigma_p = 0.131$). Personality is a statistically significant determinant of sons' earnings, and reduces the unexplained portion of the correlation in earnings from 68 to 64 percent. While this may seem a trivial decrease, remember that cognitive performance (IQ score) decreases the explained variance by only 2 percentage points. Personality makes a unique contribution to the explanation of familial similarities in earnings independent of cognitive performance, tenure, and schooling; however, a significant portion of the transmission of earnings remains unaccounted for by the full behavioral model.

The inclusion of human capital and personality variables improves

TABLE 7.4
Selected Regression Results for the Father-Son Estimation of $\Omega_{p'p}$

Variables	Earnings Equation β (t-stat)	Tenure Equation β (t-stat)	Schooling Equation β (t-stat)	Personality Equation β (t-stat)
Education	0.236 (2.638)	−0.097 (−1.040)		
IQ	−0.018 (−0.197)	0.091 (0.957)	0.595 (9.881)	
Tenure	0.125 (1.863)			
Residual Rotter	−0.200 (−2.941)	−0.117 (−1.672)	−0.056 (−1.039)	
Father perm. lnY	0.175 (2.309)	−0.190 (−2.466)	0.137 (2.293)	0.015 (0.160)
Parent Rotter				0.237 (2.592)
Adjusted R^2	0.170	0.118	0.456	0.055

Notes: Only standardized regression coefficients and t-statistics for variables relevant to the decomposition are reported; full regression results appear in the appendix. Residual Rotter is the Rotter measured in 1968 with age effects extracted. The number of observations in each regression is 195.

our understanding of the transmission of earnings, and indicates that a nontrivial portion of the transmission of earnings is mediated by personality and human capital variables (seen by the reduction of the direct effect from 0.249 to 0.160). While personality contributes to this explanation, the magnitude by which similarities in personality account for the transmission of earnings is unclear from the results in table 7.3. The magnitude by which personality similarities explain the intergenerational correlation in earnings is presented in equation 6 ($\Omega_{p'p}$), and estimates using the sample of matched father-son pairs from the NLS appear in table 7.4.

Using regression coefficients from table 7.4 and the correlation matrix presented in the appendix (where the total correlation in earnings ($r_{y'y}$) is 0.272 and the correlation between parents' earnings and Rotter score ($r_{y'p'}$) is −0.645), the estimate of omega ($\Omega_{p'p}$) is

$$\Omega_{p'p} = r_{y'p'}\beta_{p'p} (\beta_{ps}\beta_{sy} + \beta_{pt}\beta_{ty} + \beta_{py} + \beta_{ps}\beta_{st}\beta_{ty})/r_{y'y}$$
$$\Omega_{p'p} = -0.645(0.20)[-0.056(0.236) - 0.117(0.125)$$

$$- 0.20 - 0.056(-0.097)(0.125)]/0.272$$
$$\Omega_{p'p} = 0.0293/0.272 = 0.1077 \qquad (6)$$

The transmission of personality accounts for almost 11 percent of the father-son correlation in earnings, equivalent to estimates of the portion attributable to the inheritance of IQ estimated to range between 4.7 and 14.1 percent.[17]

Conclusions

This chapter uses a longitudinal, representative, and uniquely comprehensive data set to investigate how including a behavioral component influences the transmission of earnings. The main empirical results that arise from this research indicate that (1) controlling for human capital variables, personality makes a contribution to explaining the transmission of earnings from fathers to sons and (2) 11 percent of the total father-son correlation (or about one quarter of what we can explain) is accounted for by the transmission of personality.

Personality, as measured by the Rotter score, is an important factor in explaining similarities in the economic success of parents and their children. While schooling and cognitive performance are able to explain portions of the intergenerational transmission of earnings, together they explain only about 30 percent of the familial transmission. This chapter finds that personality is able to elucidate a significant mechanism by which families transmit economic status. The inclusion of personality, controlling for education, tenure, and cognitive performance, is estimated to reduce the unexplained portion of earnings transmission by 4 percentage points—more than twice that of cognitive performance. While an improvement, the results also indicate that over 60 percent of this transmission remains unaccounted for using this extended behavioral model.

Extending the human capital model to include a behavioral component is also found to make a significant contribution to our understanding of the intergenerational transmission of earnings. By decomposing the correlation between fathers' and sons' permanent earnings, the transmission of personality is estimated to account for 11 percent of the total transmission $(\Omega_{p'p})$, and almost 25 percent of what we can explain about the transmission of earnings. This finding is of significant magnitude, equivalent to the average findings on the proportion of the intergenerational transmission of earnings explained by the transmission of cognitive skills (Bowles and Nelson 1973). While human capital variables account for a significant portion of the transmission of earnings, it seems that the economic opportunities of children are limited by familial similarities in personality.

This research suggests that behavioral models of the transmission of earnings are able to explain significant proportions of the transmission of earnings not accounted for by human capital variables. While the Rotter score is no smoking gun, it increases our understanding of the correlation between fathers' and sons' permanent earnings and accounts for almost 25 percent of what we know about how earnings are transmitted from father to son. It is clear that researchers concerned with understanding and developing social policy related to economic mobility should be as concerned with the impact of the transmission of personality in the household as with the transmission of cognitive performance.

APPENDIX

This chapter uses data from the National Longitudinal Surveys (NLS) sponsored by the Bureau of Labor Statistics of the U.S. Department of Labor. These surveys are chosen because they contain large and nationally representative samples, information on personality traits, and allow parents from the mature men cohort to be paired with their sons in the young men cohort. Parent-child pairs are extracted from the data using the household identification number (variable number R300) provided in each sample. Members of the mature men cohort are between the ages of 45 and 59 in 1966, and individuals from the young men cohort are between the ages of 14 and 24 in 1966.

The personality variable evaluated in each of the data sets is the Rotter scale of externality (locus of control). The Rotter score measures the degree to which "the individual perceives that the reward follows from, or is contingent upon, his own behavior" (Rotter 1966, 1). Individuals measured to be more internal believe that they have control over their life and that success is the result of hard work and personal effort rather than luck, fate, or destiny. This research uses the singular Rotter score because it is designed to measure the degree of control one believes to have over his or her own life rather than measures including the degree of control over outcomes faced by others.

Two econometric problems arose with the use of the 1968 Rotter: (1) for some respondents in the young men cohort this evaluation was not exogenous to labor market experience and (2) variation in the Rotter score may in part be due to age effects. This first potential problem is addressed by comparing the estimates using all father-son pairs with full information with those from a smaller sample including only sons who were still in school when the Rotter was evaluated in 1968. Descriptive statistics and correlations for the smaller sample are presented in tables 7.A1 and 7.A3, respectively. Regression results are not qualitatively different for the two samples, with the larger group resulting in a smaller estimated coefficient on the Rotter score in earnings equations (see table 7.A5). Therefore, the results using the larger sample of father-son pairs are not upwardly biased by the possible endogeneity of personality and are chosen for analysis. The second potential problem is an age effect in the Rotter score. To remove the influence of age from the Rotter score, it is regressed on age and predicted residuals are used as a measure of Rotter free from age effects (what I call the Residual Rotter).

$$\text{Rotter68} = b_{AR}\,(\text{Age68}) + \mu_R$$
$$\text{Residual Rotter} = \text{Rotter68} - b_{AR}\,(\text{Age68}) = \mu_R$$

Variables of interest from parents include the log of father's permanent income created as the log of mean self-reported earnings from 1966–1968 (R0080200, R0134300) and the mean value of parents' Rotter scores measured in 1969 (R0160200, R0132900). In addition to this Residual Rotter is evaluated in 1968 when respondents are between the ages of 14 and 22, variables from the young men cohort (sons) include the quintile of IQ score in 1968 (R0171600), highest grade completed by 1976 (R044200), the log of son's permanent adult income (which is the log of mean self-disclosed earnings in 1980 and 1981 between the ages of 28 and 39 [R0635500, R0784700]), if son lived in the south in 1980–81 (R0640400, R0805800), race of son (R0002300), and tenure in current job in 1980 (created from R0601200). Responses with income equal to zero are not included. Descriptive statistics and correlations for all variables appear in the following paragraphs.

THE CORRECTION FOR MEASUREMENT ERROR

We know that observed variables are often measured with error where the observed measure of a variable (X_i) is the truth (X_i^t), with error (u_i):

$$X_i = X_i^t + u_i$$

Assuming that the errors are independently and identically distributed with zero mean and covariance $(E(\mu_i) = \text{cov}\,(X_i^t, \mu_i) = 0)$, then

$$\text{var}\,(X_i) = \text{var}\,(X_i^t) + \text{var}\,(u_i),$$

and the reliability of the observed measure (ρ_{Xi}) is the proportion of the variance in the observed measure accounted for by the variance in the true measure (Angrist and Krueger, 1998):

TABLE 7.A1
Descriptive Statistics for Seventy-One NLS Father-Son Pairs

Variables	Obs.	Min.	Max.	Mean	Standard Deviation
Parents:					
Log of permanent earnings	71	5.42	10.29	8.84	0.764
Rotter score	71	4.00	12.00	7.80	2.13
Sons:					
Log of permanent earnings	71	6.91	10.76	9.77	0.569
IQ quintile	71	1.00	5.00	3.25	1.40
Residual Rotter	71	−4.65	5.35	0.181	2.42
Education	71	9.00	18.00	13.92	2.06
Job tenure	71	0.00	15.00	5.73	3.99
Age	71	24.00	26.00	25.39	0.727
White	71	0.00	1.00	0.845	0.364

Notes: Descriptives are for parents and sons with full information and sons in school in 1968 when Rotter was evaluated. The Residual Rotter is the predicted error from regressing child Rotter on age, preventing the variance in Rotter from accounting for age effects.

TABLE 7.A2
Descriptive Statistics for 195 NLS Father-Son Pairs

Variables	Obs.	Min.	Max.	Mean	Standard Deviation
Parents:					
Log of permanent earnings	195	5.42	10.39	8.84	0.724
Rotter score	195	4.00	16.00	7.83	2.53
Sons:					
Log of permanent earnings	195	6.62	10.82	9.82	0.663
IQ quintile	195	1.00	5.00	3.30	1.47
Residual Rotter	195	−4.65	6.64	−0.161	2.34
Education	195	9.00	18.00	14.39	2.32
Job tenure	195	0.00	20.00	7.15	5.05
Age	195	24.00	34.00	28.08	2.69
White	195	0.00	1.00	0.841	0.367

Notes: Descriptives are for only matched pairs of parents and sons with full information. The Residual Rotter is the predicted error from regressing child Rotter on age, preventing the variance in Rotter from accounting for age effect.

TABLE 7.A3

Corrected Correlations for Seventy-One Father-Son Pairs from the NLS

	Parent Rotter	Father LnY	Son Educ.	Son Residual Rotter	Son LnY	Son IQ	Son White	Son Age	Son Tenure
Parent Rotter	0.622	-0.746	-0.287	0.763	-0.412	-0.096	-0.289	-0.019	0.159
Father LnY	-0.433	0.952	0.466	-0.253	0.353	0.489	0.484	0.035	-0.215
Son Education	-0.165	0.402	0.961	-0.404	0.317	0.560	0.249	-0.048	-0.369
Son Residual Rotter	0.295	-0.147	-0.232	0.622	-0.386	-0.349	0.059	-0.010	-0.190
Son LnY	-0.239	0.307	0.273	-0.224	0.952	0.202	0.036	-0.015	0.085
Son IQ	-0.057	0.433	0.492	-0.206	0.179	0.950	0.406	-0.297	-0.211
Son White	-0.180	0.452	0.230	0.037	0.034	0.386	1.00	-0.090	-0.320
Son Age	-0.012	0.033	-0.044	-0.006	-0.014	-0.282	-0.090	1.00	0.049
Son Tenure	0.094	-0.191	-0.324	-0.112	0.075	-0.190	-0.304	0.047	0.950

Notes: Correlations are only for matched parent-child pairs with full information and sons in school in 1968 when Rotter was evaluated. The Residual Rotter is the predicted error from regressing child Rotter on age, as previously discussed, to prevent the variance in Rotter from accounting for age effects. The number of observations for each correlation is 71. Values on the diagonal are correlations between true and observed variables. Uncorrected correlations appear in the lower-left quadrant while those corrected for measurement error appear in the upper-right quadrant. The data does not allow for estimation of all of the diagonal values; therefore, estimates for respondent's education and wages are taken from the paired responses with family members in other NLS data sets. Values for IQ are an average from the literature (Jensen 1980; Sternberg and Grigorenko 1997; Herrnstein and Murray 1994; Canivez and Watkins 1998), and exams are assumed to have a similar reliability. The reliability of respondents' SES is also an average from the literature (see Korenman and Winship 1999; Herrnstein and Murray 1994). Reliability estimates for Rotter are taken from five-year correlations during adulthood (1983, when respondents are ages 29–37, and 1988, when they are 34–52 years of age). These measures are higher than internal reliability measures estimated from the data, and within the range of reliabilities used in the literature (Andrisani and Nestel 1976; Applebaum and Koppel 1978; Duncan and Morgan 1981; Goldsmith et al. 1997).

TABLE 7.A4

Corrected Correlations for 195 Father-Son Pairs from the NLS

	Parent Rotter	Father Perm. LnY	Son Educ.	Son Residual Rotter	Son Perm. LnY	Son IQ	Son White	Son Age	Son Tenure
Parent Rotter	0.622	-0.645	-0.369	0.233	-0.269	-0.440	-0.479	-0.045	-0.029
Father Perm. LnY	-0.374	0.952	0.415	-0.141	0.272	0.455	0.419	0.023	-0.165
Son Education	-0.212	0.358	0.961	-0.195	0.329	0.668	0.146	0.135	-0.051
Son Residual Rotter	0.090	-0.082	-0.112	0.622	-0.283	-0.201	-0.161	-0.133	-0.130
Son Perm. LnY	-0.156	0.237	0.284	-0.164	0.952	0.254	0.108	0.143	0.111
Son IQ	-0.260	0.403	0.586	-0.119	0.225	0.950	0.425	-0.017	-0.042
Son White	-0.298	0.391	0.135	-0.100	0.101	0.404	1.00	-0.035	-0.159
Son Age	-0.028	0.021	0.125	-0.083	0.133	-0.016	-0.035	1.00	0.304
Son Tenure	-0.017	-0.146	-0.045	-0.077	0.098	-0.038	-0.151	0.289	0.950

Notes: Correlations are only for matched parent-child pairs with full information. The Residual Rotter is the predicted error from regressing child Rotter on age, preventing the variance in Rotter from accounting for age effects. The number of observations for each correlation is 195. Values on age are correlations between true and observed variables. Uncorrected correlations appear in the lower-left quadrant while those corrected for measurement error appear in the upper-right quadrant. See table 7.A3 for information on diagonal values.

TABLE 7.A5
Full Regression Results for Father-Son Pairs from the NLS

Variables	Earnings Equation Small Sample[a] b (t-stat) beta	Earnings Equation Full Sample[b] b (t-stat) beta	Tenure Equation Full Sample b (t-stat) beta	Schooling Equation Full Sample b (t-stat) beta	Rotter Equation Full Sample b (t-stat) beta	IQ Equation Full Sample b (t-stat) beta
Education	0.056 (1.334) 0.202	0.067 (2.638) 0.236	-0.239 (-1.040) -0.097			
IQ	-0.040 (-0.716) -0.099	-0.0081 (-0.197) -0.018	0.329 (0.957) 0.091	0.875 (9.881) 0.595		
Residual Rotter[c]	-0.056 (-1.830) -0.239	-0.056 (-2.941) -0.200	-0.251 (-1.672) -0.117	-0.049 (-1.039) -0.056		
Father Perm. lnY	0.208 (2.180) 0.280	0.160 (2.301) 0.175	-1.254 (-2.466) -0.190	0.368 (2.293) 0.137	0.047 (0.160) 0.015	0.454 (3.055) 0.247
Parent Rotter					0.219 (2.592) 0.237	-0.091 (-1.959) -0.164

TABLE 7.A5 (cont.)

Variables	Earnings Equation Small Sample[a] b (t-stat) beta	Earnings Equation Full Sample[b] b (t-stat) beta	Tenure Equation Full Sample b (t-stat) beta	Schooling Equation Full Sample b (t-stat) beta	Rotter Equation Full Sample b (t-stat) beta	IQ Equation Full Sample b (t-stat) beta
White						0.932 (3.442) 0.243
Tenure	0.022 (1.209) 0.153	0.016 (1.863) 0.125				
Age			0.577 (4.437) 0.308		−0.414 (−1.756) −0.123	
Adjusted R^2	0.190	0.170	0.118	0.456	0.055	0.277
Observations	71	195	195	195	195	195

Notes: The first column of equations is for the smaller sample of father-son pairs in which sons are in school in 1968 when Rotter was measured. The remaining columns are for the larger sample of father-son pairs with full information.

[a] The results from the smaller restricted sample (assuring that Rotter is exogenous to labor market experience) are not qualitatively different from the larger sample, and so the larger sample is used for analysis.

[b] The dependent variable is the natural log of sons' permanent earnings. Coefficients of interest are not qualitatively different from the inclusion of additional variables (race, age, parent Rotter, region) and their inclusion reduces the total explained variance of the model (R^2). Regression results including these variables are available from the author upon request.

[c] The Residual Rotter is the predicted error from regressing child Rotter of age, preventing the variance in Rotter from accounting for age effects. Results are not qualitatively different using either measure of child personality.

$$\rho_i = (\text{var } X_i^t / \text{var } X_i).$$

These reliabilities are used to correct the correlation according to the formula,

$$r_{i,j}^t = r_{i,j} / (\sqrt{\rho_i})\ (\sqrt{\rho_j}),$$

where r_{ij} is the uncorrected correlation, r_{xy}^t is the true correlation, and ρ_i and ρ_j represent the reliabilities for variables i and j, respectively (Munchinsky 1996; DuBois 1965; Carmines and Zeller 1979).

Because the variance of the true measure is unknown, the reliability cannot be estimated as written. Instead, the reliability is estimated from the correlation between two observed (X_{i1} and X_{i2}) measures. Knowing that the correlation between true and observed measures is equal to the square root of the proportion of the variance in the observed measure accounted for by the variance in the true measure, and assuming classical measurement error,[18]

$$r_{i1,i2} = (r_{i1,it})(r_{i2,it}).$$

and $r_{i1,it} = r_{i2,it}$, therefore,

$$r_{i1,i2} = (r_{i1,it})^2 = (\text{var } X_i^t / \text{var } X_i).$$

We can therefore replace ρ_i and ρ_j with $r_{i1,i2}$ and $r_{j1,j2}$ and correct the correlation matrix as,

$$r_{i,j}^* = r_{i,j} / (\sqrt{r_{i1,i2}})\ (\sqrt{r_{j1,j2}}).$$

REGRESSION MODELS TO ESTIMATE OMEGA ($\Omega_{p'p}$)

$$Y = \alpha_{0Y} + \beta_{y'y}Y' + \beta_{ty}T + \beta_{sy}S + \beta_{iqy}IQ + \beta_{py}P + \mu_y \qquad \text{(A7a)}$$

$$T = \alpha_{ot} + \beta_{st}S + \beta_{pt}P + \beta_{iqt}IQ + \beta_{y't}Y' + \beta_{zy}Z + \mu_t \qquad \text{(A7b)}$$

$$S = \alpha_{0S} + \beta_{y's}Y' + \beta_{iqs}IQ + \beta_{ps}P + \mu_s \qquad \text{(A7c)}$$

$$P = \alpha_{0P} + \beta_{y'p}Y' + \beta_{p'p}P' + \beta_{zy}Z + \mu_p \qquad \text{(A7d)}$$

When additional exogenous variables (Z) are included to assure coefficients, they are not subject to omitted variable bias.[19] Regression model for the IQ equation is not presented because IQ is contemporaneous to sons' personality and therefore its relationship to the transmission of personality cannot be evaluated. Full results for the IQ equation are presented in Table 7.A5.

THE DECOMPOSITION OF THE INTERGENERATIONAL CORRELATION IN EARNINGS

The correlation between parent and child earnings is decomposed to estimate the portion of the correlation in earnings that is accounted for by the transmission of personality. Equation 5 in the chapter decomposes the correlation to the sum of all standardized coefficients predicting sons' earnings times their respective correlations with fathers' earnings. From this point, each of the remaining correlations can be further decomposed as shown in equation A5:

$$
\begin{aligned}
r_{yy'} = {} & \beta_{y'y} + r_{y'iq}\beta_{iqy} + (\beta_{y's} + \beta_{yiq}\beta_{iqs} + \beta_{y'p}\beta_{ps} + r_{y'p}\beta_{p'iq}\beta_{iq} + r_{y'p'}\beta_{p'p}\beta_{ps})\beta_{sy} \\
& + (\beta_{y't} + \beta_{y'p}\beta_{pt} + r_{y'p'}\beta_{p'p}\beta_{pt} + \beta_{y'iq}\beta_{iqt} + r_{y'p'}\beta_{p'iq}\beta_{iqt} + \beta_{y's}\beta_{st} + \beta_{y'iq}\beta_{iqs}\beta_{st})\beta_{ty} \\
& + (\beta_{y'p} + r_{y'p'}\beta_{p'p})\beta_{py} \tag{A5}
\end{aligned}
$$

NOTES

1. Father-son pairs are used because they constitute the largest matched parent-child set with full information. Classical measurement error assumes that errors are independently and identically distributed with zero mean and covariance $(E(\mu_t) = \text{cov}\,(\eta_t, \mu_t) = 0)$.

2. These results are different from Loehlin (this volume) because he uses different personality traits, and this research uses measurement error correction to properly account for the low reliabilities of personality variables.

3. The Big Five personality inventory is discussed in greater detail by Loehlin in this volume and includes neuroticism, openness to experience, extroversion, agreeableness, and conscientiousness. See also Hogan, Hogan, and Roberts (1996), Barrick and Mount (1991), Tett et al. (1991), Schmidt, Ones, and Hunter (1992). For locus of control (Rotter scale) see Duncan and Morgan (1981), Dunifon and Duncan (1998), Rotter (1966), and Andrisani and Nestel (1976). Machiavellianism is a combination of a lack of emotional affect in interpersonal relations, a lack of concern for traditional morality, and low ideological commitment; see Turner and Martinez (1977) or Gable and Dangello (1994). For impulsivity (delay of gratification), see Mischel (1974) or Mischel, Shoda, and Rodriguez (1992); and for emotional intelligence, see Goleman (1995).

4. See for example, Zimmerman (1992), Solon (1992), Solon (1999), Mulligan (1997) and Behrman and Taubman (1995) who have slightly higher estimates of the intergenerational correlation using Panel Study of Income Dynamics (PSID) data.

5. Earlier studies such as Griliches and Mason (1972) and Jencks et al. (1979) estimate the returns to education to be around 5 percent; however, more recent estimates (see Ashenfelter and Zimmerman 1997) tend to be higher because of corrections for measurement error. Also, recent estimates of the returns to education are significantly higher than the returns to ability or intelligence tests. Correcting for measurement error in ability scores, Griliches and Mason (1972) find that increasing an individual's AFQT score by 10 percent increases earnings by only 1 percent. Murnane et. al (1995) estimate that the return to a one-standard deviation change in education is almost ten times larger than mathematics scores, and Cawley et. al (1996) write, "The return to a standard devia-

tion of 'g' is rivaled by that to two years of education, and can be offset by region or residence and local unemployment rates," where "g" is a measure of general intelligence (18).

6. Bowles, Gintis, and Osborne 2001b.

7. This transmission of personality from parent to child occurs through heritability (shared genetics) and shared environment in a quantifiable manner ($0.5rh^2 + pc$); however, there is little consensus about the relative influence of each.

8. The single personality traits include items such as extraversion, neuroticism, sociability, ascendance, anger, anxiety, orderliness, and diligence (Carmichael and McGue 1994; Conley 1984; Stein et al. 1986).

9. NEO Personality Inventory, 16 Personality Factor Questionnaire, Guilford-Zimmerman Temperament Survey, Minnesota Multiphasic Personality Inventory, and the California Psychological Inventory.

10. Detailed information on the correction for measurement error is presented in the appendix.

11. You will notice that an arrow is placed between parents' earnings and sons' IQ measure. This does not mean that parents literally buy their children's intelligence measures, but they can purchase services that help boost scores (SAT preparation courses, for example). This arrow is also included because measures of parental IQ are not available in the data, and so earnings are serving as a proxy for measures of parental intelligence.

12. One arrow worth noting is the link from parents' personality to child IQ. It is hypothesized that parents can act in many ways to improve their child's performance on intelligence tests. In this case, parents who are more external may not be as likely to see the benefits of exam preparatory courses as parents who are more internal—therefore linking parental personality and the child's performance on intelligence tests.

13. The standard notation, $r_{ij} = \sum_q \beta_{qi} r_{qj}$ is taken from Duncan (1971, 121) and is also used by Bowles and Nelson (1973, 41).

14. Equations are presented as A7a–A7d in the appendix, and full regression results are presented in table A5.

15. A full explanation of this process can be found in the appendix.

16. Estimates of the elasticity of sons' earnings with respect to fathers' earnings are consistent with findings by Solon (1999), especially considering that sons are between 28 and 39 years of age when permanent earnings are measured.

17. See Bowles and Gintis (2001) and Bowles and Nelson (1973).

18. This process is identical to that used by Bowles and Nelson (1973).

19. The inclusion of exogenous variables (race and age), where theoretically sensible, does not contribute to the decomposition of earnings and are included only to assure that coefficient estimates are not biased from omitted variables.

Chapter Eight

SON PREFERENCE, MARRIAGE, AND

INTERGENERATIONAL TRANSFER

IN RURAL CHINA

Marcus W. Feldman, Shuzhuo Li, Nan Li,
Shripad Tuljapurkar, and Xiaoyi Jin

RURAL Chinese society has historically been dominated by a rigid male-centered patrilineal family system, and virilocal marriage remains overwhelmingly dominant. Under this system, parents call in a daughter-in-law for each of their sons, and all sons are entitled to stay home after marriage and coreside with their parents for a period of time until family division occurs or until both of their parents pass away. A son's offspring use his father's surname to continue the family lineage. Family property is usually inherited equally among all sons, and sons are obliged to take care of their parents in their old age. By contrast, parents marry all of their daughters to other families, and these daughters as well as their future descendants are no longer regarded as the members of their natal families. All rights, productivity, and services of daughters are transferred to their husbands' families at the time of marriage, and they can neither inherit their natal family's property nor do they have any formal obligation to take care of their natal parents in old age (Das Gupta and Li 1999).

The patrilineal family system produces strong preference for sons and various forms of discrimination against daughters (Skinner 1997; Lavely et al. 2001). Son preference has been strong throughout the histories of various Asian countries, including China, Korea, and India (Dyson and Moore 1983; Das Gupta and Li 1999). In China, the phenomenon of "missing females," which existed more or less throughout the first half of the twentieth century, was exacerbated in periods of war and famine but became less serious in the 1960s–1970s (Coale and Banister 1994; Das Gupta and Li 1999).

The Chinese government has adopted a national government-guided population-control policy, which has been changing through the years. In the early 1970s, a couple was encouraged to have fewer children.

Since the early 1980s, however, couples in urban areas have been allowed to have only one child, while those in rural areas were encouraged to have one child. Those couples who could demonstrate hardships because of having only one child (e.g., not enough male laborers for agricultural fieldwork or not having a son to support them in their old age) were allowed to have an additional child three to five years after the first birth. For minorities, the policy is less strict. Since the late 1970s, a dramatic socioeconomic transition driven by economic reform and by the opening up of the country, as well as a strict population-control policy, has resulted in rapid fertility decline, with the total fertility rate dropping from 5.81 in 1970 to 1.85 in 1995. Sustained low fertility has also intensified the manifestation of son preference, as evidenced both in a rising sex ratio at birth (SRB) and in deteriorating female infant survival. For instance, SRB in China increased from 107 in 1980 to 118 in 1995, and the ratio of male to female infant mortality declined from 1.06 in 1981 to 0.75 in 1995 (Li S. and Zhu 2001).

Many studies have examined the temporal trends and regional variation in the degree to which the SRB in China is biased (Hull 1990; Johansson and Nygren 1991; Wen 1993; Zeng et al. 1993; Gu and Roy 1995; Tuljapurkar et al. 1995; Poston et al. 1997). In general, high SRB promises to be a growing problem for Chinese society, in terms of the low status of women and girls, imbalance in the future marriage market, and potential social conflicts (Hull 1990; Zeng et al. 1993; Tuljapurkar et al. 1995; Das Gupta and Li 1999). According to the Fifth National Population Census of China (taken in the year 2000), about 18.76 percent of the men aged 15 and over are never married, while for women this proportion is only about 13.75 percent. Chinese governments at various levels have been cognizant of this problem and since the early 1990s have adopted various measures to control the increase of SRB. The continuous increase in SRB since the 1990s suggests, however, that these measures have yet to be effective. In this low fertility regime, son preference plays an important role in the increase of China's SRB. It is, therefore, unlikely that government controls such as those adopted in China, or rapid economic development like that which occurred in South Korea, will change the strong son preference in the short term (Park and Cho 1995; Das Gupta and Li 1999).

Sustained low fertility has also resulted in accelerated population aging in China. According to the Fifth National Population Census of China in 2000, the population of China is 1,295,330,000, the proportion of people aged 0 to 14 is 22.89 percent, that of people aged 15 to 64 is 70.15 percent, and that of people aged 65 and above is 6.96 percent. Compared with Fourth National Population Census in 1990, the proportion of people aged 0 to 14 has declined 4.80 percent, while that of people aged 65 and above has increased 1.39 percent. Although the proportion of the population that lives in rural areas has declined from 73.77 percent in 1990 to 63.91 percent in 2000, the proportion of older people in rural areas is even higher than that in urban areas. The 2000 census shows that, in rural areas, the proportion of people aged 0 to 14 is 25.49 percent, that of people aged 15 to 64 is 67.16 percent, and that of people aged 65 and above is 7.35 percent, while these relative proportions in urban areas are 18.43 percent, 75.27 percent, and 6.30 percent respectively. Thus, the rural population has a greater burden in raising children and supporting the elderly. Related to this is old-age security, an issue that is rapidly becoming important in rural China. A reliable pension system with broad coverage has not been established in rural China, while income is not high enough for most rural couples to save for their old age (Yu 1996). That children should show filial piety to, and be responsible for the support of, their elderly parents is a widely accepted personal value and community norm in traditional Chinese culture (Ganschow 1978). In addition, relevant laws in China protect old people's legal interests and rights, and define the norm of family responsibility for elder care (Davis-Friedmann 1991).

The 1994 Annual Population Change Survey conducted by China's State Statistical Bureau shows that for 57 percent of the elderly, children or relatives provide the main source of income, 25 percent have their own income, and 16 percent live off pensions. For rural areas, however, the corresponding values are 64, 29, and 4 percent, respectively (Du and Wu 1998). Further, the 1990 census showed that 72.5 percent of the elderly coresided with their children in extended families (Du 1998). As a result, family support for the elderly, primarily provided by adult children, is and will continue to be the dominant form of care for the elderly in rural areas in the foreseeable future (Shi 1993; Gu et al. 1995; Xu and Yuan 1997). The general nature of the patrilineal family system and characteristics of virilocal marriage shape the gender pattern of old-age support. It is usually sons in a family, but not daughters, who provide necessary support for their older parents (Xu 1996; Yang H. 1996). This inevitably intensifies the existing son preference.

On the other hand, sustained low fertility has resulted in a rapidly rising proportion of couples without a son, whose old-age support in the future faces a serious challenge (Li, S., et al. 1998, 2002c). Calling in a son-in-law for one of their daughters (uxorilocal marriage) could be a realistic choice in order for these couples to continue the family lineage and secure their old age. There may be a tremendous potential demand for adoption of uxorilocal marriage in rural China. Wider practice of uxorilocal marriage may not only alleviate son preference, since uxorilocal marriages secure old age for the daughter's parents as well as guaranteeing the survival of the family name, but may also change power structures and improve women's status within the family (Li, S., and Zhu 1999; Jin and Li 2001; Jin et al. 2002). However, the strength of the patrilineal family system and the high psychological cost related to uxorilocal marriage, together with the low proportion of no-son families in populations with high fertility, have all resulted in uxorilocal marriage being historically rare throughout rural China (Wolf 1989; Chuang and Wolf 1995).

Most studies of son preference in China have focused on the manifestations of son preference, not on son preference itself (Arnold and Liu 1986; Xie 1989; Li, J., and Cooney 1993; Wen 1993; Poston et al. 1997; Graham et al. 1998). Although researchers have realized the important role played by culture in shaping fertility patterns and behaviors (Hammel 1990; Pollak and Watkins 1993), and have suggested that it would be fruitful to investigate communication of attitudes toward and behaviors in childbearing among members of a population (Bongaarts and Watkins 1996), less attention has been paid to the dynamics of son preference in China, especially its formation, transmission, and evolution, and its quantitative impact on SRB as well as its relationship to diversity of marriage forms and old-age security.

Over the past twenty years, theoretical research on cultural transmission and evolution has received considerable attention in academic circles. Several scholars have developed quantitative models for complex transmission and evolution of people's behaviors, attitudes, beliefs, and habits (Cavalli-Sforza and Feldman 1981; Cavalli-Sforza et al. 1982; Chen et al. 1982; Kumm et al. 1994; Laland 1994; Laland et al. 1995). These models provide a useful framework to address human behaviors related to son preference and other social issues. Thus, cultural transmission theory may provide an appropriate framework in which to address the transmission and evolution of attitudes and behaviors surrounding son preference, as well as their effects on actual childbearing behaviors and SRB.

Other chapters in this volume have focused on the transfer of wealth and status between generations primarily in the United States. These statistical analyses have often used techniques similar to those in behavior genetics, with regression playing an important role. Familial aggregation of wealth and status is reported in terms of estimated heritability, which can be regarded as a measure of intergenerational transmission but may also confound genetic and cultural effects. In the present study, we are interested in attitudes toward sons and daughters, what are the antecedents of these attitudes, and how attitudinal bias is translated into behaviors that discriminate against female children. These attitudes are transmitted not only within nuclear families, but within whole clans and perhaps even larger population units. The perceived inequality in the value to families (and clans) of sons and daughters translates into an important and growing sex ratio imbalance in the whole country. Intergenerational cultural transmission of this bias varies across China but for the most part results in a continuing deficit in the number of girls born. In this basic demographic sense, sons and daughters certainly have unequal chances.

Over the past five years, the Population Research Institute of Xi'an Jiaotong University in China and the Morrison Institute for Population and Resource Studies of Stanford University in the United States have jointly conducted a project on son-preference culture, marriage, and intergenerational transfer in rural China. The project uses survey data combined with theories of cultural transmission and evolution to analyze the dynamic relationship among son preference, SRB, marriage form, and intergenerational transfer in rural China. The study includes three parts: measurement of son preference and the analysis of its transmission and evolution, especially its quantitative effects on SRB; transmission and determinants of uxorilocal marriage and its relationship with son preference; marriage form and intergenerational transfer. Here we review some of the theory we have developed and the results of our surveys.

MODELS AND ESTIMATES OF SON PREFERENCE

In exploring the interaction of son preference and fertility decline on the increase in SRB, we identify two aspects of women's childbearing situation. The first, largely determined by fertility, is the *sex-selection pressure* (y), which is the probability of the random event Y, that a woman is in the *sex-selection situation*, namely, that she has no son and is able to have only one more child. Second, we define *son-preference potency* (p), as the probability that a woman has a sex-selected son, given that she is in the sex-selection situation. Obviously, son preference here is defined in terms of a woman's childbearing behavior rather than attitudes, and depends on the extent of son preference in her family, including her husband and herself.

Sex-selection pressure driven by fertility decline is a demographic effect, while son-preference potency reveals the relationship between cultural factors and individual behaviors. Thus, the factors leading to an increase in SRB are of two types: rising sex-selection pressure caused by fertility decline (y), and son-preference potency (p) determined by the economic and cultural background of a population. To formulate a relationship between son preference and SRB in the context of rural Chinese society, we make the following simplifying assumptions (Li, N., et al. 1998a, 1999): (1) sex selection is done only by women who have no previous son and are able (or permitted) to have only one more child; (2) fertility is constant over a long time; and (3) there is no mortality in the reproductive ages.

Then we have the following relation:

$$SRB = (TFR * s_0 + p * y) / (TFR - p * y), \qquad (1)$$

where TFR represents women's total fertility rate, s_0 represents normal SRB (usually about 1.05), and SRB is the observed sex ratio in the population.

Thus, the probability p of having a sex-selected son for a couple in the sex-selection situation depends on their social and cultural background. The complementary probability, $p_N = 1 - p$, is the probability that a couple have the trait of no son-preference, denoted by π_0. A couple who have trait π_0 will not have a sex-selected son when they are in the sex-selection situation. We focus on trait π_0 and its probability p_N.

The decision to have a sex-selected son for a couple in the sex-selection situation may be regarded as the result of the transmission of ideas from their parents or neighbors, or acquisition of information from outside the community about why a son is necessary. Differences in decisions made by couples in different generations may be interpreted in terms of the extent of transmission of cultural trait π_0 across generations. Although it is difficult to characterize this process of transmission in detail, its effect on changes in the value of p_N can be clarified using the general theory of cultural transmission (Cavalli-Sforza and Feldman 1981). According to this theory, individuals from a younger generation acquire the cultural trait π_0 from their parents at a vertical transmission rate C_v, given that their parents have this trait. They may also acquire π_0 from members of an older generation at an oblique transmission rate C_o, or horizontally from the mass media at a rate M_0, if their parents do not have trait π_0. For technical reasons, we assumed $C_v = C_o$.

We have constructed a dynamic demographic model including cultural transmission of son preference (Li, S., et al. 2000; Li, N., et al. 2000) and applied the model to data collected in surveys of two counties in Shaanxi province: Lueyang and Sanyuan. These surveys were carried out in 1997. In 2000 we extended the survey to include questions about intergenerational transfer of financial assistance between children and parents as well as assistance with housework and field labor. The 2000 survey was carried out in Songzi county, in Hubei province.

Sanyuan county is located in the central part of Guanzhong plain in central Shaanxi province, close to the Wei River and only 30 kilometers away from Xi'an city. The county's population was close to 390,000 in

1997. Sanyuan is rich in fertile land and its food industry has been famous in Shaanxi throughout history. Private and township enterprises
developed extensively after the 1980s, absorbing many surplus farm-
laborers. Per capita income for farmers in Sanyuan, however, is still
much lower than that for China as a whole. Sanyuan is regarded as one
of the origins of the Han Chinese population and culture, and it retains
the core elements of the traditional Yellow River culture. Because this
county is located on a plain, large family clans exist in almost every
village and are influential in village social life. Villages maintain a strict
patriarchal family system with patrilocal marriage.

Lueyang county is located in the Qing mountains in the far south of
Shaanxi province, far from Xi'an, on the borders of Sichuan and Gansu
provinces. It has a relatively small population of about 200,000. Before
the Tang dynasty, Lueyang was occupied mostly by minority Chinese
who were defeated by the Han Chinese, and most were forced to migrate
to other places. In the late seventeenth century, the Qing government
forced people in central China, where the population was dense, to migrate to southern Shaanxi, including Lueyang. Lueyang has been rich in
natural resources, especially minerals and forests. Even though its per
capita arable land is much higher than in Shaanxi and China as a whole,
Lueyang is relatively underdeveloped compared with other counties in
Shaanxi, and the standard of living is low. Most of its arable land is
mountainous and infertile, and the population relies heavily on the forests, especially wild products. The difficult conditions require hard
labor, mostly by men. In recent years, raising mushrooms has become
the major cash producer. Because Lueyang is mountainous, the size of
villages is relatively small and the ancestors of most residents were immigrants from other areas; as a result, large family clans in Lueyang are
few and unimportant to village life. The culture of Lueyang is that of
southern Shaanxi, for which the patriarchal family system is somewhat
weaker than in Sanyuan.

Songzi, located on Jianghan Plain in southwest Hubei province on the
southern side of the Yangtze River, had a population of 896,800 at the
end of 1999. Songzi is a relatively well-developed agricultural county
with fertile land that has produced the famous "Babao Cotton" for hundreds of years. The economy is based on this high-quality cotton and
related enterprises. The favorable local climate and many lakes and res-
ervoirs support production of fruit and timber as well as aquiculture. In
addition, enterprises run by villages or towns, and private ones run by
farmers, that involve agricultural by-products, textiles, and mining, are
expanding. In the late Qing Dynasty, the swampland near a riverbank
in the southeast of the county gradually became farmland, which at-
tracted many new settlers. Thus, about half of the current residents are

outsiders whose arrival is recent enough that there are few dominant family clans. As a result, the patrilineal family system in Songzi is not rigid.

Generally, minorities are rare in the three counties, whose ethnic compositions are similar; that is, the proportion of Han Chinese is overwhelming. As a result, the family planning policies in the three counties are very similar. Lueyang and Songzi, however, have fewer children per couple than does Sanyuan, and for years the former counties have been more advanced in terms of population control.

In the surveys, cluster sampling was used to select survey sites and couples. That is, in each county, we first selected one township, and then a number of neighboring administrative villages within this township, until the number of couples was more than 1,500. In Sanyuan, about 1,567 households including 1,866 couples living in 23 natural villages were included in the survey. In Lueyang, about 1,364 households, including 1,581 couples living in 46 natural villages, were included in the survey. Many measures were used to ensure the quality of interviews. There were about fourteen invalid questionnaires, and some responses had missing items, but the proportion was low. In addition, re-interviews were conducted by supervisors, and the overall proportion of inconsistent items was about 7.4 percent. The data were entered into a Foxpro database, and we randomly selected 10 percent of the data to check the accuracy and quality of data entry. The proportion of items with input error was less than 1 percent. Tests were also made for logical inconsistencies. In short, every measure was carefully implemented to ensure the quality of the field interviews, data entry, and data themselves. Errors were present but at an acceptable level, and the data can be regarded as reliable and of satisfactory quality.

Detailed information about the three counties and the surveys is available in Li, S., et al. (1998) and Jin et al. (2002).

Table 8.1 reports the numbers of births and SRB by birth cohort in the three counties. Clearly, since the 1990s there has been strong son

TABLE 8.1
Number of Births and Sex Ratio at Birth, by Birth Cohort in the Three Counties

Birth Cohort	Sanyuan		Lueyang		Songzi	
	Number	SRB	Number	SRB	Number	SRB
1930s–70s	2,394	92.4	1,854	98.5	2,024	107.8
1980s	1,324	102.8	1,039	106.6	991	106.0
1990s	891	119.5	678	96.5	589	89.4

Source: Li, S., et al. (1998), Jin et al. (2002).

TABLE 8.2
Estimated Son-Preference Potency, Sanyuan and Lueyang

County	All Women	15–29	30–44	45+
Sanyuan	0.44	0.50	0.40	0.35
Lueyang	0.08	0.06	0.03	0.20

Source: Li, N., et al. (1998b).

preference in Sanyuan but not in Lueyang or Songzi. Our surveys revealed that this SRB difference reflected differences in attitudes toward girls.

The models of son preference described earlier and the survey data permitted estimates of son-preference potency and transmission of bias disaggregated by age group in Lueyang and Sanyuan. The estimated son-preference potencies for the two counties are shown in table 8.2, while the coefficients of transmission of no preference are in table 8.3 (Li, N., et al. 1998b).

Table 8.2 shows that son-preference potency in Lueyang is extremely weak, but that it is strong in Sanyuan. These explain the high SRB in Sanyuan and the normal SRB in Lueyang.

The results reported in table 8.3 are consistent with those of table 8.2 and show that cultural transmission rates of no son-preference are higher for Lueyang than for Sanyuan. Again, this highlights that high SRB is a result of son preference, and that this preference is the result of a process of transmission. The transmission rates of no son-preference are declining in both counties, in other words, transmission rates of son preference are increasing. Thus, under the recent and current regime of low fertility, the transmission of son preference in rural China has been accelerating, leading to an increase in son-preference potency and hence in SRB (Li, N., et al. 1998b).

TABLE 8.3
Transmission Coefficients of No Son-Preference, Sanyuan and Lueyang

County	Coefficient	15–44	15–29	30–44
Sanyuan	C_V & C_O	0.50	0.24	0.59
	M_0	0.36	0.46	0.38
Lueyang	C_V & C_O	0.89	0.88	0.92
	M_0	0.94	0.79	0.97

Source: Li, N., et al. (1998b).

An important issue that has also drawn extensive attention from the government and general public concerns future trends in son preference and SRB. To explore this question, we incorporated the estimated parameters from Sanyuan and Lueyang into our demographic model with cultural transmission of son preference for the whole of China, so as to predict the future of son preference and SRB in China (Li, N., et al. 2000). First, we used data from the 1990 Population Census to estimate various initial values of cultural and population variables to use in the models for China. Then, similar to conventional high, medium, and low population projections, we assumed that a "good" situation of cultural transmission of son preference for China is similar to that in Lueyang, and a "bad" situation is similar to that in Sanyuan. That is, we used our estimated coefficients of cultural transmission of son preference in Sanyuan and Lueyang as the two possible scenarios for the whole of China. The details are described in Li, N., et al. (2000). The estimated trend for SRB is shown in figure 8.1.

Figure 8.1 reveals that if son preference in China were transmitted at rates characteristic of Lueyang, son preference would gradually decline, and SRB would become normal at equilibrium. If son preference were transmitted at rates characteristic of Sanyuan, SRB would increase to 130–135 in the long run. Under the following two conditions, the predictions using Sanyuan's parameters seem more plausible for the future of the whole of China. The first is stable fertility and the second is that the current sex-selective abortion rate remains unchanged. Applying the transmission rates of Lueyang to all of China seems too optimistic, since it would require acceptance of uxorilocal marriage throughout rural China. However, if a reliable and broad pension system were estab-

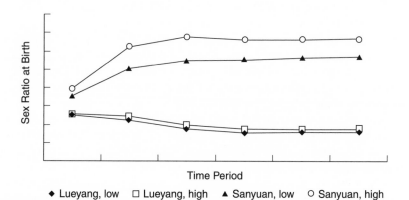

Figure 8.1 Simulated sex ratio at birth (SRB) for China's future. *Source:* Li, N., et al. (2000).

lished, or if people were willing and able to save enough for their old age, it would be possible for SRB to approach the normal value in the long run. Under such circumstances, a son would no longer be necessary to support parents financially, and, as in Lueyang, in-coming sons-in-law could provide old-age support for parents (Li, N., et al. 1998b).

MARRIAGE

Diversified Marriage Form

Why is son preference much stronger in Sanyuan than in Lueyang and Songzi under similar family planning implementation and similar levels of fertility? We claim the reason lies in the extent of acceptance and practice of uxorilocal marriage.

Marriages in rural China may be broadly classified into two categories: virilocal, where the wife leaves her natal family and moves to her husband's family; and uxorilocal, where the husband leaves his natal family and moves to that of his wife. Throughout the history of China, among Han Chinese, virilocal marriage has been almost universal while uxorilocal has been rare. Location of postmarital coresidence reflects the core elements of the rural Chinese patrilineal family system, and virilocal marriage is perceived to ensure the purity, integrity, and continuity of the family (Li, S., et al. 2000, 2001). The family system and marriage customs have been changing to some extent, but virilocal marriage remains overwhelmingly dominant in contemporary rural China (Lavely and Ren 1992) and even in big cities such as Beijing (Guo and Chen 1999).

In China, social and political status determine the mode of mate selection in the process of union formation. For the former, the better educated are also likely to enjoy a higher degree of occupational prestige; for the latter, party members and those who come from "good" families have greater potential to succeed both professionally and economically. Although people voluntarily seek out those who are like themselves (homogamy), some heterogamy always exists (Xu, X., et al. 2000). In a society where the patriarchal and patrilineal family system is practiced, some hypergamy (in which women marry up in status) is expected. In uxorilocal marriage, however, the man, rather than the woman, usually marries up since the most common cause for him to enter his wife's family is the poverty of his natal family.

With the change of assortment in the social and political status systems caused by the profound sociopolitical transformations under state socialism, patterns of assortative mating have changed (Xu, X., et al.

2000). For those couples who married before 1977, assorting by political status might have been more usual than by social status; for those who married in the economic reform era after 1978, level of education has become increasingly important. In Songzi we found that during the Cultural Revolution (between 1966 and 1976) many men whose family class-origins were "bad" married up by adopting uxorilocal marriage to elevate their status. In recent years, however, homogamy has become more common in uxorilocal marriage. More men with higher education or who come from richer families adopt uxorilocal marriage, while families calling in sons-in-law are beginning to take the family status of the other party into account in the process of choosing husbands for their daughters.

Although cultural factors defining the patrilineal family system play a decisive role in determining marriage type, demographic and economic factors may also affect an individual family's decisions, leading under some conditions to uxorilocal marriage. Uxorilocal marriage driven by demographic factors occurs in families without a son or in those that for various reasons are unable to adopt a son, and has been called "contingent" by Wolf (1989). To ensure continuity of the family lineage and for security in their old age, parents usually call in a son-in-law for one of their daughters, and either the son-in-law assumes his new family's surname as an adopted son, or one of the son-in-law's sons is assigned this family's surname to carry on the lineage. In this case, uxorilocal marriage is mainly preservative, to maintain the family lineage (Pasternak 1985), and the husband in such a uxorilocal marriage is in essence a kind of "male daughter-in-law." In a society governed by a rigid patrilineal family system, however, uxorilocal marriage usually entails high costs and stigma in terms of both individual and familial status and is therefore looked down upon by most rural communities (Pasternak 1985; Wolf 1989; Li, S., et al. 2000, 2001). Men who enter such a marriage are usually from very poor families that have more than two sons and cannot afford marriages for all their sons (Pasternak 1985). The general properties of the patrilineal family system, the high psychological costs of uxorilocal marriage, and the low proportion of son-less families in populations with high fertility, have resulted in uxorilocal marriage being rare throughout rural China. In most of the country the frequency of demographically driven uxorilocal marriages is less than or equal to that of son-less families.

Uxorilocal marriage driven by other nondemographic, mostly economic, considerations occurs in families that have at least one son but face economic constraints, including a shortage of male labor, marriage costs such as bride-price and dowry, or need for old-age support, etc. (Li, S., and Zhu, 1999; Li, S., et al. 2000, 2001). Uxorilocal marriage occurs in families deficient in male labor, where calling in a son-in-law is a means of increasing the number of male laborers in the family (Pasternak 1985; Li, S., et al. 2000); in relatively poor families, because the cost of uxorilocal marriage is inexpensive for all parties involved (Pasternak 1985); or in a family that badly needs a diligent worker who is predicted to acquire wealth, because a son-in-law coming from the outside is usually perceived as able to make more money than the natives of his adopted county (Li, S., et al. 2000, 2001). In this case, uxorilocal marriage is mainly a practical resolution of economic and other difficulties in families that already have at least one son. Wolf (1989) calls uxorilocal marriage in these situations "institutional." In general, this kind of uxorilocal marriage is rare across rural China, although it has been reported as prevalent in a few Chinese rural areas at different times. In these cases, the proportion of uxorilocal marriages is much higher than that of son-less families (Pasternak 1985; Wolf 1989; Han 1992; Chuang and Wolf 1995; Yan, M., 1995; Yan, M., and Shi 1996).

Our surveys show that the distribution of marriage forms differs in the three counties (Li, S., et al. 1998; Jin et al. 2002). In Sanyuan, virilocal marriage is overwhelmingly dominant at about 90 percent while uxorilocal marriage is rare at about only 4 percent, close to the proportion of son-less families. In Lueyang, however, the proportion of virilocal marriage is 58 percent and that of uxorilocal marriage about 32 percent. In Songzi, the corresponding proportions are 75 and 21 percent, respectively. That the frequencies of uxorilocal marriage in Songzi and Lueyang exceed those of son-less families suggests that both contingent and institutional uxorilocal marriages occur in these counties.

Uxorilocal Marriage in Lueyang and Songzi

In Lueyang and Songzi, as has historically been the case in most rural areas in China, adoption of uxorilocal marriage usually entails a written or oral contract between the incoming son-in-law and his wife's parents before marriage. A typical contract contains four elements (Li, S., and Zhu 1999). The first concerns the surname of the in-coming son-in-law. Generally, his surname is changed to his wife's, and he is regarded as an adopted son. The second concerns his children's surname. Customarily, the first child will use his or her mother's surname and the second the father's surname, ensuring that the surnames of both families are passed on. The third concerns marriage costs including bride-price and dowry, and here the bride-price of an incoming son-in-law is less than usual or totally waived. The fourth addresses old-age support of the wife's parents and inheritance of her family's property in the future. Conventionally, the incoming son-in-law is obliged to support his parents-in-law and has the right to inherit their family property. In practice, the contents of such contracts change with family structure and attitudes of family members, and differs among families (Li, S., and Zhu 1999). With recent socioeconomic changes, people do not care as much about the contract or issues related to the son-in-law's surname as in the past. Moreover, an incoming son-in-law and his children do not necessarily have to use his wife's surname. In other words, the practice of uxorilocal marriage has become more flexible than in the past.

We found that uxorilocal marriage in Lueyang and Songzi is not only a contingent variant of the Chinese patrilineal family system but also an institutional option for farmers, a phenomenon rarely observed in Han areas of rural China. In addition to the earlier mentioned individual and family considerations, acceptance of uxorilocal marriage is also closely related to the community settings of Lueyang and Songzi (Li, S., and Zhu 1999; Li, S., et al. 2000; Jin and Li 2001). First, uxorilocal marriage has historically been prevalent in Lueyang and Songzi. As an individual option for farmers, it has become part of the local community's cultural norms. Second, large family clans are not strong and their impact on members' marriage decisions is weak. Third, there are fewer community restrictions on adoption of uxorilocal marriage and less discrimination from the community against incoming sons-in-law. Further, that some infertile women in Lueyang's high mountainous areas are more likely to adopt daughters actually creates demand for uxorilocal marriage.

Individual and family factors underlying uxorilocal marriage are not the only reasons for the prevalence of uxorilocal marriage as an institutional option, since these factors also operate in other rural areas of China. The special community tolerance of uxorilocal marriage related to local sociocultural and geographic characteristics is also very important.

Cultural Transmission of Uxorilocal Marriage

Data from the 1997 survey were used to estimate the extent of cultural transmission of uxorilocal marriage in Lueyang. Marriage cohorts in Lueyang were classified into two groups: before 1978 and after 1978, so as to investigate the impact of rural economic reform on the intergenerational transmission of uxorilocal marriage (Li, S., et al. 2000). Applying the vertical cultural transmission model developed by Cavalli-Sforza and Feldman (1981), we obtained estimates of transmission parameters shown in table 8.4.

Table 8.4 shows that there exist positive transmission effects from parents to sons and daughters and positive nonparental transmission effects for the marriage cohort prior to 1978, and that the latter are more important than the former. Since 1978, the coefficients of nonpa-

TABLE 8.4

Vertical Transmission of Uxorilocal Marriage by Marriage Cohort, Lueyang

Husband's Parents' Marriage	Wife's Parents' Marriage	Before 1978		1978 and After	
		Frequency of Pair	Transmission Coefficient	Frequency of Pair	Transmission Coefficient
Uxorilocal	Uxorilocal	14	0.64	60	0.15
Uxorilocal	Nonuxorilocal	57	0.44	114	0.25
Nonuxorilocal	Uxorilocal	74	0.53	147	0.43
Nonuxorilocal	Nonuxorilocal	427	0.29	570	0.28

Source: Li, S., et al. (2000).

rental transmission have changed little while the coefficients of parental transmission have declined greatly. Further, for the marriage cohort after 1978, transmission effects from parents to daughters are positive, but those from parents to sons are negative, and nonparental transmission effects are larger than parental transmission effects. Maximum likelihood estimates of coefficients of additive vertical transmission (Cavalli-Sforza and Feldman, 1981) for marriage cohorts before and after 1978, including a_h for husband's parents, a_w for wife's parents, and a_0 for nonparents are shown in table 8.5 and are consistent with those in table 8.4.

Tables 8.4 and 8.5 suggest that rural economic reform has had little effect on nonparental transmission of uxorilocal marriage but has had strong effects on parental transmission in Lueyang. Rural economic reform since 1978 has resulted in the collective production team being replaced by the household as the basic production unit. Also there is increased mobility of farmers, and an increased circle of potential marriage partners. These have produced dramatic changes in individual and social life for farmers and have affected farmers' choices of marriage type and marriage arrangement. As a result, parental and nonparental

TABLE 8.5

Maximum-likelihood Estimates of Additive Models of Vertical Transmission of Uxorilocal Marriage, Lueyang

Marriage Cohort	a_0	a_h	a_w	χ^2	p	Number of Cases
Through 1977	0.29	0.15	0.24	0.06	>0.80	572
1978 and after	0.30	−0.11	0.08	9.89	<0.01	891

Source: Li, S., et al. (2000).

transmission of uxorilocal marriage in Lueyang are affected (Li, S., et al. 2000, 2001).

Comparison of Determinants of Uxorilocal Marriage

Logistic regression analyses (see table 8.6) show that the determinants common to the two types of uxorilocal marriage are household demographic structure, membership in large family clan, and attitude toward a man's uxorilocal marriage. For both contingent and institutional types, a husband with more brothers is more likely to engage in an uxorilocal marriage, while a wife with more siblings is less likely to engage in such a marriage. Membership in a large family clan reduces a couple's likelihood of accepting a uxorilocal marriage; a couple with a positive attitude toward uxorilocal marriage is more likely to engage in such a marriage. The observed effects are stronger for contingent than for institutional uxorilocal marriage.

The most important contributor to acceptance of institutional uxorilocal marriage in Lueyang is the parental marriage type. Table 8.4 showed that uxorilocal marriage in Lueyang is transmissible within a household and that the transmission itself has been affected by rural economic reform (Li, S., et al. 2000). Actually, only institutional uxorilocal marriage is transmissible within the household while its contingent version is not, and the transmission of institutional uxorilocal marriage is also affected by the changing social and household environment, as represented by the effect of rural economic reform on institutional uxorilocal marriage after 1978 in Lueyang. An institutional uxorilocal marriage is more likely to occur between a wife with a relatively high education level and a husband with a relatively low education level. Among couples in institutional uxorilocal marriages, the wife is more likely to have married early and to be an adopted daughter, and the husband is less likely to be an adopted son. These results also confirm that institutional uxorilocal marriage in Lueyang is mostly determined by individual and household status.

It should be noted that Lueyang is a special county, where both contingent and institutional uxorilocal marriages are common. The determinants of acceptance of contingent uxorilocal marriage reported in Lueyang, however, are basically consistent with those found in Sanyuan, a typical Chinese county, where uxorilocal marriage has been rare but most uxorilocal marriages are contingent. With sustained low fertility and an increasing proportion of son-less families, contingent uxorilocal marriage is expected to increase greatly across rural China in the foreseeable future, to provide family support for the elderly who are not covered by any social security system.

TABLE 8.6

Effects of Household and Individual Determinants on the Odds Ratios of Being in Institutional and Contingent Uxorilocal Marriage, Lueyang

Explanatory Variables	Institutional			Contingent		
	Gross Effects	Net Effects		Gross Effects	Net Effects	
		Model I	Model II		Model I	Model II
Household Factors						
Parental marriage type						
Husband's parental marriage, Uxorilocal	0.73	0.78	2.19*	1.05	1.13	1.16
Wife's parental marriage, Uxorilocal	1.88***	1.80**	3.32***	1.28	1.30	1.32
Number of siblings						
Husband's brothers						
1	1.22	1.29	1.32	2.45*	2.65*	2.65*
2+	2.35***	2.49***	2.50***	3.59***	3.68***	3.69***
Husband's sisters						
1	0.85	0.81	0.81	1.02	0.98	0.98
2+	0.74	0.75	0.74	1.24	1.17	1.17
Wife's brothers						
2+	0.56***	0.56***	0.56***			
Wife's sisters						
1	0.54**	0.59**	0.59*	0.39**	0.45*	0.45*
2+	0.46***	0.51***	0.51***	0.27***	0.30***	0.30***
Large family clan						
Yes	0.49+	0.46+	0.44+	0.10*	0.09*	0.09*
Individual Factors						
Marriage year						
1978+	0.74*	0.84	1.27	1.10	0.85	0.86
Age at marriage						
Husband						
20–24	0.85	0.75	0.78	1.25	1.15	1.15
25+	1.16	0.95	0.94	1.07	0.98	0.98
Wife						
18–22	0.64*	0.64*	0.66*	0.64	0.51*	0.51*
23+	0.50**	0.52*	0.55*	0.49+	0.57	0.57
Education						
Husband's education						
1–6	0.58**	0.71+	0.73	0.79	0.92	0.92
7–9	0.35***	0.53*	0.52*	0.54	0.73	0.73
10+	0.23***	0.33*	0.33*	0.43	0.42	0.42

TABLE 8.6 (*cont.*)

Explanatory Variables	Institutional			Contingent		
	Gross Effects	Net Effects		Gross Effects	Net Effects	
		Model I	Model II		Model I	Model II
Wife's education						
1–6	1.16	1.18	1.15	1.88*	1.92	1.92+
7–9	1.53+	1.56	1.55	2.46*	4.22	4.23**
10+	4.08***	4.87***	4.75***	4.99	9.63*	9.63+
Adoption						
Husband's adoption						
Yes	0.42*	0.47+	0.44	0.65	1.00	1.00
Wife's adoption						
Yes	2.21**	1.95*	2.03*	2.19**	1.57	1.57
Marriage Arrangement						
Self-arranged	0.81	0.87	0.88	0.55*	0.33**	0.33**
Attitude toward a man's uxorilocal marriage						
Acceptable without a son	0.73*	0.75+	0.76+	1.11	0.97	0.97
Unacceptable no matter what	0.34**	0.46+	0.48+	0.30*	0.21*	0.21*
Interactions						
HPMU[a] × M78+[b]			0.21***			0.95
WPMU[a] × M78+			0.39*			0.98
−2LL		1086***	1066***		394***	394***
Number of cases	1108	1108	1108	343	343	343

Notes: All variables are dummy categories. The mean equals percent relative to the omitted categories in the table, which are as follows: parental marriage type, nonuxorilocal marriage; number of siblings, 0; large family clan, no; marriage year, before 1978; age at marriage, 19– for husband and 17– for wife; education, 0; adoption, no; marriage arrangement, introduced; attitude toward uxorilocal marriage, acceptable no matter what.

[a] HPMU and WPMU, husband's or wife's parents are in uxorilocal marriage.

[b] M78+, marriage cohort 1978 and after.

*p < 0.05. **p < 0.01. ***p < 0.001. +p < 0.1

Source: Li, S., et al. (2002d).

INTERGENERATIONAL TRANSFER

Measurement of Intergenerational Transfer

As mentioned before, the patrilineal family system in rural China shapes the gender-based pattern of children's support for their older parents. Under this system, intergenerational transfer between parents and sons is greater than between parents and daughters, and is characterized by reciprocity over a longer period (Greenhalgh 1985). Parents usually invest greatly in sons in terms of their education, marriage, etc., and expect later repayment by being supported by their sons in their old age. By contrast, parents usually invest less in daughters in terms of their education, marriage, etc., and expect daughters to repay them before marriage by doing housework and taking care of younger siblings, etc. While a daughter's moral obligations may continue after marriage, her formal obligations to her parents end at the time of marriage (Greenhalgh 1985; Yang, H., 1996). Although dramatic social and economic transformations in rural society have brought about some changes in the traditional patrilineal family system and gender-based pattern of children's support for their older parents, the essential gender-dependent mode of old-age support remains dominant. Currently, sons are expected to provide primary support for their older parents, while daughters tend to provide supplementary support for their parents through emotional connection, care in daily life, etc. This has been reported in a few studies of old-age support in mainland China and Taiwan (Freedman et al. 1978; Lee et al. 1994; Xu 1996; Yang, H. 1996).

The intergenerational transfer addressed in our survey of Songzi includes only mutual financial transfers, housework, and agricultural labor assistance between children and their non-coresiding parents in 2000. The main reason for restricting attention to *non-coresiding* parents is that in rural China, married children coresiding with and sharing the same household economy as their parents would automatically provide economic and noneconomic help for them. In the survey, children who have separated from parental families were no longer regarded as coresiding with parents, even though they may actually have resided with their parents within the same courtyard or under the same roof.

Likelihood of Children's Help to Parents

Logistic models were employed to analyze the likelihood that children of different gender and marriage forms would provide old-age support for parents, where control variables include individual characteristics of children and parents (Li, S., et al. 2002c).

The results are shown in table 8.7 and suggest that children's proximity to their parents greatly affects their likelihood and amount of old-age support for their parents. Parents who are further away from their children tend to be less likely to receive housework and agricultural fieldwork help from their children. If parents reside within Songzi, those residing further from their children are more likely to receive financial help from these children, but the amount of financial help is the same. Parents residing outside Songzi are the least likely to receive financial help from children, and the amount of financial help is lowest. It seems that the effect of proximity on provision of support for the elderly is very important in determining substitution among various modes of intergenerational transfer. This finding is consistent with those from studies on effects of living arrangements on children's support for the elderly (Yan, S., et al. 2001).

An important finding is that while children's gender and type of marriage have significant influences on their likelihood of providing financial and housework help for parents, these factors do not affect the amount of financial support from children for parents or children's likelihood of giving agricultural fieldwork help to parents. Specifically, sons in uxorilocal and daughters in virilocal marriages are more likely to provide financial support for older parents, and daughters, especially those in uxorilocal marriages, are more likely to provide housework help for older parents. It is difficult to determine from among all types of children who actually provides more total help for their parents. It is obvious, however, that sons in virilocal marriages provide relatively less help for their parents than do other types of children.

Couples in virilocal marriages are more likely to provide financial and household support for the wife's parents. Couples in uxorilocal marriages are more likely to provide financial help for the husband's parents and housework support for the wife's parents. In other words, support from a couple in virilocal marriage is biased towards the wife's natal parents, while support from a couple in uxorilocal marriage is more balanced between their both sets of parents. As to whether virilocal couples or uxorilocal couples are stronger in support of their non-coresiding parents, our results do not give a clear answer. Our previous studies on family division, however, showed that couples in uxorilocal marriages tend to coreside longer and leave the parents later than do couples in virilocal marriages (Li, S., et al. 2002a, 2002b). Considering that in rural China couples who coreside with their parents usually share the same household economy, they would naturally provide necessary old-age support for their parents. In this context, provision of old-age support should not be worse for couples in uxorilocal marriages than for those in virilocal marriages. In fact, it may be better.

TABLE 8.7

Estimated Child's Odds Ratios of Giving Various Help to Parents in Logistic Model for Songzi

	Gross Help			Net Help		
Variable	Financial	Housework	Agricultural Fieldwork	Financial	Housework	Agricultural Fieldwork
Child Gender and Marriage						
Son/Virilocal	1.00	1.00	1.00	1.00	1.00	1.00
Son/Uxorilocal	2.39**	1.30	0.72	1.67+	1.29	0.71
Daughter/Virilocal	3.39***	1.68*	1.23	1.67**	2.01*	1.13
Daughter/Uxorilocal	0.64	3.07**	1.08	0.64	3.25**	0.92
Child Characteristic						
Age	1.02	0.98	0.99	1.01	1.01	1.00
Education	1.10*	0.99	0.98	1.09**	0.98	1.00
Number of brothers	1.16*	1.05	1.10	1.15**	1.08	1.08
Number of sisters	1.13*	0.96	1.01	1.19***	0.96	1.02
Household economy	1.11**	1.02	0.90*	1.11**	1.05	0.95
Number of offspring	0.93	0.66*	1.11	0.94	0.69+	1.06
Parent Characteristic						
Parent alive						
Both alive	1.00	1.00	1.00	1.00	1.00	1.00
Only father alive	1.10	1.25	0.73	1.09	1.52	0.92
Only mother alive	1.03	0.93	0.96	1.13	0.95	1.19
Age	0.99	0.99	1.00	1.01	0.98	1.01
Residence						
Local village	1.00	1.00	1.00	1.00	1.00	1.00

	(1)	(2)	(3)	(4)	(5)	(6)
Local township	1.44	0.77	0.47***	1.40+	0.92	0.56**
Local county	1.68*	0.33***	0.21***	1.55*	0.40**	0.33***
Other county	0.59+	0.21**	0.08***	0.67	0.25*	0.11***
Coresiding with other children	1.18	0.97	1.34	0.96	0.98	1.19
Children main source of income	2.35***			2.09***		
Can do housework						
Yes	1.00	1.00			1.00	
Partly	0.90	0.90			1.08	
No	0.92	0.92			0.94	
Can do agricultural fieldwork						
Yes			1.00			1.00
Partly			0.60**			0.83
No			0.37***			0.50***
Giving financial help to child	3.98***	1.40+	1.15			
Giving housework help to child	1.31	3.30***	2.00***			
Giving agricultural fieldwork help to child	0.80	1.57*	5.52***			
Ever helped child with child care	1.28	1.47*	1.02	1.00	1.29	1.07
-2LL	1128***	946***	1127***	1436***	768**	1226***
Number of cases	1,152	1,152	1,152	1,152	1,152	1,152

Notes: *$p < 0.05$. **$p < 0.01$. ***$p < 0.001$. +$p < 0.1$.
Source: Li, S., et al. (2002c).

The final conclusion of our study on effects of children's gender and marriage form on their provision of old-age support to parents in Songzi is that daughter's support of their elderly parents is not weaker, but may be stronger, than that of sons. Similarly, old-age support to parents for couples in uxorilocal marriages is not weaker, but may be stronger, than that of couples in virilocal marriages. In other words, in Songzi, daughters and sons are equivalent; both can carry out the family obligation and social responsibility of providing old-age support for parents and carrying on the family name for generations.

Conclusions

Intergenerational transfer has been of three kinds in the studies reviewed here. First, we have cultural transmission of attitudes toward the sex of a child manifested most widely across China as son preference. Second, we have seen transmission of marital form—virilocal or uxorilocal—across generations. This transmission is influenced by socioeconomic reforms and by local social structures in the form of large family clans. The third class of intergenerational transfers reverses that traditionally studied by Western economists in that it concerns what children provide for their parents. There is a delicate balance between the kinds of marriage and residential proximity in determining whether this upward transfer is in money or services. It is also interesting that reciprocity in transfers plays an important role beyond that of parents providing nurturance for growing children. Central to these considerations at least in the counties of China we have studied is the kind of marriage pattern approved of by the society.

There appear to be three family functions of uxorilocal marriage in Lueyang and Songzi: continuation of family lineage, old-age support, and provision of labor. In fact, virilocal marriage also has these functions, but the transfer of female laborers in virilocal marriage is not as significant as that of male laborers in uxorilocal marriage. Furthermore, virilocal marriage serves mainly the husbands' natal families, while uxorilocal marriage in Lueyang and Songzi is institutional, providing functions that are effective for both sets of natal families (Li, S., and Zhu 1999; Jin and Li 2001). Uxorilocal marriage functions socially to promote social mobility and the flow of human resources, and also to reduce son preference within families and communities. This is because although son preference reflects women's low status in their families and communities under the patrilineal family system, it also reflects farmers' practical demand for continuing their family lineage, providing male laborers and old-age security. The bilateral family functions of uxorilocal marriage to some extent resolve these practical problems. Thus, couples without a son may call in sons-in-law for their daughters to substitute for sons. Moreover, uxorilocal marriages are relatively egalitarian, which helps weaken son preference (Li, S., and Zhu 1999; Jin and Li 2001).

Our findings have important implications for the present and future of rural Chinese society. While the sustained low fertility in rural China accelerates population aging, rapid increase in the proportion of son-less families seriously challenges the traditional model of family support for the elderly, which relies fundamentally on sons. Further, low fertility and concomitant demand for old-age security intensifies the age-old son preference and decreases the survival rates of female children, as evidenced by a high sex ratio at birth and excess female child mortality (Das Gupta and Li 1999). However, in Songzi and Lueyang, the previously mentioned problems are not so serious, even though fertility is low. Songzi, for example, has almost reached zero population growth and may be regarded as providing a glimpse of the future population in rural China. However, in these places where both virilocal and uxorilocal marriages have been historically accepted and practiced, son preference is weak, sex ratio at birth is normal, and parents can receive adequate support for their old age from both sons and daughters in various marriage forms. In other words, son-less couples in Songzi can also count on their daughters and sons-in-law for their old-age security. Thus, promoting acceptance and practice of uxorilocal marriage on a large scale in areas with low fertility and a relatively high proportion of son-less families may be one of the important ways to resolve problems related to old-age security and son preference. Our viewpoints here are basically in agreement with those of other scholars on this issue (Yang, Y. 1998; Yan, M., et al. 1999; Lu 2001).

Of course, Lueyang and Songzi are unique in rural China, and broader acceptance of uxorilocal marriage may take a long time. The increasing proportion of son-less couples resulting from low fertility, however, indicates a great potential demand for uxorilocal marriage through which to provide old-age support. Sufficient increase in demand for uxorilocal marriage may overcome the resistance of the traditional patrilineal family system and community norms, and bring about important changes in marriage customs and the mode of family support for the elderly in rural areas. Community initiatives and governmental assistance could facilitate and accelerate this change (Yan, M., et al. 1999).

Chapter Nine

JUSTICE, LUCK, AND THE FAMILY

The Intergenerational Transmission of Economic

Advantage From a Normative Perspective

ADAM SWIFT

MANY regard it as unfair that a person's prospects should depend on her parent's position in the distribution of advantage. Inequalities of outcome are sometimes justified, but their being so depends on their being the outcome of a competition played on a more or less level playing field, in which all participants had something approximating equal opportunity for success. But, as parents, we seem morally justified in acting partially to further the interests of our children, at least to some extent (Nagel 1991), and few of those who value equality of opportunity argue that the family should be abolished. Now, some of the mechanisms producing the intergenerational persistence of inequality may be morally suspect, and suspect in a way that would justify attempts to deter or prevent them. Others may be legitimate, perhaps even morally required. This chapter suggests a framework for thinking about which are which.

That the family hinders the attainment of equality of opportunity is widely acknowledged by political philosophers (Rawls 1971; Fishkin 1983; Valentine and Lipson 1989; Munoz-Darde 1999). Discussion has, however, remained rather general, with little attention paid to the particular routes through which parents exert their influence—for good or ill—over their offspring's position in the distribution of advantage. Not content with measuring the degree of intergenerational association, social scientists are now engaged in the challenging task of unpacking the various causal mechanisms that produce it. Philosophers need to do something analogous, opening the black box that is "the family" to investigate in detail—and with proper attention to their variety and specificity—the moral issues raised by the things that parents do to, with, or for their children.

Developments within both social science and political philosophy increase the urgency of this task. On the empirical side, economists in the

United States have recently revised their assessment of the gross association between the incomes of parents and children. The better that association is measured, the bigger it gets. With this revision economists are, in effect, coming to hold a view about the continuing significance of intergenerational transmission in advanced industrial societies that has long been the conventional wisdom among sociologists—especially European sociologists whose tendency to conceive mobility as occurring between discrete class positions, rather than up or down a scale of income or socioeconomic status, has hindered comparison of the findings of the two research traditions (Erikson and Goldthorpe 1992, 2002; Marshall et al. 1997). As Bowles and Gintis (2002) note, previous estimates of the extent of intergenerational transmission encouraged viewing the United States as "the land of opportunity." Given this more accurate assessment, the question of what, if anything, should be done about it inevitably assumes greater importance.

But it is not simply that choosing the right parents turns out to matter more than some had thought. There has also been an increased understanding of *how* parents exert their influence. The empirical contributions to this volume seem to suggest that direct transmissions of property, and the use of economic resources to procure competitive advantage for children, are less important than many had believed. We should understand parental influence primarily to occur through other mechanisms, mechanisms that, I will suggest, can helpfully be regarded as constitutive of the family, or of the children raised in them (or of both). That does not, of course, rule out policies intended to equalize opportunities between those born to less or more advantaged parents. There remain strategies that leave families intact and seek to mitigate, neutralize, or compensate for their unequalizing effects. But it does show how deep runs the problem of reconciling the family and equality of opportunity. And it directs our attention to the question of precisely what aspects of the family should be respected.

An important development on the philosophical side has been the emergence of an approach to distributive justice sometimes known as "luck egalitarianism." Although internally heterogeneous (cf. Cohen 1989; Dworkin 2000; Arneson 2000), rejected by many political philosophers (e.g., Anderson 1999), and out of step with public opinion (Marshall et al. 1999; Swift 1999) this view—that inequalities resulting from responsible choices are just, while those due to factors beyond people's control are not—has been an important influence on much recent work on equality of opportunity. Luck egalitarianism takes seriously the intuition that it is unfair for people to be better or worse off than one another simply because of their good or bad fortune in the natural lottery, the social lottery, or indeed any lottery that they did not choose to enter

(Fleurbaey [1995, 1998] and Roemer [1998, 2000] are likely to be congenial to economists). In the current context, it is noteworthy that two of the most telling objections to luck egalitarianism direct our attention to issues raised by the intergenerational transmission of inequality.

First, it is claimed that people may deserve unequal rewards that are indeed, at least in part, the result of differential luck, as long as the luck in question can be understood as constitutive, as constituting them as the individuals they are (Hurley 1993; Miller 1999). It may be a matter of chance that some and not others possess, for example, particular genetic traits that, developed in particular environments, happen to be command a high price in the market that happens to operate at a particular place and time. But people's genetic material is constitutive in a way that makes it inappropriate to regard the return to that kind of chance as undeserved and available for redistribution on justice grounds. It is clear that one's parents play a key role in constituting one as the person one is, and not merely genetically, and so the processes by which parents transmit advantage or disadvantage to their children, and the extent to which such processes are indeed constitutive of the people their children become, is clearly, from this perspective, a crucial issue.

Second, the redistributive implications of luck egalitarianism are extremely demanding. It thus raises in especially sharp form the question of how far individuals are justified in giving special weight to their own interests and whether there are any spheres of "private" activity immune from its demands. Even G. A. Cohen, whose variant of the doctrine is particularly severe and pervasive, accepts a prerogative that limits the claims of justice, allowing individuals to pursue their own self-interest, rather than the well-being of the unluckily badly off, to some reasonable extent (1995). Whatever the precise limits of that extent, it is likely to include some element of concern for one's children. And, in any case, concern for the well-being of one's loved ones is no less plausible as a justice-limiting prerogative, qualifying as legitimate partiality rather than illegitimate selfishness, than is concern for oneself (Estlund 1998). Indeed, the family is, on plausible accounts, a sphere within which partiality is not merely morally legitimate but morally required, perhaps one where impartial thinking is positively out of place (Williams 1981). Luck egalitarians are likely to concede that parents may favor their children in *some* respects, and its advocates would do well to work out with some care precisely what it is that parents should indeed be permitted to do to, with, or for their children.

Given such a rich and varied context, and written for an interdisciplinary audience, this chapter can do little more than lay out the issues. It will explore these two ways in which parent-child relations might be thought to pose a problem for luck egalitarianism. Both aspects of that exploration will use the language of "constitution," and so let me be clear from the start that two quite different things are being "constituted." On the one hand, parents help to constitute their children *as the people they are (or become)*. If, *pace* the luck egalitarian, equality of opportunity demands only that those who are similarly constituted compete on a level playing field, then that ideal is quite compatible with strong associations between the levels of advantage experienced by parents and children. On the other hand, some parent-child interactions are constitutive of *the family* in the sense that they are integral to whatever it is that makes the family valuable. If those that are constitutive in this second sense tend to generate some inequalities of opportunity, then the reasons we have to value the family may also be reasons to accept those inequalities.

It is tempting to think of the family as belonging to the private sphere. Whereas it is possible to legislate on issues of schooling, wealth transfers, and so on, one cannot do the same with respect to private interaction within the family. What goes on there is properly immune from political action. This, certainly, is how many lay social actors, and many social scientists, conceive the issue. The state can help the pursuit of equality of opportunity only where private and public spheres intersect, and policy cannot intrude into the family. For this reason it may seem odd, or irrelevant, to talk, as I do, about which parental actions are and are not justified. If the family is private, then the moral question of how parents are justified in acting toward their children may look beside the point.

My approach may indeed be uncongenial to nonphilosophers, but it will not do simply to posit "the family" as belonging to the private sphere and thereby immune from legislation. What should be left free from legislation is precisely what we need to decide. If there are any family-related freedoms that are worthy of respect, they will emerge from careful consideration of what is valuable about the family, not by taking for granted that it is a private institution. There are, moreover, different reasons for regarding the family as beyond the bounds of state action. One might treat it that way because individuals have the right to decide for themselves how they conduct their familial affairs. But one might reach that conclusion simply because one recognized the impracticability of any attempt to enforce particular views about how those affairs should be conducted. The kind of monitoring and policing that would be needed for such a policy to succeed would be so intrusive as to destroy that which is indeed valuable about the family. So we might want to leave the family free from regulation because regulation would bring its own moral costs, not because there is no issue about which parental actions are justified. Finally, even in so far as it is true that parents have a right to conduct their relations with their children as they see fit, it remains the case that some of the actions they have the right to take may be justified while others may not. One can have the right to do wrong, or to act in ways that are, all things considered, unjustified. So even if we were to concede that significant areas of family life should, on principled grounds, be left to the discretion of those involved, it remains philosophically appropriate, if also politically less relevant, to consider which choices within that sphere of discretion are (morally) better than others.

LEGITIMATE PARTIALITY, ALLOCATIVE EFFICIENCY AND NON-IDEAL THEORY

So much for context and the normative research agenda it implies. Before attempting to lay out some of the issues that will arise as that agenda is pursued, let me register two caveats. These are points about legitimate partiality in non-ideal situations, particularly worthy of emphasis to an empirically minded, social-scientific readership that may be impatient of, or even hostile to, the utopianism or practical irrelevance that is sometimes thought to characterize the normative approach.

Illegitimate Partiality and Allocative Efficiency

Even normative philosophers care about efficiency. Social justice matters, but it matters also that people be better rather than worse off. Few, if any, would prefer an altogether fair distribution if that could be achieved only at the cost of leaving all worse off than they might otherwise be. To be sure, "efficiency" needs careful handling. Economists tend to assume that it is a matter of maximizing total output (see, e.g., Benabou 2000, whose analysis of the relation between meritocracy, redistribution, and efficiency is thereby all the more striking). But, as Roemer (2000, 29) notes, "other things can matter in judging how well a society's institutions serve its citizens." And in so far as we value economic efficiency, it is surely right to insist that the goal to be pursued incorporates distributive considerations of some kind. It is important not just that there is more but also who gets the more that there is. All that said, the conflict between equality of opportunity and allocative efficiency remains serious.

That conflict arises most starkly in relation to the direct transmission of wealth in the form of bequests. Suppose, for the sake of argument, that all bequests and inheritance of alienable property were illegitimate. One does not need to be an economist to know that it would still be a bad idea to ban them. Deprived of the opportunity to convey any of their product to their children after death, parents' economic behavior would be likely to change in catastrophic ways. The point generalizes to less restrictive conceptions of the scope of legitimate parental partiality—banning elite private schools may also have serious incentive effects. Whatever we end up deciding about the proper bounds of parental partiality, we may be morally justified in enacting policies that pander to parental motivations exceeding them. Indeed it would be morally irresponsible not to do so.

When, in what follows, I talk about "legitimate parental partiality," I mean "the kind of partiality that parents are justified in showing to their children" not "the kind of partiality that a justified policy may need to accommodate on grounds of allocative efficiency." The reader can perfectly well reject the approach to legitimate partiality to be sketched in this chapter on the ground that it fails to understand what is valuable about the family, or to give sufficient weight to the value of parental freedom. But she should not reject it on the basis that, however they may be justified in acting, parents want to favor their children, that allocative efficiency requires policies that take people as they are, wants and all, and hence that such policies should allow parents to act in ways that go beyond the scope of legitimate partiality. That claim is not disputed here.

Legitimate Partiality in Ideal and Non-ideal Contexts

Asking what justice requires that parents be allowed to do for their children, in the ideal society, is different from asking what parents are justified in doing for their children in the current, non-ideal, context. What follows will be concerned with the former.

To see how the two may diverge, suppose that, though parents do indeed have some rights over the content of their children's education, no parent has a right to send hers to an elite private school. In an altogether just society, no parent would have the option of bestowing on her offspring unfair positional advantage in the competition for desirable jobs. According to this view, and net of efficiency considerations, it would be right to abolish private schools. It by no means follows that parents are never justified in sending their children to elite private schools here and now, in societies as they actually exist today. Actions that are, in principle, wrong, and which just rules would rightly prevent, may, in practice—in the absence of those rules governing the conduct of all—be right. Perhaps the existence of unusually well-funded private schools makes the cost to one's child of sending her to a state school greater than it would be if private schools were outlawed. Perhaps the values realized by a policy preventing parents from sending their children to elite private schools are unlikely to be realized by an individual parent's decision to refrain from sending her child to such a school. (For discussion of the school case, an analogous case, and the general issue respectively, see Swift 2003; Cohen 2000; Murphy 2000.)

The example generalizes. When, I suggest that certain actions exceed the bounds of legitimate parental partiality, the claim is that, in the ideal case, those actions might justifiably be prevented. It does not follow that a parent undertaking the same action in the current, non-ideal, context is doing wrong.

Moreover, it may be that, in non-ideal circumstances, parents cannot undertake actions falling within the scope of legitimate partiality without also finding themselves doing things for their children that go beyond it. Suppose that parents may, if necessary, legitimately use their economic resources to give their children a fair chance of achieving particularly desirable outcomes—places at good universities, well-rewarded and interesting jobs, and so on. It could be that, given the options available to her, the only way for a parent to get her child that fair chance is also to get her one that is better than fair. In a polarized school system, for example, a parent could be faced with a choice between unfairly disadvantaged schools and unfairly advantaged ones. Given that, ex hypothesi, she need not settle for the former, she may legitimately opt for the latter. The unreasonably good chance she thereby bestows upon her daughter is an unintended by-product of an action undertaken for a different reason. It results from the options available to her, which are themselves the result of other people's, possibly illegitimate, choices—including their choices about policies, about what choices they and everybody else should be free to make.

We live in societies where some parents exceed the bounds of legitimate partiality while others do not do enough for their children. Rawls, whose influence does much to explain political philosophers' preoccupation with the ideal, is well aware that non-ideal theory matters too. "Obviously the problems of partial compliance theory are the pressing and urgent matters. These are the things that we are faced with in everyday life" (1971, 9.) But, he continues, "The reason for beginning with ideal theory is that it provides, I believe, the only basis for the systematic grasp of these more pressing problems. . . . At least I shall assume that a deeper understanding can be gained in no other way, and that the nature and aims of a perfectly just society is the fundamental part of a theory of justice." On the same assumption, what follows will bracket these two problems of noncompliance and consider what, in the ideally just society, parents would and would not do to, with, or for their children.

Equality of Opportunity and Constitutive Luck

For current purposes it is useful to identify just two conceptions of equality of opportunity, which I will call "radical" and "conventional" (Swift 2001). According to the radical view, associated with luck egalitarianism, all inequalities due to differential luck are unjust and give justice grounds for equalization. Taking equality of opportunity seriously means that people should not have better or worse prospects in life than one another because of things for which they are not responsible. Only then will people have an equal chance of living the life of their choice, rather than having their set of feasible options determined by factors beyond their control. It is not enough for clever poor children to have the same opportunities as clever rich children. Equality of opportunity requires also that untalented children, whether rich or poor, should have the same opportunities—for some goods (money) if not for others (places at medical school)—as talented children.

Of course, most reject the radical view. Taking equality of opportunity seriously does not mean reducing inequalities to those that result from responsible choices. It means merely removing factors that prevent the similarly talented and motivated from enjoying the same prospects of success. It requires, as Rawls (1971, 301) puts it, "equal life prospects in all sectors of society for those similarly endowed and motivated." True, as far as they are concerned, it is a matter of luck that people are unequally talented, and perhaps even unequally motivated. (It may not be a matter of luck as far as their parents are concerned, a complication to be addressed—if not resolved—later.) But equality of opportunity does not require us to compensate for differential luck of the kind that is constitutive of who people are. It requires only the removal of the social barriers and silver spoons that prevent people from competing on level terms with those constituted like them. This conception of equality of opportunity is likely to be held in conjunction with the view that people can deserve unequal rewards for the exercise of attributes that they possess unequally as a matter of luck. (See Miller 1999 for a sophisticated defense of this "conventional" conception of desert.)

The distinction that matters, on this account, is between those mechanisms that, though a matter of differential luck, are constitutive of the individual and those that are not. What is regarded as "constitutive of the individual" may be debated. Some might hold that those born with similar natural talents should not have their prospects influenced by the vagaries of childhood socialization. Others might regard those vagaries too as "constitutive" in the relevant sense: though who is socialized how is a matter of luck, socialization is constitutive of the person in such a way that justice permits, or requires, that those differentially socialized be differentially rewarded.

What parents do to, with, or for their children can be regarded as influencing their well-being in less or more constitutive ways. Some seem extrinsic, things without which their children would be better or worse off. Others seem more intrinsic: change those and what you have are different *people*. To be sure, this notion of "constitution" is vague and hard to pin down, but we can begin to explore the issues it raises by distinguishing three kinds of constitution: genetic, of the personality, and of the identity.

1. *Genetic constitution.* Parents affect the well-being of their children by influencing their genetic constitution. Though it is a matter of luck how any individual is genetically constituted, many people believe that luck of this kind is properly rewarded precisely because who people *are* is, in the relevant sense, a matter of their genetic constitution. It makes sense to think about what a particular child might have achieved if he or she had had a more encouraging home background or better schooling, whereas if we think about someone genetically different we are thinking of a different person.

2. *Constitution of personality.* Parents do things that influence their children in ways that, though not constitutive of their genetic material, are constitutive of their personalities. Some people are cheerful, some depressed. Some can defer gratification, some cannot. Some are stoical in the face of adversity, others collapse. Some are hard-working, others idle. Some of the variation in personality traits is due to variation in what parents do to, or with, or for their children. These personality traits help to explain how people fare in life and many regard this as entirely appropriate: they properly count as desert bases.

3. *Constitution of identity.* Parents also influence their children's identities: their understandings of who they are, and what matters to them. According to Brian Barry (1988, 40–41), "The details of upbringing that make for a greater or lesser thirst for educational attainment and a greater or lesser capacity to give educational institutions what they want are part of the constituents of people's personal identity. They are not necessarily to be repudiated as something that merely 'happened to them' . . . [T]he fundamental attitudes, values, behavioural traits and so on that make up people's characters would (uncontroversially) have been different had they (i.e., the identical collection of cells) been placed in different conditions, but that does not entail the conclusion that they are not *theirs* in a way that is morally relevant. . . ." Of course, the luck egalitarian may have no objection to inequalities that result from responsible choices. But, according to some views, the extent to which

the identities that generate such choices are causally influenced by parents tells against the view that such choices are indeed responsible in the way that would be needed to justify the inequality.

Whatever one thinks of these kinds of "constitution" as grounds for justifying inequalities (and I do not mean to endorse any of them), one thing should be clear. The more the intergenerational transmission of advantage occurs through constitutive mechanisms, the greater the gap between the conventional and the radical approaches to equality of opportunity. If the propensity of children to inherit their parents' position in the distribution of advantage were explained entirely by nonconstitutive mechanisms, then advocates of both approaches might agree that all the inheritance that we observe is unjust. Attention might in that case focus entirely on various kinds of equalizing strategies. If, however, that propensity were explained entirely by constitutive mechanisms, then proponents of the two approaches would disagree about whether that propensity indicated any injustice at all.

Summarising the research findings of the 1990s, Bowles and Gintis (2002) claim that while the genetic inheritance of IQ explains very little of the intergenerational transmission of economic status, genetic inheritance in general may explain a lot (the answer turns on the proper specification of the relevant statistical models). Social inheritance processes—operating through the superior wealth and educational attainments of well-off parents—explain surprisingly little of that transmission. Generally, it looks as if personality variables, and preferences that can be thought of as aspects of people's identities, are more important than had been previously acknowledged. The more the inheritance of these variables is indeed an important part of the story, as other contributors to this volume suggest, the bigger the gap between the radical and the conventional views. It seems that, in large part, economically successful parents tend to have economically successful children because they do things to, with, or for those children that result in their being constituted in ways conducive to economic success. If that is right, the choice between the conventional and the constitutive conceptions of equality of opportunity matters more than it would if the intergenerational persistence of inequality were due simply to similarly constituted children competing on unfair terms.

PARENTS, LUCK, AND THE INTERGENERATIONAL PERSISTENCE OF INEQUALITY

Parents are just one chance variable among many. Even if there were no tendency for children to inherit their parents' genes, different children would still be born with different genetic constitutions, and those, when combined with particular environments, would be more or less conducive to economic success. What is unjust, for the luck egalitarian, is not children benefiting from good or bad luck in choice of parents, but their benefiting from good or bad luck of any kind. If parents are special, that is simply because, as a matter of empirical fact, parental characteristics are especially important chance causal influences on how individuals fare.

Similarly, the intergenerational persistence of inequality is of no special relevance to the luck egalitarian. If there were a strong negative correlation between parents' and children's positions in the distribution of advantage, so that the lucky children were those born to disadvantaged parents, there might be no tendency for inequality to persist across generations; rather, mechanisms within the family would tend to produce high levels of mobility. From the point of view of radical equality of opportunity, this makes no difference. It would be no less unfair for children of the unsuccessful to profit from attributes that they have— by chance—from their parents than it is for children of the successful to do so.

The persistence of inequality across generations is relevant to luck egalitarianism only in so far as clear patterning makes manifest the extent to which inequalities in people's well-being are indeed causally related to differences among their parents. From this perspective, the contribution of social scientists is to identify the causal factors that explain why children fare differently. As it happens, they tell us, parent's location in the distribution of advantage is an influential factor. This puts the spotlight on the causal processes at work and—when those processes are disaggregated into their component mechanisms—helps us think about policies that might reduce the impact of these circumstantial factors. For example, the idea that personality differences may justly be unequally rewarded seems, to luck egalitarians, to derive some of its attraction from the belief that people are responsible for their personality traits. *Pace* Barry (1988), the more we discover about the intergenerational transmission of such traits, the less plausible it seems to regard them as worthy of unequal rewards. The conclusion is not that parents should be prevented from influencing their children's personalities. But it might make a case for reducing the extent to which a person's personality influences her position in the distribution of economic advantage.

The fact that parental characteristics are but one chance variable, and that parents' economic standing is but one of those characteristics, has implications that many regard as counterintuitive. Making family background less important means making merit a more important determinant of people's position in the distribution of advantage. To the extent that the distribution of merit is itself a matter of luck, this is simply replacing one kind of injustice with another. Luck egalitarians have no immediate interest in reducing the net effect of family background if that means increasing the effect of other morally arbitrary characteristics— even where these are quite properly regarded as "merit" (e.g., as competences relevant to the performance of occupational tasks). Achieving conventional equality of opportunity may be a good thing from the point of view of allocative efficiency, or even of individual self-realization. But, as far as justice in the distribution of economic rewards is concerned, it is not even a step in the right direction.

Whose Luck Is It Anyway?

What one's parents are like is entirely a matter of luck. What one's children are like is not. Genetic engineering only takes to a new and more explicit level the familiar fact that parents make innumerable choices that influence the way their children are. Luck egalitarians believe that people should not be better or worse off than one another due to differences in luck, but they also believe that people should reap the rewards (or suffer the costs) of their responsible choices. The well-being of their children (and, perhaps less often, their parents) is, for many, a key component of their own well-being. It is a goal in pursuit of which they make sacrifices, and one that provides a guiding orientation for many of their most important choices—where to live, how much time to spend at work, and so on. An obvious criticism of the radical approach to equality of opportunity objects that, in treating individuals as the units between which equality of opportunity is to be pursued, it fails to see that the individual's own well-being is itself tied up with that of other members of her family in such a way that equality of opportunity among individuals could be achieved only by denying those same individuals the opportunity to achieve—or fail to achieve—much of what they regard as valuable in life.

Equality of opportunity is consistent with inequality in outcomes, at least with respect to particular dimensions of advantage. From their, ex hypothesi, equal starting-points, people are free to make choices that result in their ending up with less or more of particular goods. Suppose, in that hypothetical situation, some parents regarded their children's well-being as of vital importance, and made choices designed to further it, while other parents gave their children much lower priority. (Choosing a mate on the grounds that she is likely to be a good parent qualifies as the former just as much as does choosing to work the extra hours to pay for a house in a desirable school district.) Assuming any degree of parental competence, children in the next generation would face unequal

prospects as a result. As far as the children are concerned, this is unfairness, to be rectified—in so far as that is possible—in the name of justice.
As far as the parents are concerned, it is an appropriate return to their
responsible choices. If the other parents had wanted to, they could, ex
hypothesi, have made the same choices. Compensating children for having parents who give them low priority looks like failing properly to
respect the responsible choices made by conscientious ones.

Some inequalities of outcome for parents simply are inequalities of
opportunity for children. Depending on our view about what parents
should be free to do for their children, we can think about this in two
ways: as a problematic empirical fact or as a fundamental incoherence
in the idea of equality of opportunity. Suppose we judged it normatively
unacceptable for parents to help their children in ways that tended to
produce inequalities of opportunity in the next generation. Empirically,
it is, of course, clear that parents do in fact seek to help their children,
and that the better off parents are, the better placed they are to achieve
this goal. In that case, the aim would be to insulate (justified) inequalities
of outcome in one generation from (unjustified) inequalities of opportunity in the next—so far as that goal was consistent with other values,
such as allocative efficiency (bracketed earlier), individual freedom, and
the value of the family (see next section). According to the alternative
view, however, the unequal rewards that may legitimately accrue to parents, from a position of equal opportunity, include those relating to their
children's well-being. In that case, there is a fundamental incoherence or
instability within the idea of equality of opportunity. One cannot *both*
allow people to bear the consequences of the choices that they make
with respect to their children's well-being *and* ensure equality of opportunity for all.

FAMILY VALUES AND THE PRIORITY OF FAMILIAL LIBERTIES

Those who regard the family as a valuable institution are likely to see it
as properly limiting the pursuit of equality of opportunity. In Rawls's
theory of justice, the "basic liberties"—among them freedom of association—have lexical priority over fair equality of opportunity and the difference principle. The family is an association, and, "As citizens we have
reasons to impose the constraints specified by the political principles of
justice on associations; while as members of associations we have reasons for limiting those constraints so that they leave room for a free and
flourishing internal life appropriate to the association in question"
(2001, 165).

What kinds of parental partiality are sufficiently valuable, constitutive of family values properly understood, that the freedom to engage in them must be regarded as constraining the realization of equality of opportunity? Those who would abolish private education or inheritance but would nonetheless permit parents to read their children bedtime stories are, in effect, judging that using one's money to buy a particular kind of education for one's children is not constitutive of what is valuable about the family in the same way that reading bedtime stories is. Since egalitarian aims might more easily be met by universal state-run orphanages, what exactly would be lost under such a system? (Munoz-Darde 1999) The answer—or at least the answer to be canvassed here—has something to do with emotional development and the value of intimate, loving relationships between parents and children, and between siblings (Schrag 1976).

Notice, importantly, that we must talk about "family freedoms" not "freedom of the family." Just as Rawls holds that it is certain specific liberties that are to be given priority by his conception of justice, not freedom in general, so, when it comes to the family, we should conceive the freedoms we want to protect in as much detail as possible. "Freedom of the family," "freedom of familial association," "the autonomy of the family," or "the right to raise a family" are tools too unwieldy to tackle the issues with adequate specificity.

Given our interest in the transmission of economic advantage, a parallel between familial freedom and freedom of occupational choice may be instructive. Freedom of occupational choice can be endorsed for reasons that imply no similar respect for the freedom to engage in self-seeking economic bargaining (e.g., to seek the market wage for one's occupational activity). It *may* also be the case that it is legitimately partial for individuals to seek economic rewards in this way—it may be unreasonable to expect people whose work could command a high price to desist from bargaining for something beyond what equality would yield them. But, if so, that is for reasons that go beyond those that explain the importance of free occupational choice taken on its own. One could sensibly think that people should be free not to do work they do not want to do, however valuable their doing it might be for others, without thinking that they should be free to gain greater economic advantage than others from doing whatever they do choose to do. Something similar applies in the case of parental partiality. One can believe that we should organize our society in ways that allow parents to read to their children without thinking that we must also permit those children to benefit economically from the fact that they have been read to.

Constitutive Partiality

Where to draw the line between things that parents do to, with, and for their children that are intrinsic to or constitutive of a valuable familial relationship, on the one hand, and those that are merely extrinsic or incidental, on the other, is inevitably controversial. The family is conceived quite differently in different cultures, and beliefs about what makes it valuable have changed considerably over time, and so any substantive view on the issue risks the charge of ethnocentrism and ahistoricity. Granting that an adequate defense of the view to be outlined would (and will) require years more work, here is a sketch that may at least provide some orientation. To avoid confusion, bear in mind that my aim is not to identify the core or essential features of the family as those might be revealed by anthropologists or sociologists. It is to claim something about what makes the institution of the family morally valuable; to identify the reasons we have to prefer a world in which the family exists to one in which it does not.

My approach requires us to distinguish constitutive partiality from illegitimate favoritism. Some kinds of partiality are indeed constitutive of an intimate, loving, familial relationship. A parent who treated all children as she treated her own would not be getting or providing that kind of relationship, which of course requires parents to treat their children differently, specially, and, in some ways, better than other people's children. For that relationship to exist, there must be considerable time and energy and attention given by parents to children, and great sacrifice of the pursuit of other goals—whether personal (more time pursuing career goals) or altruistic (more time in charitable endeavor). But the kind of partiality justified in this way is simply the kind needed for, or a manifestation of, the valuable relationship. The parent is not helpfully thought of as *favoring* her children over other people's, because *not* doing what she does for her children would deprive them, and her, of a very good thing without giving that thing to the others.

It is true that, even if she can't give them *that* good thing, she may be able to give them others. She could spend time teaching them to read, or earning money to buy them presents. So she is certainly favoring herself and her children over other people when she chooses to spend time developing a valuable family relationship. But this is the kind of partiality that is justified by the value of the family. Some acts of favoritism clearly go beyond this. They are things one does for one's children that are not essential elements of a valuable familial relationship. In Rawls's terms, they are not prerequisites of that "free and flourishing internal life appropriate to the association in question."

Many think that parents may legitimately do to, with, or for their children much more than is needed for intimacy and affection, or that a parent who shows no favoritism toward her children is thereby manifesting a failure of affection. A parent's bequeathing all her wealth to charity and none to her children, for example, may seem to indicate lack of love. Certainly many parents judge that acts designed to further their children's economic well-being are simply unproblematic expressions of parental love. And many regard the favoritistic transmission of economic advantage as central to what the family is all about. (They dispute my suggestion that what fundamentally makes the family valuable is the kind of intimate or expressive relationships it makes possible.) My provisional and avowedly controversial (and insufficiently defended) position is that these views are mistaken. Nonconstitutive favoritism is not justified. People who think that the family is worthy of respect because of anything to do with the transmission of property, or who think that respecting family values implies permitting bequests and other attempts to give one's children economic advantage over others, are making a mistake. It is consistent with this misperception that, given the conventional aspect to expressive acts, the widespread *belief* that bequests and other transmission mechanisms are expressions of love may be enough to make that true. Suppose a child shares the conventional belief that parents who attempt to convey economic advantage to their offspring are more loving than those who do not. Suppose her parent knows she holds that view. In that case, the parent wishing to express her love may find herself bequeathing money to her child even though she thinks that the conventional view, to which her child subscribes, is mistaken. My claim is not that economic transmissions are never properly interpreted as expressions of love or affection. It is that attempts at such transmissions are not a necessary element of a loving familial relationship.

Whether or not my particular view is correct, the proposed approach to the web of normative issues surrounding the family requires us to consider the following questions:

1. What is valuable about familial relationships? In what ways do people's lives go better if we permit family relationships that make us shrink from the idea of abolishing the family? (My answer has something to do with emotional development and intimacy.)
2. How much and what kinds of partiality-as-specialness are constitutive of that kind of relationship? What kinds of special treatment of children by parents is needed for whatever is valuable about family relationships to be realized? (My answer includes bedtime stories.)
3. What kind of partiality-as-favoritism—if any—is part and parcel of that

relationship? What kinds of favoritism toward children by parents is implied by, or necessarily accompanies, the kind of familial relationship that is valuable? (My answer is "None that is not already part of the previous answer.")

FAMILY VALUES AND THE INTERGENERATIONAL PERSISTENCE OF INEQUALITY

Clearly, our normative assessment of the intergenerational persistence of inequality will depend on how we think family values relate to the various mechanisms generating that persistence. Somebody who thinks it integral to those values that parents be permitted to act with extreme favoritism, to do what they can with their own resources to maximize their children's future economic well-being, will see things very differently from somebody who thinks that such values require us to respect only modes of interaction essential to the intimacy of the familial relationship. Suppose, for the sake of argument, that my controversial view were correct. It would then matter to what extent intergenerational persistence were indeed due to constitutive processes, such as bedtime stories (on the one hand) and extrinsic ones (such as bequests) on the other.

Intergenerational transmission of advantage that occurs through processes directly involving the fact that some parents are economically better off than others is, in principle, least worthy of respect. The bequeathing of money, the purchasing of expensive education, or of access to superior health care, are things that we might be willing to disallow. Contrast this with personality, and other "culture" variables. Suppose that well-off parents tend to produce well-off children because such parents take an unusual personal interest in their children's development, they read bedtime stories, they talk about things at the table, they instill, by their example, a positive attitude toward work, and so on. Here prevention in the name of equality of opportunity looks much more problematic. The value of close family relationships, quite apart from the sheer impracticability of policing any preventive policy, means that few would choose to equalize that way. To the extent that the reproduction of inequality across generations occurs through the transmission of cultural traits, it does so substantially (though not exclusively) through intimate familial interactions that we have reason to value and protect. Preventing those interactions would violate the autonomy of the family in a way that stopping parents spending their money on, or bequeathing money to, their children would not.

What about genes? Here, too, it looks as if prevention in the name of equality would involve excessive—and impractical—interference in what should properly be a private matter. We could require the genetically advantaged to reproduce with the genetically disadvantaged, giving all parent-pairs the same expected net genetic score and reducing the inequality that might be transmitted via that mechanism. But few would advocate such a policy. Rules about who should be allowed to have children with whom conflict with values that we have reason to care about in a different way from rules restricting parent-child interactions likely to lead to cultural transmission, but they conflict with them nonetheless.

It has been convenient for egalitarians to assume that much of the intergenerational persistence of inequality occurs through mechanisms that they would be happy for the state to block or prevent. It would be useful if the reason why inequality persisted across generations was that well-off parents bequeathed property to their children (the "family piano" conception) or used their money to buy advantages for their kids. Those mechanisms present less serious value conflicts than the dilemmas posed by culture and personality, characteristics that are transmitted via processes constitutive of the family. If social scientists are increasingly revealing the significance of these other mechanisms, they are making things harder for egalitarians. All is not lost. There are other equalizing strategies. But attention will indeed have to turn in their direction.

CONCLUSIONS: CONSTITUTIVE LUCK, CONSTITUTIVE PARTIALITY AND JUSTIFIED INEQUALITY

Other contributions to this collection suggest that one's choice of parents is more important a determinant of one's own economic well-being than had previously been recognized—at least by economists in the United States—and will indicate to many that the processes generating the distribution of such well-being are more unfair. But it seems also that the mechanisms by which economic status is transmitted from parents to children are likely to be judged more worthy of respect. This is so in two analytically distinct, though empirically overlapping, ways.

On the one hand, those mechanisms are, to a greater extent than had been acknowledged, constitutive of the individual's genetic being, personality, and identity or preferences. Rather than simply handing property down or using their economic advantage to buy their children what will increase their chances of success, parents well placed in the distribution of advantage tend to do things to, with, or for their children that constitute them as people who tend to end up occupying similar positions in that distribution. Those inclined to regard differential constitutive luck as justifying unequal desert claims will regard this as grounds for rejecting egalitarian claims that justice requires some form of compensation.

On the other hand, the inequality-reproducing actions undertaken by parents are more likely to fall within the bounds of legitimate parental partiality, even on the austere conception of those bounds sketched above. Of course that conception will indeed rule out a great deal of what parents do for their children as unjustified favoritism. Doubtless well-off parents do benefit their own children in ways that go beyond the kinds of partial action constitutive of that which is distinctively valuable about the familial relationship. Still, all things considered, recent evidence suggests that unimpeachable informal intrafamilial interactions are proving more important, relative to the favoritistic direct transmission of property and the use of economic resources to procure advantage for children, than many had thought.

Table 9.1 may help to clarify the relation between luck constitutive of the person and partiality constitutive of the family. In the top-left cell are all those things that parents should be free to do, on family-values grounds, that also constitute their children as the people they are or will become: bedtime stories, informal familial interaction, including the transmission of identity within certain limits. The bottom-left cell will include anything essential to close familial relationships—such as leisure time spent together—that takes place after children have been constituted as the people they are. Family values justify special treatment among adult members of the same family.

Many things that parents might do to constitute their children as the people they become would not also be legitimately partial, on any plausible view of the latter, let alone on my austere one. The top-right cell contains manipulative socialization (or indoctrination) together with attempts to use biotechnology genetically to engineer children designed to end up peculiarly well-placed in the distribution of economic advantage. Since schools and neighborhoods help to constitute the person, yet

TABLE 9.1

	Constitutive of Family	Not Constitutive of Family
Constitutive of Person	Spontaneous and informal parent-child interaction	Manipulative socialization, genetic engineering for economic gain
Not Constitutive of Person	Leisure time spent with family members as adults	Bequests of property

are not constitutive of the family, my view would allocate advantage-transmitting parental choices about these to this cell. The bottom-right cell contains doubly "external" processes: mechanisms that are constitutive neither of what is valuable about the family nor of the person the child becomes. The direct transmission of property as bequest is the pure case here.

Luck constitutive of the person, on the one hand, and partiality constitutive of the family, on the other, differ in their significance for the justification of inequality. Those keen to distinguish constitutive from other kinds of luck tend to hold that different constitutive characteristics, though due to chance, can help to make people unequally deserving of economic rewards. Hence the fit with the conventional conception of equality of opportunity, which seeks only "equal life prospects in all sectors of society for those similarly endowed and motivated" (Rawls 1971, 301). The thrust of talk about constitutive luck, in current debate, is to justify inequalities that would be rejected by those endorsing a more radical conception of equality of opportunity. I have said nothing in support of this inequality-justifying position.

The point of my distinction between favoritism and partiality constitutive of the family is, by contrast, precisely to cast doubt on a conventional justification of inequality. It is widely believed that parents may justifiably give special weight to their children's economic interests. Since parents are unequal with respect to the various capacities (not just economic) that can be used to further their children's economic well-being, this will justify some intergenerational transmission of advantage. The view sketched here challenges this justification by claiming that legitimate parental partiality extends only to actions constitutive of what makes the family valuable, thereby excluding many of the inequality-reproducing mechanisms judged acceptable on the conventional picture. Actions that are legitimately partial may—especially in actually existing contexts—yield the intergenerational persistence of inequality as an accidental by-product. But being a good parent is not, in principle, a matter of using your own advantage, should you have any, to do what you can to give your children an unfairly advantaged start in life.

Freedom of familial association is indeed a vital human interest and one that limits our pursuit of equality of opportunity. But unpacking the black box of the family to see exactly why it matters, and what it is that family members may legitimately do for one another, may—I think will—lead us to conclude that the constraints it imposes are less strict than is widely believed. We might still find ourselves compromising equality of opportunity, on efficiency grounds, to accommodate the favoritism of excessively partial parents. But we will be clearer about what we are doing and why.

NOTE

This chapter was written during research leave supported by the British Academy and Nuffield College, Oxford. I am very grateful to both of them. Thanks also to Herb Gintis for written comments not adequately answered here, to Jerry Cohen, and to gatherings at the Nuffield Political Theory Workshop, the London School of Economics, the University of Reading, and (under the aegis of the Asahi Glass Foundation's project on "The Possibility of Global Justice") the University of Kobe. My discussion of the family owes so much to Harry Brighouse that he shares responsibility for its errors.

REFERENCES

Abowd, John M., and David Card. 1989. "On the Covariance Structure of Earnings and Hours Changes." *Econometrica* 57 (2): 411–45.

Ahern, F. M., R. C. Johnson, J. R. Wilson, J. R. McClaren, and S. G. Andenberg. 1982. "Family Resemblances in Personality." *Behavior Genetics* 12:261–80.

Altonji, Joseph G., and Thomas A. Dunn. 1991. "Relationships among the Family Incomes and Labor Market Outcomes of Relatives." Pp. 269–310 in *Research in Labor Economics*, edited by Ronald G. Ehrenberg. Greenwich, Conn.: JAI Press.

———. 1996. "The Effects of Family Characteristics on the Return to Education." *The Review of Economics and Statistics* 78 (4): 665–71.

———. 2000. "An Intergenerational Model of Wages, Hours, and Earnings." *Journal of Human Resources* 35 (2): 221–58.

Altonji, Joseph G., and Lewis M. Segal. 1996. "Small-Sample Bias in GMM Estimation of Covariance Structures." *Journal of Business and Economic Statistics* 14 (3): 353–66.

Anderson, Elizabeth. 2000. "What Is the Point of Equality?" *Ethics* 109:287–337.

Andrisani, Paul, and Gilbert Nestel. 1976. "Internal-External Control as Contributor to and Outcome of Work Experience." *Journal of Applied Psychology* 61 (2): 156–65.

Applebaum, Eileen, and Ross Koppel. 1978. "The Impact of Work Attitudes Formed Prior to Labor Market Entry on the Process of Early Labor Market Attainment." Pp. 175–212 in *Work Attitudes and Labor Market Experience: Evidence from the National Longitudinal Surveys*, edited by Paul Andrisani. New York: Praeger.

Argyle, Michael. 1994. *The Psychology of Social Class*. New York: Routledge.

Arneson. 2000. "Luck Egalitarianism and Prioritarianism." *Ethics* 110 (2): 339–49.

Arnold, F., and Z. Liu. 1986. "Sex Preference, Fertility and Family Planning in China." *Population and Development Review* 12:221–46.

Ashenfelter, Orley, and Alan Krueger. 1994. "Estimates of the Economic Return to Schooling from a New Sample of Twins." *American Economic Review* 84, no. 5 (December): 1157–72.

Ashenfelter, Orley, and Cecelia Rouse. 1998. "Income, Schooling, and Ability: Evidence from a New Sample of Identical Twins." *Quarterly Journal of Economics* 113:317–23.

Ashenfelter, Orley, and David Zimmerman. 1997. "Estimates of the Returns to Schooling from Sibling Data: Fathers, Sons, and Brothers." *The Review of Economics and Statistics* 79 (1): 1–9.

Atkinson, A. B., A. K. Maynard, and C. G. Trinder. 1983. "Earnings: From

Father to Son?" in *Parents and Children: Incomes in Two Generations*, edited by A. B. Atkinson, A. K. Maynard, and C. G. Trinder. London: Heinemann Educational Books.

Baker, Michael. 1997. "Growth-Rate Heterogeneity and the Covariance Structure of Life Cycle Earnings." *Journal of Labor Economics* 15 (2): 338–75.

Baker, Michael, and Gary Solon. 2003. "Earnings Dynamics and Inequality among Canadian Men, 1976–1992: Evidence from Longitudinal Tax Records." *Journal of Labor Economics* 21 (2): 289–321.

Barrick, Murray R., and Michael K. Mount. 1991. "The Big Five Personality Dimensions and Job Performance: A Meta-Analysis," *Personnel Psychology* 44 (1): 1–26.

Barry, Brian. 1988. "Equal Opportunity and Moral Arbitrariness." In *Equality of Opportunity*, edited by Norman Bowie. Boulder, Col.: Westview.

Baumrind, D. 1967. "Child Care Practices Anteceding Three Patterns of Preschool Behavior." *Genetic Psychology Monographs* 75:43–88.

Becker, Gary S. 1988. "Family Economics and Macro Behavior." *American Economic Review* 78:1–13.

Becker, Gary S., and Nigel Tomes. 1979. "An Equilibrium Theory of the Distribution of Income and Intergenerational Mobility." *Journal of Political Economy* 87:1153–89.

———. 1986. "Human Capital and the Rise and Fall of Families." *Journal of Labor Economics* 4:S1–S39.

Behrman, Jere R., and Paul Taubman. 1985. "Intergenerational Earnings Mobility in the United States: Some Estimates and a Test of Becker's Intergenerational Endowments Model." *Review of Economics and Statistics* 67:144–51.

———. 1995. "The Intergenerational Correlation between Children's Adult Earnings and Their Parents' Income: Results from the Michigan Panel Survey of Income Dynamics." Pp. 229–48 in *From Parent to Child*, edited by Jere Behrman, Robert Pollack, and Paul Taubman. Chicago: University of Chicago Press.

Behrman, Jere R., Paul Taubman, and Terence Wales. 1977. "Controlling for and Measuring the Effects of Genetics and Family Environment in Equations for Schooling and Labor Market Success." In *Kinometrics: Determinants of Socioeconomic Success within and between Families*, edited by Paul Taubman. Amsterdam: North-Holland.

Benabou, Roland. 2000. "Meritocracy, Redistribution, and the Size of the Pie." In *Meritocracy and Economic Inequality*, edited by Kenneth Arrow, Samuel Bowles, and Steven Durlauf. Princeton: Princeton University Press.

Björklund, Anders, and Laura Chadwick. 2002. "Intergenerational Income Mobility in Permanent and Separated Families." Swedish Institute for Social Research, Stockholm University.

Björklund, Anders, Tor Eriksson, Markus Jantti, Oddbjorn Raaum, and Eva Osterbacka. 2002. "Brother Correlations in Earnings in Denmark, Finland, Norway, and Sweden Compared to the United States." *Journal of Population Economics* 15 (4): 757–72.

Björklund, Anders, and Markus Jäntti. 1997. "Intergenerational Mobility of

Economic Status: Is the United States Different?" Paper prepared for the American Economics Association meeting in New Orleans.

———. 2000. "Intergenerational Mobility of Socioeconomic Status in Comparative Perspective." *Nordic Journal of Political Economy* 26 (1): 3–33.

Björklund, Anders, Markus Jäntti, and Gary Solon. 2005. "Influences of Nature and Nurture on Earnings Variation: A Report on a Study of Various Sibling Types in Sweden." This volume.

Blalock, Hubert. 1964. *Causal Inferences in Nonexperimental Research.* Chapel Hill: University of North Carolina Press.

Blau, Peter Michael, and Otis Dudley Duncan. 1967. *The American Occupational Structure.* New York: Wiley.

Blau, Francine, and Lawrence Kahn. 2001. "Do Cognitive Test Scores Explain Higher U.S. Wage Inequality?" Cambridge: National Bureau of Economic Research, Working Paper 8210.

Bongaarts, J., and S. Watkins. 1996. "Social Interactions and Contemporary Fertility Transitions." *Population and Development Review* 22 (4): 639–82.

Bouchard, T. J., Jr., and J. C. Loehlin. 2001. "Genes, Evolution, and Personality." *Behavior Genetics* 31:243–73.

Bouchard, T., D. Lykken, M. McGue, N. Segal, and A. Tellegen. 1990. "Sources of Human Psychological Differences: The Minnesota Study of Twins Reared Apart." *Science* 250:223–28.

Bouchard, T. J., Jr., and M. McGue. 1981. "Familial Studies of Intelligence." *Science* 212:1055–1059.

Bowles, Samuel. 1972. "Schooling and Inequality from Generation to Generation." *Journal of Political Economy* 80: S219–51.

———. 1995. "Elusive Skills and Escalating Differences: The Place of Cognitive Abilities in the Explanation of Inequality." Manuscript. Department of Economics, University of Massachusetts.

Bowles, Samuel, and Herbert Gintis. 1976. *Schooling in Capitalist America.* New York: Basic Books.

———. 1996. "Productive Skills, Labor Discipline, and the Returns to Schooling." Working paper #1996-10. Department of Economics, University of Massachusetts.

———. 2001. "The Inheritance of Economic Status: Education, Class and Genetics." In *Genetics, Behavior and Society,* edited by Marcus Feldman. Oxford: Elsevier.

———. 2002. "The Inheritance of Inequality." *Journal of Economic Perspectives* 16:3–30.

Bowles, Samuel, Herbert Gintis, and Melissa Osborne. 2001a. "Incentive-Enhancing Preferences: Personality, Behavior, and Earnings." *American Economic Review* 91 (2): 155–58.

———. 2001b. "The Determinants of Earnings: A Behavioral Approach." *Journal of Economic Literature* 39 (4): 1137–76.

Bowles, Samuel, and Valerie Nelson. 1973. "The Inheritance of IQ and the Intergenerational Reproduction of Economic Inequality." *The Review of Economics and Statistics,* 56 (1): 39–51.

————. 1974. "The Inheritance of IQ and the Intergenerational Reproduction of Economic Inequality." *Review of Economics and Statistics* 56 (1): 39–51.

Bradley, R., and R. Corwyn. 2003. " 'Family Process' Investments that Matter for Child Well-Being." In *Family Investments in Children: Resources and Parenting Behaviors that Promote Success*, edited by A. Kalil and T. DeLeire. Mahwah, N.J.: Erlbaum.

Bureau of Labor Statistics Household Data. 1999. "Employed Persons by Occupation and Age." Table A-19.

Burtless, Gary, and Christopher Jencks. 2003. "American Inequality and Its Consequences." In *Agenda for the Nation*, edited by Henry Aaron, James Lindsay, and Pietro Nivola. Washington, D.C.: Brookings.

Cairns, R., B. Cairns, H. Xie, M. Leung, and S. Hearne. 1998. "Paths across Generations: Academic Competence and Aggressive Behaviors in Young Mothers and Their Children." *Developmental Psychology* 34 (6): 1162–74.

Canivez, Gary L., and Marley W. Watkins. 1998. "Long-term Stability of the Wechsler Intelligence Scale for Children—Third Edition." *Psychological Assessment* 10 (3): 285–91.

Capaldi, D. and S. Clark. 1998. "Prospective Family Predictors of Aggression toward Female Partners for At-Risk Young Men." *Developmental Psychology* 34:1175–88.

Card, David. 1994. "Intertemporal Labor Supply: An Assessment." In *Advances in Econometrics, Sixth World Congress*, vol. 2, edited by Christopher A. Sims. Cambridge: Cambridge University Press.

Carlson, M., and M. Corcoran. 2001. "Family Structure and Children's Behavioral and Cognitive Outcomes." *Journal of Marriage and Family* 63 (3): 779–92.

Carlson, Marcia J. 1999. "Family Structure, Father Involvement and Adolescent Behavioral Outcomes." Ph.D. diss. Ann Arbor: University of Michigan.

Carmichael, Crista, and Matt McGue. 1994. "A Longitudinal Family Study of Personality Change and Stability." *Journal of Personality* 62 (1): 1–20.

Carmines, Edward and Richard Zeller. 1979. *Reliability and Validity Assessment*. Beverly Hills, Calif.: Sage Publications.

Case, Anne, and Lawrence Katz. 1991. "The Company You Keep: The Effects of Family and Neighborhood on Disadvantaged Youth." Working Paper 3705. Cambridge, Mass.: National Bureau of Economic Research.

Case, Anne, Darren Lubotsky, and Christina Paxson. 2001. "Economic Status and Health in Childhood: The Origins of the Gradient." NBER Working Paper No. W8344.

Cavalli-Sforza, L.-L., and M. W. Feldman. 1981. *Cultural Transmission and Evolution: A Quantitative Approach*. Princeton: Princeton University Press.

Cavalli-Sforza, L.-L., M. W. Feldman, K. H. Chen, and S. M. Dornbusch. 1982. "Theory and Observation in Cultural Transmission." *Science* 218:19–27.

Cawley, John, Karen Conneely, James Heckman, and Edward Vytlacil. 1996. "Measuring the Effects of Cognitive Ability." Manuscript. Department of Economics, University of Chicago.

Charles, Kerwin Kofi, and Erik Hurst. 2003. "The Correlation of Wealth Across Generations." *Journal of Political Economy* 111 (6): 1155–82.

Chassin, L., C. Presson, M. Todd, J. Rose, and S. Sherman. 1998. "Maternal Socialization of Adolescent Smoking: The Intergenerational Transmission of Parenting and Smoking." *Developmental Psychology* 34 (6): 1189–201.

Chen, K. H., L.-L. Cavalli-Sforza, and M. W. Feldman. 1982. "A Study of Cultural Transmission in Taiwan." *Human Ecology* 10 (3): 365–82.

Chuang, Y. C., and A. P. Wolf. 1995. "Marriage in Taiwan, 1881–1905." *The Journal of Asian Studies* 54 (3): 781–95.

Clark, Todd E. 1996. "Small-Sample Properties of Estimators of Nonlinear Models of Covariance Structure." *Journal of Business and Economic Statistics* 14 (3): 367–73.

Cloninger, C. R., and I. I. Gottesman. 1987. "Genetic and Environmental Factors in Antisocial Behavior Disorders." In *The Causes of Crime*, edited by S. Mednick, T. Moffit, and S. Stack. New York: Cambridge University Press.

Cloninger, C. Robert, John Rice, and Theodore Reich. 1979. "Multifactorial Inheritance with Cultural Transmission and Assortative Mating. II. A General Model of Combined Polygenic and Cultural Inheritance." *American Journal of Human Genetics* 31:176–98.

Coale, A. J., and J. Banister. 1994. "Mortality, Race, and the Family: Five Decades of Missing Females in China." *Demography* 31 (3): 459–79.

Cohen, G. A. 1989. "On the Currency of Egalitarian Justice." *Ethics* 99:906–44.

———. 1995. "Incentives, Inequality and Community." In *Equal Freedom*, edited by Stephen Darwall. Ann Arbor: University of Michigan Press.

———. 2000. *If You're an Egalitarian, How Come You're So Rich?* Cambridge: Harvard University Press.

Cohen, P., S. Kasen, J. Brook, and C. Hartmark. 1998. "Behavior Patterns of Young Children and Their Offspring: A Two-Generation Study." *Developmental Psychology* 34 (6): 1202–8.

Conley, James L. 1984. "Longitudinal Consistency of Adult Personality: Self-Reported Psychological Characteristics across 45 Years." *Journal of Personality and Social Psychology* 47 (6): 1325–33.

Cooper, Suzanne, Steven Durlauf, and Paul Johnson. 1994. "On the Evolution of Economic Status across Generations." *American Economic Review* 84 (2): 50–58.

Corak, Miles, and Andrew Heisz. 1999. "The Intergenerational Earnings and Income Mobility of Canadian Men: Evidence from Longitudinal Income Tax Data." *Journal of Human Resources* 34:504–33.

Corcoran, Mary. 2001. Mobility, Persistence, and the Consequences of Poverty for Children: Child and Adult Outcomes." In *Understanding Poverty*, edited by Sheldon Danziger and Robert Haveman. New York and Cambridge: Russell Sage Foundation and Harvard University Press.

Costa, Paul, Jr., and Robert McCrae. 1994. "Set like Plaster? Evidence for the Stability of Adult Personality." In *Can Personality Change?*, edited by Todd F. Heatherton and Joel L. Weinberger. Washington, D.C.: American Psychological Association.

———. 1997. "Longitudinal Stability of Adult Personality." In *Handbook of Personality Psychology*, edited by Robert Hogan, John Johnson, and Stephen Briggs. San Diego, Calif.: Academic Press.

Costa, Paul T., Robert McCrae, and David Arenberg. 1980. "Enduring Dispositions in Adult Males." *Journal of Personality and Social Psychology* 38 (5): 793–800.

Couch, Kenneth A., and Dean R. Lillard. 1994. "Sample Selection Rules and the Intergenerational Correlation of Earnings: A Comment on Solon and Zimmerman." Manuscript.

Crook, M. N. 1937. "Intra-Family Relationships in Personality Test Performance." *Psychological Record* 1:479–502.

Cunningham, M. 2001. "The Influence of Parental Attitudes and Behaviors on Children's Attitudes toward Gender and Household Labor in Early Adulthood." *Journal of Marriage and Family* 63 (1): 111–22.

D'Agostino, R. B., A. Balanger, and R. B. D'Agostino, Jr. 1990. "A Suggestion for Using Powerful and Informative Tests of Normality." *American Statistician* 44 (4): 316–21.

Daniels, M., B. Devlin, and K. Roeder. 1997. "Of genes and IQ." Pp. 45–70 in *Intelligence, Genes, and Success*, edited by B. Devlin, S. Fienberg, D. Resnick, and K. Roeder. New York: Springer-Verlag.

Das Gupta, M., and S. Li. 1999. "Gender Bias and Marriage Squeeze in China, South Korea and India, 1920–1990." *Development and Change* 30 (3): 619–52.

Davis-Friedmann, D. 1991. *Long Lives: Chinese Elderly and the Communist Revolution.* Stanford: Stanford University Press.

Dearden, Lorraine, Stephen Machin, and Howard Reed. 1997. "Intergenerational Mobility in Britain." *Economic Journal* 107:47–66.

Deaton, Angus. 1997. *The Analysis of Household Surveys: A Microeconometric Approach to Development Policy.* Washington, D.C.: World Bank.

Devlin, Bernie, Michael Daniels, and Kathryn Roeder. 1997. "The Heritability of IQ." *Nature* 388 (31 July): 468–71.

Digman, J. M. 1990. "Personality Structure: Emergence of the Five-Factor Model." *Annual Review of Psychology* 41: 417–40.

Dodge, K., G. Pettit, and J. Bates. 1994. "Socialization Mediators of the Relation between Socioeconomic Status and Child Conduct Problems." *Child Development* 65 (2): 649–65.

Du, P. 1998. "Cohort Analysis of Changes of Living Arrangement of Chinese Elderly." [In Chinese.] *Chinese Journal of Population Sciences* 3: 53–58.

Du, P., and C. Wu. 1998. "Analysis of Main Sources of Income of the Chinese Elderly." [in Chinese]. *Population Research* 4:51–57.

DuBois, Philip. 1965. *An Introduction to Psychological Statistics.* New York: Harper and Row.

Duncan, G. J., and R. Dunifon. 1998. "'Soft-skills' and Long-run Labor Market Success." *Research in Labor Economics* 17:123–49.

Duncan, Greg, Ariel Kalil, Susan E. Mayer, Robin Tepper, and Monique R. Payne. 2005. "The Apple Does Not Fall Far from the Tree." This volume.

Duncan, Greg, and James Morgan. 1981. "Sense of Efficacy and Subsequent Change in Earnings-A Replication." *Journal of Human Resources* 16 (4): 649–57.

Duncan, Otis D. 1961. "A Socioeconomic Index for All Occupations." Pp.

109–38 in *Occupations and Socioeconomic Status*, edited by Albert J. Reiss, Jr. New York: Free Press of Glencoe.

———. 1968. "Inheritance of Poverty or Inheritance of Race?" In *On Understanding Poverty*, edited by D. P. Moynihan. New York: Basic Books.

———. 1971. "Path Analysis: Sociological Examples." In *Causal Models in the Social Sciences*. Chicago: Aldine.

Duncan, Otis D., and David L. Featherman. 1973. "Psychological and Cultural Factors in the Process of Occupational Achievement." Pp. 229–53 in *Structural Equation Models in the Social Sciences*, edited by Arthur S. Goldberger and Otis D. Duncan. New York: Seminar Press.

Dunifon, Rachel, and Greg J. Duncan. 1998. "Long-Run Effects of Motivation on Labor-Market Success." *Social Psychology Quarterly* 61 (1): 33–48.

Dworkin, Ronald. 2000. *Sovereign Virtue*. Cambridge: Harvard University Press.

Dyson, T., and M. Moore. 1983. "On Kinship Structure, Female Autonomy, and Demographic Behavior in India." *Population and Development Review* 9 (1): 35–60.

Eagly, Alice H. 1987. *Sex Differences in Social Behavior: A Social-Role Interpretation*. Hillsdale, N.J.: Erlbaum.

Eaves, L., A. Heath, N. Martin, H. Maes, M. Neale, K. Kendler, K. Kirk, and L. Corey. 1999. "Comparing the Biological and Cultural Inheritance of Personality and Social Attitudes in the Virginia 30,000 Study of Twins and Their Relatives." *Twin Research* 2 (2): 62–80.

Edwards, Richard C. 1976. "Individual Traits and Organizational Incentives: What Makes a 'Good' Worker?" *Journal of Human Resources* 11 (1): 51–68.

———. 1977. "Personal Traits and 'Success' in Schooling and Work." *Educational and Psychological Measurement* 37 (1): 125–38.

Efron, B. 1982. *The Jackknife, the Bootstrap, and Other Resampling Plans*. Philadelphia: Society for Industrial and Applied Mathematics.

Ellwood, David T., and Christopher Jencks. Forthcoming. "The Spread of Single-Parent Families in the United States since 1960." In *Public Policy and the Future of the Family*, edited by Daniel Patrick Moynihan, Lee Rainwater, and Timothy Smeeding. New York: Russell Sage.

England, Paula. 1982. "The Failure of Human Capital Theory to Explain Occupational Sex Segregation." *Journal of Human Resources* 17 (3): 372–84.

Erikson, Robert, and John H. Goldthorpe. 1992. "The CASMIN Project and the American Dream." *European Sociological Review* 8:283–305.

———. 2002. "Intergenerational Inequality: A Sociological Perspective." *Journal of Economic Perspectives* 16:31–44.

Estlund, David. 1998. "Liberalism, Equality, and Fraternity in Cohen's Critique of Rawls." *Journal of Political Philosophy* 6:99–112

Featherman, David, and Robert Hauser. 1976. "Changes in the Socioeconomic Stratification of the Races, 1962–73." *American Journal of Sociology* 82 (3): 621–51.

Feldman, Marcus W., Sarah P. Otto, and Freddy B. Christiansen. 2000. "Genes, Culture, and Inequality." In *Meritocracy and Economic Inequality*, edited by

Kenneth Arrow, Samuel Bowles, and Steven Durlauf. Princeton: Princeton University Press.

Fertig, Angela. 2002. "Trends in Intergenerational Earnings Mobility in the U.S." Princeton University, Center for Research on Child Well-Being.

Filer, Randall K. 1981. "The Influence of Affective Human Capital on the Wage Equation." *Research in Labor Economics* 4:367–416.

———. 1986. "The Role of Personality and Tastes in Determining Occupational Structure." *Industrial and Labor Relations Review* 39 (3): 412–24.

Finkel, D., and M. McGue. 1997. "Sex differences and Nonadditivity in Heritability of the Multidimensional Personality Questionnaire Scales." *Journal of Personality and Social Psychology* 72:929–38.

Fishkin, James. 1983. *Justice, Equality of Opportunity, and the Family.* New Haven: Yale University Press.

Fiske, D. W. 1949. "Consistency of the Factorial Structures of Personality Ratings from Different Sources." *Journal of Abnormal and Social Psychology* 44: 329–44.

Fitzgerald, John, Peter Gottschalk, and Robert Moffitt. 1998. "An Analysis of the Impact of Sample Attrition on the Second Generation of Respondents in the Michigan Panel Study of Income Dynamics." *Journal of Human Resources* 33 (2): 300–344;

Fleurbaey, Marc. 1995. "Equal Opportunity or Equal Social Outcome?" *Economics and Philosophy* 11:25–55.

———. 1998. "Equality among Responsible Individuals." In *Freedom in Economics,* edited by J. F. Laslier et al. London: Routledge.

Floud, Roderick, Kenneth Wachter, and Annabel Gregory. 1990. *Height, Health and History: Nutritional Status in the United Kingdom, 1750–1980.* Cambridge: Cambridge University Press.

Freedman, R., B. Moots, T. Sun, and M. Weinberger. 1978. "Household Composition and Extended Kinship in Taiwan." *Population Studies* 32 (1): 65–80.

Freeman, Richard B. 1994. *Working Under Different Rules.* New York: Russell Sage.

Gable, Myron, and Frank Dangello. 1994. "Locus of Control, Machiavellianism, and Managerial Job Performance." *Journal of Psychology* 128 (5): 599–608.

Gale, William G., and John Karl Scholz. 1994. "Intergenerational Transfers and the Accumulation of Wealth." *Journal of Economic Perspectives* 8 (4):145–60.

Galton, Francis. 1889. *Natural Inheritance.* London: Macmillan.

Ganschow, T. W. 1978. "Aged in a Revolutionary Milieu: China." In *Aging and the Elderly: Humanistic Perspectives in Gerontology,* edited by S. F. Spicker, K. M. Woodward, and D. D. Van-Tassel. Atlantic Highlands, N.J.: Humanities Press.

Goldberger, Arthur S. 1978. "The Genetic Determination of Income: Comment." *American Economic Review* 68 (5): 960–69.

———. 1979. "Heritability." *Economica* 46 (184): 327–47.

———. 1989. "Economic and Mechanical Models of Intergenerational Transmission." *American Economic Review* 79, no. 3 (June): 504–13.

———. 1991. *A Course in Econometrics.* Cambridge: Harvard University Press.

Goldsmith, Arthur, Jonathon Veum, and William Darity. 1996. "The Psychological Impact of Unemployment and Joblessness." *Journal of Socio-Economics* 25 (3): 333–358.

———. 1997. "The Impact of Psychological and Human Capital on Wages." *Economic Inquiry* 35 (4):815–29.

Goleman, Daniel. 1995. *Emotional Intelligence*. New York: Bantam.

Goodman R., and J. Stevenson. 1989. "A Twin Study of Hyperactivity, II: The Aetiological Role of Genes, Family Relationships and Perinatal Adversity." *Journal of Child Psychological Psychiatry* 30:691–709.

Gordon, Roger H. 1984. *Differences in Earnings and Ability*. New York: Garland.

Gottschalk, Peter, and Robert A. Moffitt. 1994. "The Growth of Earnings Instability in the U.S. Labor Market." *Brookings Papers on Economic Activity*, no. 2, pp. 217–254.

Graham, M., U. Larsen, and X. Xu. 1998. "Son preference in Anhui Province, China." *International Family Planning Perspectives* 24 (2): 72–77.

Grawe, Nathan D. 2000. "Lifecycle Bias in the Estimation of Intergenerational Income Persistence." Manuscript. University of Chicago.

———. Forthcoming. "Exceptional Mobility in the U.S. and Abroad." In *Generational Income Mobility in North America and Europe*, edited by Miles Corak. New York: Cambridge University Press.

Greene, William. 2000. *Econometric Analysis*. Englewood Cliffs, N.J.: Prentice Hall.

Greenhalgh, S. 1985. "Sexual Stratification: The Other Side of 'Growth with Equity' in East Asia." *Population and Development Review* 11:265–314.

Griliches, Zvi, and William Mason. 1972. "Education, Income, and Ability." *Journal of Political Economy* 80 (3): S74–S103.

Grusky, David, and Thomas DiPrete. 1990. "Recent Trends in the Process of Stratification." *Demography* 27 (4): 617–37.

Gu, B., and K. Roy. 1995. "Sex Ratio at Birth in China, with Reference to Other Areas in East Asia: What We Know." *Asia-Pacific Population Journal* 10 (3): 17–42.

Gu, S., X. Chen, and J. Liang. 1995. "Old-age Support System and Policy Reform in China." Paper presented at the International Conference on Aging in East-West, Seoul National University, Korea.

Guo, G., and E. Stearns. 1999. "The Social Influences on the Realization of Genetic Potential for Intellectual Development." Working paper. Department of Sociology, University of North Carolina, Chapel Hill.

Guo, Z., and G. Chen. 1999. "On Uxorilocal Marriage in Beijing with Data of 1995 One Percent Population Survey" [in Chinese]. *Sociology Research* 5: 94–104.

Haider, Steven, and Gary Solon. 2003. "Life-Cycle Variation in the Association between Current and Lifetime Earnings." Mimeo. September.

Hammel, E. A. 1990. "A Theory of Culture for Demography." *Population and Development Review* 16 (3): 455–85.

Han, C. 1992. "Uxorilocal Marriage is Good for Family Planning" [in Chinese]. *Population and Economics* 6:17–19.

Harding, David, Christopher Jencks, Leonard M. Lopoo, and Susan E. Mayer. 2005. "The Changing Effect of Family Background on the Incomes of American Adults." This volume.

Hardy, J., N. Astone, J. Brooks-Gunn, S. Shapiro, and T. Miller. 1998. "Like Mother, Like Child: Intergenerational Patterns of Age at First Birth and Associations with Childhood and Adolescent Characteristics and Adult Outcomes in the Second Generation." *Developmental Psychology* 34 (6): 1220–32.

Harris, J. R. 1998. *The Nurture Assumption.* New York: Free Press.

Harris, Y. R., D. Terrel, and G. Allen. 1999. The Influence of Education Context and Beliefs on the Teaching Behavior of African American Mothers." *Journal of Black Psychology* 25:490–503.

Hauser, Robert. 1998. "Intergenerational Economic Mobility in the United States: Measures, Differentials and Trends." Working paper. Department of Sociology, University of Wisconsin-Madison.

Hauser, Robert, and David Featherman. 1976. "Equality of Schooling: Trends and Prospects." *Sociology of Education* 49 (2): 99–120.

Hauser, Robert, and John Robert Warren. 1997. "Socioeconomic Indexes for Occupations: A Review, Update, and Critique." *Sociological Methodology* 27: 177–298.

Hauser, Robert, John Robert Warren, Min-Hsiung Huang, and Wendy Y. Carter. 2000. "Occupational Status, Education, and Social Mobility in the Meritocracy." In *Meritocracy and Economic Inequality*, edited by Kenneth Arrow, Samuel Bowles, and Steven Durlauf. Princeton: Princeton University Press.

Heckman, James, Jingjing Hsee, and Yona Rubinstein. 2000. "The GED Is a Mixed Signal." Manuscript presented at the American Economic Association meeting, Boston, Mass.

Heckman, James, Anne Layne-Farrar, and Petra Todd. 1995. "Does Measured School Quality Really Matter? An Examination of the Earnings-Quality Relationship." Manuscript. University of Chicago.

Heckman, James, and Yona Rubinstein. 2001. "The Importance of Noncognitive Skills: Lessons from the GED Testing Program." *American Economic Review* 91 (2): 145–49.

Herrnstein, Richard. 1971. "IQ." *Atlantic Monthly* 228:43–64.

———. 1973. *IQ in the Meritocracy.* Boston: Atlantic Monthly.

Herrnstein, Richard J., and Charles Murray. 1994. *The Bell Curve: Intelligence and Class Structure in American Life.* New York: Free Press.

Hertz, Thomas. 2001. "Education, Inequality and Economic Mobility in South Africa." Ph.D. diss. University of Massachusetts, Amherst.

———. 2005. "Rags, Riches, and Race: The Intergenerational Economic Mobility of Black and White Families in the United States." This volume.

Hetherington, E. M., S. Henderson, and D. Reiss. 1999. "Adolescent Siblings in Stepfamilies: Family Functioning and Adolescent Adjustment." *Monographs of the Society for Research in Child Development*, Serial No. 259, vol. 64, no. 4.

Hill, Martha. 1992. *The Panel Study of Income Dynamics: A User's Guide.* Newbury Park, Calif.: Sage Publications.

Hogan, Robert, Joyce Hogan, and Brent Roberts. 1996. "Personality Measurement and Employment Decisions." *American Psychologist* 51 (5): 469–77.

Hout, Michael. 1988. "More Universalism, Less Structural Mobility: The American Occupational Structure in the 1980s." *American Journal of Sociology* 93 (6):1358–1400.

Hull, T. H. 1990. "Recent Trends in Sex Ratios at Birth in China." *Population and Development Review* 16 (1): 63–83.

Hurley, Susan. 1993. "Justice without Constitutive Luck." *Ethics, Royal Institute of Philosophy Supplement* 35:179–212.

Hyslop, Dean. 2001. "Rising U.S. Earnings Inequality and Family Labor Supply: The Covariance Structure of Intrafamily Earnings." *American Economic Review* 91:755–77.

Insel, Paul M. 1974. "Maternal Effects in Personality." *Behavior Genetics* 4 (2): 133–43.

Jang, K. L., W. J. Livesley, and P. A. Vernon. 1996. "Heritability of the Big Five Personality Dimensions and Their Facets: A Twin Study." *Journal of Personality* 64:577–91.

Jencks, Christopher. 1980. "Heredity, Environment, and Public Policy Reconsidered." *American Sociological Review* 45:723–36.

———. 2002. "Does Inequality Matter?" *Daedalus* (Winter): 49–65.

Jencks, Christopher, et al. 1972. *Inequality: A Reassessment of the Effect of Family and Schooling in America.* New York: Basic Books.

———. 1979. *Who Gets Ahead? The Determinants of Economic Success in America.* New York: Basic Books.

Jencks, Christopher, Susan E. Mayer, and Joseph Swingle. Forthcoming. "Who Has Benefited from Economic Growth in the United States Since 1969? The Case of Children." In *What Has Happened to the Quality of Life in American and Other Advanced Industrial Nations?*, edited by Edward Wolff. Northampton, Mass.: Edward Elgar.

Jenkins, Stephen 1987. "Snapshots Versus Movies: 'Lifecycle Biases' and the Estimation of Intergenerational Earnings Inheritance." *European Economic Review* 31:1149–58.

Jensen, Arthur R. 1977. "The Puzzle of Nongenetic Variance." In *Intelligence, Heredity, and Environment*, edited by Robert Sternberg and Elena Grigorenko. Cambridge: Cambridge University Press.

———. 1980. *Bias in Mental Testing.* New York: Free Press.

Jin, X., and S. Li. 2001. "An Analysis of Uxorilocal Marriage in Rural Chinese Communities" [in Chinese]. Manuscript.

Jin, X., M. W. Feldman, S. Li, and C. Zhu. 2002. "A Survey of Marriage and Old-age Support in Songzi, China." Rev. ed. Working Paper 86. Morrison Institute for Population and Resource Studies, Stanford University.

Johansson, S., and O. Nygren. 1991. "The Missing Girls of China: A New Demographic Account." *Population and Development Review* 17 (1): 35–51.

John, O. P. 1990. "The 'Big Five' Factor Taxonomy: Dimensions of Personality in the Natural Language and in Questionnaires." In *Handbook of Personality: Theory and Research*, edited by L. A. Pervin. New York: Guilford.

Juhn, Chinhui, Kevin M. Murphy, and Brooks Pierce. 1993. "Wage Inequality and the Rise in Returns to Skill." *Journal of Political Economy* 101 (3): 410–42.

Kamin, Leon J., and Arthur S. Goldberger. 2002. "Twin Studies in Behavioral Research: A Skeptical View." *Theoretical Population Biology* 61 (1): 83–95.

Kandel, D., and P. Wu. 1995. "The Contribution of Mothers and Fathers to the Intergenerational Transmission of Cigarette Smoking in Adolescence." *Journal of Research on Adolescence* 5:225–52.

Kane, Thomas, and Cecilia E. Rouse. 1995. "Labor Market Returns to Two- and Four-Year College." *American Economic Review* 85 (3): 600–614.

Katz, Lawrence F., and David H. Autor. 1999. "Changes in the Wage Structure and Earnings Inequality." In *Handbook of Labor Economics*, vol. 3A, edited by Orley C. Ashenfelter and David Card. Amsterdam: North-Holland.

Kaufman, Bruce E. 1999. "Expanding the Behavioral Foundations of Labor Economics." *Industrial and Labor Relations Review* 52 (3): 361–92.

Kim, Yong-Seong, et al. 2000. "Notes on the 'Income Plus' Files: 1994–1997 Family Income and Components Files." Available at the Panel Study on Income Dynamics (PSID) web location: http://www.isr.umich.edu/src/psid/.

Kohn, Melvin L., and Carmi Schooler. 1982. "Job Conditions and Personality: A Longitudinal Assessment of Their Reciprocal Effects." *American Journal of Sociology* 87 (6): 1257–86.

Korenman, Sanders, and Christopher Winship. 1999. "A Reanalysis of *The Bell Curve*: Intelligence, Family Background, and Schooling." In *Meritocracy and Economic Inequality*, edited by Kenneth Arrow, Samuel Bowles, and Steven Durlauf. Princeton: Princeton University Press.

Kotlikoff, Laurence J., and Lawrence H. Summers. 1981. "The Role of Intergenerational Transfers in Aggregate Capital Accumulation." *Journal of Political Economy* 89 (4): 706–32.

Kumm, J., K. Laland, and M. W. Feldman. 1994. "Gene-Culture Coevolution and Sex Ratios: The Effects of Infanticide, Sex-Selective Abortion, Sex Selection, and Sex-Biased Parental Investment on the Evolution of Sex Ratios." *Theoretical Population Biology* 46 (3): 249–78.

Laland, K. 1994. "The Mathematical Modeling of Human Culture and Its Implications for Psychology and the Human Sciences." *British Journal of Psychology* 84: 145–69.

Laland, K., J. Kumm, and M. W. Feldman. 1995. "Gene-Culture Coevolutionary Theory: A Test Case." *Current Anthropology* 36 (1): 131–56.

Lavely, W., J. Li, and J. Li. 2001. "Sex Preference for Children in a Meifu Li Community in Hainan, China." *Population Studies* 55:319–29.

Lavely, W., and X. Ren. 1992. "Patrilocality and Early Marital Co-residence in Rural China, 1955–85." *The China Quarterly* 130:378–91.

Lee, Y., W. Parish, and R. Willis. 1994. "Sons, Daughters, and Intergenerational Support in Taiwan." *American Journal of Sociology* 99 (4): 1010–41.

Levine, David. 1999. "Choosing the Right Parents: Changes in the Intergenerational Transmission of Inequality between the 1970s and the Early 1990s." Working Paper 72. Institute for Industrial Relations. Berkeley: University of California.

Levine, David I., and Bhashkar Mazumder. 2002. "Choosing the Right Parents: Changes in the Intergenerational Transmission of Inequality—Between 1980 and the Early 1990s." Federal Reserve Bank of Chicago Working Paper 2002-08.

Li, J., and R. S. Cooney. 1993. "Son Preference and the One Child Policy in China: 1979–1988." *Population Research and Policy Review* 12:108–15.

Li, N., M. W. Feldman, and S. Li. 1998b. "Transmission of Son Preference: Estimates from a Survey in Two Counties of China." Morrison Institute for Population and Resource Studies Working Paper 76. Stanford University.

Li, N., M. W. Feldman, and S. Li. 2000. "Cultural Transmission in a Demographic Study of Sex Ratio at Birth in China's Future." *Theoretical Population Biology* 58:161–72.

Li, N., M. W. Feldman, and S. Tuljapurkar. 1998a. "A Demographic Model with Cultural Transmission of Son Preference." Working Paper 73. Morrison Institute for Population and Resource Studies, Stanford University.

Li, N., M. W. Feldman, and S. Tuljapurkar. 1999. "Sex Ratio at Birth and Son Preference." *Mathematical Population Studies* 8:91–107.

Li, S., M. W. Feldman, and X. Jin. 2002a. "Marriage Form and Duration of Post-marital Coresidence with Parents in Rural China: Evidence from Songzi." Rev. ed. Working Paper 87. Morrison Institute for Population and Resource Studies, Stanford University.

———. 2002b. "Sons and Daughters: Marriage Form and Family Division in Rural China." Rev. ed. Morrison Institute for Population and Resource Studies Working Paper 88. Stanford University.

———. 2002c. "Children, Marriage and Family Support for the Elderly in Rural China." Rev. ed. Morrison Institute for Population and Resource Studies Working Paper 89. Stanford University.

Li, S., M. W. Feldman, and N. Li. 2000. "Cultural Transmission of Uxorilocal Marriage in Lueyang, China." *Journal of Family History* 25 (2): 158–77.

———. 2001. "A Comparative Analysis of Determinants of Uxorilocal Marriage in Two Counties of China." *Social Biology* 48 (1–2): 125–50.

Li, S., M. W. Feldman, N. Li, and C. Zhu. 1998. "A Survey of Transmission of Son Preference in Two Counties of China." Morrison Institute for Population and Resource Studies Working Paper 75. Stanford University.

Li, S., M. W. Feldman, and Li Nan. 2002d. "Acceptance of Two Types of Uxorilocal Marriage in Contemporary China: The Case of Lueyang." Rev. ed. Morrison Institute for Population and Resource Studies Working Paper 85. Stanford University.

Li, S., and C. Zhu. 1999. "Analysis of Typical Couples in Uxorilocal Marriage in Lueyang, China" [in Chinese]. *Population and Economics* (Supplement): 85–93.

———. 2001. *Research and Community Practice on Gender Differences in Child Survival in China.* Beijing: Population Publishing Press.

Lillard, Lee A., and Robert J. Willis. 1978. "Dynamic Aspects of Earning Mobility." *Econometrica* 46:985–1012.

Little, Roderick J. A., and Donald B. Rubin. 1987. *Statistical Analysis with Missing Data.* New York: Wiley.

Loehlin, J. C. 1992a. *Genes and Environment in Personality Development.* Newbury Park, Calif.: Sage.

Loehlin, John C. 1992b. "What Has Behavioral Genetics Told Us about the Nature of Personality?" In *Twins as a Tool of Behavioral Genetics*, edited by T. J. Bouchard and P. Propping. New York: Wiley.

Loehlin, J. C., R. R. McCrae, P. T. Costa, Jr., and O. P. John. 1998. "Heritabilities of Common and Measure-Specific Components of the Big Five Personality Factors." *Journal of Research in Personality* 32:431–53.

Loehlin, J. C., and R. C. Nichols. 1976. *Heredity, Environment, and Personality: A Study of 850 Sets of Twins.* Austin: University of Texas Press.

Loehlin, J. C., and D. C. Rowe. 1992. "Genes, Environment, and Personality." In *Modern Personality Psychology: Critical Reviews and New Directions*, edited by G. Chapara and G. L. Van Heck. New York: Harvester Wheatsheaf.

Loehlin, J. C., L. Willerman, and J. M. Horn. 1985. "Personality Resemblances in Adoptive Families when the Children are Late-Adolescent or Adult." *Journal of Personality and Social Psychology* 48:376–92.

Lu, Y. 2001. "Childbearing Interest: Rethinking of Farmer's Childbearing Attitudes" [in Chinese]. *Population Research* 2:17–27.

Maccoby, E. 2000. "Parenting and Its Effects on Children: On Reading and Misreading Behavior Genetics." *Annual Review of Psychology* 51:1–27.

Maccoby, E., and J. Martin. 1983. "Socialization in the Context of Family: Parent-Child Interaction." Pp. 1–101 in *Handbook of Child Psychology, Vol. 4: Socialization, Personality, and Social Development*, edited by E. M. Hetherington, New York: Wiley.

Margo, Robert. 1999. "The History of Wage Inequality in America: 1820 to 1970." Working Paper 286. Levy Institute, Bard College.

Marshall, Gordon, Adam Swift, and Stephen Roberts. 1997. *Against the Odds? Social Class and Social Justice in Industrial Societies.* Oxford: Oxford University Press.

Marshall, Gordon, Adam Swift, David Routh, and Carol Burgoyne. 1999. "What Is and What Ought to Be: Popular Beliefs about Distributive Justice in Thirteen Countries." *European Sociological Review* 15:349–67.

Mayer, John D., and Peter Salovey. 1995. "Emotional Intelligence and the Construction and Regulation of Feelings." *Applied and Preventive Psychology* 4 (3): 197–208.

Mayer Susan, Christopher Jencks, and Joseph Swingle. 2001. "Trends in Children's Living Conditions: 1969–1999." Paper presented at the Levy Economic Institute, Annandale-on-Hudson, N.Y., May, 2001.

Mayer, Susan, and Leonard Lopoo. 2001. "Has the Intergenerational Transmission of Economic Status Changed?" Joint Center for Poverty Research Working Paper No. 227.

Mayer, Susan E. 1997. *What Money Can't Buy: Family Income and Children's Life Chances.* Cambridge: Harvard University Press.

———. 2002. *The Influence of Parental Income on Children's Outcomes: Report to the New Zealand Ministry of Social Development.* Wellington, New Zealand.

Mazumder, Bhashkar 2001a. "Earnings Mobility in the U.S.: A New Look at

Intergenerational Inequality." Federal Reserve Bank of Chicago Working Paper 2001-18.

Mazumder, Bhashkar. 2001b. "The Mis-Measurement of Permanent Earnings: New Evidence from Social Security Earnings Data." Federal Reserve Bank of Chicago Working Paper 2001-24.

Mazumder, Bhashkar. 2003. "Revised Estimates of Intergenerational Income Mobility in the United States." Federal Reserve Bank of Chicago Working Paper 2003-16.

Mazumder, Bhashkar. 2005. The Apple Falls Even Closer to the Tree than We Thought: New and Revised Estimates of the Intergenerational Inheritance of Earnings." This volume.

McAdams, Dan. 1994. "Can Personality Change? Levels of Stability and Growth in Personality across the Life Span." In Can Personality Change? edited by Todd F. Heatherton and Joel L. Weinberger. Washington, D.C.: American Psychological Association.

McCrae, R. R. 1989. "Why I Advocate the Five-Factor Model: Joint Factor Analyses of NEO-PI with Other Instruments." Pp. 237–45 in Personality Psychology: Recent Trends and Emerging Directions, edited by D. M. Buss and N. Cantor. New York: Springer-Verlag.

McCrae, Robert. 1993. "Moderated Analyses of Longitudinal Personality Stability." Journal of Personality and Social Psychology 65 (3): 577–85.

McCrae, Robert, and Paul Costa. 1984. "The Search for Growth or Decline in Personality." In Emerging Lives, Enduring Dispositions. Boston: Little, Brown.

———. 1994. "The Stability of Personality: Observations and Evaluation." Current Directions in Psychological Science 3 (6): 173–75.

———. 1997. "Personality Trait Structure as a Human Universal." American Psychologist 52 (5): 509–16.

McLoyd, V., T. Jayaratne, R. Ceballo, and J. Borquez. 1994. "Unemployment and Work Interruption among African American Single Mothers: Effects on Parenting and Adolescent Socioemotional Functioning." Child Development 65 (2): 562–89.

Medlund, P., R. Cederlöf, B. Floderus-Myrhed, L. Friberg, and S. Sörensen. 1977. "A New Swedish Twin Registry Containing Environmental and Medical Base Line Data from About 14,000 Same-Sexed Pairs Born 1926–58." Acta Medica Scandinavica 600 (Supplement): 5–111.

Menchik, Paul. 1979. "Intergenerational Transmission of Inequality: An Empirical Study of Wealth Mobility." Economica 46:349–62.

Michael, R. T. 1972. The Effect of Education on Efficiency in Consumption. New York: Columbia University Press.

Miller, David. 1999. Principles of Social Justice. Cambridge: Harvard University Press.

Mincer, Jacob. 1974. Schooling, Experience, and Earnings. New York: Columbia University Press.

Mischel, Walter. 1974. "Process in Delay of Gratification." Pp. 249–89 in Advances in Experimental Social Psychology, edited by Leonard Berkowitz. New York: Academic Press.

Mischel, Walter, Yuichi Shoda, and Monica L. Rodriguez. 1992. "Delay of

Gratification in Children." Pp. 147–64 in *Choice Over Time*, edited by George Loewenstein and Jon Elster. New York: Russell Sage Foundation.

Morris, P., A. Huston, G. Duncan, D. Crosby, and H. Bos. 2001. *How Welfare and Work Policies Affect Children: A Synthesis of Research*. New York: Manpower Demonstration Research Corporation.

Muchinsky, Paul. 1996. "The Correction for Attenuation." *Educational and Psychological Measurement* 56 (1): 63–75.

Mulligan, Casey B. 1996. "Work Ethic and Family Background: Some Evidence." Manuscript. Department of Economics, University of Chicago.

———. 1997. *Parental Priorities and Economic Inequality*. Chicago: University of Chicago Press.

———. 1999. "Galton vs. Human Capital Approaches to Inheritance." *Journal of Political Economy* 107 (6:2): S184–S224.

Munoz-Darde, Veronique. 1999. "Is the Family to Be Abolished Then?" *Proceedings of the Aristotelian Society* 99:37–55

Murnane, Richard, and Frank Levy. 1996. *Teaching the New Basic Skills*. New York: Free Press.

Murnane, Richard, John Willett, Jay Braatz, and Yves Duhaldeborde. 1997. "Does the Self-Esteem of High-School-Aged Males Predict Labor Market Success A Decade Later? Evidence from the NLSY." Manuscript. Harvard University Graduate School of Education.

Murnane, Richard, John Willett, and Frank Levy. 1995. "The Growing Importance of Cognitive Skills in Wage Determination." *Review of Economics and Statistics* 77 (2): 251–66.

Murphy, Liam. 2000. *Moral Demands in Nonideal Theory*. New York: Oxford University Press.

Nagel, Thomas. 1991. *Equality and Partiality*. New York: Oxford University Press.

Norman, W. T. 1963. "Toward an Adequate Taxonomy of Personality Attributes: Replicated Factor Structure in Peer Nomination Personality Ratings." *Journal of Abnormal and Social Pychology* 66:574–83.

Okun, Arthur. 1975. *Equality and Efficiency: The Big Tradeoff*. Washington, D.C.: Brookings Institute.

Osborne, Melissa. 2000. "The Power of Personality: Labor Market Rewards and the Transmission of Earnings." Ph.D. diss. Department of Economics, University of Massachusetts.

Osborne Groves, Melissa. 2005. "Personality and the Intergenerational Transmission of Economic Status." This volume.

Otto, Sarah P., Freddy B. Christiansen, and Marcus W. Feldman. 1995. "Genetic and Cultural Inheritance of Continuous Traits." Manuscript. Stanford University.

Park, C. B., and N. H. Cho. 1995. "Consequences of Son Preference in a Low Fertility Society: Imbalance of the Sex Ratio at Birth in Korea." *Population and Development Review* 21:59–84.

Pasternak, B. 1985. "On the causes and demographic consequences of uxorilocal marriage in China" Pp. 309–34 in *Family and Population in East Asian History*, edited by S. B. Hanley and A. P. Wolf. Stanford: Stanford University Press.

Patterson, G. 1998. "Continuities—A Search for Causal Mechanisms." *Developmental Psychology* 34:1263–68.

Pedersen, N. L, G. E. McClearn, R. Plomin, J. R. Nesselroade, S. Berg, and U. DeFaire. 1991. "The Swedish Adoption / Twin Study of Aging: An Update." *Acta Geneticae Medicae Gemellologiae* 40 (1): 7–20.

Peters, Elizabeth. 1992. "Patterns of Intergenerational Mobility in Income and Earnings." *Research in Economics and Statistics* 74 (3): 456–66.

Plomin, Robert. 1986. "Behavioral Genetic Methods." *Journal of Personality* 54 (1): 226–61.

———. 1999. "Genetic and General Cognitive Ability," *Nature* 402, no. 2 (December): c25–c29.

Plomin, R., R. Corley, A. Caspi, D. W. Fulker, and J. DeFries. 1998. "Adoption Results for Self-Reported Personality: Evidence for Nonadditive Genetic Effects?" *Journal of Personality and Social Psychology* 75:211–18.

Plomin, Robert, John C. DeFries, Gerald McClearn, and Michael McGuffin. 2000. *Behavioral Genetics*. New York: W. H. Freeman.

Pollak, R. A., and S. C. Watkins. 1993. "Culture and Economic Approaches to Fertility." *Population and Development Review* 19 (3): 467–96.

Poston, D. L., P. Liu, B. Gu, and T. McDaniel. 1997. "Son Preference and the Sex Ratio at Birth in China: A Provincial Level Analysis." *Social Biology* 44 (1–2): 55–76.

Price, R. A., and S. G. Vandenberg. 1980. "Spouse Similarity in American and Swedish Couples." *Behavior Genetics* 10:59–71.

Rao, D. C., N. E. Morton, J. M. Lalouel, and R. Lew. 1982. "Path Analysis under Generalized Assortative Mating. II: American IQ." *Genetic Research, Cambridge* 39:187–98.

Rawls, John. 2001. *Justice as Fairness: A Restatement*. Cambridge: Harvard University Press.

Rawls, John. 1971. *A Theory of Justice*. Cambridge: Harvard University Press.

Reiss, D., J. M. Neiderhiser, E. M. Hetherington, and R. Plomin. 2000. *The Relationship Code: Deciphering Genetic and Social Influences on Adolescent Development*. Cambridge: Harvard University Press.

Riemann, R., A. Angleitner, and J. Strelau. 1997. "Genetic and Environmental Influences on Personality: A Study of Twins Reared together Using the Self- and Peer Report NEO-FFI Scales." *Journal of Personality* 65:449–75.

Roemer, John. 1998. *Equality of Opportunity*. Cambridge: Harvard University Press.

———. 2000. "Equality of Opportunity." In *Meritocracy and Economic Inequality*, edited by Kenneth Arrow, Samuel Bowles, and Steven Durlauf. Princeton: Princeton University Press.

Rotter, Julian B. 1966. "Generalized Expectancies for Internal Versus External Control of Reinforcement." *Psychological Monographs* 80 (1): 1–28.

Rowe, David. 1993. "Genetic Perspectives on Personality." Pp. 179–95 in *Nature, Nurture and Psychology*, edited by Robert Plomin and Gerald E. McClearn. Washington, D.C.: American Psychological Association.

———. 1994. *The Limits of Family Influence: Genes, Experience and Behavior*. New York: Guilford.

Royston, P.; 1991. "Comment on sg3.4 and an Improved D'Agostino Test." *Stata Technical Bulletin* 3:23–24.

Scarpetta, Stefano, Andrea Bassanini, Dirk Pilat, and Paul Schreyer. 2000. "Economic Growth in the OECD Area: Recent Trends at the Aggregate and Sectoral Level." Organization for Economic Cooperation and Development, Economics Department Working Paper No. 248.

Schmidt, Frank, Deniz Ones, and John Hunter. 1992. "Personnel Selection." *Annual Review of Psychology* 43:627–70.

Schrag, Francis. 1976. "Justice and the Family." *Inquiry* 19:193–208.

Serbin, L., and D. Stack. 1998. "Introduction to the Special Section: Studying Intergenerational Continuity and the Transfer of Risk." *Developmental Psychology* 34 (6): 1159–61.

Serbin, L., J. Cooperman, P. Peters, P. Lehoux, D. Stack, and A. Schwartzman. 1998. "Intergenerational Transfer of Psychosocial Risk in Women with Childhood Histories of Aggression, Withdrawal, or Aggression and Withdrawal." *Developmental Psychology* 34 (6): 1246–62.

Sewell, William H., and Robert M. Hauser. 1975. *Education, Occupation and Earnings: Achievements in the Early Career.* New York: Academic.

Sewell, William, Robert Hauser, and Wendy Wolf. 1980. "Sex, Schooling, and Occupational Status." *American Journal of Sociology* 86 (3): 551–83.

Shea, John. 2000. "Does Parents' Money Matter." *Journal of Public Economics* 77 (2): 155–84

Shi, L. Y. 1993. "Family Financial and Household Support Exchange between Generations: A Survey of Chinese Rural Elderly." *The Gerontologist* 33 (4): 468–80.

Skinner, G. W. 1997. "Family systems and demographic processes." Pp. 53–95 in *Anthropological Demography: Toward a New Synthesis*, edited by D. I. Kertzer and T. Fricke. Chicago: University of Chicago Press.

Smith, James. 1999. "Healthy Bodies and Thick Wallets: The Dual Relation between Health and Economic Status." *Journal of Economic Perspectives* 13 (2): 145–66.

Smith James P., and Finis R. Welch. 1986. *Closing the Gap: Forty Years of Economic Progress for Blacks.* Santa Monica, Calif.: Rand Corporation.

Solon, Gary. 1989. "Biases in the Estimation of Intergenerational Earnings Correlations." *Review of Economics and Statistics* 71:172–74

———. 1992. "Intergenerational Income Mobility in the United States." *American Economic Review* 82 (3): 393–408.

———. 1999. "Intergenerational Mobility in the Labor Market." Pp. 1761–800 in *Handbook of Labor Economics*, vol. 3, edited by O. Ashenfelter and D. Card. Amsterdam: Elsevier Science.

———. 2002. "Cross-Country Differences in Intergenerational Earnings Mobility." *Journal of Economic Perspectives* 16:59–66.

Solon, Gary, Mary Corcoran, Roger Gordon, and Deborah Laren. 1990. "A Longitudinal Analysis of Sibling Correlations in Economic Status." *The Journal of Human Resources* 26 (3).

Stein, Judith, Michael Newcomb, and P. M. Bentler. 1986. "Stability and

Change in Personality: A Longitudinal Study from Early Adolescence to Young Adulthood." *Journal of Research in Personality* 20:276–91.

Sternberg, Robert, and Elena Grigorenko. 1997. *Intelligence, Heredity, and Environment.* Cambridge: Cambridge University Press.

Sternberg, Robert J., Richard K. Wagner, Wendy M. Williams, and Joseph Horvath. 1995. "Testing Common Sense." *American Psychologist* 50, no. 11 (November): 912–27.

Stevens, Gillian, and David Featherman. 1981. "A Revised Socioeconomic Index of Occupational Status." *Social Science Research* 10:364–95.

Stevens, Gillian, and Joo Hyun Cho. 1985. "Socioeconomic Indexes and the New 1980 Census Occupational Classification Scheme." *Social Science Research* 14:142–68.

Stoolmiller, M. 2000. "Implications of the Restricted Range of Family Environments for Estimates of Heritability and Nonshared Environment in Behavior-Genetic Adoption Studies." *Psychological Bulletin* 125:392–409.

Sullivan, Daniel G. 2001. "A Note on the Estimation of Linear Regression Models with Heteroskedastic Measurement Errors." Federal Reserve Bank of Chicago Working Paper 2001:23.

Swift, Adam. 1999. "Popular Opinion and Political Philosophy: The Relation between Social-Scientific and Philosophical Analyses of Distributive Justice." *Ethical Theory and Moral Practice* 2:337–63.

———. 2000. "Class Analysis from a Normative Perspective." *British Journal of Sociology* 51:663–79.

———. 2001. *Political Philosophy: A Beginner's Guide for Students and Politicians.* Oxford: Polity.

———. 2003. *How Not To Be a Hypocrite: School Choice for the Morally Perplexed Parent.* London: Routledge Falmer.

Swift, Adam, and Gordon Marshall. 1997. "Meritocratic Equality of Opportunity: Economic Efficiency, Social Justice, or Both?" *Policy Studies* 18:35–48.

Taubman, Paul. 1976. "The Determinants of Earnings: Genetics, Family, and Other Environments; A Study of Male Twins." *American Economic Review* 66 (5): 858–70.

Tett, Robert P., Douglas N. Jackson, and Mitchell Rothstein. 1991. "Personality Measures as Predictors of Job Performance: A Meta-Analytical Review." *Personnel Psychology* 44:703–42.

Thorndike, Edward L. 1919. "Intelligence and Its Uses." *Harper's Monthly Magazine* 140 (December/January): 227–35.

Tuljapurkar, S., N. Li, and M. W. Feldman. 1995. "High Sex Ratios in China's Future." *Science* 267:874–76.

Turner, Charles and Daniel Martinez. 1977. "Socioeconomic Achievement and the Machiavellian Personality." *Sociometry* 40 (4): 325–36.

U.S. Bureau of the Census. 2000. "Money Income in the United States, 1999." *Current Population Reports,* P-60-209. Washington, D.C.: Government Printing Office.

U.S. Bureau of the Census. 2002. "Historical Income Tables—Families." Available at http://www.census.gov/hhes/income/histinc/f04.html.

Valentine, Peter, and Morris Lipson. 1989. "Equal Opportunity and the Family." *Public Affairs Quarterly* 3:29–47.

Waller, N. G. 1999. "Evaluating the Structure of Personality." Pp. 155–97 in *Personality and psychopathology*, edited by C. R. Cloninger. Washington, D.C.: American Psychiatric Association.

Wen, X. 1993. "Effects of Son Preference and Population Policy on Sex Ratios at Birth in Two Provinces of China." *Journal of Biosocial Science* 25:110–20.

Williams, Wendy M., and Robert J. Sternberg. 1995. *Success Acts for Managers.* Orlando, Fla.: Harcourt Brace.

Wolf, A. P. 1989. "The Origins and Explanations of Variations in the Chinese Kinship System." Pp. 241–60 in *Anthropological Studies of the Taiwan Area*, edited by Chang et al. Taipei: National Taiwan University.

Wolff, Edward. 2002. "Inheritances and Wealth Inequality, 1989–98." *American Economic Review* 92, no. 2 (May): 260–64.

Xie, Y. 1989. "Measuring Regional Variation in Sex Preference in China: A Cautionary Note." *Social Science Research* 18:291–305.

Xu, Q. 1996. "A Comparative Study on Son's and Daughter's Old-Age Support for Parents" [in Chinese]. *Population Research* 5:23–31.

Xu, Q., and Y. Yuan. 1997. "The Role of Family Support in the Old-Age Security in China." Pp. 265–73 in *Twenty-Third IUSSP General Population Conference: Symposium on Demography of China*, edited by the China Population Association.

Xu, X., J. Ji, and Y. Tung. 2000. "Social and Political Assortative Mating in Urban China." *Journal of Family Issues* 21, no. 1 (January): 47–77.

Yan, M. 1995. "An Experimental Study of the Influences of Marriage Type on Women's Sex Preferences in Childbearing in Rural China" [in Chinese]. *Population Science of China* 5:11–16.

Yan, M., J. Mao, and J. Lu. 1999. "Exploring a Fundamental Way to Reduce Sex Ratio at Birth—Reforms in Marriage Customs in Daye, Hubei" [in Chinese]. *Population and Economics* 5:18–24.

Yan, M., and R. Shi. 1996. "The Role of Marriage Type in Fertility Decline in Rural China" [in Chinese]. *Population Science of China* 5:32–38.

Yan, S., J. Chen, and S. Yang. 2001. "Impact of Living Arrangement on Child's Old-Age Support for Parents" [in Chinese]. *Chinese Journal of Social Sciences* 1:130–40.

Yang, H. 1996. "The Distributive Norm of Monetary Support to Older Parents: A Look at a Township in China." *Journal of Marriage and the Family* 58:404–15.

Yang, Y. 1998. "On the Positive Impact of Uxorilocal Marriage on Aging" [in Chinese]. *Population and Family Planning* 6:31–34.

Young, Michael. 1959. *The Rise of the Meritocracy.* New York: Random House.

Yu, X. 1996. "Saving and Population Aging in China" [in Chinese]. *Population and Economics*, vol. 3.

Zeng, Y., P. Tu, B. Gu, Y. Xu, B. Li, and Y. Li. 1993. "Causes and Implications of the Recent Increase in the Reported Sex Ratio at Birth in China." *Population and Development Review* 19 (2): 283–302.

Zimmerman, David J. 1992. "Regression Toward Mediocrity in Economic Stature." *American Economic Review* 82:409–29.

INDEX